Cambridge Studies in Social and Emotional Development

General editor: Martin L. Hoffman

Advisory Board: Nicholas Blurton Jones, Robert N. Emde
Willard W. Hartup, Robert A. Hinde, Lois W. Hoffman,
Carroll E. Izard, Jerome Kagan, Franz J. Mönks,
Paul Mussen, Ross D. Parke, and Michael Rutter

Altruism and aggression

Altruism and aggression

Biological and social origins

Edited by

CAROLYN ZAHN-WAXLER

Laboratory for Developmental Psychology
National Institute of Mental Health

E. MARK CUMMINGS

Department of Psychology
West Virginia University

RONALD IANNOTTI

Laboratory of Children's Health Promotion

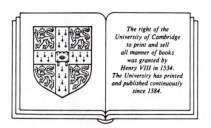

The right of the
University of Cambridge
to print and sell
all manner of books
was granted by
Henry VIII in 1534.
The University has printed
and published continuously
since 1584.

CAMBRIDGE UNIVERSITY PRESS

Cambridge

New York   Port Chester   Melbourne   Sydney

Published by the Press Syndicate of the University of Cambridge
The Pitt Building, Trumpington Street, Cambridge CB2 1RP
40 West 20th Street, New York, NY 10011, USA
10 Stamford Road, Oakleigh, Melbourne 3166, Australia

First published 1986
First paperback edition 1991

Printed in the United States of America

Library of Congress Cataloging in Publication Data

Main entry under title:
Altruism and aggression.
(Cambridge studies in social and emotional development)
Based on a conference held at the National Institute
of Mental Health, Bethesda, Md. in Apr. 1982, under
the auspices of the Society for Research in Child
Development and the Child Development Foundation.
1. Altruism in children – Congresses. 2. Aggressiveness
in children – Congresses. 3. Altruism – Congresses.
4. Aggressiveness (Psychology) – Congresses.
5. Psychology, Comparative – Congresses. 6. Socialization –
Congresses. I. Zahn-Waxler, Carolyn.
II. Cummings, E. Mark. III. Iannotti, Ronald.
IV. Society for Research in Child Development.
V. Foundation for Child Development. VI. Series.
[DNLM: 1. Aggression – in infancy & childhood – congresses.
2. Altruism – in infancy & childhood – congresses.
3. Social Behavior – in infancy & childhood – congresses.
4. Socialization – congresses. WS 105.5.S6 A469 1982]
BF723.A37A47 1986 155.4'18 85-17402

British Library Cataloguing in Publication Data

Altruism and aggression: biological and social
origins. – (Cambridge studies in social and
emotional development)
1. Aggressiveness (Psychology) 2. Altruism
I. Zahn-Waxler, Carolyn II. Cummings, E. Mark
III. Iannotti, Ronald
152.4 BF575.A3

ISBN 0-521-26834-6 hardback
ISBN 0-521-42367-8 paperback

To Morris and Rebecca Waxler with gratitude for their continuing support, encouragement, and empathy

Contents

Contributors

Robert B. Cairns
Department of Psychology
University of North Carolina
Chapel Hill

E. Mark Cummings
Department of Psychology
West Virginia University

Theodore Dix
Department of Psychology
Duke University

Kenneth A. Dodge
Department of Psychology
Indiana University

Norma Deitch Feshbach
Graduate School of Education
University of California,
Los Angeles

Seymour Feshbach
Department of Psychology
University of California,
Los Angeles

Joan E. Grusec
Department of Psychology
University of Toronto

Barbara Hollenbeck
Laboratory of Developmental
  Psychology
National Institute of Mental
  Health

Ronald Iannotti
Laboratory of Children's
  Health Promotion
Washington, D.C.

Robert F. Marcus
Institute for Child Study
Department of Human
  Development
University of Maryland
College of Education

J. M. Noel
Laboratoire d'Ethologie
  Humaine
Université de Québec à Montréal

Jaak Panksepp
Department of Psychology
Bowling Green State University

Marian Radke-Yarrow
Laboratory of Developmental
  Psychology
National Institute of Mental
  Health

John B. Reid
Oregon Social Learning Center

Ervin Staub
Department of Psychology
University of Massachusetts

F. F. Strayer
Laboratoire d'Ethologie
  Humaine

James Youniss
Boys Town Center
Catholic University

Carolyn Zahn-Waxler
Laboratory of Developmental
  Psychology
National Institute of Mental
  Health

Editorial preface

This book is the outcome of a conference held in 1982 at the National Institute of Mental Health, Bethesda, Maryland. It was funded by the Committee on Summer Institutes and Study Groups under the auspices of the Society for Research on Child Development and the Child Development Foundation. The purposes of the study groups have been (1) to organize existing scientific knowledge and (2) to define critical issues and strategies for future research on timely topics. In the Zeitgeist of the late 1970s and early 1980s, topics pertaining to socioemotional development in children have assumed special significance. Altruism and aggression are core features of both social and emotive systems in humans and infrahumans. Understanding of the etiologies and interconnections of altruism and aggression has remained elusive. They are topics that have vexed and fascinated philosophers, scientists, and other scholars over the centuries. Only recently have the tools and strategies of the biological, behavioral, and social sciences evolved to a degree of sophistication that might permit meaningful further advances in knowledge in these arenas.

The major aim of the workshop was to bring together an interdisciplinary group of scientists to discuss the interconnections of altruism and aggression within and across species. The focus was on the etiology of altruistic and aggressive behaviors in humans and nonhumans, from biological, ethological, and behavioral perspectives. We wished to discuss the role of (1) genetic transmission of affiliative and aggressive behaviors, as well as the biological (e.g., neurochemical, hormonal) correlates; (2) environmental variables (e.g., child-rearing practices, cultural patterns) that influence prosocial and antisocial behaviors; and (3) internal processes, such as affective arousal and empathy, social-inferential abilities, and cognitive attributions that may regulate the expression of selfish or kind behavior. It was hoped that such an approach would begin to foster, both in theory and in practice, a broader, more collaborative and interdisciplinary approach to the study of altruism and aggression. Through discussion of our own existing theories and programs of research that spanned a wide range of research topics, we hoped to learn more about precursors, mediators, functions, and outcomes of different kinds of altruism and aggression as well as to explore factors that link these two behavior systems. As we struggled with conceptual, methodological, and substantive issues, we began that arduous but exhilarating process of exploring new approaches and deriving fresh insights into the study of altruism and aggression. We also became acutely aware of the many unknowns that interfere with the attainment of significant new knowledge about the origins of altruism and aggression. We need continually to bear in mind the distinction between new products and true progress.

Part I of this book emphasizes biological, sociobiological, and ethological approaches to the study of altruism and aggression. Its four chapters by Panksepp, Cairns, Strayer and Noel, and Youniss explore the use of animal models in understanding both human and infrahuman behavior. Part II focuses on the development, socialization, and mediators of altruism and aggression in children. (Its chapters are by Staub; Cummings, Hollenbeck, Iannotti, Radke-Yarrow, and Zahn-Waxler; Feshbach and Feshbach; Grusec and Dix; Reid; Marcus; and Dodge.) Several of the major themes and issues of each part appear in the other part as well. Although the overlap attests to some of the conceptual and empirical untidiness that prevails in this area of research, it also illustrates the potential for fluid communication and collaboration across disciplines in a way that simultaneously takes advantage of the rich diversity of theory and approaches to the study of moral and social development. For example, the relevance of concepts pertaining to family structure and dynamics, and also of interpersonal relationships extending beyond the family, was particularly likely to emerge in chapters having both biological and behavioral orientations and in discussions of behavior in a range of species. The roles of attachment, separation distress, reciprocal interchanges, social play, parent–peer relationships, and so forth, in determining the quantity and quality of aggressive and affiliative interactions would fall under these different rubrics. The significance of emotions (e.g., empathy, anger, and guilt) as mediators was a common theme that emerged from many different theoretical camps. We attempted to foster an ethological perspective throughout the book by placing special importance on the need to explore altruism and aggression in the real lives and natural habitats of humans and other animals.

In addition to the contributors to this volume, whom we thank wholeheartedly, we were privileged to have as discussants at the conference Paul

MacLean and Martin Hoffman. Also we thank Phillip Gold, who presented data on biochemical mediators of aggression in human adults, and Steven Suomi, who presented theory and data on the development of affiliative and aggressive behaviors in rhesus monkeys. We are indebted to Geri Cooperman for the role she played in helping to organize the conference. Sincere appreciation is also extended to the following individuals who facilitated the conference and volume in a variety of ways: Rita Dettmers, Dorothy Eichorn, S. Gray Garwood, Frederick Goodwin, Jean Mayo, Herbert Pick, and Marian Radke-Yarrow. The assistance of the staff at Cambridge University Press is gratefully acknowledged, as well as the support of the Society for Research in Child Development, the Child Development Foundation, and the National Institute of Mental Health. Finally, we should like to thank family members who made it possible to explore the nature of altruism and aggression in depth. These include the following individuals: Lorrie Cummings, David Iannotti, Elizabeth Iannotti, Gail Iannotti, Morris Waxler, and Rebecca Waxler.

Carolyn Zahn-Waxler
E. Mark Cummings
Ronald Iannotti

Introduction
Altruism and aggression:
problems and progress in research

Carolyn Zahn-Waxler, E. Mark Cummings,
and Ronald Iannotti

Despite decades of research on altruism and aggression, as well as centuries of cumulative wisdom about human nature and animal life, we are still some distance from (1) having adequate scientific theories to explain their origins and patterns of expression and (2) having achieved well-developed capacities for understanding and resolving issues regarding conflict and cooperation. Problems in interpersonal relationships are equally evident within the family, within friendships, and in other social relationships of individuals within and across institutions, cultures, and nations. Negotiation and resolution of conflicts, capacities for intimacy that require empathy, and the delicate balancing of concern for others, hostility toward others, and self-interest – all are problem areas that continue to affect adversely the quality of social life. Yet they typically receive little priority relative to issues pertaining to technological advancements and mastery of the physical universe. The gap between the capacities for solving psychological problems and for solving physical or cognitive problems has often been acknowledged. As we near the end of the twentieth century, however, the mechanisms and machinery developed to master the physical universe have created serious problems.

The technology that ensued from the inventiveness of humans who constructed civilization as we know it ironically holds the potential for annihilation of all species. This calls into question what we have chosen to label as adaptive, progressive, and civilized. It also requires us to consider precisely what is meant by "survival of the fittest" in Darwinian or sociobiological terms. If fitness continues to be defined primarily in terms of characteristics that reflect physical prowess and reproductive fitness, we are likely to remain at the periphery of knowledge regarding the factors that govern our social lives. We are at a point in history where there should be special motivation to examine with meticulous care those forces within

1

and outside ourselves that determine both constructive and destructive behavioral patterns. Examination of our past, in terms of our animal heritage, our evolution as a species, and our evolution as individuals, is needed to provide a perspective on the present and the future.

A description by Janice Carter of the introduction of laboratory-reared chimpanzees back into their natural habitat presents a remarkable account of the expression of altruism and aggression expressed by a chimpanzee toward a Colobus monkey. One of the chimpanzees (Marianne) had just attacked a monkey that had entered the camp several days earlier. A second chimpanzee (Lakey), which had had some prior social interactions with the monkey, attempted to intervene in order to protect it. Carter described Lakey's response as follows: "She was clearly hysterical, screaming to the point of choking herself. With her small, outstretched, upturned hand, she was using a common begging gesture for me to intervene. She began to tug on my shirt, her stare fixing alternately on Marianne and me." Carter chose not to intervene because the ultimate goal of the project was to help the chimpanzees learn to survive in the wild. Other chimps joined in the attack, and eventually Lakey entered in as well, participating in the final kill.

This incident anticipates several of the major issues and concerns reflected in this book. One is the nature and interplay of altruism and aggression. Another is the similarities and differences in these response tendencies in different animals, within and across species. The example shows that brutal side of animal life often characterized as instinctive. But it portrays as well a capacity for altruism in animals, which we have been inclined to disregard or minimize. The example is suggestive of both the role of emotions as mediators of altruism and aggression and the role of cognition, in this case the chimpanzee's apparent understanding that someone else might be able to solve the problem that it was unable to. The potential influence of socialization agents and significant others is also dramatized. In the incident described, the person in charge chose not to control the hostility. In addition, aggressive (chimpanzee) models provided an opportunity for both imitation and contagion of aggression. A possible connection between acts of altruism and acts of caregiving is suggested as well. For example, if the incident instead had described the behavior of a mother attempting to protect or defend its offspring from danger, it would be labeled as an act of caregiving, not of altruism.

The attempt of the chimpanzee to protect the monkey was unique in that it extended (briefly) beyond kinship lines and beyond group membership. Numerous anecdotes, but few systematic data, exist regarding expressions of altruism and emotional concern for others that are more sustained and less ambivalent and that extend beyond kinship lines in infrahumans as well as humans. The search for signs of social bonding, empathy, or altruism across species as well as beyond blood lines is important. It may help determine the extent to which we view these as capabilities that are instinctive and genetically programmed for the perpetuation of our own biological families versus capacities that are more malleable and that work to aid in the perpetuation of human and animal life more generally. The fragile, tenuous nature of the emotional concern shown by Lakey and its fluid conversion to aggression (1) highlights the tremendous lability of these two response orientations, (2) indicates some of the difficulties that will be encountered in attempting to understand the logical connections between altruism and aggression, and (3) serves as a metaphor for characterizing the complex interplay of altruism and aggression in many species (humans included) throughout the course of evolution. Finally, the example documents the potential for extreme aggression in both females and males.

The urgent emotional quality of the seeking of help for another from someone in charge – the imploring look, the begging gesture – have also been documented in chimpanzees by Jane Goodall. This response constellation is virtually identical to a prosocial pattern shown by children in their second year of life. It occurs when children are in a stage of transition from helplessness to helpfulness in the face of another's distress (Radke-Yarrow & Zahn-Waxler, 1984). Children at this age are also particularly likely to seek out reassurance, guidance, or information from persons in charge, suggesting that this may be an important time, perhaps a critical period, for learning how to respond to others in distress (Zahn-Waxler & Radke-Yarrow, 1982).

Our own species, with its uniquely evolved brain, unquestionably has the greatest potential for learning (e.g., see Bleier, 1984, for a comprehensive discussion of brain–behavior interaction). But the possibility for learning altruism and aggression exists, in varying degress, in other species as well. Again, in the primate considered closest to humans, the chimpanzee, Goodall (1983) notes that (1) many of the caregiving skills and capacities for nurturing have to be learned, and (2) there are wide individual differences in socialization practices that may be implicated in the adequacy of caregiving. Goodall provides descriptions of how different chimpanzee parents deal with the aggression of their offspring. She also indicates how some primate parents serve as models of aggression and thus encourage it in their young.

Might not the same be true for altruism? Although there is a long tradition of research and a large literature on the roles of instinct and experience in social development, there is little systematic information regarding how they influence different forms of altruism and aggression across a range of species.

Origins of altruism and aggression: an evolutionary perspective

Altruism and aggression have been explored in both biological and cultural theories of evolution. Acts of altruism and acts of aggression each reflect basic patterns of social organization and life that are necessary for survival; thus, by definition, these behaviors can be said to serve adaptive functions. Procreation sets into motion actions both altruistic and aggressive that benefit and injure others. This fact of nature highlights the very distant and biological origins of these social behaviors and foreshadows the complexity of conjoint examination of the etiology of altruism and aggression. The extent to which these behaviors are part of our genetic heritage and the extent to which they are socialized or otherwise culturally transmitted from parent to offspring in both humans and infrahumans remain significant questions for research.

While the concept of survival of the fittest most readily evokes imagery of organisms that are physically strong, healthy, aggressive, and adaptively competitive for resources and territory, another feature of fitness has received less emphasis. The capacity to cooperate and share, to nurture, nourish, and protect one another (especially young offspring) can be viewed as a critical feature of fitness, evolution, and survival. Most often in sociobiological theories, these nurturing aspects of social functioning unfortunately have been viewed as a special case of selfishness in which caregivers nurture in order to perpetuate their own genes.

MacLean (1982) has taken a different point of view. He has hypothesized a link between caregiving and empathy and has discussed the role that this plays for the survival of species. According to this theory, the capability of mammals for nurturant extended caregiving toward their offspring, in contrast with the aggressive and neglectful behavior of many reptiles, which may abandon or eat their young, is the evolutionary forerunner of the development of empathy, conscience, and a sense of social responsibility. Understanding of altruism and of empathy can be sought in examination of caregiving activities because so many of the acts and associated emotions are common to both.

MacLean has speculated as well about evolutionary changes in brain structure, particularly regarding the development of neocortex, that might be associated with the development of empathy. In evolutionary models of development, the distress cries of offspring have been described as key to preventing prolonged separation and to maintaining attachments, social bonds, and a sense of family. This, in turn, makes possible the development of empathy and responsibility for others. Thus, within an ethological framework, crying can be viewed as a distress signal that serves as a releasor for adaptive, protective, and nurturing (possibly altruistic) parental caregiving behaviors (e.g., see Bowlby, 1969). Cries have also been conceptualized as activators of emotions that, in turn, may mediate caregiving behaviors (Murray, 1979). For example, Panksepp (Chapter 1) discusses the possibility of contagion of emotion (emotive resonance) of brain circuits in offspring and in their parents as important in establishing and maintaining social bonds. The cry may be a necessary, but not sufficient, condition: Cries are known to elicit anger, abuse, and aggression as well as empathy and caregiving. Although many complexities and ambiguities characterize evolutionary frameworks, they serve as a useful point of departure. The relationships among affect, altruism, and aggression have yet to be explored systematically in cross-species comparative studies of caregivers and their offspring.

An interactive framework for exploring altruism and aggression

This book is the outcome of a work-study group of scientists from a range of biological and behavioral disciplines convened to discuss the development and socialization of aggression and altruism. The goal was to explore the interaction of innate and learned factors that function as antecedents and mediators of prosocial and antisocial behaviors in different species. Development was conceived of broadly to include consideration of continuities and discontinuities of prosocial and antisocial behaviors across species, evolution, and time within the life of the individual. The focus of the conference was the biological, environmental, and individual determinants of altruism and aggression (and their interaction) during the course of development.

Biological processes implicated in aggression have been studied extensively. Through infrahuman animal studies of brain lesions, brain stimulation, and chemical intervention studies, much has been learned about the brain circuitry and structures involved in aggression (e.g., see Moyer, 1968). Hormonal and biochemical factors studied in relationship to aggression include examination of the level of monoamines in animal fights and hormone (testosterone) levels in criminals and antisocial personalities. Parallel questions concerning the biological bases of altruism have yet to be explored.

The role of environment (families, institutions, cultures) in modifying both aggression and altruism has been documented (e.g., see reviews by Parke & Slaby, 1983; Radke-Yarrow, Zahn-Waxler, & Chapman, 1983). Parental and cultural practices of discipline, instruction, modeling, reinforcement, inculcation of norms, quality of parent-child (emotional) relationships, and so on all have been implicated in the development of prosocial and antisocial behaviors in children. Much less is known about the role of rearing in social development of infrahumans.

Internal processes have been identified as mediators of kind and selfish behaviors as well. Included in this category, among other characteristics of individuals, are patterns of affective arousal (e.g., empathy), personality characteristics (e.g., self-concept or self-esteem), and cognitive factors (e.g., social-inferential abilities, cognitive attributions). Little is known about which, if any, of these processes play a role in the altruism and aggression of nonhumans. Also, these factors presumably interact in complex ways, the investigation of which will pose challenges for future research.

In summary, we were interested in several fundamental questions about connections between altruism and aggression – namely, the role of emotions as mediators, the biological origins and universality of these behaviors in other species, the developmental changes that might be expected to occur, and the factors of environment and socialization that influence altruism and aggression. From the beginning, we did not assume that we would resolve any of these issues – only that we would provide a forum for discussing them.

Two recent comprehensive literature reviews of altruism and aggression in children (Parke & Slaby, 1983; Radke-Yarrow, Zahn-Waxler, & Chapman, 1983) serve as a reminder that altruism and aggression typically are viewed as quite distinct research domains. For the most part, content areas simply do not overlap in such review chapters. Furthermore, these two topics have ridden the crests of different Zeitgeists. In developmental psychology, aggression was a popular topic of the late 1950s and the 1960s and was linked with the dominant behavioristic and neopsychoanalytic theories and approaches of that time. Research on altruism began at the tail end of that era but has been primarily a product of the 1970s, during which social-cognitive stage theories predominated. It is perhaps for this reason that we have been much less inclined to view altruism as part of our animal heritage. There are undoubtedly philosophical, theological, and ideological reasons for this bias as well. All these factors have helped make the examination of interconnections between altruism and aggression difficult at best. The remainder of this chapter considers some of the problems of definition and measurement that create special challenges for research and theory on these topics. We then provide the reader with a brief orientation to each chapter, highlighting some of the significant themes and issues that emerged.

Definitions and functions of altruism and aggression

Altruism is commonly defined as regard for, or devotion to, the interests or welfare of others; aggression is commonly understood to consist of a form of hostile encroachment upon others, according to *Webster's Seventh New Collegiate Dictionary* (1965). The form, structure, and functions of each of these behaviors vary enormously. Altruism, for example, is seen in behavioral acts of helping, sharing, sympathy, cooperation, rescue, and protecting/defending, to name a few. These behaviors can be seen across many species and may have similar or different underlying meanings. The same behavioral acts may occur for different reasons. For example, an act of rescue can be based on empathic feelings of concern for the victim that may be instinctive, or its origins may be based on behaviors that are more instrumental, calculated, or ritualized through specific socialization practices. Some of the motives and instigators may be relatively constant across species, while others will be very different. Particularly among humans, some forms of altruism are fashioned by the conventions and mores of society and of the subcultures within. Rules and standards of interpersonal conduct, learned norms of responsibility, reciprocity or equity, and so on will thus sometimes determine the circumstances under which prosocial behavior appears. Altruism may also be motivated by feelings of guilt over acts of wrongdoing committed toward others.

Parallel complexities and ambiguities exist in the domain of aggression. Many different physical and verbal forms of aggressive behaviors have been identified as well (e.g., biting, hitting, killing, verbal sarcasm, and contempt). Regarding motives for aggression that could occur across a variety of species, Moyer (1968) distinguished several categories of aggression, including predatory aggression, fear-induced aggression, territorial defense, maternal aggression (which occurs in the presence of both the young and a threat), and instrumental aggression. Still other forms of hostility occur that are specifically applicable to humans, such as aggression based on a desire to increase self-esteem through social dominance and control or reflected in planning strategies for war and combat maneuvers.

The linkages between altruism and aggression within individuals and the way in which the different patterns interact with changing developmental patterns in these domains have been virtually unexplored. From a more philosophical and evolutionary perspective, altruism and aggression are sometimes conceptualized as competing forces; a common approach is to determine which aspect of human nature will prevail. According to MacLean's theory, for example, the emergence of empathy is a relatively recent evolutionary development. Possible implications of this theory, which links increases in empathy with increases in the size of the neocortex, are that empathy is (1) greater in humans than other animals and (2) more highly developed in modern than in primitive cultures. This can be contrasted with some views of cultural evolution in which war, aggression, and violence are seen as having begun to a significant degree only when people began a settled-down way of life. Here, issues of politics, religion, economics, and the culturally imposed dominance hierarchies that ensue from the establishment of communities are thought to elevate levels of aggression and violence. In this view, we would have increased over time our potential for aggression. When one considers the developmental history of individuals, rather than of culture or species, it is interesting to note that both forces – altruistic and aggressive – are securely in place, from the first years of life. How are we to understand the different ways in which they are interconnected within individuals?

We are all aware of persons who can be both very giving and very brutal. This seems not difficult to understand if the recipients are different persons (e.g., members of an ingroup versus those of an outgroup). But many times the same individual is the recipient of extreme acts of caring and callousness. Theories characteristically do not address these complexities, particularly from a developmental perspective. Research on associations between altruism and aggression in children has produced varied patterns of findings, indicating both positive and negative associations between the two variables (see Chapters 4, 6, and 7 for more extended discussions of these issues). The positive associations could be seen as compatible with concepts of fitness and survival, if fitness is defined jointly in terms of enhanced capacity to take control of and to take care of others. Traditionally, the positive associations have been attributed to a mediating variable identified as (social) activity level, but more dynamic interpretations are also possible. The negative relationships between altruism and aggression are more intuitively obvious.

For many reasons, one would not expect simple patterns of relationships between altruism and aggression. An act of caring toward one individual can simultaneously represent an act of aggression toward another (see Chapter 4). Individuals engaged in extremely aggressive acts can simultaneously engage in acts of nurturance (e.g., a soldier who stops to rescue an infant). Some acts of altruism toward the person in need may contain aggressive components or overtones of domination; Bryant and Crockenberg (1980) describe helping that an older sibling sometimes shows to a younger sibling as intrusive, bossy, or condescending. These investigators report that such helping is associated with anger in the recipient of help. Within the same incident, too, it is possible to observe ambivalence, alternation, or shifting of prosocial and antisocial tendencies (Zahn-Waxler & Radke-Yarrow, 1982). To the extent that acts of altruism and aggression are mediated by emotions, this would help explain the lability and fluidity of expression observed in the behaviors themselves. Finally, while evolutionary and ethological theories emphasize the adaptive significance of such behaviors and emotions, both prosocial and antisocial behaviors do have maladaptive functions as well.

Many of the issues and problems raised in this introduction have a longstanding basis in the psychological literature and have been significant research issues for other disciplines as well. There are relatively few empirical data on connections of altruism and aggression and little in the way of theory as well. Investigators are not used to dealing with the two concepts simultaneously. The conference on biological and social origins of altruism and aggression was intended to take beginning steps in this direction. The final section of this chapter highlights the major themes of the substantive chapters that resulted from the workshop.

Overview of this volume

Biological and sociobiological approaches to altruism and aggression

Panksepp (Chapter 1) develops a psychobiological theory of prosocial behaviors. He hypothesizes that, while emotions such as anger–rage appear to be wired into the visceral brain of mammals, altruistic tendencies may be connected more integrally to learning processes linked, in turn, to changes in emotive systems. He summarizes knowledge concerning brain systems that mediate those types of social interactions that could provide the basis for the most common forms of altruistic behaviors. The sources of these forms of altruism are sought among (1) brain emotional systems, which mediate separation distress, which in turn may elicit altruism and caregiving in others; (2) developmental processes, which elaborate juvenile play; and (3) brain opioids, which serve as one example of brain neuromodulators that may help elaborate social bonds. Panksepp indicates that a scientifically compelling sociobiology requires an explicit wedding of evolutionary and psychobiological perspectives in order to understand social process. (We would add the need to integrate environmental perspectives as well.) He hypothesizes that mechanisms underlying helping and antagonistic behaviors may be reciprocally related and that both could be critically linked to brain opioid activity in limbic circuits. For instance, brain opioids that promote social comfort, bonding, and play presumably evoke psychological attitudes of peacefulness and trust. Conversely, opioid withdrawal promotes distress, irritability, and aggressiveness. Such reciprocal innervation may be a general property of emotive circuits in the brain.

Cairns (Chapter 2) provides an evolutionary and developmental perspective on altruism and aggression. He discusses the contributions to developmental psychology of three different biological orientations concerned with the study of the biology of social behavior: developmental psychobiology (including comparative psychology), ethology, and sociobiology. He considers as well some of the problems in attempting to provide an integration of ethological/sociological accounts of forms and functions of aggressive expression with developmental/environmental accounts. Some of the issues are illustrated through examination of (1) contributors to sex differences in aggression in different species and (2) the role of emotion arousal in the escalation of aggression. The significance of (1) sex differences (in patterns, more than frequencies, of altruism and aggression) and (2) emotional reactivity as mediating both altruism and aggression emerges in several subsequent chapters.

Youniss (Chapter 3) applies sociobiological concepts to the peer relationships of children. Parallels in sociological concepts of reciprocity (e.g., social solidarity, social cohesion) and sociobiological concepts of reciprocity (e.g., reciprocal altruism) are explored. Developmental changes in the nature of reciprocity in school-age children are described. Youniss also illustrates how specific acts of friendship between peers are very similar to the acts of altruism discussed from a sociobiological perspective by Trivers. Reciprocal social interactions with peers and the emergence of friendship as the major determinants of altruism in children are discussed in this chapter. This contrasts with the model presented by Suomi at the conference emphasizing (1) the role of both family and age-mates in influencing social development and (2) the potential of the peer groups and friends for facilitating aggression as well as altruism.

Strayer and Noel (Chapter 4) adapt ethological and sociobiological models to the study of aggression and affiliation in the preschool-age child. These contributors discuss problems that result from attempts to dichotomize prosocial behavior and aggression. For example, highly aggressive young children may be at risk for subsequent antisocial tendencies. But the aggression may also create a unique opportunity for developing (through socialization and experience) strategies for learning to control violent impulses and for becoming effectively integrated into the adolescent or adult social world. This theme is echoed by the NIMH team (Chapter 6) as well: The early, strong connections among altruism, aggression, and emotional reactivity also suggest that this is a time in life when caregivers may have a particularly potent influence. Empirical findings are presented from Strayer and Noel's research on relationships between prosocial and aggressive behaviors in the context of study of triadic conflict among young children. In their view, aggression serves to keep dominance hierarchies stable and social order is maintained, thereby preventing the occurrence of even more problematical and disruptive behaviors. It may sometimes be difficult, however, to ascertain in humans how much prosocial aggression is indeed for "the greater good" and how much of it reflects bullying and harassment that will ultimately be to the detriment of both the group and the individual (Olweus, 1979).

Social and personality approaches to altruism and aggression

The major goal of Staub's contribution (Chapter 5) is to delineate the central elements of a comprehensive theory of moral conduct in humans through analysis of the development and determinants of altruism and aggression. Particular emphasis is placed on examination of those characteristics of environment or individual that might be likely simultaneously to motivate unselfish behavior aimed at benefiting others and to inhibit harming of others; these characteristics would include prosocial value orientations, personal goals, empathy, positive social bonds, or attachments. He hypothesizes that a secure attachment is likely to be an important starting point for the development of altruism and might lessen the probability of aggression. Recent research findings on toddler-age children provide some support for Staub's hypothesis. Main and Weston (1981) report relationships among quality of attachment to parents, readiness to relate to others, and conflict behavior; Zahn-Waxler (1984) reports that securely attached children are more altruistic to their mothers in situations of distress, and Cummings, Iannotti, and Zahn-Waxler (1983) find that insecurely attached children display unusually high or low levels of aggression toward peers. The considerable research literature stimulated by the work of Sroufe and colleagues (see review by Zahn-Waxler, Cummings, & Cooperman, 1983) suggests that the quality of the social relationship with the caregiver influences later positive and negative social interactions with peers.

The examination of links between attachment and prosocial and antisocial behaviors may provide one meaningful way of exploring our commonalities with other animals. Other characteristics viewed by Staub as critical to the development of altruism and the diminution of aggression, however, have to do with uniquely human attributes, such as value orientations, self-esteem, and the capacity for self-reflection and introspection. Some of the socialization techniques that he views as particularly empathy inducing (e.g., reasoning and induction) are also likely to be practiced only by humans. Staub's approach integrates concepts from adult experimental social psychology, clinical psychology, and different areas of developmental psychology to explain altruism and aggression in humans.

The next two chapters (6 and 7) provide empirical data on the complex organization of associations between prosocial and antisocial behaviors. Cummings, Hollenbeck, Iannotti, Radke-Yarrow, and Zahn-Waxler examine the patterns of interconnection among aggression, altruism, and emotional arousal in very young children. Two different studies showed consistent patterns of association to be different for boys and girls even during the first years of life. For boys, but not for girls, aggression, altruism, and emotionality were found to be positively associated. For girls, but not for boys, aggression was found to be related positively to reparation or remorse over wrongdoing. As Cairns reminds us (Chapter 2), aggression has both innate and learned components. Different societal standards hold for aggressive behavior in girls and boys, and probably different control strategies are used with the two sexes as well. Thus, aggressive inhibition in most societies may be likely to be gender biased; that is, aggressive behavior is seen as less tolerable in girls than in boys.

The Feshbachs (Chapter 7) conceptualize the relationships between altruism and aggression. They examine how personality structure and psychodynamic processes might influence relationships between altruism and aggression; they also consider the role of antecedent developmental factors. The mediating role of empathy and an empathy-training program are described in terms of their implications for the development of altruistic behaviors and the diminution of aggression. Relationships between aggression and assertiveness are examined as well. The Feshbachs find that relationships among altruism, aggression, emotionality, and other personality attributes are strongly influenced by the child's gender. For boys prosocial behaviors are linked to empathy, cognitive skills, and a low self-concept, while in girls prosocial behaviors are linked with empathy and a positive self-concept. For boys there appear to be more connections of social behaviors and indices of emotional expressivity, consistent with the NIMH research. The less cognitively skilled boy and the boy with higher self-esteem are also likely to be aggressive. For girls aggression appears to be unrelated to cognitive competence and self-concept.

Grusec and Dix (Chapter 8) review the different socialization practices linked to prosocial behaviors, with special emphasis on the parental attributions of altruism to the child in relationship to children's internalization of values. The extent to which socialization techniques deemed effective in theories and experimental studies actually find their way into the rearing repertoires of parents is examined. Ironically, the rearing practices hypothesized and sometimes found in experimental studies to foster internalization of values (namely, attributions and empathy training) are in fact, as shown in their own naturalistic studies, used very infrequently by parents. These contributors elaborate an important distinction between aggression and the failure to be altruistic and further indicate reasons why the two may be socialized very differently.

Socialization of aggression is also the focus of Chapter 9, by Reid, on parental violence toward children. Given that most parents in the United States believe that physical coercion is sometimes a legitimate and useful discipline technique, Reid explores the conditions that enhance the probability that the parents will physically injure the child. He examines connections between abusive behavior by the parent and behavioral characteristics of the child that relate to abuse (e.g., aggression). Reid recommends discipline techniques for abusive parents that involve rapid disengagement of parent from child, physical removal of the child from the circumstances of difficulty, and minimal use of lecturing or reasoning.

Marcus (Chapter 10) discusses differences in the definitions and conceptualizations of different forms of prosocial behaviors. He indicates why prosocial behaviors such as sharing, cooperation, and helping need to be studied more as they occur in children's natural habitats. Marcus demonstrates how research conclusions, especially about developmental changes in altruism, differ systematically depending on the particular form of prosocial behavior and on the motives and intentions that influence the behaviors. He also discusses evidence for affective mediators of prosocial behavior and speculates about ways in which such models could be extended to explore relationships between emotional arousal (especially anger) and aggression.

Dodge (Chapter 11) uses a social information-processing model to explain how cognitive processes may be related to aggressive and prosocial behavior. He integrates this model with his own research, which illustrates how children's cognitive processes and their social behavior may reciprocally influence each other in a way that can perpetuate deviant aggressive behavior. In contrast to Youniss, Dodge focuses on some of the negative characteristics of peer relationships that contribute to the establishment of reputations for aggression and to the perpetuation of aggressive acts. Furthermore, he considers how difficulties that some children have in understanding the intentions of others might contribute to inappropriate patterns of aggression and impede successful entry into the peer group.

These substantive contributions are followed by a chapter that considers the gaps in knowledge, speculates about needed changes in the research process, and suggests new directions for research. This volume does not attempt to provide overviews of major approaches or theories or general reviews of the literature on altruism, aggression, and related topics of morality and social cognition. These can be found elsewhere (e.g., see Rest, 1983; Parke & Slaby, 1983; Radke-Yarrow, Zahn-Waxler & Chapman, 1983; Shantz, 1983).

References

Bleier, R. (1984). *Science and gender: A critique of biology and its theories on women.* New York: Pergamon (Athene Series).

Bowlby, J. (1969). *Attachment and loss* (vol. 1). New York: Basic Books.

Bryant, B., & Crockenberg, S. (1980). Correlates and dimensions of prosocial behavior: A study of female siblings with their mothers. *Child Development, 51*: 529–544.

Cummings, M., Ianotti, R., & Zahn-Waxler, C. (April 21–24, 1983). The affective environment and aggression in young children. Society for Research in Child Development, Abstracts from the Biennial Meeting, vol. 4. Detroit, Michigan.

Goodall, J. (1983). *In the shadow of man.* Boston: Houghton Mifflin.

Loeber, R. (1982). The stability of anti-social and delinquent child behavior: A review. *Child Development, 53*: 1431–1446.

MacLean, P. D. (May 18, 1982). Evolutionary brain roots of family, play and the isolation call. Adolf Meyer Lecture, American Psychiatric Association, Toronto, Canada.

Main, M. & Weston, D. (1981). The quality of the toddler's relationship to mother and father: Related to conflict behavior and the readiness to establish new relationships. *Child Development, 52*: 932–940.

Moyer, K. W. (1968). Kinds of aggression and their physiological basis. *Communications in Behavioral Biology, 2*: 65–87.

Murray, A. (1979). Infant crying as an elicitor of parental behavior: An examination of two models. *Psychology Bulletin 86*: 193–215.

Olweus, D. (1979). Stability and aggressive reaction patterns in males: A review. *Psychology Bulletin, 86*: 852–875.

Parke, R. D., & Slaby, R. G. (1983). The development of aggression. In P. H. Mussen (Ed.), *Carmichael's manual of child psychology* (4th ed., vol. 4), E. M. Hetherington (Vol. Ed.). New York: Wiley.

Radke-Yarrow, M., & Zahn-Waxler, C. (1984). Roots, motives and patterning in children's prosocial behavior. In E. Staub, D. Bar-Tal, J. Karylowski, & J. Reykowski (Eds.), *The development and maintenance of prosocial behavior: international perspectives on positive morality* (pp. 155–176). New York: Plenum Press.

Radke-Yarrow, M., Zahn-Waxler, C., & Chapman, M. (1983). Children's prosocial dispositions and behavior. In P. H. Mussen (Ed.), *Carmichael's manual of child psychology*, 4th ed., vol. 3: Socialization, personality and social development, E. M. Hetherington (Vol. Ed.) (pp. 469–546). New York: Wiley.

Rest, J. R. (1983). Morality. In P. H. Mussen (Ed.), *Carmichael's manual of child psychology*, 4th ed., vol. 3 (pp. 495–555). New York: Wiley.

Shantz, C. U. (1983). Social cognition. In P. H. Mussen (Ed.), *Carmichael's manual of child psychology*, 4th ed., vol. 3 (pp. 495–555). New York: Wiley.

Webster's seventh new collegiate dictionary (1965). Springfield, MA: G & C Merriam.

Zahn-Waxler, C. (April 1984). Empathy and aggression in toddlers. New York: International Conference on Infant Studies.

Zahn-Waxler, C., Cummings, E. M., & Cooperman, G. (1984). Emotional development in childhood. In G. Whitehurst (Ed.), *Annals of child development*, vol. I (pp. 45–106). Greenwich, CT: JAI Press.

Zahn-Waxler, C., & Radke-Yarrow, M. 1982. The development of altruism: Alternative research strategies. In N. Eisenberg (Ed.), *The Development of Prosocial Behavior* (pp. 109–137). New York: Academic Press.

Part I

Biological, sociobiological, and ethological approaches to the study of altruism and aggression

1 The psychobiology of prosocial behaviors: separation distress, play, and altruism

Jaak Panksepp

The hope that functionally unitary brain circuits will be discovered for global concepts such as altruism and aggression remains unrealistic. Those labels are only class identifiers for diverse behavior patterns that may share outward similarities but that arise from several distinguishable neural systems.

Only preliminary biological understanding of altruism and aggression can be distilled from existing knowledge concerning emotive systems of the brain. We know approximately which brain circuits are essential for elaborating several forms of aggression (i.e., predatory, rage, and competitive). All run through the hypothalamus, interconnecting higher and lower areas of the visceral brain. As the available information has been reviewed extensively (e.g., see Adams, 1979; Moyer, 1976; Valzelli, 1981), those systems receive little further attention here.

No comparable circuits for altruistic behaviors have yet emerged from brain research. Indeed, the concept of altruism remains troublesomely vague in the study of animal behavior, and the diverse helping behaviors that could be subsumed under this concept (depending on one's definition) may be less directly coupled to activities of hard-wired emotional circuits than the above-mentioned aggressive tendencies. Whereas circuits for several distinct emotions, including anger–rage, anxiety–fear, separation–panic, and curiosity–expectancy appear to be wired into the visceral brain by the genetic heritage of mammals (albeit the behavioral competence of this heritage is refined by experience) (for review, see Panksepp, 1981a, 1982), altruistic tendencies may be linked more integrally to learning processes coupled to changing levels of activity in such emotive systems. For instance, brains of all social vertebrates have circuits that generate separation distress (which may provide the essential impetus for human affective experiences ranging from sorrow to panic)(Panksepp, Herman, Vilberg, Bishop & DeEskinazi, 1980; Panksepp, 1981b). Repeated arousal of such aversive brain states may help establish learned behavioral patterns designed to

19

reduce the incidence of those emotions in the future. Such emotive circuits could also unconditionally promote helping behaviors. For instance, mild arousal of the circuit in adult animals, as would occur during the crying of a child, may evoke "concerned" states that promote care-giving behaviors, thereby reducing the intensity of perceived distress in both helper and the helped. Similarly, the resonance of other emotive circuits among nearby animals, such as those of fear and anger, could yield coordinated behavioral patterns beneficial to others.

Of course, in humans, higher cognitive-fantasy mechanisms and cultural evolution could promote helping behaviors independently of such circuits, but even "cold" forms of altruism, such as the value of charity, may have arisen historically from an unconditional appreciation of the dictates of brain systems that mediate basic emotions. Still, it must be emphasized that no substantive neurological evidence about brain mediation of altruism exists. Consequently, the aim of this chapter is to summarize knowledge concerning brain systems that mediate those types of social interactions that should be the basis for the most common forms of altruistic behaviors and, more theoretically, to seek the sources of altruism among (1) brain emotional systems that mediate separation distress, (2) developmental processes that elaborate juvenile play, and (3) brain neuromodulators, such as brain opioids, that may help elaborate social bonds.

Specifically, it will be argued that brain opioids constitute the brain neurochemical system, for which we have the most extensive evidence for a key role in the specific control of social-affective processes. Accordingly, it is postulated that available knowledge concerning physiological, anatomical, and behavioral controls of opiate addiction provides a conceptual scheme within which the biological basis of social bonding (hence altruism) can begin to be analyzed (Panksepp et al., 1980; Panksepp, 1981b). It is acknowledged, however, that such a theoretical scheme is only one compelling entry point into the study of underlying processes. Many other brain systems (some of which presently remain unidentified, no doubt) will eventually be found to influence social affect. Considering how little basic biological knowledge exists in this area, however, the "opioid hypothesis" is rather vigorously argued to provide a robust and provocative sounding board for future thinking in the area.

Altruism, sociobiology, and psychobiology

The emerging discipline of sociobiology has linked the concept of altruism to kin selection and has restricted it to those helping behaviors that tend to reduce the survival, hence the reproductive advantage of the purveyor of help (for reviews, see Barash, 1982; Kurland, 1980; Lopreato, 1981). Although an eminently logical and rigorous definition, there is no convincing evidence that such personally maladaptive behavioral patterns are genetically ordained in any vertebrate. Even the emission of alarm calls, tentatively taken as a line of potential evidence for such extremes of altruism in birds and mammals, remains to be empirically linked to a reduction of individual survival. As emphasized by Trivers (1971), warning calls may increase the probability that nearby strangers will be caught. Although it remains undemonstrated that any specific mammalian helping behavior is genetically coded (with the exception of maternal behavior), it is easy to see how such behaviors could arise experientially from activities of brain emotive circuits (see Hoffman, 1981; Panksepp, 1982), which were originally selected for the selfish purpose of sustaining the integrity of an individual organism. Through certain circuit sensitivities (e.g., perceptually induced resonance of emotive circuits between nearby animals), emotional brain systems may evoke contagious interanimal mood states from which altruistic behaviors arise.

For instance, pain responses in one animal may unconditionally activate distress circuits in brains of nearby animals, promoting behaviors that minimize distress in both. Such seeking of emotional relief may have direct survival value for the recipient and indirect (genetic) survival value for the altruist. However, the proximal underlying mechanism is presumably related to the rebalancing of activity in emotional circuits, and only in a distal sense may such behavior also help keep the genetic ledger in the black. The existence of such genetic advantage would not imply, however, that the altruistic behavior emerges through any kind of genetically dictated kin recognition. For geographic and historical reasons, animals are more likely to be bonded to relatives than genetic strangers, making it likely that expressions of altruism will typically benefit relatives, without the intervention of ghostly genetic imperatives. Although there may be some weak remnant of innate kin-recognition ability in mammals (e.g., Hepper, 1983; Wu, Holmes, Medina, & Sackett, 1980), the brunt of the responsibility for being committed to one's clan seems likely to arise from bonding processes that are associative in nature.

Thus, the old common-sense definition of altruism, which includes behaviors that promote the welfare of other living creatures but that do not necessarily decrease the personal survival probability of the altruist, will be sustained as the conceptual guide for the present psychobiological analysis. It is assumed that the biological nature of bond-formation and the nature of emotional circuits that mediate distress will be key processes through which the biological sources of altruism will be unraveled. Also if one relaxes the definition of altruism, as advocated here, to include all behaviors that assist the welfare of others, maternal behavior becomes a major biological process from which the sources of altruism should be sought. Clearly, the proximal causes of altruism must arise from a psychoneurological, rather than a sociobiological, analysis. The sociobiological synthesis that Wilson (1975) promised cannot materialize without an understanding of the brain mechanisms governing social emotions. A scientifically compelling sociobiology cannot exist without an explicit marriage of the evolutionary and psychobiological perspectives for the study of social processes. Toward that end, the emerging knowledge concerning brain control of social behavior (gregariousness and play, maternal behavior, sexual behavior, dominance, social displays, affective vocalizations, and imprinting) in birds and mammals is summarized in the Appendix at the end of this chapter. A warning, however: The theoretical perspective advocated in this chapter may convey a feeling that there is a great deal more closure on our knowledge of the relationship of brain mechanisms and social behavior than actually exists. Let me hasten to emphasize that we are only on the near shore of substantive knowledge in the area, and there are many alternative ways to interpret the facts summarized.

The opioid hypothesis of social affect

On the basis of similarities between narcotic addiction and social dependence, we have hypothesized that brain opioid systems (for review, see De Wied & Jolles, 1982; Henry, 1982; Miller & Cuatrecasas, 1978; Snyder & Childers, 1979) participate in the elaboration of social emotions. The logic is straightforward: The loss of social support precipitates a decrease in brain opioid activity, yielding withdrawal symptoms, as emotive circuits that mediate loneliness–panic states are activated or disinhibited. Reestablishment of social contact may, among other neural changes, activate endogenous opioid systems, alleviating separation distress, and strengthening social bonds. In view of conclusive evidence that brain opioids inhibit emotions arising from social isolation, I predict that fluctuating activity in underlying emotive systems (see Panksepp, 1982) will prove a contributing factor in the emission of altruistic behaviors. Using the prosocial categories summarized in the appendix to this chapter, the evidence for opioid involvement in social affect stacks up as follows (for more extensive reviews of our past work, see Panksepp, 1981b; Panksepp et al., 1980; and Panksepp, Siviy, & Normansell, 1985).

Opioid effects on social behaviors

Affective vocalizations. Our most extensive evidence arises from the study of separation-induced distress vocalizations (DVs). Opioid alkaloids and peptides are especially effective in reducing separation distress; opiate receptor-blocking agents (e.g., naloxone and naltrexone) can increase DVs, especially when animals are separated with several conspecifics (Panksepp, Bean, Bishop, Vilberg, & Sahley, 1980). It should be emphasized, however, that the antagonist effects have proved quite fickle from one experiment to another. Clearly, injections of opiate antagonists do not increase DVs in an obligatory manner, suggesting that opioids merely modulate the throughput system for separation distress. Our best guess is that a cholinergic pathway may be the throughput circuit, for DVs are triggered in a highly stereotyped and repetitive manner by injections of curare into the fourth ventricle region of the chick (Panksepp, Normansell et al. 1983). In any case, the effects of opiate receptor agonists are strong and unambiguous, displaying considerable pharmacological specificity (Panksepp, Meeker, & Bean, 1980). The separation response can be inhibited with doses as low as 50 and 10 picomoles of morphine and β-endorphin administered intraventricularly (J. Panksepp & P. Bishop, unpublished data). To our knowledge, these are among the smallest doses of neuroactive agents to have yielded reliable behavioral effects. Conversely, opiate withdrawal can increase DVs (Newby-Schmidt & Norton, 1981), suggesting that social withdrawal symptoms are aggravated by the central state accompanying narcotic withdrawal (see Fig. 1.1).

Furthermore, brain systems that mediate DVs are situated within high opiate receptor zones (Herman, 1979), and artificial activation of brain opioid systems with stimulation of the periaqueductal gray matter reduces the activity of distress vocalization circuitry (Herman & Panksepp, 1981). Preliminary work with different opiate receptor agonists and antagonists suggests that the μ receptor is essential for the modulation of distress that has been observed. For example, protected forms of met-enkephalin are more powerful than protected forms of leu-enkephalin in decreasing DVs. It is noteworthy that anatomical mapping of opioid systems in the bird brain has affirmed that met-enkephalin-like immunoreactive cell bodies, fibers, and terminals are located in the neighborhood of vocalization circuits (de Lanerolle, Elde, Sparber &, Frick, 1981; Ryan, Arnold, & Elde, 1981). In unpublished lesion studies, we have found that damage to dorsomedial thalamic zones from which DVs can be electrically evoked will reduce natural separation DVs in guinea pigs, dogs, and chickens.

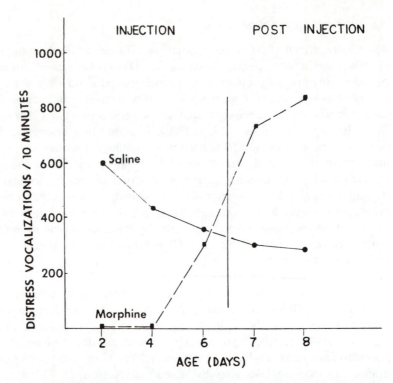

Figure 1.1. Young chicks were injected intraperitoneally with 10 mg/kg of morphine sulfate or saline vehicle for 3 days 20 min before a 10-min period of social isolation, during which distress calls were automatically recorded (as described in Panksepp et al., 1980). Vocalizations during withdrawal (24 and 48 hr after the last morphine injection) were reliably increased compared with control levels, suggesting that opioid withdrawal acted synergistically with social withdrawal.

Gregariousness and play. Activation of brain opioid systems can decrease gregariousness (Panksepp, Najam, & Soares, 1979), but the same doses of morphine can also increase social play (Panksepp, 1979) and learned homing behavior during extinction (Panksepp & DeEskinazi, 1980). Preliminary neurochemical information from subtractive autoradiography work affirms that brain opioid systems are active during social interactions (Panksepp & Bishop, 1981). The effects of naloxone on gregariousness, as measured by time together, have not been uniform in our hands (Panksepp et al., 1979), under a variety of test situations (L. A. Normansell & Panksepp, unpublished data, 1982). However, File (1980) reported decreases in social interaction between rats, and Kavaliers (1981) found naloxone to reduce schooling tendencies in goldfish. Likewise, we have uniformly observed a reduction in juvenile play between naloxone-treated rats in more than a dozen separate studies (Panksepp, 1979; Jalowiec, Panksepp, DeEskinazi, & Bishop, 1980). In an obedience-training situation, dogs are less obedient but more socially solicitous after treatment with naloxone and more obedient but less solicitous after being given morphine (Panksepp, Conner, Forster, Bishop, & Scott, 1983).

Some of the above effects may seem paradoxical, and indeed opiate effects on gregariousness are difficult to predict a priori. Such pharmacological maneuvers reduce intrinsic modulation in the underlying neurochemical curcuits, yielding brain states that surely do not occur in real life. For instance, although an animal treated with naloxone may be found to experience a shift toward an internal state of increased social need, it may simultaneously be unable to obtain the rewards from social interactions that it would under normal conditions (Panksepp, 1981b). The resultant approach–avoidance conflict could yield opposite predictions, depending on the nature of the underlying motivational gradients and the specific social tasks employed.

Although naloxone given to adult humans has not generally produced severe emotional responses, it is noteworthy that a recent high-dose study demonstrated a marked increase in tension–anxiety, hostility and bewilderment and led to a deterioration of cognitive functioning in response to the drug (Cohen, Cohen, Pickar, Weingartner, & Murphy, 1983). Furthermore, from the perspective that opioid systems should be especially responsive in childhood (Panksepp, 1981b), it might be anticipated that the most unambiguous affective changes would be seen in the younger organisms.

Dominance. Using our rat play paradigm, during which stable dominance relationships evolve (Panksepp, 1981c), we have evaluated the capacity of opiate drugs to modulate "social strength," with the prediction that opiate agonists would facilitate and opiate receptor antagonists would reduce dominance. In one study, dominance relationships were permitted to develop during a 4-day predrug period, followed by 7 days of drug treatment (at 1 mg/kg, subcutaneously for the first 5 days and 2 mg/kg for the last 2 days) followed by 4 days of no treatment (Fig. 1.2). Morphine given to submissive animals did temporarily increase assertiveness, as indicated by frequency of pinning (Fig. 1.2 top), and naloxone given to dominant animals reduced pinning (Fig. 1.2 middle), but the effects were not significant. When one animal received morphine and the other naloxone (Fig. 1.2 bottom), the morphine animals increased in dominance to a much greater extent. (Note, that no dominance is apparent during the baseline period in these groups because half of the dominant and half of the submissive

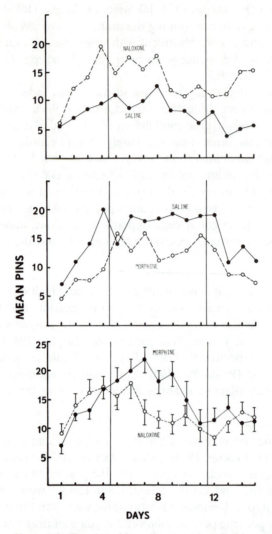

Figure 1.2. The play of juvenile rats was studied by measuring pinning behavior (as described in Panksepp, 1981). During the first 4 test days, with no drug treatments, the dominance pattern was monitored. (Top) The dominant animal was given 1 mg/kg of naloxone, and the submissive rat, saline carrier 20 min before testing (N = 10 pairs). (Middle) The submissive animal was given 1 mg/kg of morphine and the dominant animal saline (N = 10 pairs). (Bottom) One-half the dominant and one-half the submissive animals received morphine and one-half received naloxone (N = 20 pairs), yielding the clearest drug-induced separation in dominance. Drug testing was continued for 7 days, with drug dosage doubled for the last 2 test days. Four days of postdrug testing were conducted. Tests were on successive days, starting when animals were 25 days of age. Animals were individually housed at all times except during the 5-min test periods depicted.

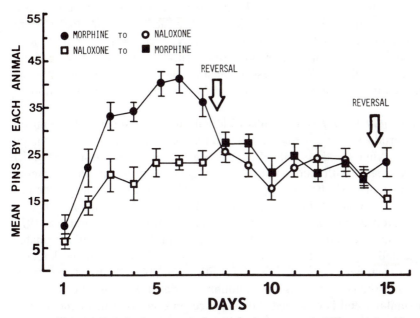

Figure 1.3. Animals were tested as in the bottom panel of Figure 1.2, with one animal receiving 0.5 mg/kg of morphine and the other 0.5 mg/kg of naloxone. Drug treatment was instituted from the first test period, starting at 22 days of age. Animals were tested thereafter every other day until they were 50 days of age. Following the 7th test, drug conditions were reversed. After the 14th test, the original drug conditions were reinstituted for one 5-min test period.

animals received each drug.) Taken together, however, these effects were not particularly robust, perhaps because of the power of social learning that had developed during the 4 days of baseline testing. When the same manipulations were done from the very beginning of testing, the separation of animals with respect to drug treatments is strong (Fig. 1.3), but the influence of social learning again seems apparent in the failure of groups to reverse when drug conditions were reversed (after the seventh day of testing). Essentially identical effects were observed in naloxone treated animals pitted against controls. But morphine was not effective in evoking robust and consistent dominance against saline-treated animals, suggesting that endogenous opioid activity in normal rats is sufficient to sustain a high level of assertive competence (Jalowiec et al., 1980).

Such results suggest that "social strength" may emerge from high activity of brain opioid circuits. How, then, can we explain that high levels of stress (Amit, Brown, & Amit, 1980), including social stress (Miczek, Thompson, & Shuster, 1982), also activate opioid systems? Perhaps medium levels of arousal of opioid systems promote assertiveness and social competence, while lower levels lead to social consequences (e.g., defeat), which can yield compensatory release of brain opioids. Such homeostatic responses may serve not only to alleviate stress but to facilitate psychological states that promote social dispersal. Alternatively, perhaps stress-induced analgesia is largely a matter of mistaken identity, actually reflecting relief-induced analgesia. Most stress-induced analgesia procedures test for pain reduction after an animal is removed from a highly stressful situation.

Maternal behavior. Our results with maternal behavior have been mixed. In certain species, naloxone has dramatically reduced maternal competence, while in others little effect has been observed. For instance, BALB mice treated with naloxone exhibited a qualitative disruption in maternal competence. Mothers did not systematically return pups back to the nest (Vilberg, Bean, Bishop, Porada, & Panksepp, 1977). Similar effects were observed in an unspecified mouse strain by Brown and Peterson (1979) using long-term delivery of naltrexone. In Long-Evans rats, approximately one-half of the mothers tested have exhibited higher retrieval latencies after treatment with naloxone than with saline, but all animals did return pups to the nest (J. Panksepp, unpublished data). In Swiss-Webster mice, a similar trend is observed. For instance, in one experiment the average latency to begin retrieving was 165 sec after naloxone injection (1 mg/kg, intraperitoneally), 28 sec after control injection ($p<.01$), and 18 sec after morphine injection (1 mg/kg), but only modest differences were found among groups in terms of number and speed of pup retrieval once maternal behavior was initiated. On the average, morphine-treated animals retrieved a pup every 1.5 sec, the saline-treated mothers every 2.2 sec, and the naloxone-treated group every 3.7 sec. In four dogs we tested, maternal retrieval of dispersed pups was severely disrupted. Although all mothers rapidly sought out the pups, three dropped them repeatedly and returned home alone.

A study of maternal aggression in Swiss-Webster mice has yielded dramatic results. Mothers treated with naloxone exhibited slightly more defensive fighting with an intruder than did controls, but morphine-treated mothers (1 mg/kg) exhibited a clear disregard for male intruders, often exhibiting no maternal defense at all. One mother permitted a male intruder to eat her pups (Bean & Conner, 1979). These results suggest that reduced brain opioid activity promotes a central state comparable to that which occurs when the safety of offspring is threatened, while activation of brain opioid activity blocks the perceptions of such threat.

Sexual behavior. If brain opioid activity fulfills social needs, it could be hypothesized that opiate blockade would facilitate seeking of specific social gratification, such as sex. Indeed, opioid systems interact with the brain systems that regulate sex-steroid secretion (Cicero, Schainker, & Meyer, 1979; Hahn and Fishman, 1979), and naloxone has been found to facilitate sexual behavior in rats (Gessa, Paglietti, & Pellegrini Quarantotti, 1979; McIntosh, Vallano, & Barfield, 1980; Myers & Baum, 1979). In dogs we have observed an increase in genital self-grooming after naloxone injections (J. Panksepp & Conner, unpublished data). It is also noteworthy that in primates, only a generalized tendency for increased prosocial activity – that is, mutual grooming among animals – rather than increased sexual activity was observed (Meller, Keverne, & Herbert, 1980). Such effects are congruent with the proposal that opiate receptor blockade increases the arousal of brain circuits that promote seeking of social contact.

Social displays. We have analyzed the effects of opiates on tail wagging in dogs. Naloxone yields a striking increase in socially induced tail wagging and low doses of morphine decrease such wagging, again suggesting that opioid systems control the desire for social interaction (Davis, 1980). Furthermore, the ability of naloxone to increase canine tail wagging with no increase in distress vocalizations indicates that opioid receptor blockade does not simply evoke a generalized state of distress, but a more subtle state that may be more accurately portrayed as increased social need (perhaps loneliness, in everyday language).

Imprinting and learning. Morphine has a powerful effect in sustaining social habits in the absence of any primary reinforcement, while naloxone speeds extinction of such habits in juvenile rats using a discriminated homing task (Panksepp & DeEskinazi, 1980). In studies of chick imprinting, we have found that naloxone does not block the development of a following response, although animals exhibit increased separation distress vocalizations (J. Panksepp, P. Bishop, & G. Davies, 1981, unpublished data). Thus, emotional measures of imprinting, as indicated by the ability of a familiar stimulus to reduce distress vocalizations, are reduced by opioid blockade (Panksepp et al., 1980). Using a discriminative choice situation with chicks that had been exposed to colored crumpled paper balls during the first 3 days of life, we found that naloxone given during acquisition trials does reduce subsequent correct choice behavior between blue and green stimuli but not between red and blue stimuli (Panksepp, Siviy, Normansell, White, & Bishop, 1982).

Summary. Taken together, these results indicate that opiate receptor blockade increases the social need of animals. Although some of the above findings appear paradoxical at first glance, they are consistent if we consider the underlying emotional states these drugs may produce – a feeling of heightened social need after treatment with naloxone and of fulfillment of social needs and corresponding increase in "social strength" after low doses of morphine. Even some of the side effects of opiate treatment, such as the nausea commonly observed after initial opiate administration in some species, suggest linkage to a social affect hypothesis. For example, many species feed their young by vomiting ingested food. Perhaps increased endogenous opioid activity rising from social stimulation promotes this food-sharing reflex.

In the context of the above theory, it is also not surprising that social isolation modifies the number of brain opiate receptors (Bonnet, Miller, & Simon, 1976) and that naloxone is perceived to be more aversive in socially housed than in solitary animals (Pilcher & Jones, 1981). However, the direct analysis of brain opioid systems in a social context remains rudimentary (e.g., Panksepp & Bishop, 1981), but a biological understanding of altruism will require a clarification of such processes.

Kin recognition

Granted the sociobiological tenet that the roots of "altruistic" behaviors are embedded in an evolutionary past based on genetic selfishness that has come to be extended to relatives, the key biological issue that needs clarification is how the brain elaborates kin recognition. The identification of genetic relatives may have weak innate components, as appears to have been demonstrated by Hepper (1983) and by Wu and colleagues (1980), perhaps mediated by such attributes as odor, appearance, or manner of behaving, but it remains likely that most kin recognition within at least mammalian and avian species arises from brain emotional systems that mediate social bonding. Thereby, both kin-related "altruism" and kin-unrelated "reciprocal altruism" could be explained by a common brain process – that which mediates the formation of social attachments. Although brain neurochemical mechanisms for social bonding remain to be identified, brain opioid activity stands as the only nominated candidate.

Indeed, opiate receptors are especially high in brain areas that have been implicated in imprinting, as well as in sensory circuits that would be essential for kin recognition. In chick brains, both the intermediate medial hyperstriatum ventrale (IMHV) and lateral forebrain – areas implicated in imprinting (as summarized in the Appendix) – are high opiate-receptor zones (Fig. 1.4). Chicks are especially adept at visual imprinting, and their

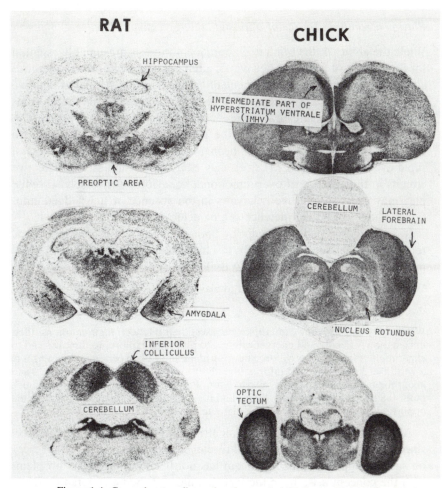

Figure 1.4. Coronal autoradiographs of rat and chick brains 30 min after administration of tritiated diprenorphine (using methods described in Panksepp & Bishop, 1981). Brain areas important in the elaboration of social processes have high opioid receptor densities, as described in the text.

optic tecta are extremely rich in opiate receptors. In less visually oriented animals such as rats, olfactory systems may be more influential in social bonding; the rodent amygdala and medial thalamus, areas that process olfactory information, are rich in opiate receptors. Also, the high density of opiate receptors in the inferior colliculus in mammals may promote auditory-affective recognition of kindred animals, both learned and unlearned.

Play as a common source of altruistic and aggressive behaviors

While the ability of the brain to elaborate emotions is presumably essential for the genesis of prosocial behaviors, adult competence probably requires substantial exercise and refinement of the genetically mandated emotive circuits of the newborn. There is reason to suppose that brain mechanisms have evolved to ensure that coherent social adaptations will evolve epi-genetically from the activities of the genetically provided circuits. Two brain mechanisms seem to ensure proper maturation of emotive processes: rapid eye movement (REM) sleep may exercise and mold brain affective circuits in the absence of overt emotional behaviors. Conversely, juvenile play may exercise emotive behaviors in the absence of full-fledged emotional states so that competence can be achieved before it is needed.

It is commonly believed that play both exercises and refines instinctual tendencies (e.g., see Smith, 1982); this hypothesis is succinctly summarized in a flyer to be found with LEGO Building Set playthings:

Why is it so important for your child to play?

it asks, and it answers:

When children play, they exercise their senses, their intellect, their emotions, their imagination – keenly and energetically . . . to play is to explore, to discover and to experiment. Playing helps children develop ideas and gain experience. It gives them a wealth of knowledge and information about the world in which they live – and about themselves. So to play is also to learn. Play is fun for children. But it's much more than that – it's good for them, and it's necessary . . . play gives children the opportunity to develop and use the many talents they were born with.

Although theories of play are plentiful, physiological data are scarce, since they must come from animal research, for which controlled research on such a supposedly fuzzy concept has not been popular. The problems with the concept arise from the fact that most of the behaviors that occur during play are also observed in adult organisms, and if the brain controls are no different at the two ages, a separate category called play is super-fluous. Although similarities in the underlying controls must surely be found, there are also several unique aspects of play behaviors: (1) the lack of seriousness (e.g., ineffective biting as opposed to real biting), (2) the unique sequential attributes (e.g., rapid fluctuation between unrelated response sequences), and (3) the motivational characteristics (e.g., play fighting is a positively motivated behavior, while adult emotional aggression has an aversive emotional tone).

No generally acceptable behavioral definition of play has yet been proposed – indeed it seems unlikely that one could be generated. Nevertheless, exploration of the psychobiological perspectives may permit us to deal realistically with those processes that remain inadequately defined. For example, many innate brain processes probably exist whose intrinsic multidimensionality prevents adequate behavioral definitions. Although the existence of such processes may be denied (as behaviorism has all too often done), it seems more realistic to assume their existence (if practically everyone can recognize their manifestations in everyday life) and then to work intentionally toward neurally linked definitions of the processes. Because play has to be generated by distinct brain activities, a lasting definition would specify the locations and properties of the circuits instigating the behavior universally recognized as play. Accordingly, play would come to be scientifically defined with respect to concrete brain processes that generate the myriad behaviors traditionally subsumed by the concept. Although we are still unable even to approximate a neurobiological definition, I would postulate that the neural substructure has an executive command component that has wide ramifications in the brain (similar in design, perhaps, to those that instigate major emotions (Panksepp, 1982) and that probably has access to the multitude of pattern generators for various emotive behaviors. Thus, it may have relationships, both in design and anatomical proximity, to executive mechanisms that generate REM sleep. Because of such divergent controls, it becomes understandable why a simple behavioral definition of play has remained persistently elusive.

In any event, considering the ease with which social play of rats can be studied in the laboratory, amplified by prior social deprivation and operationalized by the measure of pinning behavior (Panksepp & Betty, 1980; Panksepp, 1981c), a systematic analysis of how the brain controls such behavior is now feasible. In obvious ways, such work may link well with analyses of altruism, dominance, and kin recognition.

Considering that males and females assume measurably distinct social roles in most animal societies, it is to be expected that brain mechanisms that trigger play would differentially affect male and female behavioral propensities during play. Assertive–aggressive tendencies are more likely to be aroused in males, while in females, flight and prosocial inclinations may be differentially facilitated. Sachs and Harris (1978) report that male lambs exhibit more mounting and butting during play, while females are more likely to gambol. Lancaster (1971) reports that female vervet monkeys engage in more play-mothering than do males. Still, the meaning of apparent gender differences in play remains ambiguous.

Gender differences in play. Gender differences in rough-and-tumble play have been observed in monkeys, with males typically being more assertive (Goy, 1978; Owens, 1975). Some investigators have also observed comparable though modest sex-based differences in rats (Beatty, Dodge, Traylor, & Meaney, 1981; Meaney & Stewart, 1981; Olioff & Stewart, 1978; Poole & Fish, 1976), but such effects are not always apparent (Panksepp & Beatty, 1980; Panksepp, 1981a). In cats, gender differences in play are also modest (Barrett & Bateson, 1978) and largely attributable to the sex composition of the litters from which animals come – the more males in the litter, the more timid the females (Caro, 1981).

Our impression is that gender differences in the play of socially isolated rats using a paired-encounter procedure are practically nonexistent. Even in mixed-sex play pairs, male rats do not routinely play more than females when animals are young. Near puberty, however, males do begin to predominate over females, but they also weigh more, and it is clear that body weight is an important variable in the development of play dominance (Panksepp, 1981c). Since a considerable amount of social learning is elaborated during play, the so-called higher playfulness of males, which has so often been reported in animals observed in complex social environments, may be secondarily due to the consequences of androgens promoting heaviness and aggressiveness rather than to any intrinsic difference in the vigor of the underlying play circuitry. Thus, a meaningful interpretation of differences will require carefully controlled social reinforcement histories of animals, indicating the value of the paired-encounter procedure for studying play (Panksepp, 1981c) over more naturalistic approaches.

Neuropharmacology of play. In our initial pharmacological analysis of play (Fig. 1.5), low doses of morphine were found to increase play behavior in socially isolated rats, while decreasing play in socially housed animals; naloxone decreased play in both (Panksepp, 1979). Other pharmacological effects were also apparent. Psychomotor stimulants, which quiet and reduce the play exhibited by hyperkinetic children, also reduce play in rats (Beatty, Dodge, Dodge, White, & Panksepp, 1982). Unlike the reciprocal results observed in the opiate system, catecholamine receptor-blocking agents (chlorpromazine and haloperidol) have failed to increase play; in fact, these agents have reduced it; they have also failed to attenuate the effects of amphetamine. Similarly, tricyclic antidepressants (imipramine, desimipramine, and chlorimipramine) decrease play, while benzodiazepine anxiolytics (chlordiazepoxide) have little effect (for recent review see Panksepp, Siviy and Normansell, 1984).

Serotonin manipulations on play are powerful and clear cut. Since this neurochemical system generally inhibits all waking behaviors, we anticipated that social play would be reduced; both the serotonin-releasing agent fenfluramine and the serotonin receptor agonist quipazine were found to

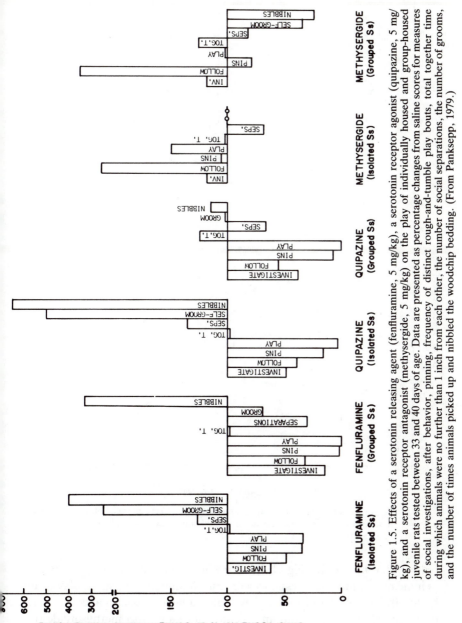

Figure 1.5. Effects of a serotonin releasing agent (fenfluramine, 5 mg/kg), a serotonin receptor agonist (quipazine, 5 mg/kg), and a serotonin receptor antagonist (methysergide, 5 mg/kg) on the play of individually housed and group-housed juvenile rats tested between 33 and 40 days of age. Data are presented as percentage changes from saline scores for measures of social investigations, after behavior, pinning, frequency of distinct rough-and-tumble play bouts, total together time during which animals were no further than 1 inch from each other, the number of social separations, the number of grooms, and the number of times animals picked up and nibbled the woodchip bedding. (From Panksepp, 1979.)

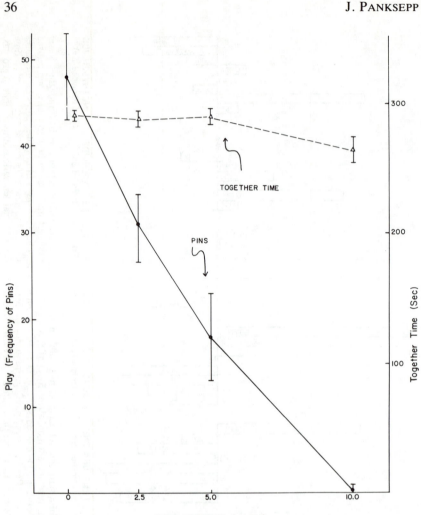

Figure 1.6. Dose–response data for fenfluramine effects on social play and together time during a 5-min test session in individually housed animals between the ages of 32 and 38.

reduce play markedly (Fig. 1.5). The effects have been very systematic, as indicated in the dose–response curve for fenfluramine, where play could be totally eliminated (10 mg/kg) without reducing maintenance of social proximity (Fig. 1.6). Serotonin receptor blockade with methysergide has not had a powerful effect on play, even though social investigation and following behaviors are slightly increased. We have attempted to determine whether social isolation amplifies play fighting partially by reducing brain serotonin activity, but neither parachlorophenylalanine (PCPA), a tryptophan hydroxylase inhibitor, nor feeding young rats tryptophan-free diets increased play. Both reduced play markedly, perhaps simply because the animals felt ill.

Cholinergic analysis of play indicates that muscarinic receptor blockade with scopolomine and atropine reduces play (Thor & Holloway, 1983). Likewise nicotine reduces play; this may be a specific effect, since the nicotinic receptor-blocking agent mecamylamine has yielded modest increases in pinning behavior (see Panksepp, et al. 1984).

It is to be anticipated that most psychopharmacological treatments will have effects on play, leading to great difficulty in winnowing essential processes from less pertinent ones. It may be appropriate to expect that specific controls will yield opposite effects with receptor agonists and antagonists; from that perspective, brain opioids are the only systems that have compelling support for a specific role in play. Indeed, subtractive autoradiography affirms that opioids may be released during play (Panksepp & Bishop, 1981).

Brain circuits and play: the case of ventromedial hypothalamic lesions. There is no compelling neuroanatomy for play processes. Specific brain circuits surely elaborate play, but a theory is needed to guide the search. Perhaps localization of brain opioids may serve such a function, but opioid systems are ubiquitous, touching most parts of the brain. Considering that social play resembles aggression – indeed some have studied it as such (Taylor 1980) – it is reasonable to expect that play fighting and real fighting will share many brain controls. Indeed, amygdala lesions reduce both aggression and play, and septal lesions can increase both behaviors (Beatty, Dodge, Traylor, Donegan, Gooding, 1982; Grossman, 1978; Meaney, Dodge, & Beatty, 1981; Siviy, Panksepp, & White, 1983).

As summarized in Figure 1.7, large amygdala and septal lesions have lasting effects on juvenile play throughout early life. It is noteworthy that the septal area is relatively free of opioid receptors, while receptor fields are dense in the amygdala (Panksepp & Bishop, 1981). It will be interesting to determine whether there can be a general principle that play is reduced by damage to brain areas enriched in opiate receptors. In any case, as with pharmacological approaches, there will be great problems in delineating that brain damage is actually disrupting play circuits as opposed to the many subsidiary processes that surely contribute to play competence, such as attention, learning, and various sensorimotor abilities. It is to be hoped that workers in the field will devote considerable effort to unraveling such issues.

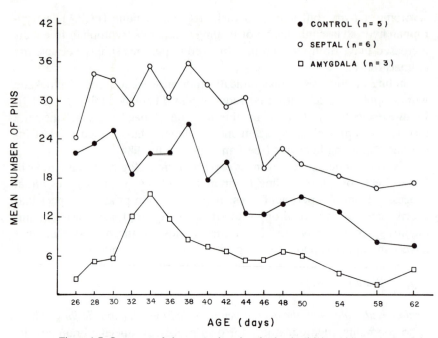

Figure 1.7. Ontogeny of play curves in pairs of animals with large bilateral amygdala and septal lesions and sham-operated controls (surgeries administered at 21 days of age). After recovery from surgery, rats were housed individually and given 5-min opportunities to play, in like-lesioned pairs, every other day until 48 days of age and every 4 days thereafter. Lesions of the septal area (damage extending laterally to ventricles, dorsally to corpus callosum and ventrally to anterior commissure) resulted in stable increases in amount of pinning, whereas lesions of amygdala (encompassing all major nuclear groups) resulted in marked reductions in play.

In any event, the executive mechanisms for aggression and play are likely to be different. That is, play is a positively motivated behavior (Humphreys and Einon, 1981), while the emotions accompanying rage are aversive (Panksepp, 1971a). Also, brain mechanisms of play are probably linked to emotional processes that promote interanimal trust, so that assertive gestures, which might provoke defensive attitudes among strange adults, are interpreted as friendly rather than threatening. Indeed, the brain mechanisms of "trust" that promote play may be the same as those that promote social comfort and bonding. For such reasons we would suggest that the ability of low doses of morphine to reduce separation distress and to increase play (Figs. 1.2 and 1.3) reflect the same emotional effect.

To evelute further the relationships among interanimal aggression, trust, and play, a brain area was selected for study, damage of which has been established to produce aggressive "sociopathic" tendencies in adult animals. The most spectacular rage observed in subjects with restricted brain damage is that evoked by ventromedial hypothalamic (VMH) lesions. VMH-lesioned animals become highly irritable and intolerant of stimuli that had provoked no anger preoperatively. Wheatley (1944) first described VMH-induced rage in cats, and it has now been extensively studied in other species as well as in humans (Reeves & Plum, 1969). How would such brain damage change social play?

As a prelude to such an investigation, Panksepp (1971b) performed a brief study that measured the effects of VMH lesions on the appreciation of submissive tendencies in other adult rats. Familiar animals usually resolve their differences through ritualized gestures that communicate dominance and submission. To determine whether massive VMH damage modifies such social sensitivity, the level of fighting between preselected aggressive and passive rats was measured in a situation in which fighting was systematically provoked by foot shock. In normal rats, passive animals seemed more influential in controlling the overall level of aggression than the aggressive ones, as summarized in Figure 1.8a. Thus, while the most passive animal (rat 4) did not fight much, regardless of which normal aggressive animal it was pitted against, the most assertive of the passive animals (rat 1) exhibited considerable fighting with every aggressive animal. When these same passive rats were pitted against four rats with VMH lesions, a different profile emerged. The viciousness of the lesioned animals provoked high levels of defensive fighting from every passive animal. Only the most passive rat refused to fight (sticking its nose in a corner of the test chamber), but this behavior did not deter the VMH-lesioned animal, which repeatedly provoked battle by biting the passive animal on the back. VMH-lesioned animals had apparently become insensitive to the peaceful attitudes of their companions; this finding raises the possibility that inhibitory influences from the medial hypothalamus normally promote harmonious and peaceful interactions among members of a species. It is noteworthy that a major brain opioid system, that containing β-endorphin, emanates from this part of the brain (Fig. 1.8b).

Accordingly, the investigation set out to determine the effects of such lesions on play in juvenile rats (Panksepp, unpublished observations, 1981). Five rats were surgically prepared with bilateral anodal VMH lesions at 24 days of age, and five animals received sham operations. They were socially isolated from their family groups 2 days later, and the first play test was conducted 2 days after isolation (at 28 days of age). For the first 2 days, VMH-lesioned animals were paired with controls, and for the next

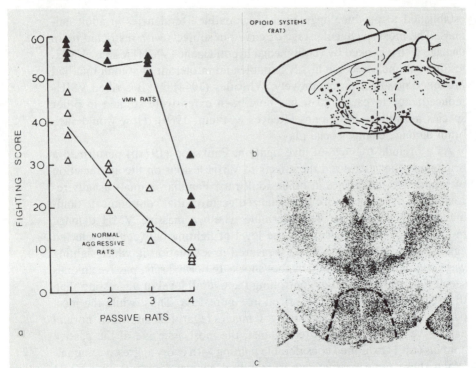

Figure 1.8. Shock-elicited fighting between normally passive rats pitted first against normally aggressive rats and then against animals with large medial hypothalamic lesions that had elicited a clear rage syndrome (a). All passive animals were paired against all aggressive animals in round-robin fashion. The approximate size of lesions is summarized on a frontal hypothalamic section depicting opiate receptor distributions (c) (according to Panksepp, 1971b). The schematic (b) summarizes brain opioid systems on a parasaggital view of the rat brain. Triangles indicate the medial hypothalamic location of β-endorphin cell bodies, and wavy lines indicate projection pathways from these cells; large squares indicate approximate locations of major enkephalin cell clusters, while smaller groups of squares depict high-density enkephalin terminal fields.

5 days, controls were tested with each other in round-robin fashion, while VMH animals were pitted against each other. For the last three tests, the original control–VMH lesion pairings were reestablished.

The results were striking. During the first days of testing, controls became intensely intimidated by VMH animals. What started as apparent play snowballed into serious aggression. What little pinning did occur was exhibited by the VMH-operated animal, but rapidly the control animals sought to avoid all contact with lesioned animals, which seemed as willing to bite as to play. Subsequently, when the control animals were paired against each other, they remained wary during the first few sessions, but gradually relaxed. The number of playful pins increased from an average of 1.4 per session to 11.6 per 5 min during the rehabilitation period. Although this was much lower than the 30–50 pins per 5 min that would normally be expected from animals of this age, it was clear that the normal rats were beginning to reexhibit playful social interactions. Meanwhile, the VMH-lesioned animals, pitted against their own kind, ended up in vicious fighting, with serious biting and squealing. Such animals rapidly learned to fear each other. While they exhibited 10.4 pins during the first session (mostly during the course of fierce fighting), the amount of pinning declined across days to a low of 2.6 pins per 5 min. This was real and earnest fighting, for pin durations of longer than 1 min were observed during which both animals assumed tense, open-mouthed, gasping postures. Normal play–pin durations do not exceed several seconds and are characterized by a relaxed attitude. When lesioned and control animals were again reunited, the controls started to initiate play, but VMH-operated animals responded with highly defensive attitudes. Successful play never materialized. For instance, during the final (tenth) session of the series, the average number of pins for the 5-min test period was 1.1. But, it appeared as if the tables were turned now. The control animals roamed around the test chamber confidently, while the VMH-lesioned rats typically remained frozen in sustained defensiveness. However, as a result of the occasional scuffles that arose when the paths of the animals crossed, the controls began to exhibit wariness once again. The VMH lesions were large, encompassing the entire medial hypothalamus, as schematically depicted in Figure 1.8c.

In summary, VMH lesions changed young rats from friendly protagonists to irritable combatants. Not only does this indicate that young animals have the requisite neural circuits for exhibiting true rage, but their aggressive impulses are under active inhibition emanating partially from the medial hypothalamus. In this context, it is noteworthy that septal lesions, which can provoke a transient postoperative rage in adult animals, markedly increase friendly play among young rats (Beatty et al., 1982). We have also studied this phenomenon (Siviy et al., 1983); it seems that contrary to VMH lesions, which disinhibit adultlike rage, septal lesions yield a dematurational effect, with animals beginning to behave psychologically younger than their chronological age (i.e., generally more impulsive and emotional). They play more but are not more dominant. Perhaps biopsychological maturation, whereby juvenile behavioral patterns characterized by friendly fighting are changed to adult patterns characterized by serious competition, arises partially from the accruing inhibitory influence of septal circuits. Such inhibition may be essential for cognitive mediation of higher forms of altruism. Likewise, perhaps social sensitivities, which arise from social bonding to yield friendly and helpful behaviors toward kin, are mediated partially by inhibitory influences arising from medial hypothalamic circuits. Indeed, Adams (1979) proposed that a "consociate modulator," which controls within-species relationships, may be situated in that part of the brain. Whether such a process might be controlled by the resident β-endorphin cells concentrated in this part of the brain is unknown, but in preliminary work we have been unable to disable VMH lesion-induced irritability with the small doses of morphine (≤ 1 mg/kg) typically used in our sociobehavioral research. However, a somewhat higher dose of morphine of 3.5 mg/kg, which is still low compared with traditional standards, has been found to attenuate VMH lesion-induced irritability (Bernard, Welch, Emberley, & Fielding, 1974).

Play and the sources of competition and altruism. Our analysis of brain circuits of play is being guided by the anatomy of brain opiate systems, the general prediction being that damage to areas rich in opioids may reduce play. On the basis of this strategy, we have tentatively identified the para-fascicular area at the mesodiencephalic juncture to contain circuitry essential for normal play (Siviy et al., 1983), but a vast series of behavioral controls need to be conducted before any brain area can be considered a definitive candidate. However, independent of such basic biological questions concerning mechanisms that control play, a systematic study of play may provide some important tools for probing the sources of altruism. Presumably animals exercise their emotional faculties during social play. If it is true that a substantial biological understanding of altruism must arise from the study of brain emotional circuits, then play may be one major avenue through which such positive potentials of emotional circuits become expressed.

Consider one possible approach: While pairs of animals are permitted to play, one is mildly punished at selected intervals. Do the other animals later become better attuned to the emotion generated by this maneuver? When future opportunities are provided for animals to alleviate the suffering of their companion, are they more willing to provide assistance? Will they respond more readily to the distress calls of infants? Are play companions more willing to share resources when placed in competitive situations?

Conclusion

Although existing facts do not lend themselves to definitive conclusions concerning brain sources of altruism, it seems likely that the mechanisms underlying helping and antagonistic behaviors are reciprocally related, and both could be critically linked to brain opioid activity in limbic circuits. For instance, brain opioids, which promote social comfort, bonding, and play, presumably evoke psychological attitudes of peacefulness and trust. Conversely, opioid withdrawal promotes distress, irritability, and aggressiveness (Lal, O'Brien & Puri, 1971; Thor & Teel, 1968). Such reciprocal innervation may be a general property of emotive circuits in the brain (Panksepp, 1982).

Presumably the mammalian nervous system must be capable of elaborating social emotions in order for altruistic behaviors to occur. When distress or threat is evoked in one animal in the presence of others to whom it is bonded, helping behaviors may be encouraged by the resonance of appropriate neural circuits. Conversely, among strangers the same environmental stimuli that provoke mutually beneficial behaviors among bonded individuals may evoke only irritability and self-serving behavioral tendencies.

Although this chapter emphasizes the role of brain opioids in the elaboration of social processes, certainly many other brain systems participate in those functions as well; conversely, brain opioids subserve other functions than social affect. Indeed, in accord with the widespread distribution of endorphin, enkephalin, and dynorphin systems in the brain, opiate effects have been observed on practically all behaviors that have been studied. Does this mean that we should be more than usually skeptical of the propositions addressed here? I think not, for the social processes have been demonstrated to be especially sensitive to opiate effects, and it is almost a truism that social processes affect practically everything an animal does. Also, the concordance among crying circuitry, other social processes, and opioid systems is remarkably good. Furthermore, the localization of opiate circuitry appears to be a reasonably good guide in our ongoing search for play circuitry in the brain. Still, considering the intricacies of the underlying neural machinery for any behavior, many of the findings described herein may eventually be subsumed by broader principles such as opioids mediating pleasure or habits in the brain (Panksepp, 1981b). But then, attachments occur not only to kin and other nearby organisms, but also to places and objects, and even to ways of behaving. All such bonds may share neurochemical similarities, albeit in somewhat different regions of the brain. Is it too farfetched to hypothesize that the ability of the brain to elaborate social bonds evolved from earlier processes such as territorial bonds? Both provide comfort and confidence, yielding essential emotional states in which animals can exert dominion over their affairs and, with a little experience, we hope, altruistic behaviors toward kindred creatures that are threatened.

In any event, an understanding of emotional circuits seems an essential precondition for unraveling the sources of altruistic behaviors, for they lie at the very root of behavioral patterns in which others are helped. Although this approach is surely different from the sociobiological perspective on altruism, it is also an essential step onto the quicksilver path of truth. All mammalian helping behaviors may ultimately arise from the nurturant dictates of brain systems that mediate social bonding and maternal care. The distress of separation and the satisfactions of maternal nurturance may be the emotional poles between which the stream of altruistic intent flows; we shall have a substantive sociobiology of human and animal behavior when the physiological mechanisms governing such processes have been more fully deciphered.

Appendix

Brain mechanisms of prosocial behavior

Essential brain areas for prosocial behavior appear to be situated sub-cortically, among the primitive circuits of the visceral–limbic–emotional brain conceptualized by MacLean (1949, 1973). Preliminary knowledge is available for brain organization of gregariousness, maternal behavior, dom-inance, sexual behavior, social displays, affective vocalizations, and social bonding. Although no substantive psychobiological work exists on altruistic behaviors, it seems likely that a neurological understanding of the above behaviors will be essential to an understanding of the sources of altruism. The following survey of recent work in the area is not intended to be comprehensive, but rather an entry point for accessing key trends in the available literature.

Gregariousness and play. Although septal lesions have been found to cause a temporary increase in aggressive reactivity in rats (Brady & Nauta, 1953; see review in Isaacson, 1982), they also result in long-term facilitation of peaceful gregariousness in rats (Johnson, 1972; Jonason & Enloe, 1971; Meyer, Ruth, & Lavond, 1978) and increased visual contact between cats (Glendenning, 1972). Such prosocial effects are caused by damage to me-dial rather than to lateral zones of the septum (Poplawsky & Johnson, 1973) and arises from damage to the ventral and antero-lateral fibers con-nections of the area (Poplawsky, 1975). The fact that such effects are not observed in some species (Johnson, Poplawsky, & Bieliaukas, 1972) may indicate that septal damage generally releases species-typical affective tendencies; thus, constitutionally solitary species may exhibit little facilitation of social behavior (Booth, Meyer, & Abrams, 1979).

Conversely, amygdaloid lesions reduce social contact in rats (Jonason & Enloe, 1971) and monkeys (Kling, 1976). Combined lesions of amygdala and septal area counterbalance each other, yielding relatively normal social contact maintenance (Jonason, Enloe, Contrucci, & Meyer, 1973). Lesions of the medial and anterior lateral hypothalamus also decrease contact time, whereas interpeduncular, habenula, dorsomedial and ventral tegmental, and cingulate cortex damage have little effect on gregariousness (Enloe, 1975; Poplawsky & Johnson, 1973).

Locus ceruleus lesions tend to produce timid rats that remain in their burrows but that exhibit high levels of "friendly" social interactions. Conversely, animals with substantia nigra lesions are willing to spend much time outside their burrows and are highly aggressive, especially toward animals with locus ceruleus lesions (Eison, Stark, & Ellison, 1977). Pharmacological reduction of brain catecholamine activity yields decreased social interaction in rats (Ellison, 1976), monkeys (Redmond, Maas, King, Graham, and Dekirmenjein, 1971), and humans (Williams, 1971). Increased gregariousness of rats with septal lesions has been simulated by reducing brain serotonin activity by some workers (Dalhouse, 1974) but not by others (Raleigh et al., 1980).

Maternal behavior. The hormonal control of maternal behavior has been thoroughly reviewed by Rosenblatt, Siegel, and Mayer (1979). Initial induction of maternal tendencies seems directly attributable to the hormonal changes that precede parturition, namely, increased estrogen and reduced progesterone secretion. Postparturition maintenance of maternal behavior seems largely hormone independent and due to stimulating effects from the young. Progress in elucidating brain mechanisms has been modest. As for all the social behaviors discussed herein, each global category can be dissected into components, most of which remain to be adequately separated in physiological studies (e.g., onset and maintenance of specific maternal behaviors such as suckling, cleaning, pup retrieval, nest building, and maternal defense). Also, the interpretation of most psychobiological studies is compromised by the possibility that social changes may result from disruption of diverse support systems (ranging from sensorimotor processes to hormone secretions) rather than from direct modification of social-behavior control circuits. However, as far as maternal behavior is concerned, neither decortication (Murphy, MacLean, & Hamilton, 1981) nor hypophysectomy (Lamb, 1975) markedly disrupts maternal behaviors (although lactation is compromised by the latter manipulation), suggesting that the limbic lesion effects observed are probably due to direct effects on maternal behavior control circuits.

Septal lesions seriously disrupt all aspects of maternal behavior (Carlson & Thomas, 1968; Slotnick & Nigrosh, 1975), and similar defects have been observed in animals with hippocampal damage (Kimble, Rogers & Hedrickson, 1967). Basolateral amygdaloid lesions induce rats to cannibalize their pups, while corticomedial amygdaloid and stria terminalis lesions can facilitate maternal behavior (Fleming, Vaccarino, & Luebke, 1980).

Dorsomedial preoptic lesions eliminate active components of maternal behavior, such as retrieval and nest building (Terkel, Bridges, & Sawyer, 1979; Jacobson, Terkel, Gorski, & Sawyer, 1980), whereas damage to several inputs to this area, including stria terminalis and the medial corticohypothalamic tract, do not (Numan, 1974). Furthermore, the disruption of active maternal behaviors in animals in which knife cuts were made around the preoptic area could be obtained independent of disrupting passive behaviors such as nursing and without hampering female sexual responsivity (Marques, Malsbury, & Daood, 1979; Numan, 1974). The facilitation of maternal behavior by estrogen has also been localized to the preoptic area (Numan, Rosenblatt, & Komisaruk, 1977), but no comparable site for progesterone inhibition of maternal behavior has been identified (Numan, 1978), even though progesterone injected into this area does trigger sexual receptivity in the estrogen-primed ovariectomized female (Ward, Crowley, Zemlan, & Margules, 1975).

Most hypothalamic lesions have relatively little effect on maternal behavior, although not surprisingly ventromedial damage leads to cannibalism and lateral hypothalamic lesions to maternal neglect (Holloway & Stevenson, 1967), perhaps because of disruption of nonspecific appetitive-emotive control circuits. Since most higher limbic and hypothalamic information flows through the ventral tegmental corridor, it is also not surprising that damage to that area disrupts maternal behavior (Gaffori & Le Moal, 1979).

The neurochemical control of maternal behavior is poorly understood. Mothers whose brain serotonin has been depleted tend to kill their pups (Copenhaver, Schalock, & Carver, 1978). Whereas central norepinephrine depletion can disrupt initiation of maternal behavior, it has little effect on maintenance (Rosenberg, Halaris, & Moltz, 1977). Early brain dopamine depletion may actually facilitate maternal behavior later in life (Piccirillo, Alpert, Cohen, & Shaywitz, 1980). Catecholaminergic blocking agents and stimulants severely disrupt maternal behaviors (Fraňková, 1977; Piccirillo et al., 1980), but it is hard to specify what dose levels of these pharmacological agents can be considered in the "physiological range."

Sexual behavior. The vast literature on sexual behavior has been extensively reviewed (Pfaff, 1980, 1981); I would merely emphasize that male and female behaviors are distinctly organized, with medial hypothalamus being especially influential in instigating female sex behavior, while preoptic and lateral hypothalamic cues contribute more to male sexual behavior. Septal lesions can release sexual reflexes in both males and females (Nance, Shyrne, Gordon, & Gorski, 1977), but in males the effect is only observed if brain damage is inflicted before puberty (McGinniss & Gorski, 1980).

The interaction of early social play with the development of sexual behavior is especially intriguing. Although preoptic lesions can abolish sexual behavior in individually weaned male rats, extended opportunity for juvenile play can protect the sexual impulse from such brain damage (Twiggs, Popolow, & Gerall, 1978). Also, proceptive behaviors of female rats (e.g., ear wiggling, hopping, darting, and presenting) can delay the decline in male sexual vigor produced by castration (Madlafousek, Hlinak, & Beran, 1976). Thus, although certain limbic circuits are important substrates for sexual behaviors, subtle behavioral interactions that occur between animals in real life can modify the course of the subsequent behavioral syndrome.

Dominance. Similar subtleties are found in studies of dominance. For instance, Mezei and Rosen (1960) gentled young rats for 5 min per day between 13 and 25 days of age and found them to be dominant over unhandled animals in a food competition situation. Equally intriguing is the tendency of female hamsters to exhibit entrained estrus with respect to the dominant animal in the group (Handelmann, Ravizza, & Ray, 1980). The expected relationship between social dominance in males and gonadal activity is becoming increasingly apparent (Mazur, 1976). Although the concept of dominance can no longer be viewed in monolithic terms (Berenstein 1981) because various types of dominance do not intercorrelate highly (Baenninger, 1970), it is noteworthy that the same brain areas found essential for the other social behaviors discussed above also modulate social dominance.

Rosvold, Mirsky, and Pribram (1954) originally demonstrated that amygdala lesions generally reduced dominance status of rhesus monkeys. Although such an effect has not been observed in all species, such as golden hamsters (Bunnell, Sodetz, and Shalloway, 1970), perhaps due to differences in lesion location, reduced dominance has been observed in rats (Bunnell, 1966) and guinea pigs (Levinson, Reeves, & Buchanan, 1980).

Septal lesions have been found to reduce social dominance in male rats rather consistently (Constanzo, Enloe, & Hothersall, 1977; Gage, Olton, & Bolanowski, 1978; Levinson et al., 1980; Miczec & Grossman, 1972), although the general disinhibition of emotional behavior can also yield apparent increases in dominance at times (Bunnell, Bemporad, & Flesher, 1966). When septal lesions are restricted to the lateral zone, which tends to reduce aggressiveness, septal-lesioned animals uniformly lose status, apparently by being easily threatened (Levinson et al., 1980). Animals with basolateral amygdaloid lesions apparently become status losers for another reason – although willing to fight, their capacity to defend themselves effectively seems compromised (Levinson et al., 1980).

The peripheral hormonal and physiological sequelae of dominance relationships are beginning to be characterized (Conner, 1972; Mazur, 1976). Reductions of brain catecholamine activity reduce assertiveness, while reduction of brain serotonin activity promotes brain states needed for dominance (Ellison, 1976).

Social displays. Knowledge concerning brain organization of social displays remains sparse, perhaps because of difficulties in bringing such behaviors under tight experimental control. MacLean (1981) surmounted these problems with the phallic-trump display of squirrel monkeys and has demonstrated that globus pallidus output pathways running through the lateral hypothalamus are essential for the generation of such dominance-greeting gestures.

Affective vocalizations. A considerable amount of social communication is conveyed by sound, and the widespread neural circuits controlling affective vocalizations in various species have been thoroughly reviewed by Jürgens (1979). Vocalization zones are hierarchically mediated throughout the limbic system (De Molina & Hunsperger, 1962) by at least four interacting neural systems. Motor coordination is controlled by lower brainstem nuclei, especially the nucleus ambiguus. Primitive coupling of vocal patterns with motivational states may occur in circuits that relay from amygdala and basal forebrain areas to midbrain tegmentum and central gray areas. Operant vocalizations, independent of specific motivational states, appear to be elaborated in anterior cingulate cortex. Finally, a cortical laryngeal area (corresponding perhaps to multimodal speech cortex in humans) appears to be concerned with volitional and motor coordination aspects of primate vocalization. The vocalization circuitry of birds has also been unraveled (Nottebohm, 1980), and brainstem circuits for simple affective vocalizations are remarkably similar to those found in mammals (Andrew, 1973; J. L. Brown, 1969; Phillips & Youngren, 1974, 1976).

The neurochemistry of affective vocalizations remains poorly understood despite extensive recent work on analyzing systems that control separation distress vocalizations (*vide supra*). As with other social behaviors, it is to be anticipated that serotonin will generally reduce affective vocalizations; indeed, a reduction in hissing in cats has been found following facilitation of serotonin activity (Panksepp, Zolovick, Jalewiec, Stern, & Morgane, 1973). Perhaps counteracting catecholaminergic arousal systems will be found to promote a variety of affective vocalizations.

As with the other social control systems, the psychobiological aspects of the behavioral subtleties elaborated by vocalization systems remain to be studied. For instance, social deprivation enriches the cowbird's song in ability to attract the attention of females while concurrently increasing the ire of competing males (West & King, 1980). Thus, the same sensory input can yield distinct perceptual-affective responses, depending on the hormonal background of the recipient.

Social bonding. Experimental work on imprinting has been pursued most extensively in avian species; consequently, the neural analysis of social bonding has been restricted largely to birds. Early ablation work by Hess (1959) implicated the posterior poles of the cerebral hemispheres in the mediation of imprinting (Hess, 1959); more recent work by Salzen and colleagues (1975, 1979) has affirmed a role for the posterior lateral forebrain. Concurrently, radioactive uracil uptake studies have implicated the anterior forebrain roof in imprinting (Bateson, Horn, & Rose, 1975; Horn, Rose, & Bateson, 1973), and more recent work has delimited the critical anterior area to the IMHV (Horn, McCabe, & Bateson, 1979). Not only do lesions of this area severely impair imprinting, but electrical stimulation of the IMHV yields frequency-specific generalization of imprinting to visual stimuli (Horn, McCabe, & Bateson, 1979). Imprinting also activates this brain area as determined with 2-deoxyglucose autoradiography (Kohsaka, Takamatsu, Aoki, & Tsukada, 1979). The IMHV receives visual input from the optic tectum and may receive auditory and somatosensory inputs from the neostriatum (Bradley and Horn, 1978). It sends efferents to the archistriatum intermedium tissue, which appears to control the somatic sensorimotor system (Bradley & Horn, 1979), yielding a cascade of controls that should be essential for imprinting.

References

Adams, D. B. (1979). Brain mechanisms for offense, defense, and submissions. *The Behavioral and Brain Sciences, 2*, 201–242.

Amir, S., Brown, Z. W., & Amit, Z. (1980). The role of endorphins in stress: Evidence and speculations. *Neuroscience and Biobehavioral Reviews, 4*, 77–86.

Andrew, R. J. (1973). The evocation of calls by diencephalic stimulation in the conscious chick. *Brain, Behavior and Evolution, 7*, 424–446.

Baenninger, L. P. (1970). Social dominance orders in the rat: Spontaneous food, and water competition. *Journal of Comparative Physiology and Psychology, 71*, 202–209.

Barash, D. P. (1982). *Sociobiology and behavior*. 2nd ed. New York: Elsevier.

Barrett, P., & Bateson, P. (1978). The development of play in cats. *Behaviour, 66*, 106–120.

Bateson, P. P. G., Horn, G., & Rose, S. P. R. (1975). Imprinting: Correlations between behavior and incorporations of (^{14}C) uracil into chick brains. *Brain Research, 84*, 207–220.

Bean, N. J., & Conner, R. (1979). Effect of morphine and naloxone on maternal aggression in the mouse. Paper presented at Midwestern Psychological Association meeting, Chicago, IL.

Beatty, W. W., Dodge, A. M., Dodge, L. J., White, K., & Panksepp, J. (1982). Psychomotor stimulants, social deprivation and play in juvenile rats. *Pharmacology, Biochemistry and Behavior, 16*, 417–422.

Beatty, W. W., Dodge, A. M., Traylor, K. L., Donegan, J. C., & Gooding, P. R. (1982). Septal lesions increase play fighting in juvenile rats. *Physiology & Behavior, 28*, 649–652.

Beatty, W. W., Dodge, A. M., Traylor, K. L., & Meaney, M. J. (1982). Temporal boundary of the sensitive period for hormonal organization of social play in juvenile rats. *Physiology & Behavior, 26*, 241–243.

Berenstein, I. S. (1981). Dominance: The baby and the bathwater. *The Behavioral and Brain Sciences, 4*, 419–457.

Bernard, P., Welch, J., Emberley, J., & Fielding, S. (1974). The behavioral effects of morphine in rats with septal hypothalamic lesions. In J. Singh & H. Lal (Eds.), *Drug addiction* (Vol. 3). (pp. 297–307). Miami: Symposia Specialists.

Bonnett, K. S., Miller, J. M., & Simon, E. J. (1976). The effects of chronic opiate treatment and social isolation on opiate receptors in the rodent brain. In H. W. Kosterlitz (Ed.), *Opiates and endogenous opioid peptides* (pp. 335–343). Amsterdam: Elsevier.

Booth, C. L., Meyer, P. M., & Abrams, J. (1979). Changes in social behavior of mice with septal lesions, *Physiology & Behavior, 22*, 931–937.

Bradley, P., & Horn, G. (1978). Afferent connections of hyperstriatum ventrale in the chick brain. *Journal of Physiology (London), 278*, 46P.

Bradley, P., & Horn, G. (1979). Efferent connections of the hyperstriatum ventrale in the chick brain. *Journal of Anatomy, 128*, 414–415.

Brady, J. V., & Nauta, W. J. H. (1953). Subcortical mechanisms in emotional behavior: Affective changes following septal forebrain lesions in the albino rat. *Journal of Comparative and Physiological Psychology, 46*, 339–346.

Brown, D., & Peterson, G. R. (1979). Effects of chronic opiate receptor antagonism on aspects of maternal behavior in mice. *Neuroscience Abstracts, 50*, 550.

Brown, J. L. (1969). The control of avian vocalizations by the central nervous system. In R. A. Hinde (Ed.), *Bird vocalizations* (pp. 79–96). Cambridge: Cambridge University Press.

Bunnell, B. N. (1966). Amygdaloid lesions and social dominance in hooded rats. *Psychonomic Science, 6*, 93–94.

Bunnell, B. N., Bemporad, J. R., & Flesher, C. K. (1966). Septal forebrain lesions and social dominance behavior in the hooded rat. *Psychonomic Science, 6*, 207–208.

Bunnell, B. N., Sodetz, F. J., & Shalloway, D. I. (1970). Amygdaloid lesions and social behavior in the golden hamster. *Physiology & Behavior, 5*, 153–161.

Carlson, N. R., & Thomas, G. J. (1968). Maternal behavior of mice with limbic lesions. *Physiological Psychology, 66*, 731–737.

Caro, T. M. (1981). Sex differences in the termination of social play in cats. *Animal Behavior, 29*, 271–279.

Cicero, T. J., Schainker, B. A., & Meyer, B. R. (1979). Endogenous opioids participate in the regulation of the hypothalamic-pituitary-luteinizing hormone axis and testosterone's negative feedback control of luteinizing hormone. *Endocrinology, 104,* 1286–1291.

Cohen, M. R., Cohen, R. M., Pickar, D., Weingartner, H., & Murphy, L. (1983). High-dose naloxone infusions in normals. *Archives of General Psychiatry, 40,* 613–619.

Conner, R. L. (1972). Hormones, biogenic amines, and aggression. In S. Levine (Ed.), *Hormones and behavior* (pp. 209–234). New York: Academic Press.

Constanzo, D., Enloe, L. J., & Hothersall, D. (1977). Effects of septal lesions on social dominance in rats. *Behavioral Biology, 20,* 454–462.

Copenhaver, J. H., Schalock, R. L., & Carver, M. J. 1978. Para-Chloro-D, L-phenylanalnine induced filicidal behavior in the female rats. *Pharmacology, Biochemistry & Behavior, 8,* 263–270.

Dalhouse, A. D. (1974). Social cohesiveness, hypersexuality and irritability induced by PCPA in rats. *Physiology & Behavior, 17,* 679–686.

Davis, K. L. (1980). Opioid control of canine social behavior. Unpublished Ph.D. dissertation, Bowling Green State University.

de Lanerolle, N. C., Elde, R. P., Sparber, S. B., & Frick, M. 1981. Distribution of methionine-enkephalin immunoreactivity in the chick brain: An immunohistochemical study. *Journal of Comparative Neurology, 199,* 513–533.

De Molina, A. F., & Hunsperger, R. W. (1962). Organization of the subcortical system governing defense flight reactions in the cat. *Journal of Physiology (London), 160,* 200–213.

De Wied, D., & Jolles, J. (1982). Neuropeptides derived from pro-opiocortin: Behavioral, physiological and neurochemical effects. *Physiological Reviews, 62,* 976–1042.

Eison, M. S., Stark, A. D., & Ellison, G. (1977). Opposed effects of locus coeruleus and substantia nigra lesions on social behavior in rat colonies. *Pharmacology, Biochemistry & Behavior, 7,* 87–90.

Ellison, G. (1976). Monoamine neurotoxins: Selective and delayed effects on behavior in a rat colony. *Brain Research, 103,* 81–92.

Enloe, L. T. (1975). Extralimbic mediation of emotionality and social cohesiveness effects. *Physiology Behavior, 15,* 271–276.

File, S. E. (1980). Naloxone reduces social and exploratory activity in the rat. *Psychopharmacology, 7,* 41–44.

Fleming, A. S., Vaccarino, F., & Luebke, C. (1980). Amygdaloid inhibition of maternal behavior in nulliparous female rats. *Physiology & Behavior, 25,* 731–743.

Fraňková, S. (1977). Drug induced changes in maternal behavior of rats. *Psychopharmacology, 53,* 83–87.

Gaffori, O., & Le Moal, M. L. (1979). Disruption of maternal behavior and appearance of cannibalism after ventral mesencephalic tegmentum lesions. *Physiology Behavior, 23,* 317–323.

Gage, F. H., Olton, D. S., & Bolanowski, D. (1978). Activity, reactivity, and dominance following septal lesions in rats. *Behavioral Biology, 22,* 203–210.

Gessa, G., Paglietti, E., & Pellegrini Quarantotti, B. (1979). Induction of copulatory behavior in sexually inactive rats by naloxone. *Science, 204,* 203–205.

Glendenning, K. K. (1972). Effects of septal and amygdaloid lesions on social behavior of the cat. *Journal of Comparative and Physiological Psychology, 80,* 199–207.

Goy, R. W. (1978). Development of play and mounting behavior in female rhesus virilized prenatally with esters of testosterone or dihyrotestosterone. In D. J. Chivers & J. Herbert (Eds.), *Recent advances in primatology,* Vol. 1: *Behaviour* (pp. 449–462). London: Academic Press.

Grossman, S. P. (1978). An experimental "dissection" of the septal syndrome. In K. Elliott

& J. Whelan (Eds.), *Functions of the septohippocampal system*. Ciba Foundation Symposium 58 (New Series) (pp. 227–260). Amsterdam: Elsevier.

Hahn, E. F. & Fishman, J. (1979). Changes in rat brain opiate receptor content upon castration and testosterone replacement. *Biochemistry and Biophysiology Research Communications, 90*, 819–823.

Handelmann, G., Ravizza, R., & Ray, W. J. (1980). Social dominance determines estrus entrainment among female hamsters. *Hormones & Behavior, 14*, 107–115.

Henry, J. L. (1982). Circulating opioids: Possible physiological roles in central nervous function. *Neuroscience & Biobehavioral Reviews, 6*, 229–245.

Hepper, P. G. (1983). Sibling recognition in the rat. *Animal Behavior, 31*, 1177–1191.

Herman, B. H. (1979). An exploration of brain social attachment substrates in guinea pigs. Unpublished Ph.D. Dissertation, Bowling Green State University.

Herman, B. H., & Panksepp, J. (1981). Ascending endorphin inhibition of distress vocalization. *Science, 211*, 1060–1062.

Hess, E. H. (1959). Imprinting. *Science, 130*, 133–141.

Hoffman, M. L. (1981). Is altruism part of human nature? *Journal of Personality and Social Psychology, 40*, 121–137.

Holloway, A., & Stevenson, J. A. F. (1967). Effect of various ablations in the hypothalamus on established pregnancy in the rat. *Canadian Journal of Physiology and Pharmacology, 45*, 1081–1091.

Horn, G., McCabe, B. J., & Bateson, P. P. G. (1979). An autoradiographic study of the chick brain after imprinting. *Brain Research, 168*, 361–373.

Horn, G., Rose, S. P. R., & Bateson, P. P. G. (1973). Monocular imprinting and regional incorporation of tritiated uracil into the brains of intact and "split-brain" chicks. *Brain Research, 181*, 506–514.

Humphreys, A. P., & Einon, D. F. (1981). Play as a reinforcer for maze-learning in juvenile rats. *Animal Behavior, 29*, 259–270.

Isaacson, R. L. (1982). *The limbic system*. New York: Academic Press.

Jacobson, D. D., Terkel, J., Gorski, R. A., & Sawyer, C. H. (1980). Effects of small medial preoptic area lesions on maternal behavior: Retrieving and nest building in the rat. *Brain Research, 194*, 471–478.

Jalowiec, J., Panksepp, J., DeEskinazi, F., & Bishop, P. (1980). Opioid control of play and social dominance. *Neuroscience Abstracts, 6*, 856.

Johnson, D. A. (1972). Developmental aspects of recovery of function following septal lesions in the infant rat. *Journal of Comparative and Physiological Psychology, 78*, 331–348.

Johnson, D. A., Poplawsky, A., & Bieliaukas, L. (1972). Alterations of social behavior in rats and hamsters following lesions of the septal forebrain. *Psychonomic Science, 26*, 19–20.

Jonason, K. R., & Enloe, L. J. (1971). Alterations in social behavior following septal and amygdaloid lesions in the rat. *Journal of Comparative and Physiological Psychology, 75*, 286–301.

Jonason, K. R., Enloe, L. J., Contrucci, J., & Meyer, P. M. (1973). Effects of simultaneous and successive septal and amygdaloid lesions on social behavior of the rat. *Journal of Comparative and Physiological Psychology, 83*, 54–61.

Jürgens, U. (1979). Neural control of vocalization in nonhuman primates. In H. D. Steklis & M. J. Raleigh (Eds.), *Neurobiology of social communication in primates* (pp. 11–14). New York: Academic Press.

Kavaliers, M. (1981). Schooling behavior of fish: An opiate-dependent activity. *Behavioral Neural Biology, 33*, 379–401.

Kimble, D. P., Rogers, L., & Hedrickson, C. W. (1967). Hippocampal lesions disrupt maternal, not sexual, behaviors in the albino rat. *Journal of Comparative and Physiological Psychology, 63,* 401–407.

Kirzinger, A., & Jürgens, U. (1982). Cortical lesion effects and vocalization in the squirrel monkey. *Brain Research, 233,* 299–315.

Kling, A. (1976). Frontal and temporal lobe lesions and aggressive behavior. In W. L. Smith & A. Kling (Eds.), *Issues in brain/behavior control* (pp. 11–22). New York: Spectrum Publications.

Kohsaka, S., Takamatsu, K., Aoki, E., & Tsukada, Y. (1979). Metabolic mapping of chick brain after imprinting using (^{14}C)2-deoxyglucose techniques. *Brain Research, 172,* 539–544.

Kurland, J. A. (1980). Kin selection theory: A review and selective bibliography. *Ethology and Sociobiology, 1,* 255–274.

Lal, H., O'Brien, J., & Puri, S. K. (1971). Morphine-withdrawal aggression: Sensitization by amphetamines. *Psychopharmacology, 22,* 217–223.

Lamb, M. E. (1975). Physiological mechanisms in the control of maternal behavior in rats: A review. *Psychological Bulletin, 82,* 104–119.

Lancaster, J. B. (1971). Play-mothering: The relation between juvenile females and young infants among free-ranging vervet monkeys (*Cercopithecus aethiops*). *Folia Primatology, 15,* 161–182.

Levinson, D. M., Reeves, D. L., & Buchanan, D. R. (1980). Reductions in aggression and dominance status in guinea pigs following bilateral lesions in the basolateral amygdala or lateral septum, *Physiology and Behavior, 25,* 963–971.

Lopreato, J. (1981). Toward a theory of genuine altruism in *Homo sapiens. Ethology and Sociobiology, 2,* 113–126.

MacLean, P. D. (1949). Psychosomatic disease and the "visceral brain": Recent developments bearing on the Papez theory of emotion. *Psychosomatic Medicine, 11,* 338–353.

MacLean, P. D. (1973). A triune concept of the brain and behavior. In T. Boag & D. Campbell (Eds.), *The Hincks Memorial Lectures* (pp. 6–66). Toronto: University of Toronto.

MacLean, P. D. (1981). Role of transhypothalamic pathways in social communication. In P. J. Morgane & J. Panksepp (Eds.), *Handbook of the hypothalamus,* Vol. 3, Pt. B: *Behavioral studies of the hypothalamus* (pp. 259–287). New York: Marcel Dekker.

Madlafousek, J. M., Hlinak, Z., & Beran, J. (1976). Decline of sexual behavior in castrated male rats. Effects of female precopulatory behavior. *Hormones and Behavior, 7,* 245–252.

Marques, D. M., Malsbury, C. W., & Daood, J. T. (1979). Hypothalamic knife cuts dissociate maternal behaviors, sexual receptivity, and estrous cycling in female hamsters. *Physiology and Behavior, 23,* 347–355.

Mazur, A. (1976). Effects of testosterone on status in primate groups. *Folia Primatology, 26,* 214–226.

McGinnis, M. Y., & Gorski, R. A. (1980). Effects of neonatal septal lesions on reproductive behavior of male and female rats. *Hormones and Behavior, 14,* 191–203.

McIntosh, T. K., Vallano, M. L., & Barfield, R. J. (1980). Effects of morphine β-endorphin and naloxone on catecholamine levels and sexual behavior in the male rat. *Pharmacology, Biochemistry & Behavior, 13,* 435–441.

Meaney, M. J., Dodge, A. M., & Beatty, W. W. (1981). Sex-dependent effects of amygdaloid lesions on the social play of prepubertal rats. *Physiology & Behavior, 26,* 467–472.

Meaney, M. J., & Stewart, J. (1981). A descriptive study of social development in the rat (*Rattus norvegicus*). *Animal Behavior, 29,* 34–45.

Meller, R. E., Keverne, E. B., & Herbert, J. (1980). Behavioral and endocrine effects of naltrexone in male talapoin monkeys. *Pharmacology, Biochemistry and Behavior, 13*, 435–441.

Meyer, D. R., Ruth, R. A., & Lavond, D. G. (1978). The septal social cohesiveness effect: Its robustness and main determinants. *Physiology and Behavior, 21*, 1027–1029.

Mezei, T. C., & Rosen, J. (1960). Dominance behavior as a function of infantile stimulation in the rat. *Archives of General Psychiatry, 3*, 53–56.

Miczek, K. A., & Grossman, S. P. (1972). Effects of septal lesions on inter- and intra-species aggression in rats. *Journal of Comparative Physiology and Psychology, 79*, 37–45.

Miczek, K. A., Thompson, M. L., & Shuster, L. (1982). Opioid-like analgesia in defeated mice. *Science, 215*, 1520–1522.

Miller, R. J., & Cuatrecasas, P. (1978). Enkephalins and endorphins. *Vitamins and Hormones, 36*, 282–297.

Moyer, K. E. (1976). *The psychobiology of aggression*. New York: Harper & Row.

Murphy, M. R., MacLean, P. D., & Hamilton, S. C. (1981). Species-typical behavior of hamsters deprived from birth of the neocortex. *Science, 213*, 429–461.

Myers, B., & Baum, M. (1979). Facilitation by opiate antagonists of sexual performance in the male rat. *Pharmacology Biochemistry and Behavior, 10*, 615–618.

Nance, D. M., Shyrne, J. E., Gordon, J. H., & Gorski, R. A. (1977). Examination of some factors that control the effects of septal lesions on lordosis behavior. *Pharmacology, Biochemistry and Behavior, 6*, 227–234.

Newby-Schmidt, M. B., & Norton, S. (1981). Development of opiate tolerance in the chick embryo, *Pharmacology, Biochemistry and Behavior, 15*, 773–778.

Nottebohm, F. (1980). Testosterone triggers growth of brain vocal control; nuclei in adult female canaries. *Brain Research, 189*, 429–436.

Numan, M. (1974). Medial preoptic area and maternal behavior in the female rat. *Journal of Comparative and Physiological Psychology, 87*, 746–759.

Numan, M. (1978). Progesterone inhibition of maternal behavior in the rat. *Hormones and Behavior, 11*, 209–231.

Numan, M., Rosenblatt, J. S., & Komisaruk, B. R. (1977). Medial preoptic area and onset of maternal behavior in the rat. *Journal of Comparative and Physiological Psychology, 91*, 146–164.

Olioff, M., & Stewart, J. (1978). Sex differences in the play behavior of prepubescent rats. *Physiology and Behavior, 20*, 113–115.

Owens, N. W. (1975). Social play behavior in free-living baboons (*Papio anubis*). *Animal Behavior, 23*, 387–408.

Panksepp, J. (1971a). Aggression elicited by electrical stimulation of the hypothalamus in albino rats. *Physiology and Behavior, 6*, 321–329.

Panksepp, J. (1971b). Shock-induced fighting: Passive vs. aggressive rats. *Communications in Behavioral Biology, 6*, 233–235.

Panksepp, J. (1979). The regulation of play: Neurochemical controls. *Neuroscience Abstracts, 5*, 172.

Panksepp, J. (1981a). Hypothalamic integration of behavior: Rewards, punishments, and related psychological processes. In P. J. Morgane and J. Panksepp (Eds.), *Handbook of the hypothalamus*, Vol 3, Pt. B., *Behavioral studies of the hypothalamus* (pp. 289–431). New York: Marcel Dekker.

Panksepp, J. (1981b). Brain opioids – a neurochemical substrate for narcotic and social dependence. In S. J. Cooper (Ed.), *Theory in psychopharmacology* (pp. 149–175). London: Academic Press.

Panksepp, J. (1981c). The ontogeny of play in rats. *Developmental Psychobiology, 14*, 327–332.

Panksepp, J. (1982). Toward a general psychobiological theory of emotions. *The Behavioral and Brain Sciences, 5,* 407–468.

Panksepp, J., Bean, N. J., Bishop, P., Vilberg, T., & Sahley, T. L. (1980). Opioid blockade and social comfort in chicks. *Pharmacology, Biochemistry and Behavior, 13,* 673–683.

Panksepp, J., & Beatty, W. W. (1980). Social deprivation and play in rats. *Behavioral and Neural Biology, 30,* 197–206.

Panksepp, J., & Bishop, P. (1981). An autoradiographic map of (^{3}H)diprenorphine binding in rat brain: effects of social interaction. *Brain Research Bulletin, 7,* 405–410.

Panksepp, J., Conner, R., Forster, P. K., Bishop, P., & Scott, J. P. (1983). Opioid effects of social behavior of kennel dogs. *Applied Animal Ethology, 10,* 63–74.

Panksepp, J., & DeEskinazi, F. G. (1980). Opiates and homing. *Journal of Comparative and Physiological Psychology, 94,* 650–663.

Panksepp, J., Herman, B. H., Vilberg, T., Bishop, P., & DeEskinazi, F. G. (1980). Endogenous opioids and social behavior. *Neuroscience and Biobehavioral Reviews, 4,* 473–487.

Panksepp, J., Meeker, R., & Bean, N. J. (1980). The neurochemical control of crying. *Pharmacology, Biochemistry and Behavior, 12,* 437–443.

Panksepp, J., Najam, N., & Soares, F. (1979). Morphine reduces social cohesion in rats. *Pharmacology, Biochemistry and Behavior, 11,* 131–134.

Panksepp, J., Normansell, L., Siviy, S., Buchanan, A., Zolovick, A., Rossi, J., & Conner, R. (1983). A cholinergic command circuit for separation distress? *Neuroscience Abstracts, 9,* 979.

Panksepp, J., Siviy, S., & Normansell, L. (1984). The psychobiology of play: Theoretical and methodological perspectives. *Neuroscience and Biobehavioral Reviews, 8,* 465–492.

Panksepp, J., Siviy, S. M., & Normansell, L. (1985). Brain opioids and social emotions. In M. Reite & T. Fields (Eds.), *Biology of social attachments and separation* (pp. 3–49). New York: Academic Press.

Panksepp, J., Siviy, S., Normansell, L., White, K., & Bishop, P. (1982). Effects of β-chlornaltrexamine on separation distress in chicks. *Life Sciences, 31,* 2387–2390.

Panksepp, J., Zolovick, A. J., Jalowiec, J. E., Stern, W. C., & Morgane, P. J. (1973). Fenfluramine: Effects on aggression. *Biological Psychiatry, 6,* 181–186.

Pfaff, D. W. (1980). *Estrogens and brain functions.* New York: Springer-Verlag.

Pfaff, D. W. (1981). Theoretical issues regarding hypothalamic control of reproductive behavior. In P. J. Morgane & J. Panksepp (Eds.), *Handbook of the hypothalamus,* Vol. 3, Pt. B: *Behavioral studies of the hypothalamus* (pp. 241–258). New York: Marcel Dekker.

Phillips, R. E., & Youngren, O. M. (1974). A brain pathway for thalamically evoked calls in birds. *Brain Behavior and Evolution, 9,* 1–6.

Phillips, R. E., & Youngren, O. M. 1976. Pattern generator for repetitive avian vocalization: Preliminary localization and functional characterization. *Brain Behavior and Evolution, 13,* 165–178.

Piccirillo, M., Alpert, J. E., Cohen, D. J., & Shaywitz, B. A. (1980). Effects of 6-hydroxy-dopamine and amphetamine on rat mothering behavior and offspring development. *Pharmacology, Biochemistry and Behavior, 13,* 391–395.

Pilcher, C. W. T., & Jones, S. M. (1981). Social crowding enhances aversiveness of naloxone in rats. *Pharmacology, Biochemistry and Behavior, 14,* 299–303.

Poole, T. B., & Fish, J. (1976). An investigation of individual, age and sexual differences in the play of *Rattus norvegicus* (Mammalia: Rodentia). *Proceedings of the Zoology Society, 179,* 249–260.

Poplawsky, A. (1975). Effects of septal-fiber knife cuts in rat open-field social behavior. *Physiology and Behavior, 15,* 177–184.

Poplawsky, A., & Johnson, D. A. (1973). Open field social behavior of rats following lateral or medial septal lesions. *Physiology and Behavior, 11*, 845–854.

Raleigh, M. J., Brammer, G. L., Yuwiler, A., Flannery, J. W., McGuire, M. T., & Geller, E. (1980). Serotonergic influences on social behavior of vervet monkeys (*Cercopithecus aethiops sabeaus*). *Experimental Neurology, 68*, 322–334.

Redmond, D. E., Maas, J. W., King, A., Graham, C. W., & Dekirmenjien, H. (1971). Social behavior in monkeys selectively depleted of monoamines, *Science, 174*, 428–430.

Reeves, A. G., & Plum, F. (1969). Hyperphagia, rage and dementia accompanying a ventromedial hypothalamic neoplasm. *Archives of Neurology, 20*, 616–624.

Rosenberg, P., Halaris, A., & Moltz, H. (1977). Effects of central norepinephrine depletion on the initiation and maintenance of maternal behavior in the rat. *Pharmacology, Biochemistry and Behavior, 6*, 21–24.

Rosenblatt, J. S., Siegel, H. I, & Mayer, A. D. (1979). Progress in the study of maternal behavior in the rat: Hormonal, nonhormonal, sensory, and development aspects. In J. S. Rosenblatt, R. A. Hinde, C. Beer, & M. C. Busnel (Eds.), *Advances in the study of behavior*, Vol. 10 (pp. 225–311). New York: Academic Press.

Rosvold, H. E., Mirsky, A. F., & Pribram, K. H. (1954). Influence of amygdalectomy on social behavior in monkeys. *Journal of Comparative and Physiological Psychology, 47*, 173–178.

Ryan, S. M., Arnold, A. P., & Elde, R. P. (1981). Enkephalin-like immunoreactivity in vocal control regions of the zebra finch brain. *Brain Research, 229*, 236–240.

Sachs, B. D., & Harris, V. S. (1978). Sex differences and developmental changes in selected juvenile activities (play) of domestic lambs. *Animal Behavior, 26*, 678–684.

Salzen, E. A., Parker, D. M., & Williamson, A. J. (1975). A forebrain lesion preventing imprinting in domestic chicks. *Experimental Brain Research, 24*, 145–157.

Salzen, E. A., Williamson, A. J., & Parker, D. M. (1979). The effects of forebrain lesions on innate and imprinted colour, brightness and shape preferences in domestic chicks. *Behavioral Processes, 4*, 295–313.

Siviy, S., Panksepp, J., & White, K. (1983). Neuroanatomical substrates of juvenile play in rats. *Neuroscience Abstracts, 9*, 535.

Slotnick, B. M., & Nigrosh, B. J. (1975). Maternal behavior of mice with cingulate cortical, amygdala, or septal lesions. *Journal of Comparative and Physiological Psychology, 88*, 118–127.

Smith, P. K. (1982). Does play matter? Functional and evolutionary aspects of animal and human play. *The Behavioral and Brain Sciences, 5*, 139–184.

Snyder, S. H., & Childers, S. R. (1979). Opiate receptors and opioid peptides. *Annual Reviews of Neuroscience, 2*, 35–64.

Taylor, G. T. (1980). Fighting in juvenile rats and the ontogeny of agonistic behavior. *Journal of Comparative and Physiological Psychology, 94*, 953–961.

Terkel, J., Bridges, R. S., & Sawyer, C. H. (1979). Effects of transecting lateral neural connections of the medial preoptic area on maternal behavior in the rat: Nest building, pup retrieval and prolactin secretion. *Brain Research, 169*, 369–380.

Thor, D. H., & Holloway, W. R. Jr. (1983). Scopolamine blocks play fighting behavior in juvenile rats. *Physiology and Behavior, 79*, 414–418.

Thor, D. H., & Teel, B. G. (1968). Fighting of rats during post-morphine withdrawal: Effect of prewithdrawal dosage. *American Journal of Psychology, 81*, 439–442.

Trivers, R. L. (1971). The evolution of reciprocal altruism. *Quarterly Review of Biology, 46*, 35–57.

Twiggs, D. G., Popolow, H. B., & Gerall, A. A. (1978). Medial preoptic lesions and male sexual behavior: Age and environmental interactions. *Science, 200*, 1414–1415.

Valzelli, L. (1981). *Psychobiology of aggression and violence*. New York: Raven Press.

Vilberg, T., Bean, N., Bishop, P., Porada, K., & Panksepp, J. (1977). Possible relations between brain opiates and social behaviors. *Neuroscience Abstracts, 3*, 303.

Ward, I. L., Crowley, W. R., Zemlan, F. P., & Margules, D. L. (1975). Monoaminergic mediation of female sexual behavior. *Journal of Comparative and Physiological Psychology, 88*, 53–61.

West, M. J., and King, A. P. (1980). Enriching cowbird song by social deprivation. *Journal of Comparative and Physiological Psychology, 94*, 263–270.

Wheatley, M. S. (1944). The hypothalamus and affective behavior in cats. *Archives of Neurology and Psychiatry, 52*, 296–316.

Williams, H. L. (1971). The new biology of sleep. *Journal of Psychiatric Research, 8*, 445–478.

Wilson, E. O. (1975). *Sociobiology: The new synthesis*. Cambridge, MA: Harvard University Press.

Wu, H. M. H., Holmes, W. G., Medina, S. R., & Sackett, G. P. (1980). Kin preference in infant *Macaca nemestrina*. *Nature (Lond.), 285*, 225–227.

2   An evolutionary and developmental perspective on aggressive patterns

Robert B. Cairns

The quiet revolution in the study of social behavior that began during the 1970s is in its second decade, and most of its tenets now seem less revolutionary than they once were. The revolt had both a positive and a negative message. On the negative side, it was a rejection of the then-dominant view that all features of personality development and social adaptation could be explained by social learning experiences of one sort or another. As useful as concepts of social reinforcement and modeling were in accounting for individual differences in social behaviors in the short run, they failed to explain continuity over the life-span. The general problem – as recognized by early critics such as John Bowlby (1969), Harry Harlow (1958), Lawrence Kohlberg (1969), T. C. Schneirla (1966), Z-Y. Kuo (1967), and K. Lorenz (1965) – was that social learning theories omitted too much information about the adaptive properties of the developing person. These properties included age-related changes in biological structure and function, in cognitive abilities, and in affective expression. Nor was there robust empirical support for the primary child-rearing propositions of social learning theory (e.g., Yarrow, Campbell, & Burton, 1968). Enthusiasm for the study of social processes in children temporarily lapsed.

By the mid-1970s, social developmental issues became once again the focus of vigorous and broad-based exploration, albeit from fresh methodological and theoretical perspectives. Of the new proposals that were offered, some of the more novel and influential ones concerned biological–evolutionary contributions to social development. The evolutionary perspectives of ethology and sociobiology promised both to broaden the boundaries of child psychology and to integrate its concerns with those of related sciences, including population biology, genetics, ecology, and anthropology. Along with fresh proposals on the explanation of familiar phenomena (including aggression and attachment), modern evolutionary theory has been concerned with the origins of prosocial processes such as altruism, cooperation, and social organization.

58

This was not the first time that students of child behavior have been called upon to merge their concerns with those of biological colleagues. The scientific study of child development began with an embryologist (Preyer, 1888–1889) and was nurtured in an evolutionary framework (Baldwin, 1895; Hall, 1904). However, the first attempts to integrate child development and evolutionary theoretical formulations led to some unhappy outcomes, including G. S. Hall's recapitulation theory, F. Galton's eugenics movement, and the enduring nature–nurture debate on individual differences in IQ (Gould, 1981). Accordingly, it seems prudent to scrutinize the steps by which the two areas of inquiry may be linked, and to subject the alternatives to critical evaluation.

Not all features of the contemporary evolutionary and psychobiological theory have been welcomed by child developmentalists. That skepticism seems well founded. For the most part, evolutionary investigators who have been most outspoken about the dominant role of biological factors in personality development have tended to ignore or underestimate the complexities of human socialization. On this score, Tinbergen (1972b) warned about the dangers of "ethologism." In the absence of compelling empirical information on the matter, thoughtful proposals on behavioral–biological integration in development often degenerated into simplistic assertions concerning nature and nurture and which was dominant.

Investigators in child development traditionally have encountered a dilemma in dealing with biological accounts of social interaction. On the one hand, the relevance of growth-related changes in structure and ability to changes in social skills cannot be gainsaid, and few developmentalists would advocate ignoring modern evolutionary theory. On the other hand, the reduction of human experience to psychobiological processes can involve a high price. One of the costs has been that the inherent richness of individual differences in human personality and social relationships tends to be submerged or redefined in comparative and evolutionary formulations. Given the choice, most child psychologists will opt for accentuating psychological richness and ignoring biological mechanisms, with good reason.

The argument set forth in this chapter is that students of human development need not compromise their area of scientific expertise in order to accommodate the concepts of developmental biology or population genetics. Indeed, it is a first responsibility of child psychologists to remind our sister sciences of the subtlety of distinctively human behaviors and to offer precise analysis of their determinants and dynamics. But this goal is not inconsistent with the critical integration of biological concepts – whether evolutionary or psychobiological – in the research program and theoretical proposals of child psychology. Such an integration is inevitable if social development is seen as representing the child's unique accommodation to biological, environmental, and cognitive change over ontogeny. The challenge for contemporary research is to determine how this integration is achieved at each ontogenetic stage and how different weights should be assigned to the components over the course of development (Cairns & Valsiner, 1984).

After presenting introductory comments on evolutionary and psychobiological concepts, this chapter illustrates some implications of the orientation by focusing on the development of gender differences in aggressive behavior patterns.

The biological bases of social development

There are currently three separable proposals on how a developmental–biological integration might productively proceed. The multiplicity arises because there are distinguishably different biological proposals to select from, each of which carries different implications for the study of social development. Any attempt to summarize the alternatives is likely to be misleading, and the present one is no exception. Happily several extended treatments of the matter for child developmentalists have recently been published (see, for instance, Hoffman, 1981; Hinde, 1983; Gottlieb, 1983; Sameroff, 1983) and some earlier discussions are still relevant (e.g., Chagnon & Irons, 1979; Cairns, 1979; Dawkins, 1976; Wilson, 1975). The following discussion highlights those ideas and concepts that seem especially relevant to the issues of this chapter.

The three distinct biological orientations have been concerned with the study of the biology of social behavior: developmental psychobiology (including comparative psychology), ethology, and sociobiology. The commonalities among these orientations outweigh their differences. Not only do these orientations have in common the goal of making explicit linkages between biology and social behavior, but they share two foundational scientific assumptions about what kinds of linkages exist and how to study them.

One of these shared assumptions concerns the evolutionary continuity among species. Accordingly, certain behavioral processes and problems may be effectively explored in closely related species (as determined by common class membership, or common family membership), while others cannot. On this count, the human–nonhuman discontinuity that separates child psychology from animal behavior is a formidable but not insurmountable obstacle. Indeed, the animal–human separation in comparative generalization is not as great as the embryo–infant–adult separation in developmental generalizations. In both cases, proposals on generalization demand a matrix of similarities and differences, and the validity of the generalizations depends on the extent of identity in the several component processes. In other words, a "polythetic" standard (Jensen, 1968) should be employed, whereby similarities and differences are simultaneously assessed across relevant dimensions of comparison, such as behavioral function, developmental sequence, and component systems. One cannot leapfrog from mice to monkeys to men without ado on the basis of a single salient similarity, that is, a "monothetic" generalization.

A second shared assumption is that social patterns are intimately related to other features of biological and ecological adaptation and that they should not be divorced from them. Behavior is the leading edge of individual accommodation, not the trailing end of evolutionary adaptation. It differs from more enduring features of the organism (including physical structures and physiological processes) in that it provides a highly flexible, variable, and modifiable mode of accommodation. Behavior thus can be rapidly adjusted to changing conditions of survival. Given the dynamic and reciprocal potential of social behavior patterns, they can both reflect ecological and interactional conditions and determine what those conditions should be. Feedback can be either internal or external, hence the corollary bidirectional proposal: namely that the child's social acts are embedded in a social matrix of influences that the child has helped construct by prior actions.

It is useful as well to draw certain distinctions among biological approaches to social development. The matter is confounded by the propensity for quite different approaches to define themselves in exactly the same way; that is, as the "biology of behavior" (compare, for instance, Eibl-Eibesfeldt, 1974, with Wilson, 1975). This ambiguity serves to blur important differences among orientations in emphasis and interpretation.

Ethology: theory and method

Modern ethology has been in business for about 50 years, since Konrad Lorenz published his landmark paper on imprinting (Lorenz, 1935). The basic theory extends back at least 100 years (Romanes, 1884). It would be exceptional if drastic modifications had not been made in the theory and its methods over this period of vigorous study. On that score, ethology has not proved an exception. There are now as many branches of European ethology and clusters of theorists as there are in its American cohort, social learning theory. Like social learning theorists, ethologists propose certain core and shared beliefs that transcend family differences. These shared beliefs are both theoretical and methodological. The theoretical proposition is that phylogenetic (i.e., evolutionary) adaptations are significant determinants of social and nonsocial behavior patterns in individuals, both human and nonhuman. The methodological commitment follows directly from the theoretical one, namely, that the appropriate study of behavior is in natural or ecologically valid settings. Thus, ethologists are naturalists first of all. On this matter, Chance (1975) noted that "the behavioral sciences came into existence as a result of historical accident and not logical requirements, otherwise ethology would have been the first, not the last, discipline to emerge, because observation and description are what is needed before analysis."

But not necessarily before evolutionary theory. On this count, classical ethology in the work of Lorenz (1966) and Eibl-Eibesfeldt (1974) provides explicit explanations for how attachments emerge, when aggressive acts appear, and why love and hate occur together. These explanations were framed in terms of an evolutionary model of behavior not unlike that implicit in Freudian theory. The resemblance is probably not by chance, since both models drew on common motivational assumptions about the inherent nature and operation of evolutionarily adapted drives, notably aggression and affiliation.

Description, in the research of traditional ethologists, serves to identify behavioral homologues or similarities in the behavioral patterns of two species that share a common ancestry. One step toward this identification is the establishment of an *ethogram* – the behavioral repertoire of the species as it occurs within a species-typical environment. Once established, these behavioral characters may be treated as if they were morphological features of the species in the analysis of similarities and differences with closely related species, hence the importance of the identification of fixed action patterns (FAP), more recently referred to as modal action patterns (MAP). These FAP (or MAP) may then be employed as phenotype units for the analysis of commonalities across species.

Of special interest to child psychologists has been the ethological study of social attachment phenomena (Hinde, 1983). Comparative psychologists (Harlow, 1958; Hebb, 1958) and zoologists (Scott, 1962) deserve credit for having initially explored the problem of social attachment behavior in nonhuman mammals, including dogs, sheep, and monkeys. Nonetheless, the studies that claimed the imagination of child psychologists during the 1970s were investigations of human infants interpreted from a psychoanalytic–ethological perspective. Accordingly, Bowlby (1958, 1969) linked the psychoanalytic theory of object relationships with the ethological concepts of instinctive behaviors and innate releasing mechanisms. This synthesis provided an influential account of the early mother–child relationship. Ainsworth (1972) and colleagues vigorously extended psychoanalytic–ethological formulation of species-typical patterns to the study of individual differences in normal and presumably at-risk infants.

The naturalistic bias of ethological methods has supported the study of behavior as it occurs within the social system, as well as the social system itself. Although social hierarchies were not discovered by ethologists, the discipline has significantly extended our understanding of their functions, properties, and mechanisms in several species, including free-ranging primates (e.g., Kummer, 1968; von Lawick-Goodall, 1968). This concern has been productively extended to studies of social dominance hierarchies in young children (e.g., Strayer & Strayer, 1968; see also Chapter 4, this volume) and adolescents (Savin-Williams, 1979). In general, the form of the social structure and its inflexibility are presumed to be a function of the frequency and intensity of aggressive acts. For instance, Savin-Williams (1979) proposed that the relatively weak dominance structures among adolescent girls reflects the modest likelihood of aggressive expression among girls as compared with boys.

Of the modifications in ethological theory directly pertaining to the study of aggressive and prosocial behaviors in children, two of the more important involved a revision of the motivational assumptions of the model (Hinde, 1970) and a revised view of the effects of early experience (Bateson, 1966). Because of the problems associated with the assumption of drive-specific energy and the heritability of unitary drive structures, contemporary neoethologists have vigorously explored the functional development of attachment, aggressive, and interactive behaviors in particular species, including humans. In addition, because of the accumulated evidence on the study of plasticity in the effects of early experience, the proposal that there are critical periods in early life experience has been drastically modified. The concept of imprinting, for example, has been reevaluated to take into account that the early exposure experiences for the affiliative behavior in precocial birds and mammals is neither as time bound nor as irreversible as once believed (e.g., Bateson, 1966; Einsidel, 1975). The term "sensitive period" is now generally preferred to "critical period," along with the appreciation that subsequent experiences can often exercise a powerful influence on social and sexual preferences (Bateson, 1978; Immelmann & Suomi, 1981).

Although ethological studies are conducted within an evolutionary framework, it is explicitly recognized that multiple levels of determinants could be operative in the control of behavior. N. Tinbergen (1972a) addressed this matter when he observed that the issues of causation could be divided into three separate questions that differ primarily in the time scale involved, each of which asks, What makes this happen? First, of the short-term cycles in behavior (such as the tendency to eat, sleep, and mate), one might ask what controls the onset and termination of such behaviors, by examining the physiological and behavioral machinery underlying them. Second, the individual's whole life can be considered as a cycle, and changes in behavior over ontogeny can be studied to identify causes. Third, evo-lutionary changes in behavior may occur over generations, and the time unit may be an eon. Tinbergen pointed out that despite some overlap, causation studies refer to three different problems that require different research strategies and different theoretical concepts. Wilson (1975) makes a similar point in his distinction between proximal (short-term, develop-mental) causes and ultimate (evolutionary) ones.

Sociobiology

Although the birthdate of sociobiology is ordinarily given as 1975 (when E. O. Wilson's influential volume, *Sociobiology: A New Synthesis*, was published), the birth occurred some 11 years earlier, with the publication of W. D. Hamilton's brilliant contributions in the *Journal of Theoretical Biology* (1964). In two companion articles, Hamilton argued that Darwin-ian theory provided a reasonable account for why individuals fought or competed with each other but that it inadequately explained why organisms should cooperate or sacrifice themselves for others. Why, then, the ubiquity of cooperation and integration, even altruism, across species? Hamilton pointed out that, under special circumstances, self-sacrifice is the best strat-egy for preserving one's genes (through transmission to the next genera-tion). Altruistic acts – in which one gave one's own life so that others might live – was not necessarily a paradox for the new Darwinian theory. The act could make perfectly good genetic sense if the recipients were closely related to the altruist. The key lies in the concept of "inclusive genetic fitness," which may include not only the surviving offspring produced by the altruist (i.e., his "genetic fitness") but the beneficiaries of the action of the altruist as well. The closer the genetic ties between the altruist and the beneficiaries, the more likely it is that the "inclusive fitness" of the altruist would be enhanced. So it makes better genetic sense for a man to sacrifice himself for a sister or her offspring than, say, for the children of his own wife if he has serious doubts about their paternity (see Kurland, 1979).

But it seems restrictive to limit the genetic determination of altruism simply to members of one's own close family. To correct for this limitation,

Trivers (1971) proposed that one's "inclusive fitness" might be enhanced, even among unrelated beneficiaries, if the altruists' behavior were to produce feedback that would benefit the altruists' progeny (or other persons closely related to them). Such a state of affairs would obtain if the act of altruism were to produce reciprocal acts of altruism, some of which would be directed toward the relatives of the original altruist. This outcome could result, say, if there were a norm of reciprocity within the society such that unrelated individuals would sacrifice their own welfare so that others might benefit. This genetic strategy should work if there are no cheaters, or only a few of them.

But if there is a norm for reciprocity, why cannot there be other evolutionarily workable ways in which to relate to members of the society and thereby enhance the inclusive genetic fitness of its members? On this matter, geneticist Maynard Smith (1974) proposed that reciprocal altruism was an example of the more general possibility that there are evolutionarily stable strategies (ESS) characterizing societies and species. An ESS may be defined as a "strategy which, if most members of a population adopt it, cannot be bettered by an alternative strategy" (Dawkins, 1976). What makes the strategy better or worse is measured by whether it contributes to the genetic fitness of the members of the population. Maynard Smith (1974) develops in mathematical terms why certain interactional strategies (i.e, the "hawk" strategy, or winner-take-all) are unlikely to become stable for a society, since they would lead to species extinction or an evolutionary cul-de-sac. More generally, ESS include but are not limited to interpersonal strategies. They may refer to rearing strategies, mating strategies, or even reproduction strategies (e.g., a 50–50 split in sex ratio is more stable than a 75–25 or 10–90 division).

Sociobiology – and the biological reductionism and determinism implicit in its proposals – has not been without criticism. To the contrary, it has generated controversy that spilled over from the pages of the *Journal of Theoretical Biology* and the *American Psychologist* to those of the *Boston Globe*, *New York Times*, and *Newsweek*, among others. Assaults have been leveled at the assumptions adopted, at the data reported, and at the presumed political and economic implications of sociobiological ideas. The main points of attack may be outlined as follows:

1. *Theoretical*: includes several criticisms of sociobiology:
   a. Reifies dynamic behavior patterns, portraying complex interactive processes such as kindness or aggression as stable entities within the person
   b. Inappropriately assumes a simple isomorphic relationship between genes, hormones, and behavior, without attention to the reciprocal mechanisms of social interaction

    c. Appeals to word magic and monothetic criteria in generalizing disparate processes from ants to mice to humans by such terms as "aggression" and "altruism" (Distinctively human concepts are redefined to apply to fundamental animal behaviors, then applied back again to the human level with concepts that have been subtly altered in meaning and severely reduced in process. The conceptual confusion that has been generated extends beyond semantics.)

  2. *Empirical*: includes several criticisms of sociobiology:

    a. Ignores much of the available empirical literature in developmental studies on the causes, plasticity, and adaptive properties of human social behavior over time and circumstances

    b. Fails to consider the role of developmental regulation and feedback, assigning ontogeny to a minor role in the "fine-tuning" of evolved behaviors

    c. Appeals to the results of human behavioral genetics studies which characteristically misinterpret genetic variance by including the effects of interactional and social factors

    d. Fails to address directly the mediational mechanisms that provide the most powerful controls for the adaptive behaviors

  3. *Political*: includes the belief that sociobiology may be employed as an apology for the social and economic policies of meritocracy and discrimination (sexual, economic, racial) in the same ways that early versions of social Darwinism were employed to justify eugenics and maintenance of the status quo

The scientific criticisms – namely, the points summarized in 1 and 2 on theory and data – have been raised in various forms over the past 10 years by researchers from diverse disciplines, including anthropology (e.g., Sahlins, 1975), evolutionary biology (e.g., Gould, 1981), and psychology (e.g., Cairns, 1977). Whether the introduction of political–economic matters in the debate by researchers has done more to clarify or to confuse the basic scientific issues is hard to judge. Virtually any kernal idea in biological or developmental science, if taken seriously by an informed public, can be shown to have major ramifications for the social and political order, and sociobiology is no exception. In any case, one of the most recent and vigorous scientific–political critiques of sociobiology has been provided in the book, *Not in our genes* (1984), written by Lewontin, Rose, and Kamin, who are, respectively, an evolutionary geneticist, a neurobiologist, and an experimental psychologist.

Beyond the controversy sociobiology arouses – and the basic points of scientific criticism cannot be ignored in any thoughtful consideration of its claims – this orientation of evolutionary biology presents us with a theory that is rich in content, using descriptive terms and ideas that resonate immediately with those used by developmental psychologists. It has the additional advantage of exposing the flaws of contemporary psychological emphases that depict only the dark side of aggressive adaptations. The sociobiological formulation promotes a broad evolutionary view of social organization and social adaptation.

Developmental psychobiology

What I label "developmental psychobiology" encompasses approaches that are less novel for child psychology because they reflect a concern with the immediate proximal controls of behavioral and biological phenomena. These approaches include virtually all investigators who examine the problems of social development within the context of comparative psychology. Among representatives of this broad orientation, perhaps the most familiar are H. Harlow (1958), J. P. Scott (1958; 1962), D. O. Hebb (1953), T. C. Schneirla (1966), Z-Y. Kuo (1967), W. Mason (1980), and G. Gottlieb (1983), each of whom has been associated with the exploration of some distinctive feature of animal social development. However, unlike the other two biological orientations we have just covered, no dominant or integrative theory has emerged. Nevertheless, it is possible to identify certain theoretical assumptions common to developmental psychobiologists.

Two of the guidelines are metatheoretical in that they refer to biases on how explanatory concepts should be evaluated and on how research should proceed. T. C. Schneirla (1966), in particular, consistently stood for the need to exercise parsimony in explanation. One of the problems he found with "instinctual" explanations, for instance, was that they require special drives and dispositions to explain behaviors that might be more efficiently explained in terms of general quantitative principles. It is not that instinctual explanations are wrong so much as they are inadequate, providing answers when more questions are called for. A second metatheoretical bias is a preference for induction in scientific explanation. One begins with the analysis of a phenomenon, obtaining information about its development, regulation, and functional consequences in adaptation before offering explanations about its origins and determinants. This scientific strategy can be contrasted with the then-, and still-, dominant view in psychology that hypotheticodeductive research is preferred, where one begins with an expectation and the phenomenon either confirms or disconfirms the prediction. Empirical research in the inductive approach is concerned with description and discovery; empirical research in the hypotheticodeductive approach is concerned with demonstration and rejection of the null hypothesis.

The comparative-developmental orientation also has a general commitment to the organismic study of behavior. This means, among other things, that behavior is an essential component of the organismic system. It is considered a system because the organism is more than what is under the skin; it includes feedback with other organisms, with the physical environment, and with the changes in endogenous states. This organismic approach may be summarized in the following six principles (from Cairns, 1979):

1. During the course of development, endogenous and exogenous contributions to behavior become inseparably coalesced. Among other things, this means that "holistic theory conceptualizes all processes of progressive organization in consecutive early stages of development as fused, coalescing maturational and experiential functions" (Schneirla, 1966, pp. 288–289). No need to worry about how genetics and experience and maturation interact – they necessarily lose their separate identities in the developmental fusion. The problem then remains, for developmental researchers, to describe the processes of fusion, and not to generate hypotheses about proportional influence (such as 80% environment, 20% heredity, or vice-versa).

2. For social behaviors, developmental analyses must be concerned with the acts of other organisms and the reciprocal relationships that are formed with them. Bidirectional and feedback effects can occur both within and between organisms. Infants, for example, "design" their own mothers. Social acts of the infant (activity toward the mother, including suckling) can change her biological state of readiness for further maternal actions toward the infant.

3. Development shows continuity such that the organization of behavior and biological status at one stage provides the basis for organization at the next succeeding stage. This does not mean, however, that all processes persist throughout life, nor does it mean that behaviors must remain stable across stages. To the contrary, the organismic assumption requires that development be essentially a dynamic process that promotes continuing accommodation and reorganization over time.

4. The study of any behavioral phenomenon involves a need for multiple levels of analysis. This is a direct correlate of the assumption that there are interlocked systems (endogenous and exogenous) fused in the regulation of behavior. Hence the investigator must be prepared to assess internal states (including hormonal levels, morphological status, and/or neurological activity) as well as external ones (including the acts of other individuals and contextual/ecological factors). As Kuo (1967) put it, "the study of behavior is a synthetic science" (p. 25).

5. The fifth principle concerns the basis for generalization of one's observations across species and across ages in a given species. In general, the investigator must be as attentive to differences as to similarities in organization. What appears to be the same phenomenon of attachment, aggression, or altruism in two different species may be the same only in limited ways. The whole matrix of similarities and differences throughout development should be made explicit before considering cross-specific generalizations. The judgment should then be made on the basis of *polythetic* criteria (i.e., on multiple relevant characteristics) rather than a monothetic criterion (i.e., a single salient shared property). Jensen (1967) discusses the distinction and problem of generalization in detail.

6. The organism is continuously active throughout the course of embryo-
logical and postnatal development, into maturity. The developmental accommodations are not restricted to the very early ontogenetic stages, but
the processes continue to be active from conception to death.

Developmental psychobiology may be seen as a foundation for a theory
and not as a theory in itself. It is clearly open ended with respect to the
problem, say, of how aggressive behaviors develop, become regulated, and
are controlled in the course of living. What the orientation does provide
are guides as to how one should investigate developmental issues and how
to develop inductive answers to questions about their origins, maintenance,
and regulation.

Differences in conception and emphasis

Even a brief outline of the major views on behavioral biology suggests
some differences that could have significant implications for child psychologists. Consider first the matter of proximal determinants and accommodations during the course of development. Much of the content and
concern of developmental psychobiology is involved in the question of how
the system works, as well as its immediate and ontogenetic controls. This
matter is of special interest for ethologists, particularly neoethologists. But
it is only of peripheral concern for sociobiologist E. O. Wilson (1975), who
considers developmental modifications to involve fine-tuning the major
or ultimate evolutionary determinants. This difference in focus – on proximal or evolutionary factors – is not a trivial one, for it has multiple implications for how investigations in human development might proceed most
profitably.

Another point of difference concerns the content of the theory. Developmental psychobiology in its several forms hardly qualifies as a coherent
theory of behavioral biology. Instead, it provides propositions that eventually may constitute foundational assumptions for a theory capable of
yielding specific predictions as to the nature of social accommodations and
why they occur. On the other hand, sociobiology offers explanations for
behavioral patterns and motives that transcend taxonomic classes, species,
and phyla. The unit of the explanation is the gene, or confederations of
genes; thus, the accounts offered are indeed general to all living organisms,
not merely to particular individuals or populations or species. Sociobiology
has the additional advantage of the use of specific categories of behavior,
including "altruism," "spite," "aggression," "rape," "selfishness," and
"cooperation," that resonate with the sorts of behavioral categories employed in human personality development. As noted above, this claim for

generality of social motives across all forms of animal life has generated well-earned criticism because of its biological reductionism, monothetic generalizations, and inattention to developmental dynamics.

The dual genesis of aggressive behaviors

The universality of aggressive behaviors across cultures and across species has been broadly accepted as proof of behavioral evolution and a puzzle for developmental psychology. It is a puzzle because there seem to be few redeeming features for this dark side of human nature. At one point, Freud proposed the activity as the outcome of an instinct for destruction or the return to the quiescence of the inorganic world by the destruction of the self and of others (Bibring, 1969; Freud, 1959). Accordingly, aggressive behavior has generally been viewed within psychology as devoid of social merit for human beings – the very antithesis of survival. It is seen as something to be controlled in oneself and inhibited in others, especially in one's own children. Even in those contemporary treatments in which it is recognized that aggression "works" or "pays" (see, e.g., Bandura, 1973; Buss, 1962), it is seen as a bogus effectiveness, much as counterfeiting, fraud, or lying may be useful in the short term but eventually disastrous for the individual and the society.

This section presents an outline of an alternative conception based on the premise that aggressive behaviors are ubiquitous because they represent a convergence of evolutionary adaptations and developmental accommodations. They persist in individuals and in the society because they are functional for personal and social adaptation. This revised conception of the behavior pattern in children and adolescents does not mean, however, that developmental explanations may be reduced to phylogenetic terms. On the contrary, the distinctive human capabilities for cognitive strategies, including deception, permit the development of interpersonal aggressive patterns that are as novel as they are effective. All this is to say that evolutionary processes are themselves dynamic and susceptible to change, and development may be one of the primary mechanisms for initiating such change (de Beer, 1958).

The ultimate determinants of evolutionary analysis and the proximal determinants of developmental psychobiology provide explanations about aggressive patterns at two levels of discourse. If there exists collaboration in ontogeny and phylogeny one might expect to find at least some common ground in the two approaches to the problem.

Evolution and gender differences

Modern evolutionary theory suggests that a revised view should be taken of the occurrence of aggressive behavior (Dawkins, 1976; Lorenz, 1966; Maynard Smith, 1974; Wilson, 1975). For both sociobiology and ethology, aggressive acts serve a purpose. This purpose is directly related to the more general evolutionary goal of *any* behavior pattern; namely, the conveying of one's genes to the next generation. Within the ethological framework of aggressive behavior described by Konrad Lorenz (1966), the acts serve different purposes for males and females because of the different roles they play in reproduction. Among males, aggressive acts facilitate mate selection, such that the most "fit" will enjoy reproductive priority in access to females. It also promotes optimal levels of population distribution (through the establishment and defense of territories) and the establishment of societal structures (hierarchies of social status) within the society. This social organization, in turn, diminishes the need for continued conflict about access to the resources of the population, including access to fertile females.

Females within this evolutionary framework may also find aggressive behavior to be adaptive, but under different circumstances. For females, access to reproductively active males is less of a problem than is the protection of the young. (For males in societies in which there is a high level of promiscuity and indiscriminate sexual activity, brood protection may not be an especially wise investment of energy. Not so for females, who breed a limited number of offspring.) It might be expected that females would show strongest tendencies to attack during the period when they are reproductively active, and particularly when they have neonatal and weaning young. In the case of males, there is a need to protect their access to resources – or more important – to ensure that their young will have access to resources. On this count, it would be consistent with a sociobiological perspective to expect that females would show some propensity to inhibit the actions of those who might diminish the resources, particularly other females who could then produce litters of their own.

The evolutionary perspective holds that aggressive behavior is both functional and inevitable. It also implies certain sex and age differences might be expected, and that there is a special relationship between aggressive behavior and reproductive states. Although a good deal of discussion (and controversy) has surrounded the problem of sex differences implied by evolutionary speculations, less attention has been given to the equally important age-developmental expectations. Given the presumed adaptive functions of aggressive behavior, it should be immediately linked to the developmental-gender status of the individual and the victims of aggressive acts should show a high level of developmental-gender specificity. The foregoing implies that the highest levels of aggressive expression would occur during those periods of the males' life in which they are reproductively active and that the bulk of their aggressive expression would be directed toward same-sex competitors (i.e., other reproductively active males, as opposed to females and immature males). Among females, there would also be an age-developmental bias in aggressive expression. As in the case of males, such a bias would be associated with periods of reproductive activity, with the highest likelihood during periods in which the female is with her own immature young. But females must have resources to live upon, and so must their offspring. Hence there should be a bias against unfamiliar conspecifics, including strange males who would destroy their offspring, and new females who would intrude on the resources and produce additional young.

One central problem can be raised for evolutionary accounts: Why shouldn't there be more aggression? Why should the fighting stop as long as there are resources to be protected, and victims to be controlled, chased away, or otherwise regulated? On the surface, such a "hawk" interpersonal strategy would appear to be the most efficient means to enhance genetic fitness. However, as Maynard Smith has pointed out, this effective short-run strategy is not likely to pay off in the long run in "inclusive genetic fitness." "Fighting to the death" is likely to have low payoffs for the individual in genetic transmission if all of one's opponents are likely to reciprocate with the same strategy. In any case, Maynard Smith (1974) argued that the to-the-death solution, if adopted by all members of the society, would be unlikely to become stable from one generation to the next, hence could not qualify as an evolutionarily stable strategy.

Evolutionary formulations have been treated with some skepticism by child developmentalists. The hazards in evolutionary theorizing about human behavior have been amply demonstrated in the reductionistic speculations on the matter endorsed by various authors, from G. S. Hall (1904) to E. O. Wilson (1975). We must agree with Tinbergen's assessment that "professional students of human behaviour have, in rejecting some of Lorenz's claims, thrown away the baby with the bathwater, and so the Ethology of Man finds itself at the moment in a false position: over-acclaimed by many, shrugged off by others" (Tinbergen, 1972b, p.vii). Sociobiology presents a similar dilemma for developmentalists in the 1980s, and that is a pity. Despite its pitfalls, an evolutionary perspective to social developments – including aggressive behavior patterns – can provide a

biological perspective that has been missing from developmental formulations of the past half-century.

Development and gender differences in human beings

Probably the most parsimonious developmental answer to the question,
"Why aggression?" is that, for humans, "Aggression works." This answer
is implied in the above evolutionary accounts in that it is presumed that
the winners, not the losers, of aggressive encounters are the ones who gain
access to females, achieve high status, gain resources, and ensure prosperity
for their babies. Notwithstanding psychological legends to the contrary,
punishment is an effective short-term means of controlling, inhibiting, and
redirecting behavior, including social actions (Cheyne & Walters, 1970;
Church, 1963; Solomon, 1964). During the course of living, hurtful acts
performed by one member of an interchange typically have the effect of
producing an immediate change in the ongoing behavior of the other individual. What is hurtful or harmful to the other is highly dependent on
the strength, cognitive capacity, and abilities of the aggressor as well as
the vulnerability, sensitivity, and cognitive status of the victim. In any case,
pain – or the events that signal it – serves to redirect behavior in an
interchange. This basic lesson seems to be learned early in the life of most
young (e.g., Homberg, 1980). Nor does it appear to be a lesson they ever
forget.

Given the bias within each individual toward (1) internal organization
and the reduction of stress, and (2) interpersonal synchrony and mutual
accommodation, why should conflicts arise between individuals? One developmental answer is that the actions required for intrapersonal organization do not always coincide with those required for interpersonal
organization. On such occasions, something must give – either the organized behavior of one person, or the organized behavior of the other. If
neither person can or will accommodate to the acts of the other, and both
remain in the interaction, some form of behavioral disruption is inevitable.
Interference with an organized response pattern – whether the interference
is called "punishment," "aggression," or "coercion" – is likely to produce
resistance by the victim and a heightened level of arousal (e.g., Mandler,
1964). For the same reason, if each person in the interaction operates
according to the same ground rules, there should be reciprocal resistance
to the interference. So two 12-month-old children may tug at the same
toy, and the two teenage brothers may get into an argument over which
program they should watch on TV, and the argument may escalate into a
vicious assault.

Whatever resolutions may be reached at one stage of development may not be valid or workable at later stages because of inevitable ontogenetic changes. As the infant become a child and the child becomes an adolescent, a host of modifications affect the individual's capabilities to resist interference, and the other person's options to create interference. Such reorganizations of behavior and cognitive status in development force changes in social and familial organization. Shifts in role and dominance relationships bring about differences in the ways in which interpersonal synchrony is achieved and in the limits placed on each other's actions. For example, two of the obvious and powerful changes that occur in development are those associated with morphology and cognition. Human male and female adolescents experience a major differentiation in the trajectory and form of morphological development. This sexual dimorphism could be expected to be integrated with and supportive of differential societal standards for male and female behavior as well as sex-related differences in the form and content of methods of mutual control.

It is in the area of cognitive competence that human social development is most likely to have effects distinctively different from those of nonhumans. Children and adolescents gain increasingly flexible techniques based on verbal communication as they move from infancy to childhood to adolescence. These distinctively human strategies for interference include symbolic information and misinformation. For example, an "apology" or a "confession" might be viewed as one way in which to restructure the past and modify future attributions. In many contexts, it can defuse a stressed relationship or otherwise diminish the tendency for future reciprocal aggression. Such cognitive capabilities, perfected in adolescence, open the door to a whole range of advanced social strategies whereby deception and misdirection might be employed in controlling the direction of relationships. It seems reasonable to expect that these techniques might be employed by boys and girls differently when they emerge at puberty.

Toward an integrated account

To attempt an integration of ethological/sociobiological accounts of aggressive expression in animals with developmental/interactional ones is a hazardous business. Nonetheless, there does appear to be sufficient common ground in the explanations to permit us to offer some preliminary proposals on the matter. We first outline these proposals, then illustrate some recent findings relevant to them. The above evolutionary considerations suggest four propositions on the development of aggressive behavior:

1. The capacity for the developmental emergence of hurtful patterns of in-

terchange is inherent in all mammalian species, including human beings. Accordingly, no specific learning experiences are required for the establishment of the behavior, although the interchanges may be learnable (i.e., either inhibited or facilitated by prior experiences).

2. Strong age and sex differences in aggressive behavior should typically appear, emerging most prominently at puberty. For males, the most intense levels of hurtful and destructive behavior should appear during the stages of heightened reproductive activity.

3. At the point in development when sexual dimorphism emerges – at puberty in human beings – physical aggression should play a less prominent role for females than for males. Moreover, there should be concomitant differences in the gender of the victims such that males should express more frequent and intense physical aggression toward other males than toward females. The above propositions must be qualified to the extent that distinctive species adaptations occur in such characteristics as sexual dimorphism, breeding strategy (including duration of prematurity), and cognitive and interactive capabilities. Cognitive development in human beings is a case in point. Children and adolescents develop an ability to employ alternative cognitive strategies of interpersonal control. The cognitively mediated controls may be either indirect (e.g., manipulating events and attitudes in the social network) or direct (e.g., assaults on another's self-esteem).

4. Because direct physical aggression is likely in most societies to be gender-biased, that is, the behavior is seen as less tolerable in girls than in boys, it follows that in adolescence and early adulthood, indirect alternatives of interpersonal control and punishment, including social ostracization and alienation, should occur with higher frequencies among girls than boys.

The last proposition returns us to the problem: why not more aggression? The functions offered in ethology and sociobiology supplement those suggested in a developmental analysis. On the one hand, evolutionary analyses point to the importance of social structures, including the development of roles, dominance hierarchies, ritualized actions and counteractions, and symbolic forms of aggressive expression. On the other hand, developmental–interactional analyses have pointed to the individual strategies that children may adopt in their relationships, including failure to respond to provocation and the redirection or deflection of the interchange to new channels. For children and adolescents, developmental solutions have emphasized the distinctively human strategies of information transmission, including apologies, confessions, and deceptions. Which techniques are employed presumably depend on the role and circumstances of the individual, including the skills and competences of those with whom they interact.

Developmental emergence of sex–age differences

The four propositions provide a useful framework for organizing otherwise puzzling findings on age and gender differences in aggressive expression.

To varying degrees, these propositions run counter to intuition and psychological theories of the establishment of aggressive behavior. As the relevant empirical evidence has recently been reviewed elsewhere (e.g., see Cairns, 1979; Cairns & Cairns, 1985; White, 1983), some illustrative findings are abstracted here.

First, is learning necessary? Here the distinction between establishment and change is critical. For the establishment of aggressive behavior in ontogeny, no special lessons, training, or modeling experiences seem required for any of the nonhuman species in which appropriate experiments have been conducted. The experiments include studies of isolation and cross-specific rearing in order to ensure that the social learning experiences of the individual are controlled. As Eibl-Eibesfeldt (1964) and Lorenz (1966) argued, the behavior is exhibited in animals that have been maintained in isolation from conspecifics since birth or very early in ontogeny. The outcome has now been established in several mammalian and avian species (Cairns, 1979). The effects of training for aggression in mice indicate, paradoxically, that training procedures inhibit the behavior, and there is little or no gain over mere isolation (Cairns, 1979). Analyses of the psychobiological effects induced by isolation have shown that the procedure serves to facilitate aggressive expression through the induction of states of heightened reactivity and arousability, which serve in turn to escalate aggressive expression (Cairns & Nakelski, 1971; Cairns & Scholz, 1973). Further analysis of learning contingencies indicates that aggressive expression and inhibition are highly learnable but they are not initially established through specific learning processes.

For human beings, no adequate experimental study of aggressive establishment has been conducted, and it is unlikely that one can be. Observational studies of aggressive behavior development in infants and young children, although informative, cannot be conclusive on the contributive role of learning. Nonetheless, it has been observed that approximately 50% of the actions displayed by children aged 12–15 months toward same-age peers may be classified as assertive or coercive, diminishing to 17% at 42 months (Holmberg, 1980; also Goodenough, 1931). It would be useful to determine whether similar proportions are observed in other societies and whether a systematic age decline occurs in proportion of assertive acts. On the other hand, there is ample evidence that aggressive behaviors are learnable in humans. The conditions of learning are highly relative to the circumstances of the individual, the role of the other, and the quality of the interchange (Parke & Slaby, 1983).

Few attempts have been made to plot the occurrence of aggressive behavior as a function of age and sex in nonhuman species (Cairns & Hood,

1983). The available information appears to be consistent with the second proposition. For instance, the longitudinal development of fighting in male mice shows a sharp increase at days 30–45, the period of onset of sexual maturation in this species (Cairns, MacCombie, & Hood, 1983). It should also be noted that this developmental stage describes the period in which the differences arise between lines that have been genetically selected for "high" and "low" aggression (Fig. 2.1). Further analysis shows a convergence between lines at later maturity that is partly attributable to the effects of repeated testing (Fig. 2.2). This conclusion was reached by comparing repeatedly tested animals with male siblings who were tested on but one occasion. This cosibial research design controls for between-litter genetic differences and replicates the pubertal effect of aggressive onset. The single-test cosibial animals show diminished convergence between high- and low-aggressive lines at later maturity. Little information is available on development of aggressive behaviors in females, regardless of species.

As noted by Cairns & Cairns (1985), the available crime and behavioral evidence consistent with the proposition that the differences between males and females in aggressive expression sharply increase at puberty and early adulthood. For the prototypical crime of violence – murder – a clear relationship exists among age, sex, and the rate of arrests. According to recent national statistics on arrests for violent crimes, the most aggressive persons in the United States are boys 17–19 years of age. There is an age-related rise in the rate of arrests of females for crimes of violence, but the increase is much less sharp for females. Overall, the differential rate of arrests for violent crimes is approximately 10 to 1 in the years of highest risk, diminishing as a function of age (Crime in the United States, 1983) (Fig. 2.3). These robust effects have recently been discussed by Greenberg (1985; but note that Greenberg argues for an asymptote somewhat later than shown in Fig. 2.3).

The data available from direct observation of "normal" boys and girls before and during adolescence yield a picture that is not inconsistent with the crime statistics. For instance, Cairns, Cairns, and Ferguson (1984) reported an age-related increase in observed and self-reported aggressive acts in boys aged 9–10 to 13–14. The increase was obtained for males, but not for females (see also Cairns & Cairns, 1984). Ferguson calls this acceptance of aggressive solutions the "brutalization norm." Moreover, in a population of unselected children/adolescents, Cairns & Cairns (1985) found an age-related increase among females in the employment of the social network as an instrument for aggressive expression. Seventh-grade girls, but not boys, reported instances of social ostracism and alienation, as opposed to direct confrontation. The gender difference in the use of social

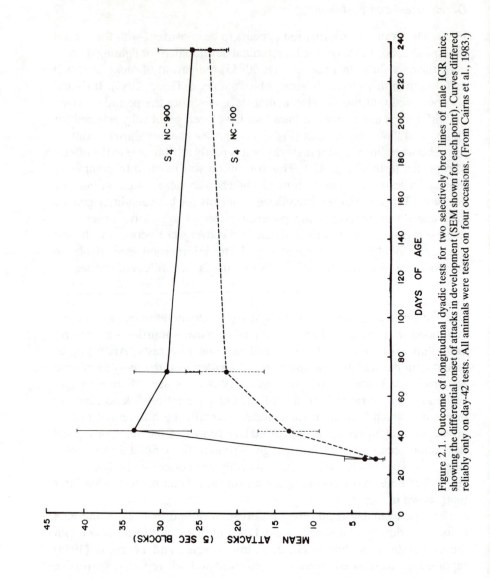

Figure 2.1. Outcome of longitudinal dyadic tests for two selectively bred lines of male ICR mice, showing the differential onset of attacks in development (SEM shown for each point). Curves differed reliably only on day-42 tests. All animals were tested on four occasions. (From Cairns et al., 1983.)

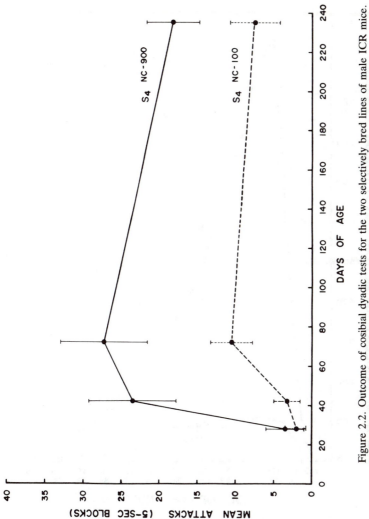

Figure 2.2. Outcome of cosibial dyadic tests for the two selectively bred lines of male ICR mice. In contrast with the information shown in Figure 2.1, each animal was tested on only one occasion. The animals were full sibling littermates to the animals tested in the longitudinal test; thus the convergence at mid-adulthood in Figure 2.2 represents the combined effects of repeated testing and developmental changes. (From Cairns et al., 1983.)

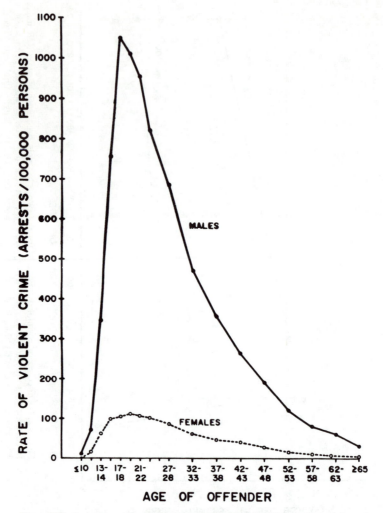

Figure 2.3. Arrest rates for violent crime by males and females as function of age. (From *Crime in the United States, 1982,* and *United States Census Report, 1980.*)

cliques as "attack groups" increased as the girls entered adolescence (Cairns & Cairns, 1985).

In sum, the empirical information relevant to the proposition that gender differences in aggressive expression become magnified at puberty is fragmentary but provocative. A potential conceptual advantage of the biological perspectives is that they may help identify gaps in the empirical evidence on the developmental dynamics of gender differences.

Conclusions

This chapter began with the observation that the child-rearing studies of 20 years ago taught us that social learning theory was in itself inadequate to solve the problems of social development. The research of the past 10 years teaches a similar lesson about evolutionary theories. Neither ethology nor sociobiology is sufficient, in itself, to account for the main features of social development in children, for they do not focus on the developmental origins of aggressive and altruistic behaviors. To a greater or lesser extent, evolutionary models have given short shrift to the problems of essential concern to child psychologists. These include the need for guidelines on how to understand individual differences in the development of complex emotional and behavioral states, such as those involved in aggressive and altruistic patterns. The more general problem is that the social behaviors reflect a fusion of factors. Any workable theory of social development must give explicit attention to both evolutionary *and* developmental functions, and to how they coalesce at successive developmental periods to reproduce distinctive individual patterns.

It would be a grave mistake, as well as regressive, to conclude that what biological approaches have to offer students of social development is not of central importance. The contributions have been both methodological and theoretical. The emphasis on direct and naturalistic observation is a primary legacy of ethology to psychology, as has been the psychobiological integration of experimental and observational procedures. Beyond method, there have been clear theoretical gains for developmental investigators, particularly with respect to the thorny issues of why one might expect age and sex differences. The tradition in developmental psychology has been to approach the questions of age and gender differences atheoretically or in terms of grossly defined dichotomies (e.g., biological determinism or social norms; nature or nurture; genetics or learning). Evolutionary and psychobiological functions suggest that sex differences should not be invariant with respect to age, but should emerge in puberty and converge in later maturity.

The question has been asked, Can ethology or sociobiology contribute to the understanding of behavioral development? Obviously they can, if not always in the ways originally envisioned. It seems reasonable to ask, in addition, Can studies of development contribute to the understanding of behavioral evolution? Here again there is strong evidence for an affirmative answer. Beyond the fact that developmental analyses are essential to the enterprise of cross-specific generalization, they can also inform about the nature of the developmental shifts that contribute to evolutionary changes. In this regard, it has been proposed that modest changes in gender development rate or sequence (i.e., heterochronies) can produce sharp changes in descendent generations (e.g., Cairns, MacCombie, & Hood, 1983; de Beer, 1958; Gould, 1977; Mason, 1980; Piaget, 1978). In the long run, ontogenetic studies of behavior may be as crucial to understanding behavioral evolution as the other way around. In either case, they are necessarily intertwined.

Evolutionary theories of social behavior have considered behavior to be like other biophysical structures that have evolved in natural history. One upshot of this reification – viewing behavior as structure – is that behavioral propensities are assumed to be conserved, unchanged, across generations. Since the biological substrates for, say, aggression and altruism, have evolved over hundreds or thousands of generations, it has been assumed that they are inevitable in the ontogeny of each person. Hence the predetermined nature of human nature. This emphasis on the nondevelopmental, static properties of evolved behavioral patterns is ironic in light of the kernel idea that evolution is the dynamic force in adaptation. This static emphasis also supports a fatal error in theoretical conception.

The problem with the concept of behavior as structure is that it overlooks the dynamic functions of social interactions. Social behaviors – as opposed to nonsocial ones – should be especially vulnerable to change in both phylogeny and ontogeny. To the extent that behavioral patterns serve as a leading edge of biological adaptation, they constitute that part of the organismic system that is most flexible. On this proposition, even the most fundamental social relationships should be open to rapid modification should circumstances require it. For example, it would make little survival sense for immature mammals to persist in their original social attachments if the mother should die. If the infant is to survive, adoption by a substitute mother should not only be possible, it should be very rapid. Such adoptions presuppose social plasticity in both the infant and the foster mother. Similarly, it could be disastrous for species to fail to undergo rapid evolutionary changes in social behavior and organization should abrupt local changes in social ecology demand it.

The outcomes of behavioral–genetic studies of microevolution are consistent with the view that social behavior processes are open to extreme and rapid change, if the changes in adaptational requirements are themselves extreme and sudden. For instance, Fuller and Thompson (1978) report no failures of attempts to selectively breed for particular social patterns, whether in males or females. The genetic effects on complex social behaviors, including aggressive ones, are rapid and robust. They appear full-blown in a short time, usually by three generations and often after a single generation (e.g., Cairns, MacCombie, & Hood, 1983). The very rapidity of these microevolutionary changes belies the commonly accepted belief that changes in complex social patterns require hundreds or thousands of generations to evolve. Moreover, the same social patterns that are susceptible to microevolutionary pressures are highly vulnerable to ontogenetic ones (Cairns, MacCombie, & Hood, 1983). Developmental studies of the aggressive behaviors indicate that they are rapidly and effectively "fine-tuned" to individual experience and local social rearing conditions.

This view that social interactions serve as the leading edge for organismic adaptation suggests three propositions regarding the collaboration between ontogenetic and evolutionary factors, namely:

1. The role that evolutionary–genetic factors play in the modifications of systems of social interchange is very great. Complex social behavior processes are more susceptible to rapid modification and reorganization through genetic manipulation than are complex nonbehavioral structures.
2. The role of developmental factors is even greater. Since most systems of social interchange are highly vulnerable to developmental change, they will be conserved in ontogeny only if the social conditions prevailing during development are conducive to preservation.
3. Stability of social patterns in both microevolution and individual development should be observed only to the extent that the adaptational conditions remain relatively constant and unchanging. This conservatism comes about because social processes are constrained by multiple organismic, social, and ecological factors. But when changes occur in these constraints, social patterns should be susceptible to rapid modification.

Evolutionary–developmental accounts of social behavior do not require reification. To the contrary, the dynamic conception of social interchanges provides a better fit than the static one to the puzzling empirical findings on microevolution. Furthermore, the same genetic–biological stuff can be organized differently in the course of development to bring about drastically different patterns of social adaptation. The results on genetic regulation and developmental change are not incompatible. To the contrary, they are precisely what one should expect if (1) social behavior processes were the leading edge for biological adaptation, and (2) ontogenetic and phyletic mechanisms collaborate in achieving optimal accommodations.

One enduring problem for behavioral biology has been the unfortunate biological reductionism implicit in many of its proposals. Social processes have been seen as subsidiary to biochemical and neurological mechanisms. According to the present view, such reductionism is not merely misleading, but it reverses the actual processes of evolution and development. Biochemical and physiological mechanisms are the servants of social adaptation, not the other way around.

The last point is key to this discussion. To the extent that students of children's social behavior and those of animal social behavior behave as if they dwell in different lands, both areas stand to suffer. Evolutionary theorists have effectively reminded child psychologists of basic gaps in their analysis, including the role of altruism, reciprocity, and biological preparedness in the synchrony of social behaviors. They also underscore the importance of mounting a unified scientific assault on matters of social structure and social behavior. On the other hand, the static and reductionist depictions of socialization embodied in recent evolutionary accounts underscore the need for child psychologists to speak with greater authority, precision, and directness about the nature of developmental dynamics. The understanding of social development can no longer be considered the exclusive business of a single enterprise, whether developmental psychology, ethology, or sociobiology. The thoughtful merger that now seem to be in progress should benefit science.

References

Ainsworth, M. D. S. (1972). Attachment and dependency: A comparison. In J. L. Gewirtz (Ed.), *Attachment and dependency* (pp. 97–137). New York: Wiley.

Baldwin, J. M. (1897). *Social and ethical interpretations in mental development: A study in social psychology*. New York: Macmillan.

Bandura, A. (1973). *Aggression: A social learning analysis*. Englewood Cliffs, NJ: Prentice-Hall.

Bateson, P. P. G. (1966). The characteristics and context of imprinting. *Biological Reviews, 41*, 177–220.

Bateson, P. P. G. (1979). How do sensitive periods arise and what are they for? *Animal Behaviour, 27*, 470–486.

Bibring, E. (1969). The development and problems of the theory of instincts. *International Journal of Psychoanalysis, 50*, 293–308.

Bowlby, J. (1958). The nature of the child's tie to his mother. *International Journal of Psychoanalysis, 39*, 350–373.

Bowlby, J. (1969). *Attachment and loss (Vol. 1)*. New York: Basic Books.

Buss, A. (1961). *The psychology of aggression*. New York: Wiley.

Cairns, R. B. (1977). Sociobiology – A new synthesis or an old cleavage? *Contemporary Psychology, 22*, 1–3.

Cairns, R. B. (1979). *Social development: The origins and plasticity of development*. San Francisco: Freeman.

Cairns, R. B., & Cairns, B. D. (1985). The developmental–interactional view of social behavior: Four issues of adolescent aggression. In D. Olweus, J. Block, & M. Radke-Yarrow (Eds.), *The development of antisocial and prosocial behavior* (pp. 315–342). New York: Academic.

Cairns, R. B., Cairns, B. D., & Ferguson, L. D. (1984, April). *Aggressive behavior in elementary school children: Gender similarities, differences, and developmental continuities.*

Paper presented at the Eighth Biennial Meeting of the Southeastern Conference on Human Development, Athens, GA.

Cairns, R. B., MacCombie, D. M., & Hood, K. E. (1983). A developmental–genetic analysis of aggressive behavior in mice. *Journal of Comparative Psychology*, *97*, 69–89.

Cairns, R. B., & Nakelski, J. S. (1971). On fighting in mice: Ontogenetic and experiential determinants. *Journal of Comparative and Physiological Psychology*, *71*, 354–364.

Cairns, R. B., & Scholz, S. D. (1973). Fighting in mice: Dyadic escalation and what is learned. *Journal of Comparative and Physiological Psychology*, *85*, 540–550.

Cairns, R. B., & Valsiner, J. (1984). Child psychology. *Annual Review of Psychology*, *35*, 553–577.

Chagnon, N. A., & Irons, W. (1979). *Evolutionary biology and human social behavior: An anthropological perspective*. North Scituate, MA: Duxbury.

Chance, M. R. A. (1975, May). Letter. *Human Ethology Newsletter*, pp. 1–5.

Cheyne, J. A., & Walters, R. H. (1970). Punishment and prohibition: Some origins of self-control. In *New directions in psychology* (Vol. 4, pp. 281–366). New York: Holt, Rinehart, and Winston.

Church, R. M. (1963). The varied effects of punishment on behavior. *Psychological Review*, *70*, 369–402.

Crime in the United States. (1982). Washington, DC: Government Printing Office.

Dawkins, R. (1976). *The selfish gene*. Oxford: Oxford University Press.

de Beer, G. (1958). *Embryos and ancestors*, 3rd ed. London: Oxford University Press.

Eibl-Eibesfeldt, I. (1961). The fighting behavior of animals. *Scientific American*, *205*, 112–122.

Eibl-Eibesfeldt, I. (1975). *Ethology: The biology of behavior*, (2nd ed.). New York: Holt, Rinehart, and Winston.

Einsidel, A. E. (1975). The development and modification of object preferences in domestic White Leghorn chicks. *Developmental Psychobiology*, *8*, 533–540.

Freud, S. (1959) *Collected papers*. New York: Basic Books.

Fuller, J. L., & Thompson, W. R. (1978). *Foundations of behavior genetics*. 2nd ed. St. Louis, MO: Mosby.

Geen, R. G., & Donnerstein, E. I. (1983). *Aggression: Theoretical and empirical reviews*. (2 vols). New York: Academic Press.

Goodenough, F. L. (1931). *Anger in young children*. Minneapolis: University of Minnesota Press.

Gottlieb, G. (1983). The psychobiological approach to developmental issues. In P. H. Mussen (Gen. Ed.) and J. J. Campos & M. M. Haith (Vol. Eds.), *Handbook of child psychology: Vol. 2. Infancy and developmental psychobiology*. (4th ed., pp. 1–26). New York: Wiley.

Gould, S. J. (1977). *Ontogeny and phylogeny*. Cambridge, MA: Harvard University Press.

Gould, S. J. (1981). *The mismeasure of man*. New York: Norton.

Greenberg, D. F. (1985). Age, crime, and social explanation. *American Journal of Sociology*, *91*, 1–21.

Hall, G. S. (1904) *Adolescence: Its psychology and its relation to physiology, anthropology, sociology, sex, crime, religion, and education* (2 vols.). New York: Appleton.

Hamilton, W. D. (1964). The genetical theory of social behavior. I, II. *Journal of Theoretical Biology*, *7*, 1–52.

Harlow, H. F. (1958). The nature of love. *The American Psychologist*, *13*, 673–685.

Hebb, D. O. (1953). Heredity and environment in mammalian behavior. *British Journal of Animal Behaviour*, *1*, 43–47.

Hinde, R. A. (1970). *Animal behavior: A synthesis of ethology and comparative psychology* (2nd ed.). New York: McGraw-Hill.

Hinde, R. A. (1983). Ethology and child development. In P. H. Mussen (Gen. Ed.) and

J. J. Campos & M. M. Haith (Vol. Eds.), *Handbook of child psychology: Vol. 2. Infancy and developmental psychobiology* (4th ed., pp. 27–94). New York: Wiley.

Hoffman, M. L. (1981). Is altruism part of human nature? *Journal of Personality and Social Psychology, 40*, 121–137.

Holmberg, M. C. (1980). The development of social interchange patterns from 12–42 months. *Child Development, 51*, 448–456.

Immelmann, K., Barlow, G. W., Petrinovich, L., and Main, M. (1981). *Behavioral development: The Bielefeld Interdisciplinary Project*. Cambridge: Cambridge University Press.

Immelmann, K., & Suomi, S. (1981). Sensitive phases in development. In K. Immelmann, G. W. Barlow, L. Petrinovich, & M. Main (Eds.), *Behavioral development: The Bielefeld Interdisciplinary Project* (pp. 395–431). Cambridge: Cambridge University Press.

Jensen, D. D. (1967). Polythetic operationism and the phylogeny of learning. In W. C. Corning & S. C. Ratner (Eds.), *Chemistry of learning: Invertebrate research* (pp. 43–63). New York: Plenum.

Kohlberg, L. (1969). Stage and sequence: The cognitive-developmental approach to socialization. In D. A. Goslin (Ed.), *Handbook of socialization theory and research*. Chicago: Rand McNally.

Kummer, H. (1968). *Social organization of hamadryas baboons: A field study*. Chicago: University of Chicago Press.

Kuo, Z-Y. (1967). *The dynamics of behavior development: An epigenetic view*. New York: Random House.

Kurland, J. A. (1979). Paternity, mother's brother, and human sociality. In N. A. Chagnon & W. Irons (Eds.), *Evolutionary biology and human social behavior: An anthropological perspective*. North Scituate, MA: Duxbury.

Lawick-Goodall, J. van. (1968). Behaviour of free-living chimpanzees of the Gombi Stream area. *Animal Behavior Monographs, 1*(3), 161–311.

Lewontin, R. C., Rose, S., & Kamin, L. J. (1984). *Not in our genes: biology, ideology, and human nature*. New York: Atheneum.

Lorenz, K. Z. (1935). Der Kumpan in der Umwelt des Vogels. *Journal of Ornithology, 83*, 137–213; 289–413.

Lorenz, K. Z. (1965). *Evolution and modification of behavior*. Chicago: University of Chicago Press.

Lorenz, K. Z. (1966). *On aggression*. New York: Harcourt, Brace, and World.

Mandler, G. (1964). The interruption of behavior. In D. Levine (Ed.), *Nebraska Symposium on Motivation* (Vol. 12, pp. 163–219). Lincoln: University of Nebraska Press.

Mason, W. A. (1960). The effects of social restriction on the behavior of rhesus monkeys: I. Free social behavior. *Journal of Comparative and Physiological Psychology, 53*, 582–589.

Mason, W. [A.] (1980). Social ontogeny. In P. Marler & J. G. Vandenbergh (Eds.), *Social behavior and communication*. New York: Plenum Press.

Maynard Smith, J. (1974). The theory of games and the evolution of animal conflict. *Journal of Theoretical Biology, 47*, 202–221.

Parke, R. G. & Slaby, R. G. (1983). The development of aggression. In P. H. Mussen (Gen. Ed.) & E. M. Hetherington (Vol. Ed.), *Handbook of child psychology: Vol. 4. Socialization, personality, and social development* (4th ed., pp. 547–641). New York: Wiley.

Piaget, J. (1978). *Behavior and evolution*. New York: Pantheon.

Preyer, W. (1888–1889) *The mind of the child* (2 vols.). New York: Appleton.

Romanes, G. J. (1884). *Mental evolution in animals*. New York: Appleton.

Sahlins, M. D. (1976). *The use and abuse of biology: an anthropological critique of sociobiology*. Ann Arbor, MI: University of Michigan Press.

Sameroff, A. (1983). Developmental systems: Context and evolution. In P. H. Mussen (Gen.

Ed.) & W. Kessen (Vol. Ed.), *Handbook of child psychology: Vol. 1. History, theory, and methods* (4th ed., pp. 235–294). New York: Wiley.

Savin-Williams, R. (1979). Dominance hierarchies in groups of early adolescents. *Child Development, 50,* 923–935.

Schneirla, T. C. (1966). Behavioral development and comparative psychology. *Quarterly Review of Biology, 41,* 283–302.

Scott, J. P. (1958). *Aggression.* Chicago: University of Chicago Press.

Scott, J. P. (1962). Critical periods in behavioral development. *Science, 138,* 949–958.

Solomon, R. L. (1964). Punishment. *American Psychologist, 12,* 239–253.

Strayer, F. F. & Strayer, J. (1976). An ethological analysis of social agonism and dominance relations among pre-school children. *Child Development, 47,* 980–999.

Tinbergen, N. (1972a). *The animal in its world: Explorations of an ethologist.* London: Allen & Unwin.

Tinbergen, N. (1972b). Foreword. In N. Blurton Jones (Ed.), *Ethological studies of child behaviour.* Cambridge: Cambridge University Press.

Trivers, R. L. (1971). The evolution of reciprocal altruism. *Quarterly Review of Biology, 46,* 35–57.

White, J. W. (1983). Sex and gender issues in aggression research. In G. Geen & E. I. Donnerstein (Eds.), *Aggression: Theoretical and empirical reviews* (Vol. 2, pp. 1–26). New York: Academic Press.

Wilson, E. O. (1975) *Sociobiology: The new synthesis.* Cambridge, MA: Harvard University Press.

Yarrow, M. R., Campbell, J. D., & Burton, R. V. (1968). *Child rearing: An inquiry into research and methods.* San Francisco: Jossey-Bass.

3   Development in reciprocity through friendship

James Youniss

The concept of reciprocity has played a central role in sociological explanations of social solidarity and social cohesion (Gouldner, 1960; Sahlins, 1965). It has a similar role in social biology through Trivers's (1971) notion of reciprocal altruism. Recent studies of children's friendship indicate that major components of moral or prosocial development appear within this relationship during the preschool period. If reciprocity does indeed prove to be a defining characteristic of friendship (Hinde, 1976; 1979; Youniss, 1980), studies of the development of reciprocity may provide fresh insight into prosocial development that has been overlooked by most theorists.

The aim of this chapter is to present an analysis of the concept of reciprocity, as demonstrated in the development of prosocial behavior in children. First, uses of the concept of reciprocity in sociology and social biology are reviewed; the discussion focuses on aspects of the concept that appear most useful for developmental interest. Next, findings on children's friendships are summarized insofar as they bear on reciprocity and on prosocial behavior. Both reviews are then conjoined in a theoretical analysis in which a distinction is drawn between the child as an individual agent and the child as conceived through membership in interpersonal relationships. Finally, the chapter concludes with a discussion of the implications of the latter viewpoint both for developmental psychology and for social biology.

Social cohesion

Sociologists face the difficult task of having too many data to explain regarding social behavior. For any behavior that seems conducive to social cohesion, say, cooperation, there is a counterbehavior that potentially leads to the opposite result, in this case, competition. Their problem, then, is in finding a base from which to account for both types of behavior and, simultaneously, to explain how society continues to persist rather than

88

deteriorate. Gouldner's (1960) statement on reciprocity may be considered seminal because it addresses both sides of the problem and provides a basis for reapproaching central questions from a fresh perspective.

Gouldner begins with the question of why particular social patterns (e.g., customs, political parties) survive or persist. The question is considered within the context of functionalist theory and bears on the sociological matters of macrostructure. At the time Gouldner wrote, for example, political parties, or machines, were seen as passé and ready to be replaced by government run by the more rational means of systems organization. The issue was and remains important for a sociology based on functionalist premises, for reasons not immediately pertinent to the present discussion. Gouldner's answer to the question, however, is germane because he argues that formal social structures might not be causal entities that determine behavior, but rather that behavior may be the causal force that sustains certain structures. To wit, he suggests that machine politics survives because it is based on an elemental exchange that is beneficial to the machine and its members. Simply put, the members' services to the machine are contingent on the machine's services to the members, and vice-versa.

After considering alternate statements on reciprocity from other sociologists, Gouldner hypothesizes that reciprocity is a norm, in the sense of being a fundamental mechanism, and is universal, not culturally relative. He reduces reciprocity to two minimal requisites: "(1) people should help those who have helped them, and (2) people should not injure those who have helped them" (p. 171). He explicates as follows. When person A offers a positive initiative to person B, the latter incurs an obligation and a debt. The debt is to return a positive initiative to A, and the obligation is not to harm A while person B is in debt. Furthermore, it can be seen that when B lives up to the debt and obligation, both persons enter a special relationship. For example, after B has reciprocated, the debt and obligation are passed back to A, who should now return the positive initiative and, meanwhile, is obliged not to harm B.

Gouldner points out that application of the norm supplies society with the kind of glue that makes cohesion possible. Persons who participate in reciprocal exchanges are drawn closer together both in the debts they share and in the obligations they feel toward one another. He calls the norm "a kind of all-purpose moral cement" that stabilizes human relationships and functions of its own accord and may not need other supporting sociological structures. In this regard, he views reciprocity as a "starting mechanism" that functions in the early phases of group formation before it evolves into formal and customary statuses, rules, and duties. The implication is interesting, since the norm would help explain why any person would risk the first step in initiating a positive gesture or why any other person would reciprocate and so set up the beginnings of a longer-term relationship.

This brief summary omits several issues that Gouldner covers in his paper. Among other things, he addresses two problems pertinent to developmental psychology. One is the potential differences that might follow from relative statuses between A and B. Specifically, A and B may be equals, or A may be in a superior position to B. Gouldner suggests that these differences may have interesting differential implications for cohesion or survival. The second problem concerns the issue of equivalence in what A and B exchange. Technically, if B were to pay back precisely what A had originally given, there might be no need for A to feel further indebted. To this Gouldner suggests that cohesion might be better served when initiatives and paybacks are less than precisely equivalent; in such cases, there would be carryovers in debts over time.

Sahlins (1965) follows up on Gouldner's ideas from an anthropological perspective. One of his major contributions is the demonstration that Gouldner's hypothesis regarding universality of the norm could be supported by a scan of diverse cultures. Sahlins shows how the norm may be seen to underlie a remarkable variety of cultural customs which, taken on their own, appear as unique rituals having little in common. The value of his approach is to show how reciprocity as a starting mechanism may have given rise to practices that take on their own dynamics but share in common the central principle of reciprocity.

In addition, Sahlins provides a clarifying discussion of Gouldner's concern for the problem of equivalence. Briefly, Sahlins suggests that the terms of exchange depend on the degree of relationship between the participants. When the relationship is "distant," such as with a buyer and seller in an economic transaction, the terms are definite. The buyer offers something for a specified price and the seller gets that something for a prescribed cost. In "close" relationships, however, the terms are harder to quantify and, given the sheer numbers as well as varieties of interaction, it is easy to see that closely related persons reciprocate in equivalent but not identical acts. For example, in a long-term spouse relationship, each partner might give and take of material and personal resources for which a strict accounting would not be possible and for which neither could specify what, at any moment in time, is being returned for what else, at some past or future moment. It would follow that these persons, and not some objective system, are determinants of what qualifies as equivalence. This means, among other things, that an observer outside the relationship might have difficulty knowing precisely what is being reciprocated for what in a close relationship.

Reciprocal altruism

Trivers (1971) carries the concept of reciprocity over to biological evolution in an attempt to resolve inherent problems with altruism. At issue is the risk an organism takes when help is extended to another organism. Although the stake need not be the life of the donor, the donor is at least diminished in some way. When the stake is the life of the altruistic actor, that organism is likely to be dropped from the gene pool for altruistic behavior. Indeed, one can argue that cheaters, defined as organisms who accept donations from others but who do not reciprocate, may have advantages for survival. Thus, Trivers's task is to account for the persistence of altruism as well as for the elimination of cheating. To these ends, he introduces the concept of reciprocity to altruism as follows: "if the drowning man reciprocates [the act of being saved] at some future time, and if the survival chances are then exactly reversed, it will have been to the benefit of each participant to have risked his life for the other" (p. 36).

Among other considerations, Trivers attempts to outline conditions that contribute to greater chances of selection for reciprocal altruism. These conditions include (1) an extended period of contact that, other things being equal, should maximize the number of potential occasions for reciprocal altruism; (2) a low dispersal rate in geography, so that there will likely be repeated interactons among the same set of "neighbors"; and (3) interdependence, also called "mutual dependence," which tends to keep a small number of persons in continued contact. Trivers illustrates these points in a review of observations from several species and of a variety of types of behavior.

He then goes on to apply his model speculatively to humans, beginning with a list of types of cases that might represent reciprocal altruism. They are (1) helping in time of danger, (2) sharing food, (3) helping the less able (the ill or dependent children), (4) sharing tools, and (5) sharing knowledge. In this section, Trivers amends the preconditions listed above to account for human situations as well. Two of his several points stand out. One is that despite its meeting some of the above conditions, the parent–child relationship provides little occasion for reciprocal altruism. This is because, first, "The relationship is usually so asymmetrical that few or no situations arise in which an offspring is capable of performing an altruistic act for the parents" (p. 38) and second, in a dominance relationship, the less dominant organism is not so capable of helping the more dominant (p. 38).

The other point pertains to different relationships in which reciprocal altruism is more likely because the above conditions obtain and because the persons are in similar positions. "The most important parameters to specify for individuals of a species are how many altruistic situations occur and how symmetrical they are" (p. 38). As an example, Trivers chooses friendship as a relationship that best fits these parameters. In this he cites Darwin, who suggested that altruism would likely evolve in organisms that "live in stable social groups and have the intelligence and other mental qualities necessary to form a system of personal friendships and animosities that transcend the limits of family relationships" (p. 48). Trivers does not probe deeply into friendship but notes that it contains many features that make it a candidate for reciprocal altruism. For example, when a cheater fails to reciprocate, the partner may cut the cheater off from future aid. This is possible in a voluntary relationship but less likely in a relationship as fixed as that between parent and child.

Finally, Trivers deals with the question of "developmental plasticity of those traits regulating altruistic and cheating tendencies and responses to these tendencies in others" (p. 53) and suggests that "no simple developmental system is likely to meet all these requirements" (p. 53) – the requirements being the several conditions that appear to be prerequisite to altruistic behavior. Naive altruism will not suffice, since it could be thwarted by cheating. At a minimum, any developmental theory must take into account judgment in the cognitive vein, in terms of both the individual's altruistic education and learning of the may societal mechanisms that may have arisen not only to enhance altruism but to guard against its abuse as well. Consequently, Trivers concludes that cognitive, social, and moral development are all implicated in the acquisition of a "regulating system [in which] adaptive, altruistic behavior must be dispensed with regard to many characteristics of the recipient . . . , of other members of the group, of the situation . . . , and of many other parameters" (p. 53).

Reciprocity in children

In many instances, the study of children's social behavior has been constrained by a peculiarity in the method of measurement. Observers have tended to code behavior for the individual child with no specific regard to the social context in which the behavior occurred. The typical report lists behaviors such as "aggression," "talking," or "contact" according to frequencies for either groups or individuals or both. One could not tell from these data (1) the actual flow of behavior, (2) which behaviors are likely to precede or follow which, or (3) whether the interactions from which these frequencies were lifted have patterned sequences. Thus, while the behaviors are claimed to be "social," they are unfathomable with respect to social origins.

During the past decade, the problem has begun to be remedied through studies of children's interactions. The focus has been on sequences in studies driven by the general question of whether there is order in children's social exchanges. It is worth noting that several of these studies were stimulated by an inaccurate interpretation of Piaget's writings. Throughout these studies, one finds Piaget set up as a straw man claiming that young children are egocentric, unattentive to others in social situations, and apt to speak in collective or parallel monologues. It will be shown that Piaget (1932; see also Youniss 1981a) actually took a different stand toward children's capacity for sociality and that his position is quite helpful in clarifying the role of reciprocity in children's social interactions. Nevertheless, hyperbolic use of Piaget was heuristic for shifting focus toward the study of children's interactions.

Two types of studies are of interest to the present discussion. The first looks at peer interactions in infants aged roughly 12–24 months. One representative study is reported by Lewis, Young, Brooks, and Michalson (1975) whose observations showed that infant peers manifest a high degree of sharing of toys, mutual contact and visual regard, turn-taking, and sequential imitation. Furthermore, rates of these sequences were found to vary according to the partners with whom the infants were paired. For example, infants interacted most with peers with whom they were familiar, next most with newly met peers, next with their mothers, and least with adult strangers.

When reciprocity is defined as the sequential exchange of like act for like act, infants' interactions with peers are found to display considerable reciprocal exchange. Mueller and Lucas (1975) support the findings reported by Lewis et al. in addition to offering a fine-grained analysis of precise sequences, which they have organized into a three-stage scheme. Their youngest infants often acted in parallel fashion, as if they were independent agents, although not exclusively so. Their stage-three subjects, however, showed "mutual attention," "turn-taking" in verbal dialogues, and sequential "role reversals" in sequences that resulted in sustained interactive chains. Mueller and Lucas conclude from these data that their subjects manifested true social behavior in the sense that each child's action was contingent on, and directed toward, the other child's action. Furthermore, these workers conclude that chained sequences illustrate the capacity to sustain mutual play over a period of time, so that the chain itself becomes the object of mutual regard.

The second type of study concerns play in preschool children when play is accompanied by more sophisticated dialogue and conversation than is possible in infants. Garvey and Hogan (1973) were among the first to document that, in preschoolers' play, social speech is the rule and not the exception, when defined as "speech that is strictly adapted to the speech of the behavior of the partner" (p. 563). They report conversations in which the partners jointly worked on themes, indicating mutual engagement. For example, one child introduced a topic, the other added to it by way of question or comment, one then took a further step, and so on, until the two had carried out the theme more fully. According to Garvey and Hogan (1973), mutual engagement, rather than egocentric monologues, is dominant, and turn taking, akin to Mueller and Lucas's (1975) role reversals, is a primary underlying mechanism.

A second representative study of this genre was reported by Cook-Gumperz and Corsaro (1977). The data were taken from a nursery school setting and consist of records of conversations. They report detailed transcripts in which the participants spontaneously generated conversations without intervention from the investigators. These workers approached the data to document children's conversational competence rather than asking whether children were able to overcome egocentrism. Furthermore, they used categories of analysis unconstrained by the presumption that individuals' acts are discrete; instead, they looked for cases in which sequences of actions were organized into conversational units (cf. Garvey & Hogan's social speech).

Several patterns of conversation are reported verbatim. The common feature found across transcripts is that preschoolers use conversation to "*arrive* at a *shared meaning*" (p. 427). To do this, children were found to allocate roles, ask questions, offer criticism, clarify earlier statements, and negotiate differences. These procedures are seen by Cook-Gumperz and Corsaro (1977) as means for the social production of reality. There can be little doubt that the subjects were manifesting two levels of co-construction: (1) in conversation itself, and (2) the topic or reference of conversation. The latter is most evident in the creation of fantasy situations that begin with such initiatives as, "Let's play," and continue as the partners allocate imaginary roles and create objects whose reality base is the preceding conversation, which they themselves had constructed together.

Role taking

The foregoing studies were selected in order to make two central points about reciprocity. First, an elemental form of reciprocity is evident in very young children's peer interactions. It appears as an exchange of actions in which the second act in a sequence is directed to the first, the third to the second, and so on. Second, reciprocity implies more than a blind exchange of like act for like act. For children, reciprocity may also have the deeper meaning of social construction. One reason that children interact reciprocally is that they are cooperating in the production of ideas, in which each contributes to a third thing, which is the product of their social interaction. These points are not easily separated without risking loss of the significance of the data.

The Cook-Gumperz and Corsaro study is the most forthright in marking the distinction dividing theoretical viewpoints toward social development. From their perspective, children are partners in interactions that could not have persistence or direction were the children primarily discrete individuals or actors. They are actors in a joint effort that may begin in two discrete views or ideas. But once their actions are conjoined, the starting points merge into a third view or idea. The new view comes from conjoining of the partners whose actions continually build on reference to earlier moments in the sequence that is being co-constructed.

The more conventional position taken toward children's social behavior is found in a prevalent version of the role-taking concept. As many theorists pose the concept, children are egocentric and must come to realize that other persons may have different views – perceptual, conceptual, or emotive – from theirs. It follows that the key to social development lies in the recognition that there are multiple viewpoints. Once this breakthrough is made, children can begin to adopt the viewpoints of others. Thereafter, the child's own viewpoint becomes socially modified and is no longer egocentric.

At its heart, this stance toward role taking is predicated on several uninspected assumptions, the major one being that children are individualistic and consequently asocial. Another assumption is that egocentrism is broken through with advances in cognition, to wit, the recognition of other views and, later, use of new capacities to acquire these other views for oneself. The cognitive addendum only reinforces the assumption about individualism because the child's own cognitive capacities and skills are the means to social life. Children on their own are thought to be responsible for reaching out to others in order to grasp what others think or feel; the "other" is much like the proverbial stoneface and the child much like a detective who must use personal wits to pierce the surface and discover who or what the other really is.

The data just reviewed are representative of studies that suggest that it is time to try out a different theoretical perspective. The evidence demonstrates that children are not what the conventional role-taking concept says and that they do not interact as the concept prescribes. For example, children do not act as if one were passively holding onto a thought or feeling that the other would have to try to guess at through active seeking. On the contrary, children freely express to each other what they know and how they feel. They do so in the most blatant ways. They say aloud what they think and feel. They ask questions of one another. They clarify apparently misunderstood messages. They resist messages with which they disagree. And they endorse actions they agree with.

According to the conventional concept, the problem is to get children to take the role of others and to stop being egocentric in their own roles. The data on children's social interactions show that this may not be the central problem at all. Rather, the question of interest stems from the starting point of social construction and pertains to the development of procedures through which children cooperate as partners in interpreting reality. What differentiates younger from older children are procedures that become more effective in producing reality jointly. It follows that role taking is a misnomer when it refers to the image of an active seeker struggling to know what a passive other has inside the mind. A more accurate term would be "role making," because it refers to interactive behavior through which partners construct roles (ideas, themes, feelings, and opinions) together and in public.

Friendship

In recent years, a literature has evolved on the topic of children's friendship. Several studies have yielded results that fit together in showing consistency in the way children define friendship and in indicating systematic changes in the definition of friendship from about age 6 to age 12 or 13 (cf. Bigelow, 1977; Bigelow & LaGaipa, 1975; Selman & Jaquette, 1977; Youniss, 1980; Youniss & Volpe, 1978). This section highlights these findings with reference to reciprocity and the co-construction of reality. Examples selected from my own work reflect the findings of other studies as well. First, a prefatory note is in order. The data come from a general method having the following features. Children are interviewed by an adult and respond to questions verbally. The questions specify situations in terms of participants (two friends) as well as outcome (a conflict). The task is to give an account of an interaction; for example, "Tell me how two friends who just had a fight about X got together again and became friends like they were before." Accounts of interactions are scored according to forms of exchanges, with the categories being decided upon according to dominant groupings in age levels. Of the several hundred children aged 6–7 who were asked questions about interactions through which peers showed each other that they were friends, the overwhelming majority described either of two interactions: reciprocal sharing of material possessions or playing together. These interactions are coded by form as symmetrical (exchange of like acts) and are also coded by content (material goods and play activities).

The development of reciprocity

The common finding in most studies of friendship is that at the beginning school age, around 6–7 years, children in general define friendship through symmetrical reciprocal acts, that are positive in nature (e.g., "He lets me ride his bike; then I let him ride my bike," or "She says, 'Let's play dolls?' and then I say, 'Ok, we'll play dolls.'"). At the same age, negative symmetrical exchanges indicate nonfriendship or, in children's words, not liking or not being friends (e.g., "He hit me, so I hit him," and "She called me a name, so I called her a name. Then I told her I didn't like her and she said she didn't like me too"). These seemingly simple accounts bear on the concept of reciprocity in several interesting ways:

1. Children are consistent in saying that their interactions follow the symmetrical reciprocal form.
2. The form bespeaks of an equality between children since whichever act one child initiates, the other child returns in kind.
3. In estimating the results of interactions, one cannot distinguish the interactants. Both get in the end the same benefit (or cost).
4. The participants are obviously described as equipotential agents because each is capable of duplicating the other's action.
5. The accounts seem to derive from the initial act since, once it occurs, subsequent acts follow in sequence. These features conform to Hinde's (1976, 1979) formal definition of symmetrical reciprocity and fit Piaget's (1932) depiction of reciprocity as the constituting rule of peer relations.

It has been suggested that reciprocity at this age level is a literal practice that determines friendship (Youniss, 1980). When peers exchange positive initiatives, they are friends. When they exchange negatively, they are not friends. Nor are they friends when a positive initiative is offered by one child and not reciprocated by the other. At this age level, friendship seems to be an off-again, on-again relationship, wholly dependent on the practice of reciprocity. This might help explain why young children believe that they can have many friends, that friendships can be made easily, and that peers who do them a bad turn are no longer their friends.

Reciprocity and relationship

When reciprocity alone defines a relationship, it is difficult to sustain that relationship over time. This point became evident to us from children's accounts. The problem can be posed as a matter of lack of direction. According to the rule of reciprocity, the second of two acts may, by right, be identical to the first. Thus, if A shares, B may share something too. If A hurts B, B may retaliate. And if A asserts an opinion, B may assert an opinion as well. Since all three kinds of reciprocal actions occur in peer associations, there is nothing in the practice per se upon which a relationship can be built in a singular direction. With peers as equipotential actors, any interaction is likely to go in a positive direction or a negative direction or lead to an impasse. The total of experiences, then, is something like a stalemate in the long run, with variations from moment to moment, depending on the acts that happen to initiate interactions.

It is not surprising that at about 9–10 years of age children see friendship as more than a matter of the practice of reciprocity. First, they perceive friendship as voluntary. Second, it is selective. Third, children who decide to be friends view each other as equals. Fourth, this equality refers to rights because the friends begin to perceive one another as individuals with different personalities, strengths, and weaknesses. Given these changes in conceptions of friendship, it follows that literal symmetry will no longer serve to work for older children. At this time, they transform the practice into a principle that can be summarized as follows: Friends merit equal and fair treatment.

The above points are evident in several examples. When asked to describe what one friend did to show kindness to another friend, 9– and 10-year-old children typically began by posting a deficit state in the friend, such as illness, depression, having trouble studying for a test, or loneliness. Given the deficit state, kindness ensued when the other friend acted to relieve the friend in need, even if only to sympathize. Furthermore, when asked what the recipient would do next, children were clear that in most cases, the needy friend could and would do nothing. As some children put it, there was little the recipient could do, since he or she was in no state to return the kindness, and the friend who was kind did not need anything at that moment. But, they added, should the roles be reversed on some later occasion, the previous recipient would act to relieve the earlier actor when the need came up.

A second type of illustration involved what children thought about unkindness. They commonly described a deficit state that was followed by no action, such as seeing a friend in need, and walking away. In other words, unkindness is in the act of omission. In order for this to constitute unkindness, an obligation would have to fail to be met. Many children explained that this obligation ensued from an earlier occasion when the friend who was now in need had helped the friend who presently walked away. Both results, then bear on the above components of friendship conceptions and demonstrate that the principle of reciprocity has replaced the naive practice of reciprocity evident in younger children.

The relationship of friendship

Children about 12–13 years of age made further additions to the friendship conception. One of the most notable was found in the realization that friendship is an enduring relationship requiring particular procedures to meet its maintenance. For example, friendship could be sustained in spite of occurrences of negative reciprocity, omitted reciprocity, fights, arguments, and conflicts of several sorts. A rift in friendship was seen as a momentary breach that could be repaired when the friends took recourse in procedures such as offering apology or compensation or acknowledging fault while promising better behavior in the future.

These points are illustrated in a 12-year-old girl's description of a case of conflict and repair between herself and her best friend:

If they're playing a game and [one is] not too good at it, you want to be on the winning team, so you don't pick her.... "she can't throw and she can't catch." [*What would the offended girl do next?*] She wouldn't feel too good. If she were doing something you couldn't do, she would do it back, like not want you on a team or something. [*Then what would the first girl do?*] Later that night it would probably bother me. I would apologize and say, "You can't do things I can do and I can't do things you can do. I'm sorry. Next time you can be on my team because games are just for fun." [*Then what would the other one say?*] She would probably say, "Don't worry about it. We're still friends." And we would be friends. (Youniss, 1980, p. 251)

A second addition to friendship at this age pertains more directly to the consequences of reciprocity as seen through the mutuality it may engender. A theme found in most studies is that friends understand each other and seek each other out to construct consensus about thought and feelings. Friends are likely to construct roles together, not through a kind of hide-and-seek, but by consensus-making communication. For example, in our studies, subjects said that a mark of best friendships was open discussion of ideas and emotions. Friends do this in private when others are not around. They present their inner feelings for one another's comments, criticisms, comparisons, and endorsement. This is the apparent basis of what Sullivan (1953) has called consensual validation. Moreover, it leads children to sense that friends understand them more than their mothers, fathers, brothers, or sisters.

One can see this as a form of reciprocal self-disclosure, which it literally is. But it is equally a case of cooperative construction of reality. The dynamics are interesting. Children realize that, by opening up to friends, they expose themselves by revealing weaknesses and risking the charge that they are odd or different. They spontaneously admit to the point but add that they are confident that friends will not embarrass them or take advantage of the inside information. Part of their assurance comes from the reciprocity in which each knows enough about the other so that both feel protected from exposure to persons outside the relationship. At this point, the bigger fear is losing the relationship, not just for the personal risk involved but equally for loss of one's co-constructing partner.

Developmental implications

Studies of friendship bring an interesting fresh perspective to the consideration of reciprocity. Researchers have observed a consistency in the practice of reciprocity by peers and friends aged 12 months to 13 years. They have also found an accompanying developmental course that may be described as moving from the literal practice, to the articulation of principle, to the realization of the dynamics of relationship. Early in life, peers in general serve the ends of reciprocity. But soon after the school age begins, children meet the impasse brought by literal practice. Subsequently, they select from their peers a few with whom they can construct the principle and find ways to practice it while adapting to the data of individual differences. These few become friends.

In what has been conventionally called the latency period, children seem to be quite active in experiencing friendships and in learning about the demands as well as advantages of voluntary interpersonal relationships. A key to development at this time occurs as friendship gives rise to those procedures by which they contribute equally to the co-construction of reality. Friends act as equally powerful agents who together can decide on ideas, arbitrate feelings, and otherwise reach consensus judgments. They need not agree on all things, yet each must be heard from and both must be respected. Differences do come up. When they do, procedures are needed to settle conflicts and repair breaches, hence, the principle of fair treatment. Fairness in the face of individual difference develops even further during adolescence (Youniss & Smollar, 1985). In the broader theoretical considerations of reciprocity proposed by Gouldner or Trivers, reciprocity remains a more or less fixed mechanism that takes no account of its participants. Recent findings on children's friendship bring in the developmental dimension at two levels. First, reciprocity develops conceptually from a literal practice (e.g., turn taking; retaliation) to a refined principle that is understood through rights and obligations. Second, as children develop in conceptions of the friendship relationship, reciprocal interactions take on new meanings. Examples include: acts of omission signifying a relational breach, the protection derived from mutual self-disclosure, and the use of discussion to negotiate toward consensual validation of thoughts and feelings.

It is not clear that these developments are or should be separated. For example, consider Sahlin's point about reciprocity in close relationships. The findings for 9- to 10-year-olds illustrate his point precisely. Close friends in an enduring relationship do not have to reciprocate either immediately or on identical terms. Indeed, when friends offer positive initiatives, recipients may not be in a position to reciprocate. But the bond of friendship imposes an obligation that carries over to some future time. Moreover, when the reciprocation occurs, it is adapted to the needs that pertain at that point. Thus, the reciprocity is known only to the friends who have their own construction of what constitutes equivalence.

Piaget (1932) suggests a possible clarification, seeing the practice of reciprocity as the constituting rule of relatively immature conceptions of relationship. An example would be the on-again, off-again nature of 6-year-olds' friendships, which are dependent on the literal practice of reciprocity. Later, however, reciprocity becomes reconstituted as a principle of relationship. At that point, the practice of reciprocity depends on the conception of relationship. In friendship, the result is the co-construction of procedures by which children seek to maintain their bond as a means of consensual validation that is not easily attainable with other persons outside the friendship domain. The reconstituted principle is essential to the relationship. But the more developed concept of relationship is more than an advance in reciprocity. It is supraordinate to reciprocity and properly belongs to the sphere of relationship (Youniss, 1980, 1983).

Theoretical implications

Many of the specific points in Trivers's analysis of reciprocal altruism bear directly on the findings of children's friendships.

1. The content of children's interactions corresponds to the content of the list of altruistic domains proposed by Trivers; helping when in danger, sharing food, helping the more helpless, sharing implements, and sharing knowledge. The match may not be incidental. In our own research, chil-

dren were free to give accounts of whichever interactions they thought fit our specification of partners and end result. It was the subjects who chose to describe friends as sharing food, sharing toys and school supplies (children's implements), helping in time of physical weakness, offering emotional support, and working together on the construction of knowledge.

2. Trivers suggests that a low dispersal rate promotes reciprocal altruism. It is interesting that children not only draw their friendships from classmates, whom they regularly see, but spend considerable time with their friends outside class hours. Time spent together and the wide variety of incidents that friends encounter together make for altruistic opportunities that non-friends do not have.

3. A check against cheating occurs when individuals are mutually dependent on one another. Mutual dependence increases the likelihood that the need to be a recipient of another's altruism will shift back and forth between friends. After about 9 or 10 years of age, children recognize this condition in their friendships. They say that friends alternate from giving to receiving positions. They also see that friends are individuals with different strengths and weaknesses; mutual dependence comes from the repeated experience of one's strengths compensating for the other's weaknesses, and vice versa.

4. Trivers notes that reciprocal altruism is unlikely between the young and their adult caretakers because the former generally have little to offer to the latter, due to huge differences in capacities as well as possession of resources. This asymmetry is not the case in friendship despite the fact that children appreciate the importance of individual differences, which they handle by constructing the principle of fair and equal treatment. Moreover, since any friendship covers so many different instances and domains of living, a balance can be achieved between giving and receiving, with symmetry obtaining across instances within the friendship.

5. Trivers proposes that reciprocal altruism is enhanced when individuals maintain contact over long periods of time. As was seen after about 10 years of age, children claim that friendship is an enduring relationship (see also, Youniss & Smollar, 1985). This may be more than wishful musing on their part. Fischer (1977) reports that friendships established at that time are, in fact, likely to endure. Adult men report that many of the friendships they now have began in childhood or early adolescence.

6. Trivers considers the number of reciprocal relationships important to altruism. The fewer in number, the more exclusive and the greater the opportunity for reciprocity. Unquestionably, after about 12 years of age, children consider friendship an exclusive relationship (Youniss & Smollar, 1985). For example, acts of omission are unkind only within the context of friendship wherein the principle of reciprocity applies. For another example, mutual self-disclosure not only occurs within friendship but is unlikely to occur elsewhere, since outside its reciprocal boundaries disclosures entail risks, while within friendship reciprocity protects the partners and even draws them closer together.

All these points bear on the suggestion made by Trivers that the development of reciprocal altruism within ontogeny may be complex and difficult to sort out. I do not mean to simplify the matter, but theorists seem to have ignored an important avenue for the development of reciprocal altruism. Childhood friendships are grounded in the practice of reciprocity and follow a developmental course that covers the several conditions that enhance the opportunities for, and the understanding of, reciprocal altruism. This is not to imply that altruism, empathy, and other prosocial behavior originate only in peer relationships. There is evidence that children become agents in prosocial episodes at around 2 years of age and that their parents are the recipients. Some of these acts are difficult to distinguish from imitative performances, but other seem to be innovative as well as designed to assist the recipient (e.g., Hay, 1979; see also Radke-Yarrow, Zahn-Waxler, & Chapman, 1983).

It is not yet clear just how experiences within the parent–child relationship carry over developmentally to relationships with peers. But the possibility that one is a forerunner to the other seems plausible (e.g., Arend, Gove, & Sroufe, 1979; Zahn-Waxler, Cummings, McKnew, & Radke-Yarrow, 1984). Still, there is a bias in developmental theories against the role that peer relationships in general and friendship in particular may play in prosocial development (cf. Advisory Committee, 1976). The bias is accompanied by a tendency to make adults the keepers of society without whom children would revert to the savagery depicted in Golding's *Lord of the Flies*. The bias is unwarranted by the findings on children's friendship.

The data are not amenable to a romantic view of childhood friendships. In the accounts we have gathered, children readily admit to the difficulties within friendship. Friends fight, argue, hurt each other, let one another down, reveal secrets, and otherwise cheat, in the vein described by Trivers. However, for most breaches, children stipulate procedures designed to repair rifts and bring friends back on an even keel. Most important, friendship is voluntary, and friends have a definite weapon to use in meeting repeated cheating. They can step out of one friendship and enter another, leaving the cheater alone, without a relationship to depend on. Reciprocal altruism is not automatic but comes only from the intricate dynamics that evolve in dealing with real friendships.

The individual in relationships

The foregoing considerations of children's friendship and its development raise a question that pertains to most analyses of reciprocity. The question may be introduced as follows. In our work on friendship, we initially evaluated children's accounts of interactions in an attempt to decide which partner gained and which gave, under a presupposition of cost and benefit. We were stymied because the accounts did not permit separation between giver and receiver. Cost and benefit were applicable only to a given moment or event. But children, after 9 years of age, did not consider events as discrete. Instead, they described events within the context of an ongoing relationship. In the long run, A gave as much as B, and A received as much as B. A clear cost–benefit analysis would have to look to the relationship itself as the primary beneficiary – that is, the benefits derived by individual friends come from the relationship.

Developmental psychology, which has had some difficulty in appreciating friendship, has an equal problem with relationship. This problem may be attributable to an overemphasis on individualism; for example, that impetuousness, hedonism, and egocentrism are natural features of children that have to be overcome before prosocial or moral life proper can begin. It is suggested here that such properties may be consequences of certain kinds of relationships (cf. Piaget, 1932). It is also proposed that development may proceed through relationships so that to understand individuals fully, one must first grasp the relationships from which the individual is derived.

One of the possible underpinnings of this orientation is found in a borrowing from evolutionary thinking, which gives priority to individual self-interest and competition. This is not the only perspective one can take toward evolution. Trivers's position offers a viable alternative, with its emphasis on reciprocity. Another is found in Humphrey (1976), who proposes that natural selection has favored "*social* foresight and understanding"; that is, "man's intellect is thus suited primarily to thinking about people and their institutions" (p. 312). In referring to the individualist model, Humphrey chooses the analogy of chess playing, which, he says, "misses a crucial feature of social interaction. For while the good chess player is essentially selfish, playing only to win, the selfishness of social animals is typically tempered by what, for want of a better term, I would call *sympathy* . . . a tendency on the part of one social partner to identify himself with the other and so to make the other's goals to some extent his own" (p. 313).

Humphrey's central point is that intelligence has been adapted through dealings not only with "nature," but with problems pertaining to persons and society. One of the clearest voices that represent this perspective is that of Kropotkin (1902), who attempted to expand the individualistic orientation of social Darwinists of his day. He granted his opponents the evolutionary principle of competition among individuals. At the same time, he argued for a second law of evolution that was equally powerful and basic. He called this the law of mutual aid through which individuals cooperated in the service of one another's and the species' survival. For Kropotkin, the error of evolutionary thinking of his time, was in failure to recognize the simultaneity of two laws because of a blinding emphasis on the individual as the only unit of analysis.

It is interesting that the view taken by Kropotkin is called "anarchistic" because he argued against social contract theory which supported state control over individual lives. Kropotkin believed that when individuals were left to their own devices, both laws of evolution would take over and government would not be needed to enforce the social contract and protect persons from their inherent competitive savagery. Governance, he proposed, was ensured through the law of mutual aid, which did not have to be administered from without. This was because cooperation had been selected for and was part of the human evolutionary heritage.

Kropotkin is, of course, an extreme voice, perhaps even an idealist. But, he offers a broader context for viewing evolution than the orientation toward individualism which psychologists ordinarily presuppose. Developmentalists seem to hold to one law of evolution, that favoring the individual, with no conscious concern that there may be a second law regarding mutual aid that is equally fundamental in evolution. It is hoped that this chapter will encourage exploration of a broader approach to evolutionary thinking and will help provoke interest in the study of the individual in relationships. This is not the individual who uses intelligence to develop social skills through the prodding of already socialized adults. Rather, it is the individual whose intelligence is social in origin and who develops in the most natural of ontogenetic settings – interpersonal relationships, in general, and friendship in particular (Youniss, 1980; 1981b, 1983).

References

Advisory Committee on Child Development. (1976). *Toward a national policy for children and families.* Washington, DC: National Academy of Sciences.

Arend, R., Gove, F. L., & Sroufe, L. A. (1970). Continuity of individual adaptation from infancy to kindergarten. *Child Development, 50,* 950–959.

Bigelow, B. J. (1977). Children's friendship expectations. *Child Development, 48,* 246–253.

Bigelow, B. J., & LaGaipa, J. (1975). Children's written descriptions of friendship: A multidimensional analysis. *Developmental Psychology, 11,* 857–858.

Cook-Gumperz, J., & Corsaro, W. A. (1977). Social-ecological constraints on children's communicative strategies. *Sociology, 11,* 411–434.

Fischer, C. S. (1977). *Networks and places: Relations in the urban setting.* New York: Free Press.

Garvey, C., & Hogan, R. (1973). Social speech and social interaction. *Child Development, 44,* 562–568.

Golding, W. (1955). *Lord of the flies.* New York: Coward-McCann.

Gouldner, A. J. (1960) The norm of reciprocity: A preliminary statement. *American Sociological review, 25,* 161–178.

Hay, D. F. (1979). Cooperative interactions and sharing between very young children and their parents. *Developmental Psychology, 15*, 647–653.

Hinde, R. A. (1976). On describing relationships. *Journal of Child Psychology and Psychiatry, 17*, 1–19.

Hinde, R. A. (1979). *Toward understanding relationships*. London: Academic Press.

Humphrey, N. K. (1976). The social function of the intellect. In P. P. G. Bateson & R. A. Hinde (Eds.), *Growing points in ethology* (pp. 303–317). London: Cambridge University Press.

Kropotkin, P. (1902). *Mutual Aid*. London: Sargent.

Lewis, M., Young, G., Brooks, J., & Michalson, L. (1975). The beginning of friendship. In M. Lewis & L. A. Rosenblum (Eds.), *Friendship and peer relations* (pp. 27–66). New York: Wiley.

Mueller, E. & Lucas, T. (1975). A developmental analysis of peer interactions among toddlers. In M. Lewis & L. A. Rosenblum (Eds.), *Friendship and peer relations* (pp. 223–257). New York: Wiley.

Piaget, J. (1932). *The moral judgement of the child*. London: Routledge Kegan Paul.

Radke-Yarrow, M., Zahn-Waxler, C., & Chapman, M. (1983). Children's prosocial dispositions and behavior. In P. H. Mussen (Ed.) *Carmichael's manual of child psychology* vol. IV, (pp. 469–546). New York: Wiley.

Sahlins, M. D. (1965). On the sociology of primitive exchange. In M. Banton (Ed.), *Relevance of models of social anthrology*. New York: Praeger.

Selman, R. S. & Jaquette, D. (1977). Stability and oscillation in interpersonal awareness. *Nebraska Symposium on Motivation, 25*, 262–304.

Sullivan, H. S. (1953). *The interpersonal theory of psychiatry*. New York: Norton.

Trivers, R. L. (1971). The evolution of reciprocal altruism. *The Quarterly Review of Biology, 46*, 35–57.

Youniss, J. (1980). *Parents and peers in social development*. Chicago: University of Chicago Press.

Youniss, J. (1981a). Moral development through a theory of social construction: An analysis. *Merrill-Palmer Quarterly, 27*, 385–403.

Youniss, J. (1981b). A revised interpretation of Piaget (1932). In I. E. Sigel, D. M. Brodzinsky, & R. M. Golinkoff (Eds.), *New directions in Piagetian theory and practice*, Hillsdale, NJ: Erlbaum

Youniss, J. (1983). Piaget and the self constituted through relations. In W. F. Overton (Ed.), *The relationship between social and cognitive development*. Hillsdale, NJ: Erlbaum.

Youniss, J., & Smollar, J. (1985). *Adolescent relations with mothers, fathers, and friends*. Chicago: University of Chicago Press.

Youniss, J., & Volpe, J. (1978). *A relational analysis of friendship*. In W. Damon (Ed.), *Social cognition*. San Francisco: Jossey-Bass.

Zahn-Waxler, C., Cummings, E. M., McKnew, D. H., & Radke-Yarrow, M. (1984). Altruism, aggression, and social interactions in young children with a manic-depressive parent. *Child Development, 55*, 112–122.

4   The prosocial and antisocial functions of preschool aggression: an ethological study of triadic conflict among young children

F. F. Strayer and J. M. Noel

Few of the conceptual distinctions in the study of human development are as fundamental, yet as fragile, as the dichotomy of prosocial and antisocial behavior. Both the ultimate strength and the inevitable weakness of this distinction arise from its direct focus on the complex relationship between the individual and his social world. A special preoccupation with the individual in relationship to society was evident in the earliest formulations of the emerging social sciences (James, 1890). However, the historical roots of the prosocial–antisocial distinction can be traced to earlier political and moral reflections on the nature of "good" and "evil" (Masters, 1983). In its simplest form, prosocial activity can be defined as that which is good or beneficial for the social group; by contrast, antisocial refers to that which is harmful to, or disruptive of, social life. That these two concepts are linked to abiding historical concerns about the nature of human conduct attests to their likely importance in any scientific study of human behavior. However, such historical antecedents also suggest important limits as well as potential misuses of these descriptive constructs in the study of human development.

The value of the prosocial–antisocial dichotomy in the description of human activity is most readily apparent when confronted with extreme behavioral contrasts. For example, lying, cheating, and stealing are generally less valued as social acts than giving, helping and sharing. Similarly, aggressive activities such as fighting and competing are usually less desirable than altruistic behaviors that involve caring and comforting. However, a simple dichotomous classification of social behavior neglects the fact that both the value and the social impact of any specific action is dependent on the immediate behavioral context and/or social setting in which it occurs. Aiding and comforting a collective enemy is socially undesirable, while misinforming or harming such a foe is often applauded by members of one's own community. The issue here surpasses the simple identification of general norms that characterize an appropriate reference group for the initiator of a specific action. The evaluation of human conduct requires consideration of more diverse kinds of contextual information that clarify the potentially multiple functions of social action. The meaning or significance of both altruistic and aggressive behavior can only be revealed through a pragmatic analysis that moves progressively from the level of the individual, to the immediate social group, then to the larger cultural context, and finally to a consideration of human society itself.

Problems in specifying the prosocial or antisocial nature of human action become even more complex when placed within the historically meaningful contexts of human development and cultural evolution. Rapidly changing notions about "the collective good" add a dimension of relativity to judgments about the value of individual behavior. Revolutionary movements and political resistance have been seen historically as extreme embodiments of antisocial tendencies in the short term, but subsequently they have often been reinterpreted as beneficial contributions to the emergence of a new social order. Similarly, in the short run, a highly aggressive child may be characterized as having antisocial tendencies. However, early aggressive experience may contribute directly to the development of effective means of controlling violent impulses later in life. Aggressive children elicit qualitatively different types of social feedback from both adults and peers. When effective, such feedback may facilitate the internalization of collective values and ultimately leads to a more developed capacity to evaluate the relative costs and benefits of specific actions from the perspective of the individual and the social other. From this viewpoint, early activities may be ultimately beneficial if they facilitate a more effective integration of the child into the adolescent or adult social world.

The above examples of prosocial or antisocial behavior illustrate the need to distinguish among (1) unique and multiple consequences of social actions, (2) immediate and long-term advantages of particular behavioral adaptations, and (3) normative and contextual expectations about socially appropriate conduct. Such distinctions are essential for a heuristic approach to the study of social development, which attempts to provide a more complete, multilevel analysis of how individual activity influences, and is influenced by, the specific context in which it occurs. Such an approach to the study of aggressive and altruistic behavior places human action more clearly within its social, developmental, and cultural settings. Emphasis on contextual influences reduces the very real danger of unintentionally imposing local normative expectations from one's own social class, or subculture, as a presumed "objective" and "value-free" framework for the scientific analysis of social behavior.

A concrete example of how normative expectations bias our views about behavioral development is evident in the different interpretations of the basic goals of peer socialization during early childhood. Among North American preschool teachers few topics are as widely discussed, and as generally unresolved, as the problem of social conflict within the early peer group. Many preschool programs are in fact explicitly designed to reduce or eliminate aggressive and competitive interaction, and to increase or facilitate reciprocal aid and support. However, seldom do these programs address basic questions about the adaptive significance of aggressive and competitive behavior for the young child. Nor do they often consider the potential importance of such activites as the child's integration into the stable peer group. Instead aggression and competition are assumed to be self-serving in nature and inherently antisocial because of the potential harm that they present for others. These assumptions have begun to be questioned by ethological research on naturally occurring conflict among preschool children. These studies suggest that many forms of aggressive activity are not necessarily disruptive for preschool social life; in fact, some may stabilize the social structure of the early peer group.

Ethological studies of preschool conflict

The earliest ethological studies of child development did not categorize children's behavior in terms of its apparent social value (Grant, 1969; Blurton-Jones 1972a). These investigations attempted instead to document the full range of morphologically distinct action patterns observable in children's naturally occurring play activities. Descriptive accounts of naturally occurring activities were subsequently analyzed with a view toward understanding the adaptive signficance of various components of the individual child's behavioral repertoire. For example, in a now classic study, Blurton-Jones (1972b) demonstrated basic differences between children's "rough-and-tumble" play and peer aggression. His analyses of observational data showed that these two morphologically similar forms of activity do not have strong temporal associations – that is, there is not a general tendency for one form of activity to lead directly to the other. Furthermore, individual children who often engaged in one form of such behavior do not necessarily tend to initiate high levels of the other. Such findings underscore the importance of distinguishing between aggressive play and more serious social conflict in our accounts of individual differences in aggressive behavior. For example, previously documented sex-based differences in early antisocial tendencies may be somewhat misleading because they fail to account for the greater tendency among boys to participate in rougher forms of social play.

The ethologists' preoccupation with the adaptive significance of children's behavior offers an important bridge between the conceptual frameworks underlying research on animal social behavior and those characterizing psychological studies of children's social development. A much more direct link between psychological approaches to prosocial and antisocial activity and ethological studies of child behavior was elaborated by McGrew (1972), who suggested that morphologically defined behavioral units could be scaled according to their relative probability of leading to the continuation of social exchange between interacting partners. According to McGrew, "rough-and-tumble play" (or quasi-agonism) is functionally different from aggressive behavior because it is usually embedded within longer social episodes where members of the dyad, or subgroup, maintain their association in spite of the often brusque or even forceful acts that comprise their interaction. By contrast, aggressive and competitive acts, although morphologically similar to forms of "rough-and-tumble play," lead more directly to the termination of social participation. Such activities mitigate against the individual's continued involvement in the ongoing activities of the group, and thus have a disruptive effect on group life.

McGrew's (1972) functional scheme for classifying cohesive and dispersive forms of agonistic behavior parallels conceptual framework developed by field researchers studying social behavior among nonhuman primates (Kummer, 1968). The earliest theoretical efforts to explain the nearly universal sociality of nonhuman primates emphasized a continuing dialectic between cohesive and dispersive forces underlying the stability and organization of any social group (Carpenter, 1942; Zuckerman, 1932). In general, these early theorists held that individuals initially congregated together because of specific advantages derived from the collective exploitation of ecological resources, and/or mutual defense against predation. Advantages associated with such social cooperation favored the evolution of stronger natural attraction among conspecifics. However, increased associations also led to more frequent occasions for intraspecific conflict that tended to disperse the social unit. Ultimately the equilibration of the opposing cohesive and dispersive tendencies was achieved through the development of social systems that prescribed social roles during dyadic conflict and facilitated the development of less severe, or ritualized, expressions of aggressive tendencies. In this sense, the group dominance hierarchy represents a prosocial, or cohesive, mechanism that regulates aggressive behavior especially during times of stress, and thus minimizes the absolute level of dispersive activity within a social group. Implicit in this view is the notion that some aggressive actions have prosocial functions, since their natural consequence is the establishment of a social order that reduces aggression and ultimately benefits each group member by assuring the stability and continuity of the social unit.

Although dominance relationships and group status hierarchies have been studied extensively in a large variety of nonhuman primates, substantially less attention has been accorded the analysis of the nonaggressive underpinnings of social organization. The earliest models of primate social behavior, perhaps anticipating current views of sociobiology, placed primary emphasis on reproductive behavior and sexual attraction in an effort to explain why animals formed cohesive groups (Carpenter, 1956; Maslow, 1936; Zuckerman, 1932). However, at an empirical level such mechanisms do not account for the full range of observed social attraction – especially cohesive bonds that remain stable even during nonreproductive periods. More recent field and laboratory research has focused on kinship relationships, especially mother–child attachments as the potential origin of the pervasive cohesive tendencies of nonhuman primates (Harlow and Harlow, 1965; Sade, 1967). Current interests in primate social bonding reflect a necessary complement to earlier preoccupations with social aggression; however, analytic procedures for the study of cohesive activities still lag behind those that exist for dispersive social behaviors.

Ethological studies of peer group social organization

The extension of ethological concepts and methods to the study of children's adaptation within stable peer groups has been influenced extensively by research preoccupations from both primate ethology and developmental psychology. Child ethologists also directed their primary attention toward the analysis of dispersive, or antisocial components of the child's behavioral repertoire. However, unlike earlier social scientists, ethological researchers provided a somewhat different account of antisocial activities by describing social conflict in terms of more neutral patterns of agonistic interaction, rather than in terms of motivationally laden categories such as violence, hostility, and/or intent to harm. In addition, by exploring the concept of social dominance among young children, these studies stressed that some forms of agonistic exchange may have potentially positive or beneficial consequences for the organization and stabilization of the early peer group.

During the 1970s, a number of independent researchers reported empirical evidence documenting the existence of social dominance hierarchies as an organizational feature of preschool groups (Abramovitch, 1976; Hold, 1976; Misshakian, 1976; Sluckin & Smith, 1978; Strayer & Strayer, 1976). Simultaneously, ethological studies with older children began to suggest that social dominance persisted as a unifying aspect of peer group social organization throughout the grade school and adolescent periods (Omark, Omark, & Edelman, 1976; Savin-Williams, 1976; Weisfeld, Omark, & Cronin, 1980). More recently, some investigators have begun to verify the theoretical assumption in ethology that the establishment of a group dominance hierarchy contributes to the reduction of intragroup aggression (La Frenière and Charlesworth, 1983).

Following these initial efforts to document the nature of dominance hierarchies, researchers began to explore how other, more positive, forms of social activity are related to group dominance status. Although some of the preliminary findings indicated that social dominance may be directly related to patterns of peer friendship and popularity (Strayer, 1980b), social attention (Abramovitch & Strayer, 1978), imitation, and leadership (Savin-Williams, 1980; Strayer, 1980a, 1981), other findings cast doubts on the central role of social dominance as the major organizing principle for social behavior in the early peer group (Vaughn & Waters, 1980, 1981). The way in which different forms of prosocial behavior are organized and coordinated within the peer group remains an important issue in ethological research on child behavior. Undoubtedly, a complete answer to such questions will require a consideration of environmental factors influencing the social activities of the peer group, as well as maturational factors controlling patterns of social participation during early development.

Recent research suggests that the organization of dispersive and cohesive activities might differ systematically in relationship to age and previous social experience of peer group members. For example, Misshakian (1980) and colleagues reported different patterns of social conflict between children in a mixed-aged peer group. Similarly, Strayer (1980a, 1981) reported quite similar social dominance hierarchies for 4- and 5-year-old children but also showed that prosocial activities are related to status in different ways at each age level. More recent cross-sectional studies of preschool groups have revealed stable dominance structures among children aged 1 to 5 years (Strayer, Jacques, & Gauthier, 1983). In addition, analyses of affiliative activity in these same groups indicate a significant coordination between dominance status and friendship only among 4- and 5-year-olds (Strayer & Trudel, 1984). These preliminary findings indicate that the organization of peer activity varies in important ways during the first five years of life. However, few researchers have attempted to provide direct information concerning the processes underlying the emergence and the development of peer group social organization.

The lack of information on the development of social structure in the peer group reflects certain conceptual and methodological limits in earlier research on child development. Most scientists working with very young children have studied primary attachment or maternal dependence as the principal sphere of social change during the first 2 or 3 years of life (Maccoby & Masters, 1970; Bowlby, 1969, 1972). Other researchers have examined differences in early peer experience as well as parallel differences in social styles as primary determinants of the child's adaptation within the early peer group. Although such studies provide important information about the antecedent conditions associated with individual differences in patterns of adjustment to the peer group, they offer less insight into the dynamic processes that lead to the emergence of structured social groups.

Processes underlying the development of social structure have been addressed most directly by researchers working on the sociobiology of small groups. For example, Chase (1979, 1981) suggests that social organization in a stable group is an emergent property of interactive processes between three or more individuals. This perspective stresses that the analysis of social structures cannot be reduced to a simple calculus of individual differences. Chase's analyses of triadic conflict in animal societies show that certain patterns of tripartite interaction lead inevitably to asymmetrical social relations and to the emergence of transitive dominance hierarchies. Although such forms of triadic conflict have been extensively examined among nonhuman primates (de Waal, 1978; Kummer, 1968; Moore, 1982), triadic participation has seldom been studied in groups of young children.

Triadic social conflict among children

Many of the frequently observed bouts of social conflict among preschool children are not restricted to just two participants. Often children intervene in bouts of dyadic conflict between their peers or expand an aggressive episode by involving a third group member in the originally dyadic bout. Four possible patterns describe how a bystander can become involved in an ongoing episode of dyadic conflict. Two of these triadic patterns involve coalitions, in which a third child assumes a prosocial or supportive role by providing aggressive help to one of the original members of the dyad. By contrast, during episodes of redirected conflict, the bystander becomes involved because one of the original participants has attacked him. Both of these latter patterns can be viewed as antisocial, as they involve the spread of aggression without support or help to another group member.

Figure 4.1 provides a schematic representation of the four possible forms of triadic aggression that have been discussed by Chase (1979, 1980). To facilitate the discussion of these triadic patterns, the labels (1) Defense, (2) Alliance, (3) Generalization, and (4) Displacement are used. These

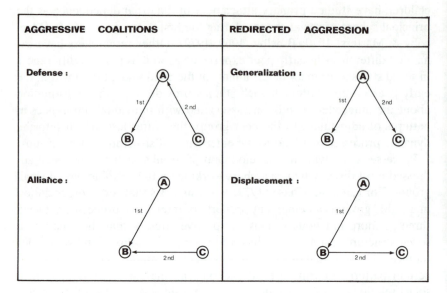

Figure 4.1. Schematic representations of basic structures of triadic conflict.

labels are not intended to prejudge the motivational dispositions of the participants in the triadic episode, but rather are used descriptively to distinguish between the dynamics of aggressive exchange within an observed subgroup of three children. In each illustration, the first act occurs between individuals A and B. The subsequent act, which involves C, determines the structure of the triadic episode. When C attacks A (the original aggressor), the patterns involve defense of B by C. When C attacks B (the original victim), the episode entails on alliance of C with A against B. When A directs aggression toward C, the episode reflects the generalization of social conflict by A. Finally, when B attacks C, the triadic bout involves displacement of aggression by B.

Although these four patterns of triadic conflict can be observed in most preschool settings on a daily basis, little systematic research has been conducted to document the relative frequency of either coalitions or redirected aggression. Even less is known about how participation in such conflict may be related to other parameters of early social adjustment. The present research examines the nature of such conflict within stable groups of socially experienced preschool children. Our initial questions concerned the relative occurrence of these forms of triadic conflict as well as the quality of behavioral activity displayed in such episodes. Subsequently, we examined how interactive roles within such triadic bouts were related to more traditional ethological measures of dominance and friendship within the stable preschool peer group.

Methods

The participants in this study were 48 French-speaking children who attended a community day-care center in the central urban region of Montreal. The children, who ranged in age from 48 to 72 months (mean 66 months, SD = 8.40), were members of the oldest group at the center during three different academic years. Group A was observed in 1977–78, group B in 1979–80, and group C in 1980–81. Most children had had at least 2 years of previous preschool experience. The day-care center provided services for a large variety of social classes, including tradesmen, professionals, students, and welfare recipients. Approximately 30% of the children came from single-parent homes. Daily activities for each of the three groups were divided into periods of nonintrusive structured activity, relatively unsupervised free play, and meal- and naptime. Most children attended the center for a full day (9:00 A.M. to 5:00 P.M.). Each class had a permanent male and a permanent female teacher, who were occasionally replaced by part-time staff of either sex.

Video records of social behavior were obtained for the 1977–78 group. In this study, eight 5-min focal samples were recorded for each child throughout an 8-week observational period at the end of the academic year. Both of the other two groups were observed using direct observation procedures. Group B was also observed at the end of the academic year, while group C was observed during three different seasons – the Fall, the Winter, and the Spring of their school year. Focal sampling procedures involved a minimum of 24 5-min periods for each child in the latter two studies. Supplementary scan sampling of occurrences of social conflict was also collected for all three groups (Altmann, 1974). This supplementary information was used to complete the description of social dominance relations as well as to augment the frequency of triadic episodes for each of the three groups.

Records of social exchange in each group were coded in sequence using a minimal four-item syntax. This coding syntax required that each observation record include the code of the initiator of an act, the action, the target, and the target's response to the initial behavior. If one of the required elements in this syntax could not be specified, the social exchange was not included for analysis. The description of behavior required noting specific elements selected from a Social Action Inventory (Strayer, 1980b). The behavioral categories included in the current analyses are summarized

Table 4.1. *Principal categories and patterns of social behavior*

Class and category	Behavioral patterns
	Initiated actions
Affiliation	
Attention	Glance, gaze, look, watch, turn toward
Signal	Beckon, point, show, wave–smile, play face
Approach	Step toward, walk toward, run toward, follow
Contact	Touch, pat, kiss, hold hands, shoulder hug
Agonism	
Attack	Bite, hit, grab, kick, pull, push, throw at, assault
Threat	Fragment hit, kick, throw, chase, facial display, body display
Competition	Object struggle, steal, supplant
	Sequence terminators
Affiliation	
Reorient	Look away, look to other, turn away, turn toward other
Withdraw	Step away, walk away, run away, approach other
Agonism	
Submission	Gaze avert, crouch, cringe, flinch, cry
Retreat	Step back, flee
No response	Ignore, miss

in Table 4.1. Although the precise coding scheme varied for the three groups, each study involved obtaining extensive measures of both agonistic and affiliative activities of each child during a minimum period of 4 weeks.

Data were taken from video records in multiple passes by separate teams of observers. In the analysis of agonistic behaviors, activities of the focal child and of any other group members who were visible on the television monitor were noted. However, only the former measures were used to calculate aggressive rate measures for children in this study. In the direct-observation procedures, social behaviors were coded in sequence as they occurred. A change of social partners or a period of 10 sec between the offset of one action and the onset of another were used to separate sequences of dyadic social exchange. Reliabilities for the use of each coding framework were assessed using both correlational and agreement procedures. Reliability indices were consistently 80% in direct observation and were slightly higher for the coding of selected behaviors in the 1977–78 video samples.

The nature of children's triadic conflict

Our first set of questions concerned the form and relative frequency of the four possible patterns of triadic conflict discussed above. From the 10 hr

Table 4.2. *Frequency of observed forms of triadic conflict*

	Group A ($n = 15$)	Group B ($n = 16$)	Group C ($n = 17$)	Total
Defense	10	17	14	41
Alliance	5	10	21	36
Generalization	14	10	21	45
Displacement	12	9	15	36
Total	41	46	71	158

of videotaped interaction for group A, 41 episodes of triadic conflict were noted. For group B, 46 episodes were coded during slightly more than 32 hr of field observation. Finally for group C, 71 episodes were available from three observational sessions scheduled during the full academic year. Triadic conflict appeared an average of 4.1 times per hour in our video records but on the average less than twice per hour in the direct-observation data. This difference reflects the different observational techniques that were employed in the three studies. In general, one of every five or six episodes of dyadic conflict involved a third peer group member.

Table 4.2 presents a descriptive summary of the frequency of each form of triadic conflict for each of our three groups. Defense made up 26% of the total 158 observed episodes. Generalization occurred slightly more often and accounted for 25% of the total. Alliance and Displacement occurred less often, each contributing 23% to the total data base. It is important to note that the relative distribution of triadic conflict varied across the three groups. Redirected aggression was most evident in group A (63% of total triadic conflict) and was least evident in group B (41% of total). In group C, coalitions and redirected aggression each accounted for 50% of the total episodes. The inclusion of 30 additional episodes provided by the supplementary scan procedures did not alter this general view of the relative frequency of the four patterns of triadic conflict.

Finally, seasonal analyses for group C showed a relatively balanced use of the four triadic patterns during the Fall but showed a marked increase in Generalization during the Winter months when, because of the Montreal climate, children were usually required to stay indoors for their entire day. There was a corresponding increase in Alliances during the Spring when outside playground activities again predominated during freeplay periods. Such inter- and intragroup variation in the frequency of patterns of triadic conflict suggests that both social and physical factors of the group ecology

Table 4.3. *Transition matrices for prosocial and antisocial triadic conflict*

	Second act			
First act	Attack	Threat	Competition	Total
Coalitions				
Attack	17	6	12	35
Threat	7	4	6	17
Competition	11	1	13	25
Total	35	11	31	77
Redirected aggression				
Attack	12	3	7	22
Threat	5	8	9	22
Competition	9	5	23	37
Total	26	16	39	81

may have important determining influences on the nature of triadic conflict within the stable preschool group.

Our analyses of the behavioral content of triadic conflict focused on the relative use of attacks, threats and competition as initial and secondary components of conflict. Of the 316 acts observed in the episodes of triadic conflict, 42% involved competition, 37% aggressive attacks, and 21% forms of nonverbal threat. This general trend was also evident in separate analyses for first and second acts; it reflected, in large measure, the baseline frequencies of the three categories of conflict in simple dyadic exchange.

Subsequent questions concerned whether the form of behavior differed substantially as a function of the type of triadic conflict observed. We wanted to examine whether there was a possible trend toward the use of "matching" or "escalation" strategies during triadic conflict. Table 4.3 shows first-order transitions for the aggressive content of our observed examples of triadic conflict. Inspection of these transition matrices suggests that physical attacks are slightly more evident in support episodes, whereas competition occurs slightly more frequently in redirected bouts. For both categories of triadic conflict, there is a trend to match attacks with attacks and competition with competition. However, this trend is significant only for redirected aggression (chi square (4) = 11.94, $p < .05$). Thus only for this latter category of triadic conflict is there a clear tendency to conserve the quality of aggressive participation from one dyadic context to the next.

Individual profiles and participation in triadic conflict

Although the preceding descriptions provide preliminary evidence about the nature of triadic conflict among preschool children, they do not show how participation in such activities is related to other behavioral characteristics of the preschool child. Nor do these simple descriptive analyses add much to our understanding of how the social dynamics within the context of the preschool peer group differentially influence the use of prosocial and antisocial behavior during this period of development. These latter questions require a more comprehensive analysis of the peer group social ecology that provides the social context for the observed instances of triadic conflict in our three groups.

Our previous research on the social ecology of stable groups has distinguished different analytic procedures that focus on either the behavorial ecology or the social organization of the preschool group (Strayer, 1980a, 1980b). Behavorial ecology refers to the quality of behavioral actions and exchanges observed within a particular group. Pertinent measures include individual rates of specific actions, or classes of actions, relative time allocated to different forms of social participation, as well as relative frequencies of different forms of social exchange. All these measures are similar to behavioral indices traditionally used in psychological research on individual differences in behavior. They offer potential indices for predicting whether children with certain social profiles or interactive styles are more inclined to participate in triadic conflict, as either the original aggressor, the initial victim, or the bystander.

Behavioral measures of individual differences in social activity were computed by summing the total number of agonistic and affiliative acts that were initiated by children during periods of focal observation. These frequency scores were subsequently converted to measures of hourly rate in order to compare the three different social settings. In each group, less than 10% of the observed social activity involved initiation of agonistic behaviors. However, the absolute value of the obtained rate measures differed according to the observational coding procedures. Behavioral rate estimates from the video recordings were substantially greater than those obtained from the direct observation field procedures. To control for this methodological artifact, subsequent correlational analyses of individual differences were based on a standardized rate score for each group.

The first two columns in Table 4.4 show the correlations obtained between the initiation and receipt of affiliative activities and the frequency with which children assumed the different possible roles in triadic conflict. There was no significant tendency for the two initial participants in a De-

Table 4.4. *Correlations between triadic roles and individual behavioral profiles*

Triadic patterns role	Affiliation		Agonism	
	Initiation	Receipt	Initiation	Receipt
Defense				
Aggressor	.03	.09	.33	.68[b]
Target	−.05	.00	−.08	.28
Defender	.28	.35[a]	.63[b]	−.05
Alliance				
Aggressor	.57[b]	.61[b]	.69[b]	.22
Target	.08	.01	.07	.49[b]
Ally	.50[b]	.51[b]	.47[b]	.06
Generalization				
Aggressor	.44[b]	.40[b]	.74[b]	.04
Target 1	.18	.31	.26	.23
Target 2	.14	.11	.17	.52[b]
Displacement				
Aggressor	.15	.22	.33	.21
Target/Aggressor	.27	.29	.44[b]	.61[b]
Target 2	−.08	−.09	−.07	.10

[a] $p < .05$, $df = 46$.
[b] $p < .01$, $df = 46$.

fense episode to initiate or receive more affiliative behaviors from other peer group members. However, children who intervened as defenders in these triadic episodes tended to receive significantly more affiliative acts from their peers. Similarly, both aggressive participants in triadic alliances were significantly more likely to initiate and receive affiliative behaviors, whereas the targets of such alliance were not characterized as being involved in more or less than the average level of affiliative exchanges. Similar analyses for triadic roles in redirected aggression reveal only two significant correlations. Contrary to our intuitive expectations, the aggressors in the Generalization episode were involved in significantly more affiliative exchanges, both as initiators and as targets.

The latter two columns in Table 4.4 provide corresponding correlations for roles in triadic episodes and individual differences in the initiation and receipt of aggressive behavior – these latter measures do not include agonistic behaviors that were already scored as parts of triadic conflict. The correlational findings indicate that aggressors (A) in Defense episodes generally received more aggressive acts from their peers, whereas defenders (C) tended to be more highly aggressive. The target child in Alliances also usually received more aggression from his peers, while both the aggressor and his ally tended to be more aggressive than the average child in their group. Similarly, the initiators of Generalization episodes were also significantly more aggressive, whereas only their second victim tended to receive more than his or her share of aggressive acts. Finally, in displacement episodes, the initial victim (B) both initiated and received more aggressive acts than the average child.

Social relationships and participation in triadic conflict

Although the preceding analyses provide information on the behavioral styles of participants in triadic conflict, they do not reveal much about the social context of such tripartite interaction. Other measures of social functioning may provide better prediction about how individuals differ in their involvement in triadic conflict. Clearly the nature of the social relationship between two children could have important determining influences on how they participate in bouts of triadic conflict. For example, we might expect that friends would be more inclined to engage in mutual prosocial support or perhaps that the dominant member of a dyad would be more likely to redirect aggressive interventions toward the subordinate.

In contrast to the preceding analyses, which emphasized frequency of social contact, consideration of relational constraints on triadic participation requires an examination of how regularities in patterns of social exchange between members of a dyad are associated with their involvement in these conflict episodes. Figures 4.2 and 4.3 provide a visual résumé of the affiliative and dominance relations obtained for each of our three groups. Each group had a relatively complex cohesive network, with a tendency toward same-sex affiliative cliques. The dominance structure for each group was highly rigid and linear. In the first two groups, position in the dominance hierarchy was not directly related to gender. However, in group C, there was a marked gender difference in dominance status; virtually all the boys were ranked above all the girls. The nature of both the cohesive and agonistic social structures presented in Figures 4.2 and 4.3 corresponds well with previous ethological findings on social dominance and cohesive relations among 5-year-old children (Strayer, 1980a, 1980b).

The results of the analyses of relational constraints on participation in triadic conflict are presented in Table 4.5 Once again, both agonistic and affiliative categories are compared with triadic interactive roles. These relational findings provide a somewhat different view of how affiliative and agonistic are related to roles in triadic conflict. For social defense, only dominance covaries with observed interactive roles. In both cases, the

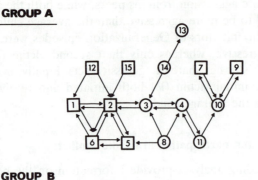

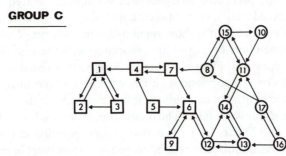

Figure 4.2. Behavioral sociograms of the affiliative networks for the three preschool groups.

defender (C) was dominant to both of the original participants. Somewhat surprisingly, the defender did not appear to intervene differentially on behalf of his own preferred affiliative partners. Dominance relations were also significantly related to triadic alliances. Both the initiator of these episodes and his ally tended to be dominant to their mutual victim. In addition, as expected, the ally selectively supported his own preferred affiliative partners during these tripartite bouts.

The pattern of social relationships in the Generalization episode is by

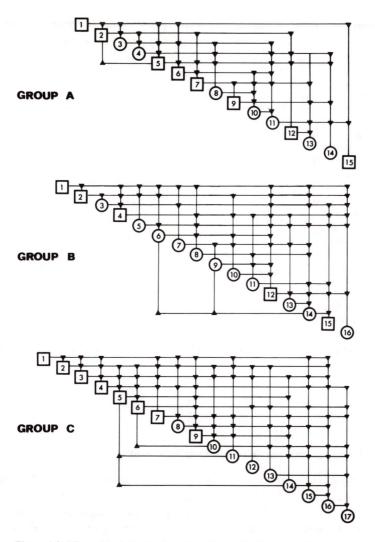

Figure 4.3. Hierarchical dominance networks for the three preschool groups.

far the most complex. As expected, the initiator (A) was usually dominant to both victims but, quite surprisingly, the initiator also tends significantly to prefer both of these latter children as affiliative partners. A somewhat similar result was evident in Displacement episodes. Dominance relationships again significantly followed the lines of observed aggression, but the initial target in Displacement episodes appeared to favor differentially this child's own affiliative playmates as targets for displaced aggression.

Table 4.5 *Social relationships between participants in triadic conflict*

Triadic patterns	Initiator friend to target (%)	Initiator dominant to target (%)
Defense		
A initiates to B	20	66
C initiates to A	20	79[c]
C initiates to B	23	71[a]
Alliance		
A initiates to B	24	79[c]
C initiates to B	23	71[a]
C initiates to A	34[c]	50
Generalization		
A initiates to B	28[b]	79[c]
A initiates to C	26[a]	86[c]
B initiates to C	18	61
Displacement		
A initiates to B	19	72[a]
B initiates to C	30[b]	73[a]
A initiates to C	24	66

Note: X^2 analysis on raw frequencies, with expected values 50% for dominance and 13% for affiliation.
[a] $p < .05$.
[b] $p < .01$.
[c] $p < .001$.

Social status and participation in triadic conflict

Our final set of analyses were designed to examine how the child's position in the group social structure was related to involvement in triadic conflict. Social status is not necessarily identical to being aggressive or being generally dominant over many peers. For example, even though one child may be the most aggressive and most domineering member of a particular group, that child might never direct aggression toward or dominate another particular group member. If an occasional attack by the other child provokes this child either to withdraw or to submit, the established dyadic dominance relationship is clearly not in this child's favor. Such situations, in which a less aggressive child dominates a more aggressive peer, are often observed among young children; they simply reflect the fact that having the highest frequency of aggressive acts, or dominance exchanges, is not identical to having the highest dominance status within the social unit.

Generally, an examination of the complete set of dyadic dominance re-lationships in a stable group permits the derivation of a linear status struc-ture. In the present example, the aggressive child would have a group dominance role inferior to that of the less aggressive child in question.

Similar analytical techniques for the derivation of cohesive group struc-ture have been applied to the study of affiliative activities within the pre-school peer group. In each case, distinctions can be made between the behavioral ecology analyses that stress frequency and rate measures of individual action, and the organizational analyses that emphasize asym-metries or reciprocities in dyadic relationships and social roles within the stable group. At the end of the preschool period, control and influence seem to be hierarchically structured and highly correlated with agonistic dominance status (Strayer, 1981). By contrast, cohesive activities are struc-tured according to a network of reciprocity, consisting of preferred social partners and central and periphal group roles (Strayer, 1980a). This latter network maps almost perfectly onto the network of altruistic choices that emerge from the analysis of dyadic helping, sharing and cooperation (Strayer, Wareing, & Rushton, 1979).

The status of children in the dominance and affiliative structures of the peer group may also be systematically related to their probability of par-ticipating in triadic social conflict. Perhaps more popular children are more able to attract the support of their peers, whereas less affiliatively integrated group members are more often selected as the target of redirected aggres-sion. Similarly, higher group dominance status may be associated with individual prerogatives in terms of generalizing or displacing aggression. In addition, high-status individuals may have certain social responsibilities in terms of defending more subordinate group members. The following analyses address these questions about how a child's affiliative and dom-inance status predict interactive roles in triadic conflict. For the cohesive network, a rank measure of affiliative centrality was calculated following the procedure developed in earlier research (Strayer, 1980a). For domi-nance, a rank measure of hierarchical position was contrasted with fre-quencies of participation in triadic conflict.

Table 4.6 shows the results of this final analysis. Level of integration in the cohesive structure of the peer group was not significantly related to interactive roles in triadic conflict. Alternative measures of popularity, such as the number of times a child was chosen as a significant social target, or the number of behavioral preferences expressed, also failed to relate sys-tematically to triadic interactive roles.

By contrast, dominance status was significantly related to interactive roles for three of the triadic conflict patterns. In Defense, the bystander

Table 4.6. *Correlations between triadic roles and social status*

	Dominance rank	Affiliative integration
Defense		
Aggressor	.03	.12
Target	−.14	.06
Defender	.56[a]	.21
Alliance		
Aggressor	.40[a]	.26
Target	−.16	.25
Ally	.33	.24
Generalization		
Aggressor	.58[a]	.11
Target 1	.12	−.11
Target 2	−.08	.05
Displacement		
Aggressor	.20	−.02
Target/Aggressor	−.01	.21
Target 2	−.18	−.04

[a] $p < .01$; $df = 46$.

(C) tended to be a high-status group member. Similarly, the original aggressor in both Alliance and Generalization episodes seemed also to be high ranking in the group dominance hierachy. Although these final results underscore that high-status children have certain prerogatives in terms of directing aggression toward subordinate group members, they also indicate that dominant peer group members attract social support in the form of aggressive alliance, and discharge certain responsibilities in terms of defending other group members. It is interesting to note in this context that the preceding analysis of affiliative relationships suggests that such defense is not necessarily reserved for the dominant child's personal friends.

Concluding remarks

The major focus of this study draws heavily from the past work of Ivan Chase (1979, 1980, 1981), who has pioneered recent advances in the study of interactive processes leading to the emergence of small group social structures. Chase's theoretical and empirical research suggests that linear dominance hierarchies are a direct result of the developing patterns of triadic conflict during periods of group formation and group stabilization.

The essence of Chase's argument is that only two forms of triadic conflicts – Alliance and Generalization – lead logically to transitive aggressive relationships. According to Chase, it is precisely these two patterns that account for nearly 85% of observed triadic conflict during group formation. Defense and Displacement appear as more frequent forms of triadic conflict only after the linear dominance structure has been firmly established.

Whether similar changes in the nature of triadic conflict are also evident in the interactions of preschool children during the academic year or in the structuring of a peer group during early childhood must be addressed in future studies. Although it is apparent that the integration of individuals into a social unit places important limitations on their subsequent social activities, it has often been less clear how to analyze developmental changes in the organization of the peer group. In this regard, the conceptual approach for the inductive analysis of social relationships and group status represents the most important contribution of this chapter. Peer relations and status within the peer group social structure provide the context for a more detailed examination of the dynamics of individual action. Our current approach has stressed basic distinctions among four levels of social description. The first two, which summarize the behavioral ecology of a social group, entail the identification of individual differences in initiated social behavior as well as differences in the frequency of different forms of social exchange. These two levels of analysis provide basic information concerning the behavioral settings that characterize the peer group. Subsequent analysis of the regularity and diversity of social exchanges for specific dyads reveals larger categories of social participation that can be used as converging measures of emerging social relationships. Finally, analysis of general principles that summarize the organization of these established relationships provides an empirical basis for the identification of structures that characterize the stable social unit; as well as measures of individual status differences that reflect differential social adaptation.

Although our focus on triadic social conflict provides some preliminary insights concerning the nature of prosocial and antisocial aggression, the extension of this research perspective should offer a more complete understanding of how social behavior changes during the course of preschool development. Application of the current analytic framework to the study of social organization within groups of younger children will provide the opportunity to examine the developmental origins of social relationships and group structures. Such developmental research might also determine the importance of triadic interaction for the organization and stabilization of the early peer group. The extension of a triadic framework in the analysis of other forms of social exchange could also offer more comprehensive information about how both affiliative and dominance structures vary in form and function during the course of early development.

Such questions about the nature and function of peer interaction must remain central themes in future studies of children's social adaptation. We still have very little information about when or how dyadic relationships and group social structures emerge as stable characteristics of the child's social world. Even if such structures develop quite early, they might not necessarily fulfill a social regulatory function until later in the preschool period. For example, if dominance hierarchies control intragroup conflict, reductions in total aggressive activity may only be evident as the group status structure becomes well established. When children become more familiar with and better able to predict the social dynamics of their peer group, they should also begin to select among available social settings and thus directly control the forms of social activity in their peer environment that in turn shape their own behavioral activity. Only at this moment should we expect the correlation between individual rates of aggression and dominance status to decrease. Finally, if more dominant children have important roles in the control of intragroup conflict, we might also expect that their defensive aid to lower-ranking peers would eventually increase their general popularity among these less dominant members of the social group. Once again, such a trend could reflect either short-term adaptations within the academic year or more long-term developments throughout the preschool period, or both. Ideally, these ontogenetic changes should be examined in a longitudinal study covering the complete span of preadult socialization. However, even cross-sectional analysis of social functioning within age-stratified preschool groups would provide new information concerning how socially cohesive and dispersive peer activities vary in both frequency and organization during the first 5 years of life.

Acknowledgments

This research was made possible by the continued collaboration of the children, parents, and staff at La Gardérie La Souritthèque. We wish to thank all members of the Human Ethology Laboratory for their assistance, as well as Teresa Blicharski for graphic illustrations, Roger Gauthier for computor programming, and Louise Champagne for word processing. Finally a special note of appreciation to the editors of this volume, and especially to Carolyn Zahn-Waxler, for the tolerance of repeated delays and encouragement to bring things to their present state of completion. Our reseach was funded by the Conseil Québécois de la Recherche Sociale, the Conseil de Recherches en Sciences Humaines du Canada, and the Fondation FCAC. Parts of the empirical data in this chapter were presented at the International Conference on Prosocial and Antisocial Behavior at Voss, Norway (1982), and at the biennial meetings of the Society for Research in Child Development at Detroit, Michigan (1983).

References

Abramovitch, R. (1976). The relation of attention and proximity rank in the preschool children. In M. Chance & R. Larsen (Eds.), *The social structure of attention*, London: Wiley.

Abramovitch, R., & Strayer, F.F. (1978). Preschool social organization. Agonistic spacing and attentional behaviors. In P. Pliner, T. Kramer, & T. Alloway (Eds.), *Recent advances in the study of communication and affect* (vol. 6). New York: Plenum.

Altmann, J. (1974). Observational study of behavior: sampling methods. *Behavior, 49*, 227–267.

Blurton-Jones, N. (1972a). Characteristics of ethological studies of human behavior. In N. Blurton-Jones (Ed.), *Ethological studies of child behavior*. Cambridge: Cambridge University Press.

Blurton-Jones, N. (1972b). Categories of child-child interaction. In N. Blurton-Jones (Ed.), *Ethological studies of child behavior*. Cambridge: Cambridge University Press.

Bowlby, J. (1969). *Attachment and loss: Vol. I. Attachment*. New York: Basic Books.

Bowlby, J. (1973). *Attachment and loss: Vol. II. Separation*. New York: Basic Books.

Carpenter, C. R. (1942). Sexual behavior of free ranging rhesus monkeys. Periodicity of estrus, homo- and autoerotic and nonconformist behavior. *Journal of Comparative Psychology, 33*, 147–162.

Chase, I. D. (1979). Models of hierarchy formation in animal societies. *Behavioral Science, 19*, 374–382.

Chase, I. D. (1980). Cooperative and non-cooperative behavior in animals. *American Naturalist, 115*, 66–76.

Chase, I. D. (1981). Social interaction: The missing link in evolutionary models. *The Behavioral and Brain Sciences, 4*, 237–238.

de Waal, F. (1978). Exploitative and familiarity-dependent support strategies in a colony of semi-free living chimpanzees. *Behaviour, 66*, 268–312.

Grant, E. C. (1969). Human facial expression. *Man, 4*, 525–536.

Harlow, H.F., & Harlow, M.K. (1965). The affectional systems. In A. Schrier, H. Harlow, & F. Stollnitz (Eds.), *Behavior of non-human primates* (Vol. 2). New York: Academic Press.

Hartup, W.W. (1970). Peer interaction and social organization. In P. Mussen (Ed.), *Carmichael's manual of child psychology*. New York: Wiley.

Hold, B. (1977). Rank and behavior: An ethological study of preschool children. *Homo, 28*, 158–188.

James, W. (1890). *Principles of psychology*. New York: Holt, Rinehart & Winston.

Kummer, H. (1971). *Primate societies: Groups techniques in ecological adaptation*. Chicago: University of Chicago Press.

LaFrenière, P. J., & Charlesworth, W. R. (1983). Dominance, affiliation and attention in a preschool group: A nine-month longitudinal study. *Ethology and Sociobiology, 4*, 55–67.

Maccoby, E. E., & Masters, J. C. (1970). Attachment and dependency. In P. Mussen (Ed.), *Carmichael's manual of child psychology*. New York: Wiley.

Maslow, A. H. (1936). A theory of sexual behavior in infrahuman primates. *Journal of Genetic Psychology, 48,* 310–336.

Masters, R. D. (1983). The biological nature of the state. *World Politics, 35,* 161–193.

McGrew, W. C. (1972). *An ethological study of children's behavior.* New York: Academic Press.

Misshakian, E. A. (1976, June). *Aggression and dominance relation in peer groups of children six to forty-five months of age.* Paper presented at the Annual Conference of the Animal Behavior Society, Denver, Colorado.

Misshakian, E. A. (1980). Gender differences in agonistic behavior and dominance relations of Synanon communally reared children. In D. R. Omark, F. F. Strayer, & D. G. Freedman (Eds.), *Dominance relations: An ethological view of human conflict and social interaction.* New York: Garland.

Moore, J. (1982). Coalitions in langur all male bands. *International Journal of Primatology, 3,* 314 (Abstract).

Omark, D.R., Omark, M., & Edelman, M. S. (1976). Formation of dominance hierarchies in young children: Attention and perception. In T. Williams (Ed.), *Psychological anthropology.* The Hague: Mouton.

Sade, D. S. (1967). Determinants of dominance in a group of free-ranging rhesus monkeys. In S. Altmann (Ed.), *Social communication among primates.* Chicago: University of Chicago Press.

Savin-Williams, R. C. (1976). An ethological study of dominance formation and maintenance in a group of human adolescents. *Child Development, 47,* 972–979.

Savin-Williams, R. C. (1980). Dominance and submission among adolescent boys. In D. R. Omark, F. F. Strayer, & D. G. Freedman (Eds.), *Dominance relations: An ethological view of human conflict and social interaction.* New York: Garland.

Sluckin, A., & Smith, P. (1977). Two approaches to the concept of dominance in preschool children. *Child Development, 48,* 917–923.

Strayer, F. F. (1980a). Social ecology of the preschool peer group. In W.A. Collins (Ed.), *The Minnesota symposia on child psychology* (Vol. 13). Hillsdale, NJ: Erlbaum.

Strayer, F. F. (1980b). Child ethology and the study of preschool social relations. In H. C. Foot, A. J. Chapman, & J. R. Smith (Eds.), *Friendship and social relations in children.* New York: Wiley.

Strayer, F. F. (1981). The organization and coordination of asymmetrical relations among young children: A biological view of social power. In M.D. Watts (Ed.), *New directions for methodology of social and behavioral science* (vol. 7).

Strayer, F. F., Jacques, M., & Gauthier, R. (1983). L'évolution du conflit social et des rapports de force chez les jeunes enfants. *Recherches en Psychologie Sociale.*

Strayer, F. F., & Strayer, J. (1976). An ethological analysis of social agonism and dominance relations among preschool children. *Child Development, 47,* 980–988.

Strayer, F. F., & Trudel, M. (1983). Developmental changes in the nature and function of social dominance among young children. *Ethology and Sociobiology.*

Strayer, F. F., Wareing, S., & Rushton, J. P. (1979). Social constraints on naturally occurring preschool altruism. *Ethology and Sociobiology, 1,* 3–11.

Vaughn, B., & Waters, E. (1980). Social organization among preschooler peers: Dominance, attention and sociometric correlates. In D. Omark, F. Strayer, & D. Freedman (Eds.), *Peer-group on human dominance and submission.* New York: Garland.

Vaughn, B., & Waters, E. (1981). Attention structure, sociometric status and dominance: Interrelations, behavioral correlates and relationships to social competence. *Developmental Psychology, 17,* 275–288.

Weisfeld, G. E. Omark, D. R., & Cronin, C. L. (1980). A longitudinal and cross-sectional study of dominance in boys. In D. R. Omark, F. F. Strayer, & D. G. Freedman (Eds.),

Dominance relations: An ethological view of human conflict and social interaction. New York: Garland.

Zuckerman, S. (1932). *The social life of monkeys and apes.* London: Routledge & Kegan Paul.

Part II

**Development, socialization, and
mediators of altruism and aggression
in children**

5   A conception of the determinants and development of altruism and aggression: motives, the self, and the environment

Ervin Staub

The time has come to develop theories and conduct research that jointly consider the most basic, central elements of moral conduct: aggression and altruism. How are such behaviors determined? What influences contribute to their occurrence? How do personal characteristics develop that make their occurrence more or less likely? A simple theory that focuses on one or two elements will necessarily be inadequate. What might be the central elements of a comprehensive theory of the development and determinants of aggression and altruism?

A major purpose of this chapter is to consider socialization and childhood experiences that contribute to the development of aggressive and altruistic behaviors. It is not possible, however, to consider their development meaningfully without understanding how such behaviors are determined. What psychological processes promote and inhibit aggression and altruism? What personal characteristics are likely to give rise to these psychological processes and to influence whether they gain expression in behavior? A reasonable strategy is to specify these characteristics and then to proceed to consider their sources in children's socialization and experience (Atkinson, 1981; Staub, 1979).

In order to understand the determinants of altruism and aggression, we have to consider three classes of influences: (1) environmental conditions that instigate or activate such behavior (e.g., someone's distress or an insult or attack), (2) personal characteristics that affect how people respond to external activators, and can also result in internal activation or initiation of altruism or aggression (e.g., empathic capacity, values, the self-concept), and (3) psychological states (e.g., empathy, anger) that are the result of activation and are the direct determinants of ways of dealing with it. Although altruism or aggression is frequently the result of environmental forces or external instigation, personal characteristics and psychological states can lead to self-instigation. Others in need can always be found. Reasons for victimization and violence can always be created.

135

Environmental instigation of altruism and aggression

Aggressive and prosocial behavior will be broadly defined. Prosocial behavior is behavior intended to benefit other people. However, the reason
for benefiting them may be to gain reciprocal benefits, or approval – that
is, some kind of self-gain. Altruism is behavior intended to help other
people for no other purpose but to improve their welfare, to benefit them.
Obviously, good feeling for having done so may follow, as may the reduction of empathic distress or the arousal of positive empathic feelings,
but the motive or reason for action is not self-related. Aggression, in the
truest sense, is behavior meant to harm others. It is important to recognize,
however, that much of aggressive behavior is in the service of other goals,
for example physical or psychological self-defense, while the actor accepts
or even takes for granted that the object of aggression will be harmed.
Such behaviors will be called aggressive, although the different motivational sources are important to recognize. Also, the motivational sources
of aggression are often likely to be mixed – hostility, the desire to harm,
added to the desire to defend the self.

The primary instigator of altruism is the need of others. The need may
result from a condition of deficiency – someone is physically hurt or injured
or a life is in danger; a person is in psychological distress or is sad or
grieving; someone is hungry or cold; individuals or groups are deprived or
unjustly treated or are suffering relative to some standard of reasonable
welfare or some standard of comparison applicable to all human beings or
to the specific class of individuals in question. The instigating power of
need may arise out of our hereditary makeup, as geneticists and recently
sociobiologists (Wilson, 1975) and psychologists have argued (see Hoffman, 1981, for an extensive discussion of biological origins of altruism),
and it may arise out of social values and socialization that transmits those
values to the young. There is likely to be an overall genetic inclination, in
my judgement (Staub, 1978b), but it is socialization and individual experience that determine the extent to which specific individuals or members
of specific cultures will respond to others' needs as activating conditions
for prosocial or altruistic action. In addition to need that results from
deficiency in someone's welfare, there can be need for help to pursue a
positive goal that will enhance someone's welfare above and beyond
a standard. A person's own state of well-being, comparison between the
self and the other person, the relationship to the other, and other factors influence the perception of, and response to, the need of others
(Staub, 1978b).

A genetic potential for aggression is also likely. Sociobiologists, particularly Wilson (1978), argue that an examination of the probabilities of aggressive behavior under certain environmental conditions, over time and across cultures, suggests that aggressive behavior is part of the human genetic makeup. In response to threat to survival or reproduction, the probability of aggression – not of any specific type, but some aggressive behavior out of the whole range of possible aggressive actions – will increase. However, the malleability of human beings is great. Culture and individual personality that evolves through socialization and experience will strongly affect, increase, or decrease the likelihood of aggression and altruism.

Consistent with the ideas of sociobiologists, psychologists found that certain conditions make aggressive behavior more likely. The primary instigators of aggression seem more varied and complex than those of altruism, but all involve loss, danger, or threat to the self. Frustration (i.e. interference with goal-directed behavior), increases the likelihood of aggression. However, many reactions other than aggression can follow frustration. Even more than frustration, physical attack such as electric shocks and psychological attack on the self (insult, humiliation) or threat to the self make aggressive reactions probable (see Baron, 1977; Averill, 1982). In sum, threat to existence, to the self-concept, and to fulfillment of goals all appear to increase the probability of aggressive responses. These conditions at times directly and physically, at other times potentially or symbolically, threaten a person's existence. Even when threat to survival is not immediate, aggressive responses can be genuinely self-protective in that attack or threat can predict later attacks. Lack of self-defense or retaliation makes continued and often more intense aggressive acts directed at the self more probable. The instigating conditions noted here can give rise to a number of motivations – anger, hostility, and the desire to harm another ("hostile" aggression); self-defense; and the defense of the self-concept. Instrumental aggression (aggression in the service of personal gain) need not be in response to instigation. Nonetheless, under difficult life circumstances, when the fulfillment of goals is difficult, instrumental aggression may increase the real or imagined probability of goal attainment.

An analysis of historical events suggests that the conditions that are likely to give rise to aggression on an individual level also increase the probabilities of violence within or between societies. Economic problems, chaos, and political disorganization within a society, increase the likelihood of violence and of scapegoating and persecution of subgroups in the society (Staub, 1982, 1984a, 1985b).

Value orientations, altruism, and aggression

Certain value orientations that children acquire during the course of socialization and experience can both contribute to positive behavior and
inhibit the likelihood of aggression. The stages of Kohlberg's (1969) moral
reasoning can be seen, for example, as describing different value orientations. Different investigations have described and assessed different moral
value orientations that characterize people, such as humanistic versus conventional (Hoffman, 1970) or rule-centered versus person-oriented (Gilligan, 1982). These have different probable (and as some research shows,
actual) consequences on behavior.

In a number of studies with adult participants, my associates and I found
that persons characterized by a moral value orientation, which I called
prosocial orientation, are more likely to respond helpfully to someone's
need. We used a variety of tests to assess prosocial orientation (Staub,
1974, 1978a, 1978b, 1980). These tests, in our view, tap three interrelated
domains: (1) a positive view or positive evaluation of human beings; (2)
concern about and valuing of other people's welfare; and (3) a feeling of
personal responsibility for others' welfare. When several weeks after the
assessment of their prosocial orientation individuals were faced with another person's need, those with a stronger prosocial orientation responded
more helpfully to either the physical (Staub, Erkut, and Jaquette, as described in Staub, 1974; and Erkut, Jacquette, & Staub, 1981), or the psychological distress of another (Feinberg, 1977; Grodman, 1979; Staub,
1978a, 1978b, 1980).

Value orientations are characterized by desired ends they specify and
associated "cognitive networks." Different value orientations are expected
to give rise to different actions. For example, an orientation to maintaining
the social order, sometimes described as a duty or obligation orientation
– in essence a conventional orientation that focuses on maintaining rules
and conventions – (Durkheim, 1961; Hoffman, 1970; Staub, 1978b, 1980)
might frequently lead to prosocial behavior. However, when a person in
need is seen as having been at fault, particularly as having brought about
his or her need by contravening societal norms or conventions, this person
may be seen as deserving his or her suffering (Lerner, 1980; Rubin &
Peplau, 1973, 1975). Individuals characterized by a concern with rules and
feelings of duty or obligation to them may be more likely to make the
judgment that victims deserve their suffering and be less helpful under
such conditions.

The extent to which the relationship between personal characteristics
such as value orientations and either prosocial or aggressive behavior has

been explored is limited. Our research on the relationship between a prosocial value orientation and prosocial behavior was briefly noted. As yet the relationship between prosocial orientation and aggression has not been explored. A strong prosocial orientation is assumed to make it less likely that motives for aggression arise, and more likely that behavior that harms other people is inhibited. Limited evidence does exist that value related personal characteristics are associated with less aggression (Baron, 1977; Kohlberg, 1969). Most research that has explored such relationships was not guided by a conception of behavior as the result of varied influences, both environmental and personal. Instead, usually a correlation between some individual characteristic and a specific behavior was investigated. Since any behavior is multidetermined, and individual characteristics and circumstances will usually join in affecting behavior, a conception of how different influences join is essential to come to understand and be able to predict the occurrence of altruistic and aggressive behaviors. Such a conception, described in more detail elsewhere (Staub, 1978a, 1978b, 1980, 1984a, 1984b) is briefly presented below. How different moral orientations and other relevant individual characteristics develop will then be considered.

Instigation, value orientations, and personal goals: a theory of social behavior

A motivational disposition, for example a strong prosocial orientation, obviously does not guarantee that such a motive will become active and gain out over other motives. Faced with another person's need, people may aim to benefit them or may choose another, self-related, end or purpose, or may continue with an already ongoing pursuit of a goal. Similarly, conditions that are instigators for aggression might give rise to aggression, or to non-aggressive self-defense, or to no outward response, or to flight. A person may also continue to work toward a blocked goal in nonaggressive ways or choose and proceed to pursue a different goal. Self-instigation also occurs, so that altruism or aggression is not merely a response to environmental conditions. *In order to understand how altruism or aggression comes about, we must consider both how people select the aims of their behavior from a multiplicity of aims, and what determines whether they actually pursue aims they selected.*

I have proposed a theory of social behavior, with the primary purpose of accounting for how prosocial behavior comes about (Staub, 1978a, 1978b, 1980, 1984b). Recently I began to extend this concept to embody aggressive behavior, as a beginning toward a comprehensive theory of moral conduct (Staub, 1984a).

The theory assumes that the characteristics of persons and their circumstances jointly affect the selection of aims. During the course of their development, people develop varied motives. In recognition of the fact that much of human behavior is purposive in character, the focus is placed on motivation to reach desired ends or to avoid aversive ones. Such motivation is conceptualized in the theory as goals (Lewin, 1938, 1948) or as personal goals, or as goal orientations. Personal goals embody desired preferences or end states. In most cases the person has developed an associated cognitive network consisting of beliefs, thoughts, elaborations, and meanings in relation to the valued outcomes. Goals are potentials that become active under certain conditions. As potentials, goals can be arranged in hierarchies according to the value or importance of each goal to a person. Environmental (as well as internal) conditions can have activating potentials for goals for one, two, or more goals. Activating potentials vary in their intensity. The activation of a goal is a function of its importance to the person, which is at least partly relative, a function of its position in the hierarchy of goals, and the intensity of the activating potential for that goal. It is possible for more than one goal to be activated; the result is goal conflict, with the actual motivation a function of the way in which the conflict is resolved. One focus of this model is how the aims of benefiting or harming others is selected from the multiplicity of a person's potential aims; another is a specification of conditions that promote or influence the expression of aims in goal-directed behavior.

Value orientations can be seen as embodying personal goals in moral domains and as incorporating both the desire for outcomes and ways of thinking – cognitive networks – in relation to the welfare of other people and to "right" or "wrong" conduct. A prosocial value orientation can be seen as embodying the personal goal of benefiting and not harming others. Research findings (Staub, 1974, 1978b) show that the stronger their prosocial orientation, the more people respond with positive behavior to activating conditions (physical or psychological distress), supporting the theoretical model. Given the nature of this value orientation, with its focus on personal responsibility for others' welfare, it can also be expected to inhibit aggression under some activating conditions.

This approach provides useful ways of explaining a variety of research findings. Consider one example. Darley and Batson (1973) asked seminary students to give a public lecture. Some, but not others, were told that they were late to the lecture; each student *then* proceeded to the building where the lecture was to be given. Those who believed they were late were more likely to pass by – practically step over – a person lying in their path than were the seminary students who were not in a hurry. Giving a public lecture probably served an important goal for these students, as it was an activity they would later engage in as part of their profession. Being late presumably intensified the focus of attention on their goal. Since the goal was in a highly active state, they were less open to the activating potential of their environment for another goal. Research findings of other psychologists (e.g., Schwartz et al., 1969; Gergen et al., 1972; and London, 1970) were discussed from the perspective of this theory in other publications (Staub, 1978a, 1978b, 1980).

Although the focus here is on prosocial value orientation as the motivational source of unselfish behavior that aims to benefit other people (or inhibits harming them), two additional motivational sources should be noted. Prosocial orientation is person centered, its focus others' welfare. However, some people, both children and adults (Karylowski, 1984; Hoffman, 1970; Gilligan, 1982; Staub, 1979) are characterized by a rule-centered moral orientation with a focus on adherence to rules or principles of conduct. The aims that arise from these two different moral orientations will be different – concern with the welfare of persons versus obligation to rules or principles.[1] In general, the precise nature of internalized rules or norms or motives (Schwartz & Howard, 1984) will affect motivation and action.

These two types of moral value orientations can have different effects on behavior, and are brought about by different socialization and experience of children. For example, Hoffman (1970) found that parental withdrawal of love was an important source of conventional moral orientation in seventh-grade boys, whereas induction was a source of humanistic orientation; these two value orientations are comparable to the prosocial and rule-centered orientations discussed here.

Empathy is the third important motivational source of altruism and potential inhibitor of causing harm to people (Staub, 1971). Empathy is currently receiving substantial theoretical and research attention (e.g., Hoffman, 1975; Batson et al, 1981; Eisenberg & Lennon, 1983). Briefly, what are the sources of empathy and the characteristics of persons that enhance their empathic potential, what is the likelihood that they will respond empathically to others, and finally what is the relationship of empathy to this model?

Possibly, one source of empathy is a primitive emotional responsiveness in the child to others' distress, which Hoffman (1975a) called primitive empathy. Another source is the cognitive elaboration of the sense of other people as separate, differentiated individuals, which Hoffman (1975a) described. This is a value-free characteristic, a cognitive knowledge and awareness. For a person to respond empathically to other people it is probably also necessary to develop a positive evaluation of other people. As Hoffman (1976) also noted, the primitive "empathy" appears to be a connection with and responsiveness to others that is not necessarily empathic; for example, the experience of the infant can be fear, rather than shared distress (Staub, 1979). Given the malleability of human beings this responsiveness can evolve not only in positive, but also in negative ways (fear and avoidance).

We can expect it to evolve as a source of empathic responsiveness only if, in addition to an elaboration of the sense of others, a positive valuing of others develops. This positive valuing is one component of prosocial orientation. Whereas empathy and prosocial orientation are not identical, the latter is a likely source of empathic response, particularly if it is accompanied by an elaborate cognitive sense of others or an in depth capacity for role taking.

Although Hoffman does not assume that a positive evaluation of human beings is a precondition for more forms of empathy, he proposes that children in the course of development discover "both that others react as persons in their own right, and that their responses are often very similar to his own. The realization that his feelings resemble those experienced independently by others in similar situations must inevitably contribute to a sense of 'oneness' which preserves and may even enhance the child's developing motivation to alleviate others' distress" (Hoffman, 1976, p. 136).

A sense of oneness with other human beings is important for identification, a basis for empathy. Experiencing a sense of oneness will depend on positive evaluation of other people; without that, the similarity of others' distress to one's own may not be noticed or acknowledged. However, a feeling of identification and a positive evaluation may have bidirectional influences on each other. Although the two are not regarded here as identical, they probably evolve under similar conditions of socialization and experience, such as warmth and inductive reasoning by parents (Hoffman, 1976; Staub, 1979). They will not evolve under conditions of hostility and rejection by parents.

Finally, a related source of empathy is the self concept, which affects the self–other bond. Empathy is, in part, an extension of the self to other people. It is not surprising, therefore, that people respond more empathically to similar others, even if the similarity is limited in nature (Krebs, 1975; Stotland, 1969). Victims of mistreatment of whole groups of people are usually defined as dissimilar, an outgroup, as "them" rather than "us" (Hornstein, 1976; Staub, 1982, 1984a). A poor self-concept makes it more difficult to extend the boundaries of the self in benevolent ways.

The preceding discussion suggests that empathy arises out of a multiplicity of sources: an emotional connectedness that evolved from primitive empathy and that may require a positive self-concept, a well-developed sense of other people, and the positive valuation of human beings. The empathic response has an emergent quality. It arises as a unitary response from these varied characteristics of persons, usually in response to environmental events. The quality of empathic response, whether it is an emotion similar to that of another person or includes a sympathetic responsiveness, needs to be further defined and investigated (Staub and Feinberg, 1980).

Hoffman (1982) proposed that sympathy is developmentally more advanced than empathy and a qualitatively different feeling. Staub and Feinberg (1980) found that empathy (which they called "parallel empathy") and sympathetic responsiveness (which they called "reactive empathy") have different behavioral correlates. Girls who showed reactive empathy on a test engaged in somewhat more positive behavior and were the recipients of substantially more positive behavior from peers. (There were no reactive empathy responses among the third- and fourth-grade boys in the study.)

One consequence of empathy can be the desire to benefit another, which diminishes one's empathic distress or gives rise to empathic enjoyment of another's increased well-being. Empathy differs from the desire to benefit another that arises from prosocial orientation in that the former does not include a feeling of responsibility for others' welfare. This difference may make prosocial orientation a more reliable source of positive behavior than empathic capacity. It is the lack of this feeling of responsibility, and the more specifically affective nature of the response, that might account for escape from empathy arousing situations, which can be one mode of reducing empathic distress (Piliavan, Dividio, Goertner, & Clark, 1981). However, escape is less likely when the affective response is sympathetic or reactive.

A conscious valuing of other people's well-being and a desire for benefiting them may not be prerequisites for empathy. Most likely, though, these characterize persons with a well-developed capacity for empathy, especially "reactive" empathy.

The emergent quality of empathic emotion gives it immediacy. However, in selecting an aim for behavior, empathy is still in competition with other motives, which give rise to the desire for one or another outcome. That is, in the current perspective empathy is a source of motivation that must be viewed in conjunction with other motivational sources such as value orientations and personal goals, for its relative influence to be understood.

Motivation alone does not determine behavior. The nature of the self-concept is also important, particularly for altruism and aggression. (This will be discussed in the next section.) Moreover, a variety of supporting characteristics are essential for motivation to be expressed in action, and sometimes for motivation to become active.

For example, competencies are important in determining whether altruistic motivation will gain expression in behavior. Frequently without seeing the possibility of reaching a desired outcome, of fulfilling a goal, the goal may not become active (Benesh and Weiner, 1982). Three types of competencies are important: a general belief in one's ability to influence events and successfully pursue goals; the capacity to generate plans of action or the knowledge of action on specific occasions; and specific competence to act in required ways, (such as the ability to swim in order to save a drowning person) (Staub, 1978a, 1978b, 1980). Other supporting characteristics sometimes include the ability to make fast decisions, if the opportunity for action might come to pass (Denner, 1968) and a role-taking capacity to perceive others' needs when those needs are not obvious. Such characteristics are seen, however, as being in the service of motivation. Without a motivational source, they will not give rise to altruistic behavior.

The self-concept and self-other connections

A substantial body of research findings shows that positive experience, such as success, luck or kindness by other people, increases subsequent helpfulness and generosity. Although negative experiences often decrease helpfulness or generosity, sometimes they do not and can even increase positive behavior (for reviews, see Rosenhan, Salovey, Karylowski, & Hargis, 1981; Staub, 1978b). This variation following negative experiences seems partly a function of the type of negative experience. For example, shared misfortune can increase a sense of communality with other people and enhance positive behavior. In some cases, after failure people might engage in positive behavior in an attempt to repair others' assessment of them, or even their self-assessment, diminished by the failure (Isen, Horn, & Rosenhan, 1973).

Why do positive and negative experiences have these effects? They can affect temporary levels of self-esteem and attention to self versus others. First, negative experiences, or even the expectation of stress or of evaluation by other people, can lead to self-preoccupation (Berkowitz, 1970). The result is diminished attention to other people and their needs. In an important study, Reykowski and Yarymovitz (1977) found that children with low self-esteem showed substantial increase in their perception of the need of another child once their self-esteem improved as a result of a series of success experiences. Second, negative experiences can result in motivation to enhance or protect the self and thereby diminish concern for other people's needs. Positive experiences can free people of self-concern, which is often present to some degree in social relationships. As a result, the ability to attend to other people's needs increases and the motivation to help others can come to the fore, becoming active and gaining expression. I am implying that the effects of positive and negative experiences, particularly of success and failure, will depend on a person's self-esteem (see also Karylowski, 1976). Moreover, differences in self-esteem will be related to altruistic behavior. However, according to the conception presented here, the influence on prosocial behavior of a person's self-concept and self-esteem, and how it is modified by current experience, will also depend on the strength of their prosocial orientation or other altruistic motivation.

Since positive and negative behaviors are expressions of the connection between the self and others, it is not surprising that how people feel about or experience themselves would affect the way they feel about others, as well as their willingness to extend themselves for others. It is interesting, in this context, that some research findings with children suggest that an extremely positive self-concept is less related to positive behavior (Reykowski & Yarymovitz, 1976) and to positive peer relations (Loban, 1953, Reese, 1961; see Staub, 1979, p. 236) than a positive but more moderate self-concept. Children with a very positive self-concept may feel sufficient unto themselves and less concerned with their connection to other children. They may have less of a sense of connectedness to others. However, the relationship between self-esteem and positive behavior would be modified by the degree of prosocial motivation that children developed and the relative importance of their prosocial versus other motives.

There are also indications that a weak sense of self, a low self-esteem, contributes to aggression. It makes it more likely that the behavior of others is perceived as threatening, as dangerous, if not physically, then at least to one's self-esteem. Certain kinds of danger, or threats to self will be more acutely experienced, or even imagined, by people who have low self-esteem or a vulnerable self-concept. The need or desire to protect the self will more easily arise and dominate other motives. The clinical literature suggests that young aggressive delinquents tend to perceive others' behavior as threatening, and they respond with what might be called pre-retaliation (Staub, 1971; Slavson, 1965). The study of violent criminals also shows that a frequent source of violence is sensitivity to insult or threat by other people. In a careful study of prison inmates who committed crimes

of violence, with other trained inmates or former inmates acting as inter-
viewers, Toch (1969) found that a large percentage (25%) of these violent
individuals reacted to mild or imagined insults. These insults gave rise to
motivation to defend their reputation or self-image. As Toch (1969) writes,
"he invariably responds with violence to defend himself against the belit-
tlement" (p. 148). Another group of violent individuals, also characterized
by feelings of worthlessness, would seek violent encounters to convince
others that they are fearless (Toch, 1969). When the defense or enhancement of the self become important goals – either as persistent individual
characteristics or aroused on specific occasions – in some individuals these
motivations are fulfilled by aggression.

Self-awareness, or knowledge of oneself, and acceptance of the varied
aspects of the self so that they become part of the self-concept can also be
of great importance in affecting altruism and aggression. Freud, Jung, and
Rogers all theorized, on the basis of their clinical experience, about the
negative consequences of individuals not being aware of certain impulses
or emotions within themselves or of not accepting them and failing to
incorporate them into their conscious self-concept. The denial of feelings
of anger or of sexual impulses can lead to the projection of such characteristics into other people. But when such characteristics are seen as wrong,
as unacceptable – which is the reason for their denial or repression – a
desire to punish them in other people can arise. That is, lack of self-
awareness and of self-acceptance and the lack of self-fulfillment that results
can be a source of hostility toward others. The existing research on the
authoritarian personality (Adorno, Frenkel-Brunswik, Levinson, & Sanford, 1950; Cherry & Bryne, 1977; Sanford, 1973) – some with better and
others with less adequate methodology – indicates that authoritarian individuals are characterized by such tendencies of denial and projection and
by the desire to punish other people who presumably have these unacceptable characteristics. Such individuals also show a tendency toward
obedience and submission to authority and a disregard for those without
power. The combination of these characteristics provides a potential for
their becoming tools of malevolent authority in perpetrating violence against
others (Staub, 1982, 1985b).

Developmental psychologists have not been much concerned with the
acceptance of aspects of the self. As an incidental finding, Hoffman (1970),
described children characterized by a conventional moral orientation as
having also learned to inhibit anger as well as sexual and other impulses
in themselves. Self-awareness and the acceptance of varied aspects of oneself have basic importance for many aspects of functioning, including ways
of relating to other people. This received substantial attention from psy-

chologists who developed theories based on clinical experience. Research exploring the origins and consequences of differences in self-awareness and self-acceptance are greatly needed.

Summary of determinants of altruism and aggression

The conception presented here identifies important influences on altruistic and aggressive behaviors. Moral value orientations and empathic potential, the sources of a person's altruistic motivation, probably diminish hostility or its expression in behavior (Staub, 1971). Their influence is also a function of their position in a hierarchy of motives. The self-concept, self-esteem, self-awareness, and self-acceptance all affect connectedness to other people. Jointly with moral value orientation and empathy, they affect openness to others' needs as opposed to a focus on the self, as well as sensitivity to instigators of aggression such as frustration or threat. Competence, role taking and other supporting characteristics affect the engagement of motivational potentials, and the expression of motives in action. To understand the development of altruism and aggression, we must understand the sources of these personal characteristics in socialization and experience.

A question of profound discussion and controversy in personality and social psychology has been the extent of consistency in behavior across different (but related) circumstances (Mischel, 1968; Mischel and Peake, 1982; Epstein, 1979). The model presented here suggests that moderate to fairly high consistency can be expected in general, and in prosocial and aggressive behaviors in particular, when a relevant goal or motive is important to a person (high in the person's hierarchy of goals) and when this person possesses positive self-esteem and supporting characteristics that lead to the expression of the goal in behavior. Still, very high consistency would not be expected because (1) the environment will at least occasionally offer a strong potential to satisfy another goal important to the person, which then gains dominance; or (2) an already active goal will interfere with the activation of the goal. The seminary students who ignored a person lying in their path in their hurry to get to their assignment provide an example of the latter.

Motivational sources in human nature

A number of basic motivational systems seem to be present at birth, or to develop as humans mature, if minimal supporting conditions exist. They are the sources of a variety of personal goals. Some are importantly involved in the development of altruistic and aggressive behaviors. How these motivational potentials unfold, however, is a function of socialization and experience.

These motivational systems or potentials include primary needs and sex. They include intrinsic motivation, an interest in stimulation and in novelty, and in the ability to manipulate and work with objects. With favorable experience, out of this, can grow a sense of agency, a belief in one's ability to influence events. As a conception of the self and the world begins to develop, it guides the way the individual makes sense of the world, of himself or herself, and of the relationship between the two (Epstein, 1973, 1980). There appears to be a strong motivation to protect and maintain one's existing self-concept, and to protect and enhance self-esteem. The relevance of this system to prosocial behavior and aggression was noted earlier.

Motivational sources of specific relevance

Certain stimuli appear to have biological meaning, such as contact comfort and crying by another infant. There is evidence that infants, on their first day of life, cry in response to crying by another infant, although not in response to the same-intensity noise (Simner, 1971; Sagi and Hoffman, 1976). This may provide support for a notion of genetically based connectedness to other human beings, a genetically based sociotropic orientation. The observation of infants and young children also indicates a tendency to respond to certain experiences with rage or anger. With increasing age, undirected forms of anger decline while anger directed at other children increases (Goodenough, 1931). How the potential for anger and for aggression that it sometimes gives rise to develops depends on socialization and experience.

Attachment, an early affectional tie to specific others, is another motivational potential present at birth. It has long been believed that the first important relationship of infants to parents represents a prototype of later relationships. Recent research findings provide support (see Sroufe, 1979).

The human infant, like the infant of many species of animals, has the capacity to form strong attachments to members of its species. Recent research findings show that the quality of attachment of infant to parents – usually the mother – varies, and that the quality of this attachment is associated with later social behaviors of the child in interactions with peers. Children who form secure attachments to their caretakers, in contrast to anxious or ambivalent attachments (Ainsworth, 1979), later manifest more effective or positive peer relations (Sroufe, 1979). In one study, secure attachment was associated with more effective peer relations when combined with early experience with peers (Lieberman, 1976). In part, the reason for these differences in social relations to peers is probably motivational. Children who experience conditions leading to secure attachment and who develop such attachment may feel safer and less anxious. They may experience less need to protect themselves. They may also experience greater positivity of feelings towards other people and would, therefore, be more motivated to approach and interact with peers. From earlier research on institutionalized infants who, because of lack of a consistent caretaker in their environment and of social stimulation and responsiveness to their needs, had no opportunity to develop attachment to an adult, we know that such children later have serious problems in their personal relationships (Thompson and Grusec, 1970).

A secure attachment, which is associated with responsiveness by caretakers to the child's needs, bodily contact, mutual gazing, as well as other types of contact (Shaffer, 1979), is likely to be an important starting point for the development of altruism and might lessen the probability of aggression. It provides a basis for positive feelings for and positive evaluation of other human beings, the most basic component of prosocial orientation. It is probably also a component of empathic responsiveness. The positive contact to a caretaker probably contributes to the beginnings of a positive self concept. The nature of continuing socialization and experience of the child is crucial, of course, to expand this rudiment of positive relatedness to other human beings, and to the self.

At the time that attachments to primary caretakers develop, stranger anxiety also appears, a fear and/or avoidance of unfamiliar individuals. This may be a rudimentary appearance of a very basic human tendency, to divide people into ingroups and outgroups, into "us" and "them" (Staub, 1982; Tajfel, 1982). In turn, we are more likely to help those we identify as "us" (Hornstein, 1976). Consistent with this is the substantially greater altruism toward mothers than toward lesser known adults in the first years of children's life (Zahn-Waxler and Radke-Yarrow, 1982). The evolving perceived similarity and identification with "us" is a source of empathy and presumably leads to the application of values that promote altruism (Krebs, 1975; Stotland, 1969).

Obviously, it is socialization and experience that shape the course of development of the early rudimentary differentiation. More varied early experience, for example, exposure to and familiarity with more people, is associated with less stranger anxiety (Shaffer, 1979). The quality of attachment also affects stranger anxiety, less stranger anxiety accompanying secure attachment. At a later age the family or tribe, identifying outsiders as dangerous, or as enemies, will further promote differentiation, while creating new boundaries along which enemies are made. The culture, including its most basic aspects, such as language can embody such differentiation. For example, among the Mundurucu, the word for non-Mundurucu also means enemy (Wilson, 1978).

Differentiation between "us" and "them" is so basic an aspect of human thinking that it is worth considering its bases in the human genetic makeup. The differentiation of the known and familiar from the unknown and unfamiliar, of which stranger anxiety is an important example, and the categorization of classes of objects by which the human mind works, may be such bases. Usually people defined as outsiders, as "them," are also devalued (Piaget and Weil, 1951). They can become the object of prejudice, hostility, and violence, even to the point of extermination. When people are so identified they come to be excluded from the application of moral value orientations (Staub, 1982, 1984a, 1984b). This seems a general principle, suggesting that extending the boundaries of "us" in the course of socialization may increase helpfulness and diminish aggression. Secure attachment, varied social experience, and socialization (and culture), which identify other human beings as similar and which positively evaluate them, would best contribute to the rudiments of prosocial orientation and empathic responsiveness applied to a broad range of people.

We are reminded of the multiple influences on aggression and altruism by the substantial degree of ingroup violence in contemporary America, such as child abuse, abuse of spouses, and the large proportion of murders occurring among intimates. It is consistent with the previous theorizing that identifying some people as part of one's ingroup will not alone determine altruism or aggression toward them. Differentiation between "us" and "them" affects the arousal and application of altruistic and aggressive motivations and their expression. However, these motivations depend primarily on the personal characteristics identified earlier.

Socialization practices and their consequences

A great deal of laboratory and socialization research shows that prosocial behavior is influenced by a combination of (1) parental warmth and nurturance, (2) *induction*, pointing out to children the consequences of their behavior on other people, and (3) firm control by parents, so that children actually behave in accordance with important values and rules (Staub, 1979, 1981).[2] These practices expand the original attachment that children develop toward important caretakers. The experience of warmth can contribute to the development of positive assumptions about human beings as well as trust in their benevolence. Induction, particularly if it is accompanied by control, can lead children to become aware of and take others' needs seriously and to feel responsible for others' welfare. By enhancing awareness of others' needs, induction can contribute to empathy.

From a theoretical perspective, warmth, nurturance, induction, control, and actual participation in positive behavior implied by control can be expected to contribute to positive assumptions about human beings and concern about, and a feeling of personal responsibility for, their welfare. These are elements of the prosocial value orientation. However, research on how socialization practices contribute to personal characteristics in general, and value orientations in particular, is quite sparse. Much of the research has been laboratory analogue research. Such research can demonstrate immediate cognitive or affective consequences of experimental treatments, which possibly mediate behavioral consequences, as for example research by Grusec and associates (Chapter 8, this volume). Having identified such cognitive and affective consequences, we can extrapolate and hypothesize that the repeated application of such "treatments" or practices by parents will lead to the acquisition of the mediating cognitive-affective tendencies, which thus become personal characteristics of children.

The limited research that has explored the relationship of parental socialization practices to children's characteristics has sometimes focused on the relationship of those practices to children's behavior (Baumrind, 1975). At other times, children's value orientations were explored, with a primary focus on the extent to which children demonstrated internalization of values. Many of the actual values assessed were proscriptive in nature, prohibiting misconduct (Hoffman and Saltzstein, 1967). However, the limited research findings that are available do show a relationship between specific parental socialization practices discussed above and the acquisition of concern about the welfare of other humans (Hoffman and Saltzstein, 1967; Hoffman, 1970, 1975b). For example, Hoffman's (1970) humanistic-flexible children, who demonstrate a value orientation similar to prosocial orientation in that it embodies concern for others' welfare, have parents who demonstrate warmth and inductive reasoning as important aspects of child rearing.

What is needed, however, is research in which the correlates of the enduring use by parents or socializing agents of the *whole pattern* of practices are identified. The more parents and socializers in other settings, such as schools, particularly in the early school years (Staub, 1981), use such a pattern, the more we can expect prosocial orientation, empathic responsiveness, and behavioral tendencies for increased altruism and less aggression in children. Practices that are expected to contribute to a rule-centered moral orientation can also be identified. For example, the focus of parents' reasoning with the child would be not the consequences of the child's behavior (and human behavior in general) on others' welfare, but the importance of adherence to rules. Very early in life, parents more or less characterized by such patterns may be selected for study, with continued assessment of the evolution of the pattern. Alternatively, parents may be willing to undergo, in the context of a study, early training in "optimum" socialization practices for the development of an altruistic behavioral disposition.

While reasonable parental control is important, it is also important that parents respond to the child's own reasoning and be willing to consider the child's point of view (Baumrind, 1975). Autocratic control has negative effects. In general, the mode of control employed by parents can be crucial. There is evidence of an association between overly power-assertive control, with a substantial amount of physical punishment, and aggressive behavior displayed by children (Aronfreed, 1968; Bandura and Walters, 1959). Such controlling practices break the connection of love and trust in other people, generate anger, and create concern in the child about his or her well-being, safety, and goodness. Thus both prosocial orientation and the self-concept may be affected. There is some evidence that the combination of power-assertive control and autocratic parenting contributes to the development of authoritarian personalities (Cherry & Byrne, 1977).

Another consequence of the mode of parental control has been shown in a study by Hoffman (1970). In assessing children's moral orientations and parental childrearing practices, Hoffman found love withdrawal to be associated with a conventional rule-oriented morality. This gained expression in concern about rules in contrast to the welfare of individuals. A characteristic of conventional children was an inhibition of expression of impulses. There are hidden elements in most parental socialization practices; a primary one is the content of what is rewarded or punished, what is promoted or inhibited. Love withdrawal may result in pervasive concern by the child about being loved and accepted as he or she is. As a result, children become cautious and therefore inhibited. Or love withdrawal may be an expression of parental sensitivity that leads to prohibiting specific behaviors, particularly expressions of anger. Certainly the effects of love withdrawal will depend on its severity, generality, and the total pattern of parental practices, including the type of behaviors which parents punish by love withdrawal. However, the possibility that extensive use of love withdrawal leads to a focus on adherence to rules and social convention, and perhaps interferes with self acceptance and self awareness, is important.

Children learn from the specific types of behaviors that are encouraged or discouraged, rewarded or punished. The example of parents and others is another mode, a highly influential one, through which specific behaviors, standards of conduct, and value placed on human welfare are learned. The influence of such examples will depend on the total context, on socialization practices, and on other experiences.

Modeling clearly affects prosocial behavior (Grusec, 1981; Eisenberg, 1982; Staub, 1979). The evidence also suggests (Barron, 1977; Eron, 1982; Maccoby, 1980; Theiss, 1983) that the more exposure children had to aggression in the course of growing up – in the form of physical punishment or violence directed at them by parents, or exposure to violence in their own families, or these combined with television aggression – the more they later demonstrate aggressive behavior. Aggression directed at them can lead children to develop hostility, mistrust, and generally negative feelings and perceptions of other people. Antagonism between boys and their fathers has itself been found to be related to the boys' aggressiveness (Bandura and Walters, 1959). Frequent and varied exposure to violence can lead to viewing aggression as a basic and acceptable mode of conflict resolution and as a basic plan or strategy toward interpersonal relationships. Competence, both in the sense of plans and strategies for the use of aggression, and for specific skills in enacting aggression, will be available.

Apart from their specific child-rearing practices, parents vary in their emphasis on prescriptive versus proscriptive orientation to morally relevant behaviors (McKinney, 1971; Olejnik and McKinney, 1973). Some parents tend to prohibit undesirable behaviors while others focus their efforts more on promoting desirable, including prosocial, behaviors in their children. Obviously, love withdrawal is a proscriptive practice, while induction can be either proscriptive or prescriptive. There is evidence that children whose parents are more prescriptively oriented are more generous (Olejnik and McKinney, 1973). The differences in personality that result from such variation are unexplored. A focus on prohibition may result in concern about doing wrong, hence reducing harmdoing but also reducing the initiative frequently required for benefiting other people. A focus on prohibition may also promote self concern, thereby diminishing attention to others' needs. Probably a balance is desirable with parents *proscribing* certain forms of aggressive behavior (without prohibiting the underlying emotions, while teaching children to constructively deal with these emotions) and of *prescribing* positive conduct.

The socialization practices that apparently contribute to a prosocial orientation and positive behavior in children are similar to those that contribute to the development of positive self-esteem, at least among boys. Coopersmith (1967) found in his research with 10- to 11-year-old boys that parents who are genuinely concerned with the welfare of their children and who use reasoning with their children, set high standards for them, and enforce these standards, had children who developed high self-esteem. It seems that the development of a positive self-esteem and of prosocial value orientation, two personal characteristics that in my view are crucial influences on both altruistic and aggressive behavior, are the result of overlapping socialization practices. These practices share an interest in and desire to promote the child's welfare, reasoning with the child, and effective control. Clearly, the antecedents of the two in parental socialization can be highly supportive of each other. Caring about the child's welfare can be expressed through nurturance and in other ways; reasoning can apply to personal relations, as in induction, and to other aspects of the child's life.

It is possible to postulate a pattern of practices that might be antecedents of all the personal characteristics that were identified as important in promoting altruism and diminishing aggression. For example, to those already mentioned we could add fostering self-reliance in children, so that they can experience and meet challenges, and experience success and reinforcement by other people for their achievements. This is an elaboration of the high standards set by parents of high self-esteem children. It would contribute to a positive self-esteem but would also promote a particular aspect of a positive self-concept, a belief in one's ability to influence events. Both by promoting such a belief and by helping develop other aspects of competence, it would enhance the likelihood that motives of any kind are expressed in action, including that of benefiting other people. At the same time, the characteristics resulting from all these practices would diminish the likelihood of aggression, for reasons discussed earlier.

It is essential that we also begin to study the sources or origins of parental socialization practices, which may be regarded as methods, in parental values and goals that underlie these methods. The goals of parents regarding the kind of child they want to raise, the everyday behavior of the child they want to promote or inhibit, as well as their own behavior or the kind of persons they themselves want to be, particularly in relation to their children, are all important (Staub, 1985a).

Natural socialization: learning by doing

Just as the ancient philosophers had proposed (see Peters, 1970), moral behavior is learned through action, through engagement in moral conduct. A prosocial behavioral tendency develops, in part, through participation in prosocial behavior. In fact, learning by doing is a hidden aspect of most socialization. The extent to which the child is or is not guided to do or to act will determine whether the child does or does not learn certain behavioral orientations. It would be unusual to have a prosocial person who, in the course of growing up, had heard a great deal about how desirable it is to benefit others but rarely engaged in helpful, charitable, or generous conduct. The same is true of achievement or other forms of conduct. It is also difficult to imagine that a person who as a child and adolescent was freely allowed to engage in aggressive behavior and has been successful in aggressing against others would not continue to behave aggressively. The development of valuing certain outcomes, an important characteristic of personal goals, as well as the learning of competencies to execute one's goals, crucially depend on actual participation in goal-directed behavior.[3]

There is substantial evidence that prior participation in prosocial behavior increases adults' subsequent positive actions (Harris, 1972; for a review of research on the foot-in-the-door phenomenon that is also an example, see DeJong, 1979; Staub, 1978) as well as children's (Staub, 1979). In the realm of aggression, there is less clear evidence, partly because clear evidence is more difficult to come by. Children allowed a substantial amount of aggressive behavior who would later exhibit aggressiveness would constitute such evidence. However, a substantial amount of aggression can be taken as an already learned aggressive behavioral tendency that then continues to demonstrate itself. Another kind of evidence might be the inhibition of aggressive behavior associated with less aggression at a later time. However, limited aggression by children can be the result of direct and forceful control, which would increase the likelihood of aggression in different settings or at later times. The combination of discouragement of aggressive behavior by reasonably enforced rules, and helping children to learn and allowing them to exercise effective self-assertion, combined with socialization practices and experience that contribute to a prosocial behavioral tendency, may be most effective in diminishing the potential for aggression.

Participation in prosocial action, particularly when it is not the result of forceful demands by adults, and when it is accompanied by induction and/or the experience of having benefited others, will have important psychological consequences (Staub, 1979). First, it will affect the evaluation of the importance of both such action and the welfare of its intended (or actual) beneficiaries, thereby promoting prosocial orientation. Second, it will result in self-attribution and the perception of oneself as a helpful person (DeJong, 1979; Grusec, 1981; Staub, 1979). Nonparticipation in aggression, when it is not the result of forceful prohibition by adults, may also result in increased concern with others' welfare and in self attribution. Induction that is offered concurrently (Staub, 1975, 1979) or prior experience that results in a network of cognitions that enter into self-guidance and the inductive interpretation of events would contribute to these changes. In other words, existing characteristics, participation, and how its meaning and effects are interpreted evolve and mutually influence each other.

Existing personality as a source of later development

The already existing personal characteristics and behavioral tendencies of children become an important source of their later development. Children shape their environment and others' response to them, which in turn affect their own further development. Through their behavioral expression, rudiments of empathic responsiveness, prosocial or rule-enforced orientation, self-esteem, and other characteristics themselves become influences on children's further development.

In one of our studies, we observed the relationship between children's behaviors and the behaviors directed toward them by their peers during the course of natural interactions in open classrooms (Staub and Feinberg, 1980). This study showed strong reciprocity in boys' aggressive behaviors. Boys who initiated aggression were also the recipients of aggressive behavior from others. Among both boys and girls, there was fairly substantial reciprocity in positive behaviors. Girls who were empathic on a test that we developed, who responded to pictures with sympathetic concern and sympathetic distress to others' fate, were the recipients of many positive behaviors from their peers. Presumably, girls who showed this kind of empathy, which we called *reactive empathy* in contrast to the *parallel* emotional reactions to others' feelings that some boys and girls demonstrated (what is usually seen as the empathic emotion) were sensitive to their peers' desires and needs. Children's aggressive behaviors, their positive behaviors, and their sensitivity to others presumably shape and form their environments and their experience. Their experiences in interactions with peers will, however, affect their feelings about themselves, their feelings about other people, and the types of strategies for interaction that they develop, master, and habitually use.

Concluding remarks

A major purpose of this chapter is to present a *conception* of how prosocial behavior comes about, as well as the relationship between influences promoting altruism and inhibiting aggression. This conception is then used to consider the development of the tendency to behave prosocially (and not behave aggressively). Certain personal characteristics are described as a basis of selecting, usually in interaction with environmental influences, the benefit of other people rather than other outcomes as one's aim and as contributing to people acting on this aim. On the basis of this view and supporting research, the development of these personal characteristics should become a focus of research on the socialization of altruistic (and aggressive) behavior. Relevant personal characteristics include broad value orientations (and the consideration of their importance relative to other values and goals), the self-concept and self-esteem, and competencies. This view implies that the development of prosocial and aggressive tendencies must be seen in the context of the development of the totality of the child's personality and social behavior.

The discussion has focused more on the development of altruistic and prosocial behavior and on how characteristics that promote altruism will inhibit aggression than on the sources and origins of aggression. Although social psychologists have paid much attention to aggressive behavior, and recently developmental psychologists have concerned themselves with the determinants and origins of altruism and prosocial behavior (Eisenberg, 1982; Grusec, 1981; Staub, 1979, 1981; Staub et al. 1984; Radke-Yarrow et al., 1984), research on the development of aggressive behavioral tendencies has been less extensive. However, some of the discussion did suggest origins of the motivation for aggression and of characteristics that contribute to its behavioral expression. The development of negative perception of people, devaluing people in general or specific groups, a negative self-concept, and plans, strategies, and skills for aggressive interactions are central elements.

There is substantial support for the "personal goal theory" account (Staub, 1978b, 1980, 1985) of how social behavior in general and altruistic behavior in particular are determined. There is also good evidence, in this writer's view, that the influences that were presented as contributing to the tendency for altruistic-prosocial behaviors actually do so. There is little evidence, however, that these influences contribute to the development of the motivations for altruistic behavior that were identified as central – prosocial orientation, or a rule-centered value orientation, and empathy – and to a positive self-concept and other supporting characteristics. Research needs to focus on collecting such evidence.

In concluding I will note some unfortunate limitations in theory and research. First, theories of the development of altruism or prosocial behavior, with some exceptions (Hoffman, 1975a), are limited or lacking. The same is true of theories of the development of aggression. In the concept presented here a theory of the determinants of altruistic-positive behavior and/or aggression is an important starting point for a theory of their development. Second, the focus of much research on development is on limited forms of altruism and aggression. We do not know whether this research is of much relevance to the development of characteristics that give rise to heroic acts by individuals, to tremendous sacrifices endured and danger accepted for the sake of saving the lives of persecuted people (London, 1970), to continued self-sacrifice of any kind to benefit other people, or even to the capacity for genuine kindness in everyday relationships. The conception presented here assumes that there are core characteristics relevant to a broad range of altruistic acts. However, special motivation and special personal characteristics are required for special forms of beneficial acts, which must be identified by an analysis of the nature of the need, the behavior required, and other properties (Smithson, Amato, & Pearce, 1983). Heroic acts require competence and a strong "action tendency" (Staub, 1974); rescuing the lives of persecuted people requires courage and perhaps an enjoyment of adventure (London, 1970); helping the poor and needy requires a view of them as deserving, rather than a belief that they are the cause of their own misfortune (Rubin and Peplau, 1973, Weiner, 1980). We also need to differentiate types of aggression and the developmental course of different types. We need research that informs us about the antecedents of people participating in a life of violence, or in torture, or genocide and other mistreatment of groups of people. To understand the latter, we must study the characteristics not only of individuals but of cultures and of social organizations as well (Staub, 1982, 1984a, 1985b).

Considering such examples of human altruism and violence, we must question and carefully analyze the extent of continuity and discontinuity, or degree of isomorphism, in the influences on and developmental origins of such behaviors among animals and humans. The recognition of the extent to which human altruism and aggression are guided by ideas and ideals is essential: we defend our self-concept when no danger to survival is present, act according to our self-concept in performing altruistic acts, or follow ideologies that offer the hope of a better life, while identifying some people as interfering with the better future that the ideology promises. While ideologies, systems of beliefs, can offer hope, meaning, a sense of significance, they have also been the origins of mass murder and genocide – as in Nazi Germany, or recently in Cambodia. Psychologists have been inattentive to such truly large-scale violence. Such symbolically based violence appears uniquely human. However, it is threatening, frustrating, and chaotic life conditions that give rise to ideologies of mass murder. Comparable environmental conditions may lead to aggression among animals.

How human beings come to deal with difficult life conditions, when these give rise to violence, and how cooperative efforts to deal with them can be promoted are important questions (Staub, 1982, 1985a, 1985b). How human beings create and come to embrace ideologies that justify the mistreatment of other people and how such mistreatment serves personal goals on both the individual and cultural-societal level must be one of our concerns.

Acknowledgement

The preparation of this chapter was facilitated and some of the research referred to was supported by NIMH grant MH23886.

Notes

1. Rule-centered moral orientations can vary in important ways that cannot be fully discussed here. They may vary in the *level* at which rules are of concern, either specific standards and norms, the conventions of the social group (Hoffman, 1970), or higher principles such as the social contract, justice, or mercy. The rules or principles may focus on obligation to persons, although frequently the implicit or explicit focus is obligation to the social group.
2. This discussion focuses on generalizations that can be drawn from past research and does not examine the intricacies of research findings that have been reviewed and analyzed by a number of workers (Eisenberg, 1982; Staub, 1979, 1981; Staub, Bar-Tal, Reykowski, & Karylowski, 1984; Yarrow, Zahn-Waxler, & Chapman, 1984). For example, both socialization research in which parental practices and child characteristics and behavior are examined and laboratory analogue research exploring influences on children's helping behavior found a *positive* relationship between parental warmth and positive behavior by children. By contrast, laboratory studies of generosity (children sharing rewards they just acquired) found no such relationship. According to one view (Staub, 1979) this is because children want to maximize their gains in a situation wherein the adult had no opportunity to transmit his or her values to the child in an effective manner. The generalizations presented here are likely to apply, however, when these practices are jointly used, in the usual contexts of the child's life (Staub, 1979).
3. Certain exceptions might exist. At least in the realm of religion, important conversion experiences have been described. St. Francis and St. Augustine are described as young men who lived a life of debauchery followed by conversion and lives of sainthood. It is probable, however, that the childhood of these important religious figures did include important influences, including some forms of learning by doing, which formed the basis of their later conversion. Religious influences were common in their days. It may also be the case that such conversion experiences, which result in the adoption of whole ideologies, may be different in nature from the gradual development of value orientations and behavioral tendencies.

References

Adorno, T. W., Frenkel-Brunswik, E., Levinson, D. J., & Sanford, R. N. (1950). *The authoritarian personality*. New York: Norton.

Ainsworth, M. D. S. (1979). Infant–mother attachment. *American Psychologist, 34*, 932–937.

Aronfreed, J. (1968). *Conduct and conscience.* New York: Academic Press.

Atkinson, W. (1981). Studying personality in the context of an advanced motivational psychology. *American Psychologist, 36*, 117–129.

Averill, J. R. (1982). *Anger and aggression. An essay on emotion.* New York: Springer-Verlag.

Bandura, A., & Walters, R. H. (1959). *Adolescent aggression: A study of the influence of child training practices and family interrelationship.* New York: Ronald.

Baron, R. A. (1977). *Human aggression.* New York: Plenum.

Batson, C. D., Duncan, B., Ackerman, P., Buckley, T., & Birch, K. (1981). Is empathic emotion a source of altruistic motivation? *Journal of Personality and Social Psychology, 40*, 290–302.

Baumrind, D. (1975). *Early socialization and the discipline controversy.* Morristown, NJ: General Learning Press.

Benesh, M., & Weiner, B. (1982). On emotion and motivation: From the notebooks of Fritz Heider. *American Psychologist, 37*, 887–895.

Berkowitz, L. (1970). Reactance and the unwillingness to help others. *Psychological Bulletin, 79*, 310–317.

Cherry, F., & Byrne, D. (1977). Authoritarianism. In T. Blass (Ed.), *Personality variables in social behavior* (pp. 109–135). Hillsdale, NJ: Erlbaum.

Coopersmith, S. (1967). *Antecedents of self-esteem.* San Francisco: Fremont.

Darley, J., & Batson, C. (1973). From Jerusalem to Jericho: A study of situational and dispositional variables in helping behavior. *Journal of Personality and Social Psychology, 27*, 100–108.

DeJong, W. (1979). An examination of the self perception mediation of the foot in the door effect. *Journal of Personality and Social Psychology, 37*, 2221–2239.

Denner, B. (1968). Did a crime occur? Should I inform anyone? A study of deception. *Journal for Personality, 36*, 454–466.

Durkheim, E. (1961). *Moral education.* New York: Free Press.

Eisenberg, N. (1982). *The development of prosocial behavior.* New York: Academic Press.

Eisenberg, N., & Lennon, R. (1983). Sex differences in empathy and related capacities. *Psychological Bulletin, 94*, 100–132.

Epstein, S. (1973). The self-concept revisited. Or a theory of a theory. *American Psychologist, 28*, 404–416.

Epstein, S. (1979). The stability of behavior: I. On predicting most of the people much of the time. *Journal of Personality & Social Psychology, 37*, 1097–1126.

Epstein, S. (1980). The self-concept: A review and the proposal of an integrated theory of personality. In E. Staub (Ed.), *Personality: Basic aspects and current research* (pp. 81–133). Englewood Cliffs, NJ: Prentice-Hall.

Erkut, S., Jaquette, D., & Staub, E. (1981). Moral judgment–situation interaction as a basis for predicting social behavior. *Journal of Personality, 49*, 1–44.

Eron, L. D. (1982). Parent–child interaction, television violence, and aggression of children. *American Psychologist, 37*, 197–211.

Feinberg, H. K. (1977). *Anatomy of a helping situation: Some personality and situational determinants of helping in a conflict situation involving another's psychological distress.* Unpublished doctoral dissertation, University of Massachusetts, Amherst.

Gergen, K. J., Gergen, M. M., & Meter, K. (1972). Individual orientations to prosocial behavior. *Journal of Social Issues, 8*, 105–130.

Gilligan, C. (1982). *In a different voice. Psychological theory and women's development.* Cambridge: Harvard University Press.

Goodenough, F. L. (1931). *Anger in young children*. Minneapolis: University of Minnesota Press.

Grodman, S. M. (1979). *The role of personality and situational variables in responding to and helping an individual in psychological distress*. Unpublished doctoral dissertation, University of Massachusetts, Amherst.

Grusec, J. (1981). Socialization processes and the development of altruism. In J. P. Rushton & R.M. Sorrentino (Eds.), *Altruism and helping behavior* (pp. 65–91). Hillsdale, NJ: Erlbaum.

Harris, M. B. (1972). The effects of performing one altruistic act on the likelihood of performing another. *Journal of Social Psychology, 88*, 65–73.

Hoffman, M. L. (1970). Conscience, personality and socialization technique, *Human Development, 13*, 90–126.

Hoffman, M. L. (1975a). Developmental synthesis of affect and cognition and its implications for altruistic motivation. *Developmental Psychology, 11*, 607–622.

Hoffman, M. L. (1975b). Altruistic behavior and the parent–child relationship. *Journal of Personality and Social Psychology, 31*, 937–943.

Hoffman, M. L. (1976). Empathy, role-taking, guilt, and development of altruistic motives. In T. Lickona (Ed.), *Moral development and behavior: Theory research and social issues* (pp. 124–144). New York: Holt, Rinehart and Winston.

Hoffman, M. L. (1981). Is altruism part of human nature? *Journal of Personality and Social Psychology, 40*, 121–137.

Hoffman, M. L. (1982). Development of prosocial motivation: Empathy and guilt. In Eisenberg, N. (Ed.), *The development of prosocial behavior* (pp. 218–231). New York: Academic Press.

Hoffman, M. L., & Saltzstein, H. D. (1967). Parent discipline and the child's moral development. *Journal of Personality & Social Psychology, 5*, 45–57.

Hornstein, H.A. (1976). *Cruelty and kindness: A new look at aggression and altruism*. Englewood Cliffs, NJ: Prentice-Hall.

Isen, A. M., Horn, N., & Rosenhan, D. L. (1973). Effects of success and failure on children's generosity. *Journal of Personality and Social Psychology, 27*, 239–248.

Karylowski, J. (1976). Self esteem, similarity, liking and helping. *Personality and Social Psychology Bulletin, 2*, 71–74.

Karylowski, J. (1984). Focus of attention and altruism: endocentric and exocentric sources of altruistic behavior. In Staub, E., Bar-Tal, D., Karylowski, J., & Reykowski, J. (Eds.) *The development and maintenance of prosocial behavior. International perspectives* (pp. 139–155). New York: Plenum.

Kohlberg, L. (1969). Stage and sequence: The cognitive-developmental approach to socialization. In D. Goslin (Ed.), *Handbook of socialization theory and research* (pp. 347–480). Chicago: Rand McNally.

Krebs, D. L. (1975). Empathy and altruism. *Journal of Personality and Social Psychology, 32*, 1134–1146.

Lerner, M. J. (1960). *The belief in a just world: A fundamental delusion*. New York: Plenum.

Lewin, K. (1938). *The conceptual representation and measurement of psychological forces*. Durham, NC: Duke University Press.

Lewin, K. (1948). *Resolving social conflicts*. New York: Harper.

Lieberman, A. F. (1976). *The social competence of preschool children: Its relation to quality of attachment and to amount of exposure to peers in different preschool settings*. Unpublished doctoral dissertation, John Hopkins University.

Loban, W. (1953). A study of social sensitivity (sympathy) among adolescents. *Journal of Educational Psychology, 44*, 102–112.

London, P. (1970). The rescuers: Motivational hypotheses about Christians who saved Jews from the Nazis. In J. Macaulay & L. Berkowitz (Eds.), *Altruism and helping behavior* (pp. 241–251). New York: Academic Press.

Macoby, E. E. (1980). *Social development.* New York: Harcourt Brace Jovanovich.

McKinney, J. P. (1971). The development of values: Prescriptive or proscriptive? *Human Development, 14,* 71–80.

Mischel, W. (1968). *Personality and assessment.* New York: Wiley.

Mischel, W., & Peake, P. K. (1982). Beyond deja-vu in the search for cross-situational consistency. *Psychological Review, 89,* 730–755.

Olejnik, A. B., & McKinney, J. P. (1973). Parental value orientation and generosity in children. *Developmental Psychology, 8,* 311.

Peters, R. S. (1970). Concrete principles and the rational passions. In J. M. Gustafson, R. S. Peters, L. Kohlberg, B. Bettelheim, & K. Keniston, (Eds.), *Moral education: five lectures* (pp. 29–57). Cambridge: Harvard University Press.

Piaget, J., & Weil, A. (1951). The development in children of the idea of the homeland and of relations with other countries. *International Social Science Bulletin, 3,* 570.

Piliavin, J. A., Dividio, J. F., Goertner, S. L., & Clark, R. D. (1981). *Emergency intervention.* New York: Academic Press.

Radke-Yarrow, M. R., Zahn-Waxler, C., & Chapman, M. (1984). Children's prosocial dispositions and behavior. In P. H. Mussen (Ed.), *Carmichael's manual of child psychology* (4th ed.) (Vol. IV, pp. 469–545). New York: Wiley.

Reese, H. (1961). Relationships between self-acceptance and sociometric choices. *Journal of Abnormal and Social Psychology, 62,* 472–474.

Reykowski, J., & Yarymovitz, M. (1976). *Elicitation of the prosocial orientation.* Unpublished manuscript. Warsaw, Poland: University of Warsaw.

Rosenhan, D. L., Salovey, P., Karylowski, J., & Hargis, K. (1981). Emotion and altruism. In J. P. Rushton & R. M. Sorrentino (Eds.), *Altruism and helping behavior* (pp. 233–251) Hillsdale, NJ: Erlbaum.

Rubin, Z., & Peplau, L. A. (1973). Belief in a just world and reactions to another's lot: A study of participants in the national draft lottery. *Journal of Social Issues, 29,* 73–93.

Rubin, Z., & Peplau, L. A. (1975). Who believes in a just world? *Journal of Social Issues, 31,* 65–89.

Sagi, A., & Hoffman, J. L. (1976). Empathic distress in the newborn. *Developmental Psychology, 12,* 175–176.

Sanford, R. N. (1973). Authoritarian personality in contemporary perspective. In Knutson, J. N. (Ed.), *Handbook of political psychology* (pp. 139–171). San Francisco: Jossey-Bass.

Schwartz, S. H., Feldman, K. A., Brown, M. E., & Heingarter, A. (1969). Some personality correlates of conduct in two situations of moral conflict. *Journal of Personality, 37,* 41–57.

Schwartz, S. H., & Howard, J. (1984). Internalized values as motivators of altruism. In Staub, E., Bar-Tal, D., Karylowski, J., & Reykowski, J. (Eds.), *The development and maintenance of prosocial behavior. International perspectives* (pp. 229–257). New York: Plenum.

Shaffer, D. R. (1979). *Social and personality development.* Monterey, CA: Brooks-Cole.

Simner, M. L. (1971). Newborn's response to the cry of another infant. *Developmental Psychology, 5,* 136–150.

Slavson, S. R. (1965). *Reclaiming the delinquent.* New York: Free Press.

Smithson, M., Amato, P. R., & Pearce, P. (1983). *Dimensions of helping behavior.* New York: Pergamon.

Sroufe, L. A. (1979). The coherence of individual development: Early care, attachment, and subsequent developmental issues. *American Psychologist, 34,* 834–841.

Staub, E. (1971). The learning and unlearning of aggression: The role of anxiety, empathy, efficacy and prosocial values. In J. Singer (Ed.), *The control of aggression and violence: Cognitive and physiological factors* (pp. 94–125). New York: Academic Press.

Staub, E. (1974). Helping a distressed person: Social, personality, and stimulus determinants. In L. Berkowitz (Ed.), *Advances in experimental social psychology* (Vol. 7, pp. 113–136). New York: Academic Press.

Staub, E. (1975). To rear a prosocial child: Reasoning, learning by doing, and learning by teaching others. In D. DePalma and J. Folley (Eds.), *Moral development: Current theory and research* (pp. 113–137). Hillsdale, NJ: Erlbaum.

Staub, E. (1978a). Predicting prosocial behavior: A model for specifying the nature of personality-situation interaction. In L. Pervin & M. Lewis (Eds.), *Internal and external determinants of behavior* (pp. 87–111). New York: Plenum.

Staub, E. (1978b). *Positive social behavior and morality: Vol. 1. Social and personal influences.* New York: Academic Press.

Staub, E. (1979). *Positive social behavior and morality: Vol. 2. Socialization and development.* New York: Academic Press.

Staub, E. (1980). Social and prosocial behavior: Personal and situational influences and their interactions. In E. Staub (Ed.), *Personality: Basic aspects and current research* (pp. 236–295). Englewood Cliffs, NJ: Prentice-Hall.

Staub, E. (1981). Promoting positive behavior in schools, in other educational settings, and in the home. In J. P. Rushton & R.M. Sorrentino (Eds.), *Altruism and helping behavior* (pp. 109–137). Hillsdale, NJ: Erlbaum.

Staub, E. (1982, June). Social evil: *The psychology of perpetrators and bystanders.* Presented at the meetings of the International Association of Political Psychology, Washington, DC.

Staub, E. (1984a). Steps toward a comprehensive theory of moral conduct: Goal orientation, social behavior, kindness and cruelty. In J. Gewirtz and W. Kurtines (Eds.), *Morality and moral development* (pp. 241–261). New York: Wiley-Interscience.

Staub, E. (1984b). Notes toward an interactionist–motivational theory of the determinants and development of prosocial behavior. In E. Staub, D. Bar-Tal, J. Karylowski, & J. Reykowski (Eds.), *The development and maintenance of prosocial behavior: International perspectives* (pp. 29–51). New York: Plenum.

Staub, E. (1985a). *Social behavior and moral conduct: A personal goal theory account of altruism and aggression.* Unpublished manuscript, Amherst: University of Massachusetts.

Staub, E. (1985b). The psychology of perpetrators and bystanders. *Political Psychology, 6,* 61–86.

Staub, E., Bar-Tal, D., Karylowski, J., & Reykowski, J. (Eds.), *The development and maintenance of prosocial behavior. International perspectives.* New York: Plenum.

Staub, E., & Feinberg, H. (1980). *Regularities in peer interaction, empathy, and sensitivity to others.* Presented at the symposium on the development of prosocial behavior and cognitions at the American Psychological Association Meeting, Montreal.

Stotland, E. (1969). Exploratory studies of empathy. In L. Berkowitz (Ed.), *Advances in experimental social psychology* (Vol. 4, pp. 271–313). New York: Academic Press.

Tajfel, H. (1982). Intergroup relations. In M. R. Rosenzweig and L. W. Porter (Eds.), *Annual review of psychology* (pp. 1–41). Palo Alto: Annual Reviews.

Theiss, A. (1983). *Violence. A problem for and of society.* Unpublished manuscript, Amherst: University of Massachusetts.

Thompson, W. R., & Grusec, J. (1970). Studies of early experience. In P. H. Mussen (Ed.), *Carmichael's manual of child psychology* (3rd ed.) (Vol. 2, pp. 567–657). New York: Wiley.

Toch, H. (1969). *Violent men.* Chicago: Aldine.

Weiner, B. (1980). A cognitive (attribution)–emotion–action model of motivated behavior: An analysis of judgments of help giving. *Journal of Personality and Social Psychology, 37*, 186–200.

Wilson, E. O. (1975). *Sociobiology: The new synthesis*. Cambridge, MA: Belknap Press (Harvard University Press).

Wilson, E. O. (1978). *On human nature*. Cambridge, MA: Harvard University Press.

Yarymovitz, M. (1977). Modification of self-worth and increment of prosocial sensitivity. *Polish Psychological Bulletin, 8*, 45–53.

Zahn-Waxler, C., & Radke-Yarrow, M. (1982). The development of altruism: Alternative research strategies. In Eisenberg, N. (Ed.), *The development of prosocial behavior*. New York: Academic Press.

6 Early organization of altruism and aggression: developmental patterns and individual differences

*E. Mark Cummings, Barbara Hollenbeck,
Ronald Iannotti, Marian Radke-Yarrow,
and Carolyn Zahn-Waxler*

Children in transition from infancy to childhood are learning rapidly about their social environment and social relationships. Their social initiations and communications are increasing in number and variety, and their level of understanding of such events is changing as well. The intricacies of giving, defending, asserting, receiving, aggressing, and negotiating begin to appear in the stream of their behavior. Individual children are soon distinguishable in their patterns of social interaction. Investigators have not found it easy to identify how prosocial and antisocial behaviors emerge along a developmental trajectory and how they become organized into adaptive and maladaptive patterns. Our interest here is in investigating patterns of development as well as individual differences in altruistic and aggressive behaviors in young children.

The concentration of research with regard to altruism and aggression has been on middle and later childhood (see reviews by Radke-Yarrow, Zahn-Waxler and Chapman, 1983, on altruism, and by Parke and Slaby, 1983, on aggression). When these behaviors have been observed in the 2- and 3-year old, there has been a tendency to attribute less than full intentionality to them. Rather, they have been conceived as random, incidental acts independent of later patterns of social behaviors. As research of recent years has greatly elaborated our knowledge of infants' and young children's social sensitivities and capacities, there has been greater interest in the early manifestations of altruism and aggression (e.g., the work of Rheingold, Hay, & West, 1976; Yarrow and Waxler, 1977; and Zahn-Waxler and Radke-Yarrow, 1982, on prosocial behavior; of Hay & Ross, 1982, on aggression) and in the predictive value of these early behaviors as precursors of later social behaviors. The studies reported here investigate both classes of behavior. Our focus is on (1) the form and organization of

165

aggression and altruism during the early years of life, (2) the stabilities and continuities in behaviors, and (3) the relations between altruism and aggression and between these behaviors and other characteristics of the child.

Altruism and aggression have been defined in a variety of ways. One criterion for prosocial behavior is action that aids or benefits another person (see review by Radke-Yarrow et al., 1983). To this definition are sometimes added stipulations concerning underlying motives or intentions. For example, an act of generosity may or may not qualify as altruistic, depending on whether it was intended as a self-serving manipulation of another or as an act performed without anticipation of external reward. Similarly, aggression has been defined both behaviorally and in terms of underlying motives. If altruism and aggression are defined in terms of outcomes, that is, whether children's behavior results in benefits or injuries to another, both altruism and aggression appear to be present by the second year of life. For example, in an observational study, Rheingold et al. (1976) found that most 18-month-old children shared something with another person on one or more occasions. Toddlers have also been observed to show cooperative behaviors (Eckerman, Whatley, & Kutz, 1975). Prosocial responding to another's distress (provision of objects, help, comfort) has also been found among 18- to 24-month-old children by Zahn-Waxler and Radke-Yarrow (1982). In the latter study, reparations for acts of interpersonal aggression were also observed; such attempts to undo harm may be taken as additional evidence for the early emergence of a moral sense or of standards of interpersonal behavior. Furthermore, the very act of reparation for aggression suggests some possible common origins or connections between acts of altruism and aggression.

Few studies, however, have been directed specifically toward analysis of children's aggression during the early years of life. The work of Hay and Ross (1982) is a rare exception to this generalization; it has provided evidence for the hypothesis that by 2 years of age, children's conflicts have social significance. That is, toddlers fight over many of the same things that adults do. Toddlers quarrel with playmates over space and resources and over social issues, including the degree of control they have over their peers' activities, the intrusiveness of their peers' social acts, and their peers' violations of social norms (Hay, 1984). The early potential for violation of norms for interpersonal behavior in promoting conflict and aggression again hints at the very early origins of a subtle and complex interplay of prosocial and agonistic behaviors.

Relatively little is known with regard to the coherence and organization of early altruism or aggression or the extent to which their early forms are predictive of prosocial and antisocial behaviors later in development. There is evidence of modest to moderate consistency across situations in altruism among preschool-age and elementary school-age children. Generally, there are positive associations in the range of +.20 to +.40 (see review by Radke-Yarrow et al., 1983). Stability of altruism over time has not often been investigated. Mussen and Eisenberg-Berg (1977) describe two studies examining stability in the early years. Block and Block (cited in Mussen & Eisenberg-Berg, 1977) found 4-year-olds identified by their preschool teachers as exhibiting prosocial characteristics to be more generous in a structured task 1 year later. Baumrind (cited in Mussen & Eisenberg-Berg, 1977) observed social responsibility and altruism in nursery school children and again 5–6 years later, when the children were in elementary school. She also found significant stability in these behaviors.

Recently Hay and Ross (1982) reported stability of aggression in 21-month-old children over a short span of time. Observations were made over 4 consecutive days. Initiations of conflict during the first 3 days were found to predict initiations of conflict with same or different partners on a fourth day. Stability over time in aggression has frequently been reported for boys, but the data are mainly on older children (Parke & Slaby, 1983). In a review of 16 longitudinal studies of aggression in males, Olweus (1979) concluded that stable individual differences in aggression have been demonstrated in preschool-age children. Loeber (1982) reports that consistency across situations in aggression predicts chronic aggressive patterns.

Relatively little information is available on developmental transformations in modes of expression of altruism and aggression during the early years of childhood (see review by Radke-Yarrow et al., 1983). With regard to aggression, a general trend is evident between very early childhood and school age toward decreased physical and increased verbal aggression (see review by Parke & Slaby, 1983). Again, however, research has provided little detail concerning changes in the content and occasion of aggressive behavior over the course of early childhood.

Studies of associations between altruism and aggression reveal no simple patterns. Conflicting theories, as well as complex findings, mark the literature relating aggression and altruism. For example, Murphy (1937) proposed that there should be a positive association between aggression and altruism in young children, as both are reflective of more outgoing or sociable personalities. Feshbach and Feshbach (1969) argued that children who are more empathic, and thus more responsive to others' distress, should be less aggressive because of the discomfort produced by pain experienced by others. Variations in the relations between altruism and aggression (e.g., Feshbach & Feshbach, 1969; Friedrich & Stein, 1973; Yarrow & Waxler, 1976; Barrett & Yarrow, 1977) depending on children's sex, age, and the precise dimensions of altruistic and aggressive behavior, are suggestive of the varied cognitions and motivations involved (Radke-Yarrow, et al., 1983). These variations are summarized in Table 6.1.

Table 6.1. *Interrelations of aggression and altruism*

Investigations	Sample characteristics	Measures
A. *Significant positive associations between altruism and aggression*		
Murphy (1937)	3–5-year-old girls and boys	Ratings of sympathy and aggression
Muste & Sharpe (1947)	3–5-year-old girls and boys	Sympathy and aggression
Friedrich & Stein (1973)	Preschool-age girls and boys	Interpersonal aggression and cooperation
Barrett & Yarrow (1977)	5–8-year-old girls and boys	Assertiveness and prosocial behavior
B. *Significant negative associations between altruism & aggression*		
Harris & Siebel (1975)	Third-grade girls and boys	Sharing and aggression against objects (a clown) (marginal association)
Rutherford & Mussen (1968)	4-year-old boys	Generosity and rating of aggression
Barrett (1979)	5–8-year-old girls and boys	Aggression and prosocial behavior (for boys high in aggression)
C. *Inconsistent or nonsignificant associations between altruism and aggression*		
Feshbach & Feshbach (1969)	4–7-year-old girls and boys	Positive association between ratings of aggression and empathy (4–5-year-old boys) Negative association between ratings of aggression and empathy (6–7: year-old boys)
Bryant & Crockenberg (1980)	5- and 11-year-old girls	No consistent associations between prosocial behavior and verbal aggression
Yarrow & Waxler (1976)	3–7½-year-old girls and boys	Positive association between aggression and prosocial behavior (for boys low on aggression) Negative association between aggression and prosocial behavior (for boys high on aggression)

The patterns of findings are compatible with earlier generalizations and interpretations about associations between altruism and aggression (Radke-Yarrow & Zahn-Waxler, 1982). Associations are positive, negative, mixed, or nonexistent, depending on qualitative characteristics of the prosocial and antisocial behaviors, or characteristics of the child and setting. If aggression is infrequent, is assertive more than hostile, and for the most part is situationally determined, this kind of aggressive quality seems to accompany the ability to intervene on behalf of another person. For children who are probably basically well adjusted in their social relationships, interpersonal aggression may provide opportunities for teaching and learning about conflict resolution and the consequences for others of one's own hurtful actions. Such experiences, in turn, may contribute to the development of sensitivity to the feelings of others and to prosocial actions. When aggression is more truly hostile and chronic (for reasons that are not yet fully understood), the resulting anger and turmoil may actively preclude expressions of empathy and concern. Cumulative research findings also suggest that the incompatibility between altruism and aggression is more likely to be seen in older than in younger children. Furthermore, there is a tendency for patterns of association to emerge more clearly for boys than for girls. (See Chapter 7 for a discussion of further interpretations of associations between altruism and aggression.)

Emotionality of the child may function as a common mediator of both altruism and aggression. Typically, however, altruism and aggression have been examined separately in relationship to the child's affective state. These studies also demonstrate no simple relationships between altruism or aggression and other dimensions of the child's social and emotional functioning. One of the few naturalistic studies to address relationships between persisting affective states and empathic behaviors was performed by Strayer (1980). She found that frequencies of children's expressions of emotion in a preschool setting, over an 8-week period, were associated with differences in empathic expressions and behaviors. Children who more frequently displayed happiness were more likely to respond sympathetically to others, whereas those who more frequently evidenced sad emotions ranked low in empathy. Momentary affective states in relation to altruism have more often been studied. In general, an induced positive affect, such as asking the child to think about a happy circumstance, has been found to increase sharing in an experimental situation (Barnett & Bryan, 1974; Isen, Heim, & Rosenhan, 1973; Moore, Underwood, & Rosenhan, 1973: Rosenhan, Underwood, & Moore, 1977; Rushton & Littlefield, 1979; Underwood, Froming & Moore, 1977). The results regarding the effects of sad thoughts or experienced failure on altruism are less consistent (see review by Radke-Yarrow, Zahn-Waxler, & Chapman, 1983). Some studies have found negative associations between sadness and altruism. A critical distinction may be whether children's sad thoughts tend to be about themselves or about others. When children think of another's distress, rather than their own, their level of generosity is comparable to that expressed when a positive affect has been induced (Barnett, King, & Howard, 1979).

Limiting the literature to that concerned with the 2- and 3-year-olds, few data can be found on the relation between emotionality or temperament and altruism and aggression. Thomas, Chess, and Birch (1968) found behavioral problems (including aggression) to be associated with more intense, persistent, distractible, irregular, and active behavior and with lower thresholds and low adaptability at early ages. With older children, a number of temperament–aggression links have been reported. Thus, Olweus (1980) found boys' temperament in early years, assessed as a composite of general activity level and intensity of temperament (calm/hot-tempered), to predict peer ratings of habitual interpersonal aggressive behavior in adolescence. Harris and Siebel (1975) found that boys tend to be more aggressive after any affect induction, whether positive or negative, whereas girls are less aggressive after each affect induction. Feshbach and Feshbach (Chapter 7, this volume) found that boys who report intense euphoric feelings when viewing other children in situations of happiness and pride are rated by their teachers as antisocial and by their peers and themselves as aggressive. Boys who report intense dysphoric feelings when viewing children in dysphoric situations tend to be helpful individuals.

The research literature on aggression and altruism, concentrated as it is on older children, necessarily cannot deal with many issues regarding the origins of prosocial and aggressive behavior. Investigation of the emergence of these behaviors during the very early childhood years is needed to provide an empirical basis for understanding of these issues. This chapter focuses on several issues pertinent to the early organization of altruism and aggression: (1) styles and patterns of altruism and aggression, (2) the continuity over time and consistency across settings of these behaviors, and (3) broader personality organization, such as interrelations among altruism, aggression, and emotionality.

Procedures

The research reported on is derived from two studies of early manifestations of altruistic and aggressive behavior (Radke-Yarrow, Zahn-Waxler, Cummings, Strope, & Sebris, 1981; Zahn-Waxler & Radke-Yarrow, 1982; Cum-

mings, Iannotti, & Zahn-Waxler, 1985). The first study involves 24 children
(11 boys and 13 girls), aged 1–1½ years who are followed for a period of
9 months, and followed again for 3 months at 7 years of age. The subjects
of the second study are 46 2-year-old children (25 boys and 21 girls) seen
twice, a month apart. The families are middle-class, generally two-parent
families.

Study 1

The first study provides data on children's altruism and aggression in the
home. Our objective was to obtain a high-density sampling of data on each
child, that is, as many behavior samples as possible, with a continuous
assessment over enough time that one could comfortably speak of "usual"
behavior and also of "development." Conventional research strategies are
not well suited to obtaining large samples of altruistic and aggressive behavior in infants and toddlers. As neither behavior occurs with high frequency, traditional observation procedures pose problems. Furthermore,
the experimental manipulations characteristically used with older children
do not readily translate for use with very young children. The research
strategy adopted here was to train mothers as one would train research
assistants to provide on-the-spot descriptive behavioral records of incidents
likely to elicit altruism and aggression. Mothers were asked to tape-record
incidents in which children were exposed to emotions of distress in others
and to provide detailed narrative accounts of these events. These incidents
included situations of emotion caused by the child (child hits a playmate
with a brush) or observed by the child (child's brother falls off the high
chair, or child's mother is crying). This resulted in a substantial sampling
of children's interpersonal aggression incidents ($\bar{X} = 14.3$ incidents during
the toddler period and $\bar{X} = 3.5$ incidents during the school-age period)
and situations providing opportunities for prosocial responding ($\bar{X} = 88.4$
incidents during the toddler period and $\bar{X} = 26.8$ incidents during the
school-age period). In addition to these naturally occurring incidents, separate records were obtained where mothers simulated emotions (e.g., pain,
sadness, and anger) in specified circumstances. Each observation record
by the mother included a report of the emotional events, the child's emotional, verbal, and behavioral reactions to the events, and the interactions
of other persons, if any, with the child. (A detailed treatment of procedures,
training, and validity and reliability assessments for this technique of studying young children's responses in the home is presented in the review by
Zahn-Waxler & Radke-Yarrow, 1982.)

Study 2

The second study used a laboratory design combining experimental and naturalistic procedures. On each of two laboratory visits, held 1 month apart, each child was observed in a half-hour play session with a familiar peer, once a peer of the same sex, and once of the opposite sex.

Peer play was observed in a room furnished as a living room–kitchenette. The play setting was patterned after a typical peer play session in the home, with mothers accessible but not highly involved. At the start of each session, mothers were asked to sit on a sofa located at one side of the living room and were provided with other activities. They were asked not to initiate interactions with children and not to interrupt children's interactions with each other, unless something occurred that made them uncomfortable or that they felt was dangerous. A standard set of toys (a rocking horse, a ball, a pull toy, a stacking toy, a doll, a hammer and ball toy, and a toy telephone) were placed on the floor before the start of each session. Children were permitted to explore these surroundings freely throughout the session.

During peer play, several experimental manipulations were introduced to alter the environmental context in which the social interactions took place: (1) changes in the affective tone of the background environment, followed by (2) a brief departure by the mother. To accomplish the former condition, two staff members, not familiar to the children, carried out some routine cleanup chores in a corner of the room. During this process, they first engaged in friendly, prosocial verbal interaction. This was followed by an angry quarrel. Later, reconciliation occurred. It is assumed that the affective climate constitutes an important set of stimulus conditions that have an impact on children. For the purposes of this study, such emotion-inducing events were introduced and interspersed with regular activities in order to heighten the probability of observing aggression and altruism in these young children. The same sequence of events was used in both sessions. The specific manipulations are outlined in Table 6.2.

Each child in the second study was also seen individually, following the peer play sessions. The child was exposed to events involving simulated, but seemingly natural, emotional distress (pain, crying). One simulation was performed by the mother and two by female experimenters. A tape-recorded infant cry was also played from an adjacent room. Elaboration of the procedures and descriptions of reliabilities may be found in Zahn-Waxler, Cummings, McKnew and Radke-Yarrow (1984) and Cummings et al. (1985). Here the interest was in the child's prosocial responding.

Table 6.2. *Contents for peer interactions in study 2*

Period	Duration (min)	Event
1	5 minutes	No intervention
2	5 minutes	Simulation of pleasant interaction between two adults
3	5 minutes	No intervention
4	5 minutes	Simulation of anger between two adults
5	5 minutes	No intervention
6	2 minutes	Two adults return and reconcile
7	1 minute	One mother leaves the room
8	1 minute	The other mother leaves
9	4 minutes	Both mothers return

Provoked aggression was observed when an unfamiliar adult unexpectedly took a turn with a toy from the child in the midst of play.

Findings

Study 1

The two research strategies have contributed differentially to information on the form, continuity, and organization of altruistic and aggressive behaviors in their emergent stages. The home study provides information on some of the features or styles of altruism and aggression. In addition to cataloging the instrumental characteristics of the children's behaviors (e.g., sharing, helping, hitting, pushing), the children's behaviors were coded on dimensions assumed to have an important bearing on their meaning, motives, and intentions.

Analyses of aggressive behavior are considered first. Each incident of aggression recorded by the mother was rated on (1) intensity of aggression, (2) persistence on the part of the child, (3) escalation in the aggression, (4) whether the aggression was accompanied by expressions of emotion (distress or anger or positive affect), and (5) whether the child offered reparation to the victim.

Significant variability was found among the children on each of the dimensions. Approximately one-third of all aggression incidents were rated as high in intensity, one-third were accompanied by distress or anger, and 27% were accompanied by laughter or smiling. Reparative behavior for their own assaults on others was attempted in fewer than 20% of incidents.

Table 6.3. *Correspondence in features of aggressive and altruistic behaviors*

Aggression		Altruism	
Feature	Stability.	Feature	Stability
Frequency	.21	Frequency	.68[b]
Intensity	.67[a]	Affective, empathic	.72[b]
Persistence	.09	Hypothesis testing	.66[b]
Escalation	−.10	Ritualistic	.51[a]
Distress or anger	.44[c]	Aggressive defense of victim	.33
Positive affect	.05	Unemotional, passive	.53[b]
Reparation to victim	.71[a]	Actively nonprosocial	.58[a]

Note: Associations in the toddler period: Comparisons of first and second half of 9 months of assessment.
[a] $p < .05$.
[b] $p < .01$.
[c] $p < .10$.

Reports for boys and girls did not differ. Because sampling of incidents by different mothers is not uniform, we are not relying on this strategy to establish frequencies in a normative sense. Our primary focus is, therefore, on the intrachild analyses of styles of responding.

The first and second halves of the 9-month observational period were examined separately to determine patterns of stability or continuity over time. (The developmental changes in children's prosocial responses and in their reparations following their own acts of interpersonal aggression are described in Zahn-Waxler and Radke-Yarrow, 1982.) Correlations between the two time periods are presented in Table 6.3. Significant stability is evident in the intensity of aggression, the extent to which it is accompanied by distress or anger, and the likelihood of making reparation following acts of aggression. Whether these stabilities are expressive of inborn temperament or of infant socialization, we assume that they would set in motion, very early, different patterns of stimulation to parents and, probably, different kinds of handling by parents.

The questions we have just explored for aggression of young children were investigated for altruistic behavior. Again, styles of response suggestive of underlying processes were the bases for analyzing the child's altruism. All incidents involving overt attempts by the child to help another person were coded. Of the total incidents of distress reported by mothers, overt helping attempts occurred in 39% of them. Although all the children were coded as altruistic on one or more occasions, there was considerable

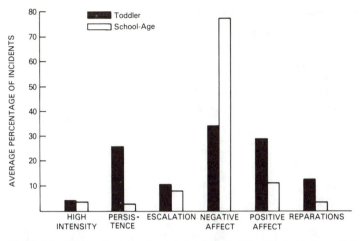

Figure 6.1. Changes in style of aggression from toddler to school-age periods.

variation in the tendency of children to respond helpfully (from 1% of incidents to 82% of incidents of distress).

Helping or altruistic style in each incident was coded as (1) affective, empathic arousal (emotional concern), (2) problem-solving or hypothesis testing (e.g., "You bump your head?" "You sad?"), (3) ritualistic behavior (e.g., "God bless you" following a sneeze), or (4) aggression in defense of the victim (e.g., child hits perpetrator). Where someone's distress brought out (5) an actively nonprosocial response (aggression or callousness regarding the victim), or (6) an unemotional passive response, this too was coded. When the individual child's styles of responding over the first 4½ months of observation were compared with ratings covering the second 4½-month period, the correlations (as for aggression) showed a high degree of stability (see Table 6.3).

Five years later, the families were contacted and again asked to make systematic reports on their children for a period of 3 months. They were also seen in a laboratory session in which simulations of distress and stories were used to probe children's prosocial and antisocial response tendencies (Zahn-Waxler, Iannotti, & Chapman, 1982). Twenty-two of the 24 families cooperated in the follow-up evaluation. Figures 6.1 and 6.2 illustrate developmental patterns in styles of aggression and altruism at the two ages, as measured by the mother's observation and reports. Children modified the characteristic manner in which they expressed aggression. In general, school-age children, although not different statistically from toddlers in the intensity of their aggression, were significantly less likely to persist, once

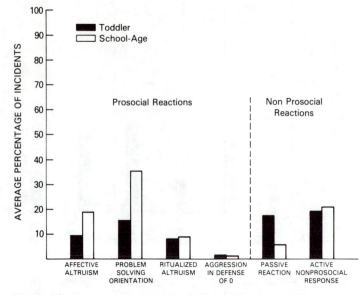

Figure 6.2. Changes in style of prosocial behavior from toddler to school-age periods.

they had produced a response in the victim [$F(1,15) = 26.43, p < .001$], were more likely to show anger or distress while aggressing [$F(1,15) = 25.52, p < .001$], and were less likely to smile or laugh as they hit someone [$F(1,15) = 12.43, p < .01$]. In addition, they were less likely to offer reparation after they had physically attacked someone [$F(1,15) = 9.01, p < .01$]. The aggression of the older children seems to be more purposeful, serious, and deliberate than the aggression of the toddlers. Boys and girls did not differ in the intensity of their aggression as toddlers, but boys were marginally more intensely aggressive during the school-age period [$F(1,15) = 4.15, p < .06$]. For altruism, profiles are similar at the two ages (see Fig. 6.2). Virtually no developmental changes occur, except for a problem-solving approach to distress, which is significantly ($p < .05$) more characteristic of the 7-year-olds.

Comparisons of the toddler period and the school-age period for individual children's styles of altruism show significant associations for overt attempts to help [$r(15) = .47, p < .05$], for unemotional passive reactions [$r(15) = .53, p < .05$], and for hypothesis testing [$r(15) = .40, p < .10$]. For aggression, a significant relation was found for reparation across time periods [$r(15) = .45, p < .05$]. One might conclude from these analyses that the child's early organization of behavior has some, albeit limited, predictive value for later development.

There are, however, alternative ways to examine continuity. Our next analytic approach attempted to evaluate components of prosocial and aggressive behavior of the individual child in a way that meaningfully represents the organization of behavior for that particular child. Thus, from the dimensions already described plus new ratings of such dimensions as "guilty" reactions and effectiveness of prosocial behavior, we derived a profile for each child, at each age. (Some measures were based on laboratory as well as the home assessments at follow-up evaluation.) This approach is described more fully by Radke-Yarrow et al. (1981). These more clinically based descriptions make it possible to examine the data for continuities in (1) important unique or idiosyncratic characteristics of children that do not occur often or in enough children to warrant correlational analysis, and (2) patterns of behavior that are logical and congruent but not identical at the two ages. An example of the latter is a child who is indiscriminately highly aggressive as a toddler but who has learned to channel this aggression by age 7 and who is now at the top of his or her group on physical aggression directed toward perpetrators of distress. On the basis of these analyses, 17 of the 24 children had compelling themes of continuity. These are seen, for example, in correspondences over time in a few children for each of the following: extreme affective intensity in altruism or aggression, in cold avoidance behavior in the face of others' distress, in combative defense of others, and so on. The following description provides further illustrations of continuities in children's patterns of aggression and altruism. Child A, age 1½–2 years, is characteristically made anxious by O's distress; he intervenes little or weakly and shows low-intensity affect and low reparation. At time 2, the same qualities are coded, except aggression has increased. Child B is initially aloof, affectively uncommitted, and avoidant of O's distress. At time 2, there is minimal concern for someone else's distress. Child C responds (T1 and T2) intensely with both affective prosocial and aggressive behavior, in addition to responding to O's distress with ambivalence. Child D is unambivalently empathic and competent in caring for others in need, both as a toddler and as a school-age child. This analytic procedure suggests that consistent patterns of coping with distress (e.g., empathy, guilt, and hostility), when broadly defined, may be deeply rooted in early developmental processes.

There was no strong evidence for continuity between laboratory assessments of children at age 7 and home measures at either age period, perhaps because the potential recipients of altruism in the laboratory were unfamiliar to the children, whereas in the home recipients were often well known. One specific response pattern noteworthy for its consistency, however, was the manner in which the child dealt with personal responsibility for another person's distress. The concept of guilt is of special developmental interest because of its potential common tie to concepts of both altruism and aggression. Children's reparations for hurting someone reflect self-attributions of responsibility that are realistic (justified guilt). Such reparative behaviors showed consistency over time. Guilt feelings also take another form, namely, misplaced self-responsibility and apparent remorse for acts the child has not committed (unjustified guilt). There was evidence of consistency over time in unjustified, misplaced guilt. Such guilt-prone behavior was in the repertoire of six toddlers. At 7 years of age, nine children manifested guilt in projective tests done in the laboratory; of the original six toddlers who had shown misplaced guilt as toddlers, five were included in this group. Commonalities were found in the rearing histories of the children who exhibited guilt: their mothers tended to use strong affective inductive methods of discipline (see Zahn-Waxler, Radke-Yarrow, & King, 1979).

The moderate consistency seen in both the altruism and aggression of such very young children suggests that these may be rather enduring features of personality that are laid down early in life. Such stability also suggests the feasibility of examining possible interconnections between altruism and aggression. The few patterns of association that occurred were high in magnitude. For girls, there was a correlation between intensity of aggression and reparation for aggression [$r(11) = .58, p < .05$]. For boys, there was an association between intensity of aggression and altruistic reactions to others' distress [$r(9) = .67, p < .05$].

Study 2

The laboratory study corroborates some of the findings of the home study and extends analyses to other issues as well. It explores stability, interconnections, and possible mediators of aggression and altruism as well as focusing more extensively on early patterns of sex differences. The emotions and behaviors coded may be briefly described as follows:

1. Frequency and duration of aggression during peer interactions were coded as were the following components of aggression:
   a. Interpersonal physical aggression (hitting, kicking, pushing)
   b. Interpersonal object struggles (attempts to grab or take another's possession)
   c. Aggression against property (throwing things against the floor or kicking toys)
   d. Intense aggression (aggression that was violent or potentially dangerous)
2. Prosocial or altruistic acts during peer interactions were coded each time the child was observed to help, share, cooperate, provide comfort or affection, or provide noninterpersonal aid (e.g., cleaning up).

3. Ratings of emotional expressiveness were made at the end of peer interactions during each session (scale of 1–4). Several types of emotions were coded:
   a. Positive affect (laughter, smiling, happy excitement, expressed facially, vocally, or bodily)
   b. Anger (angry yelling, screaming facial expressions, complaints)
   c. Distress (crying, crankiness, concerned facial expressions)
   d. Emotionality that was a composite of a, b, and c.

Global ratings of altruism and aggression were also made at the end of peer play. Children's aggressive and altruistic responses in standard distress situations were coded in categories parallel to those used for peer interactions. Summed altruism scores (i.e., of help, share, cooperate, comfort) were obtained for each of the four distress simulations. Object conflict with the adult was rated for intensity of aggression. Positive affect, anger, and distress during each of the distress simulations were coded as well.

In the home study, gender-based differences in frequencies and styles of aggression and altruism were virtually nonexistent. In the laboratory study, however, there were some reliable gender-based differences in altruism, aggression, and emotionality. Out of many possible comparisons, several significant differences were obtained. Boys exhibited more destruction of property than was shown by girls [$F(1,44) = 21.16, p < .001$]. In addition, boys showed marginally more physical aggression (hitting and pushing) than did girls [$F(1,44) = 3.59, p < .10$]. No gender-based differences, were found, however, in overall levels of interpersonal aggression (i.e., object struggles plus physical aggression). Boys and girls differed on three of nine measures of emotionality: During peer play sessions, boys showed more positive affect and overall emotionality ($p < .05$), and during conflict with the adult, they showed more distress ($p < .01$) than did girls. Two marginally significant differences were found: Girls were somewhat more responsive to infant cries than boys [$F(1,44) = 3.50, p < .10$], and boys were somewhat more reactive to their mothers'.distress than were girls [$F(1,44) = 3.94, p < .10$].

Boys and girls often differed in analyses reflecting features of behavioral organization: Boys and girls differed with regard to how their behaviors changed with the situation, how their aggression and altruism related to each other, and how these behaviors were associated with other personal characteristics. Boys' aggressive behavior showed continuity across situations (Table 6.4) in which they were interacting with different persons (same sex versus opposite sex peers, peers versus adults). By contrast, the aggressive behavior of girls appeared to be more situationally determined. Other studies (Loeber, 1982) have shown that highly aggressive children tend to be more consistent with regard to aggression across settings; there-

Table 6.4. *Stability of total aggression and altruism across different situations*

Comparisons of	Boys	Girls
Aggression		
Aggression toward boy peers and girl peers	.78[b]	.27
Aggression toward both peers, and in object conflict with adults	.48[a]	.07
Prosocial behavior		
Altruism toward boy peers and girl peers	.52[b]	.16
Altruism toward peers and altruism in standard distress situations	.02	.30
Altruism toward distressed mother and distressed stranger	−.18	.46[a]
Altruism toward distressed stranger and crying infant	.56[b]	.25

[a] $p < .05$.
[b] $p < .01$.

fore, higher correlations for boys here might be attributed, in part, to the somewhat higher levels of aggression in boys. Both boys and girls showed some consistency in their prosocial behavior across situations.

An important issue of behavioral organization concerns the relations between aggression and prosocial behavior. The correlations presented in Table 6.5 are associations based on the children's aggressive and altruistic behavior with peers. The correlations shown in Table 6.6 are between children's aggression toward peers, property, and adults, and altruism in the standard distress situations. The correlations between frequency scores for each of these behaviors most often are nonsignificant for boys and girls. Associations emerge when distinctions are made within aggressive and prosocial responding. One basic distinction concerns the intensity of the aggression. When aspects of aggression indicative of intensity (duration, escalation, or direct ratings of intensity) were considered, associations of aggression with prosocial behavior (comforting of others in emotional distress) were significant and positive for boys. This relation held whether prosocial responding was assessed in interaction with peers (Table 6.5) or in standard situations with adults and infants (Table 6.6); this also provides a replication of the association between altruism and aggression found for boys in the home study. For girls, intensity of aggression was an important factor in association with prosocial responding but only in peer interactions in which girls' intensive aggression was associated with high reparation for aggression and with cooperation. Frequency of aggression also predicted their reparation. The reaction suggests that young girls, more than boys, may attempt to undo their aggression with good behavior. Thus, the pat-

Table 6.5. *Relations between components of aggression and altruism between peers*[a]

	Boys					Girls				
Aggression	Reparation for aggression	Sharing	Help	Cooperation	Total altruism	Reparation for aggression	Sharing	Help	Cooperation	Total altruism
Object struggles										
Frequency	—	—	—	—	—	.51[b]	—	—	—	—
Duration	—	—	—	—	.60[c]	.42[b]	—	—	.50[b]	—
% escalation	—	—	—	—	.39[b]	.46[b]	—	—	.50[b]	—
Physical aggression										
Frequency	—	—	—	—	—	.70[c]	—	—	—	—
Duration	—	—	—	—	—	—	—	—	—	—

[a] A dash indicates a nonsignificant correlation.
[b] $p < .05$.
[c] $p < .01$.

Table 6.6. *Relations between peer aggression and altruism in standard distress situations*[a]

	Boys				Girls			
Aggression	To mother	To adult stranger	To infant cry	Total Altruism	To mother	To adult stranger	To infant cry	Total Altruism
Interpersonal aggression toward peers								
Frequency	—	—	—	—	—	—	—	—
Intensity	.46[b]	—	.39[b]	.55[c]	—	—	—	—
Aggression towards property (frequency)	—	.48[b]	.55[c]	.42[b]	—	—	—	—
Aggression in object conflict with adult	—	—	.52[c]	.37[d]	.48[b]	—	—	.39[d]

[a] A dash indicates a nonsignificant correlation.
[b] $p < .05$.
[c] $p < .01$.
[d] $p < .10$.

Table 6.7. *Relations among aggression, altruism, and emotional behavior*[a]

	Aggression		Altruism	
Emotional behavior	Boys	Girls	Boys	Girls
Ratings in peer interaction				
Positive affect	.52[c]	—	—	—
Distress affect	—	—	—	—
Overall emotional expressiveness	.45[b]	—	.51[b]	—
Ratings in object conflict with adult				
Positive affect	.44[b]	—	—	.46[b] ·
Distress affect	.41[b]	—	.44[b]	—
Overall emotional expressiveness	.56[c]	—	.52[c]	—
Rating in standard distress situations				
Positive affect	—	—	—	—
Distress affect	—	—	—	—
Overall emotional expressiveness	—	—	.39[b]	—

[a] Aggression is a composite measure across both peer sessions. Prosocial behavior is total frequency of altruistic responding in all standard distress situations. A dash indicates a non-significant correlation.
[b] $p < .05$.
[c] $p < .01$.

terns of association for girls, too, provide a replication of the home study that, with a different sample of children and very different methods for measuring altruism and aggression, also yielded this gender-linked connection between aggression and reparation.

Our last comparison of boys and girls is in regard to indices of emotionality in relation to prosocial and aggressive behavior (see Table 6.7). For boys, levels of aggression were positively related to several measures of positive and negative affect across different settings. Similarly, for boys, high levels of prosocial behavior were related to high levels of emotional expressiveness. No similar patterns emerged for girls.

Discussion

Two studies using two very different research strategies have provided unmistakable displays of both aggressive and prosocial behavior in toddler-age and school-age children. Stylistic features of these behaviors, more than their frequencies, show consistencies over this age period, as well as indications of continuity from toddlerhood to school age. The intentionality and organization of these early manifestations and the significance of these prosocial and antisocial behaviors as starting points along a developmental pathway seem well documented.

The organization of altruism and aggression appears to be distinctly different for girls and boys. Patterns of intense interpersonal aggressive behavior in boys are associated with prosocial responsivity in the form of comforting others in distress. These two behaviors have in common a heightened reactivity to social stimuli. The aggression shown by these children occurred most commonly after the conflict and aggression simulated by the adults. And the altruistic responses to another's distress typically followed signals for needed help. One might speculate that the aggressive 2-year-old boys, who are also emotional or easily aroused and who are prosocial in response to another's distress, have the potential for becoming highly sensitive sympathetic children or highly sensitive antisocial children. The environments to which they are exposed or the persons with whom they must cope may be significant determinants of the boys' development.

Among girls the pattern of relations between altruism and aggression is quite different. Aggressiveness among girls is associated with reparation for their own aggressive misconduct, but is not associated with a generally greater sensitivity to another's distress. Furthermore, it does not appear that the specification of an intensity dimension of aggression is critical in relations between altruism and aggression, as was the case with boys. If the connection between reparation and aggression is a causal one, the feelings of guilt or a misplaced sense of personal responsibility may be a precursor of altruism in girls. In many societies, women more than men have been assigned the role of volunteer and provider of emotional care "without thought of recompense." Indeed, assumption of this role requires a very deeply engrained sense of personal responsibility for resolving the distresses and problems of others. We are perhaps already seeing the outcome of the very early transmissions of these patterns. It is reasonable to hypothesize that aggression by girls especially cannot be tolerated because it will interfere so fundamentally with later caregiver functions. One way to heighten this sense of responsibility is to induce guilt for interpersonal aggression and transgressions.

The broader question concerns the extent to which altruism, aggression, guilt, and emotionality are genetically based or are a product of the environment. Greater emotional reactivity as a significant dimension of early temperament has been suggested in some theoretical approaches to the concept of temperament. Rothbart and Derryberry (1981) define temperament as constitutional differences in reactivity and self-regulation. Goldsmith and Campos (1982) recently proposed a model that also incorporates concepts of reactivity and self-regulation as important to temperament.

Buss and Plomin (1975) postulate that there are four basic elements of temperament: emotionality, impulsiveness, sociability, and activity. Differences in temperament could thus underlie differences in early altruism and aggression and in emotionality. Differences in temperament are usually thought to be innate. That the individual differences and patterns observed in the present study appear so early invites a genetic interpretation. However, variations in socialization practices, particularly toward boys and girls, undoubtedly begin very early.

Gender-based differences in situationality of aggression are subject to similar interpretations. Among boys significant correlations were found across settings in aggression. None of these correlations was significant for girls. This gender-associated difference may exist for many reasons: Boys' aggression may be strongly temperamentally determined. Girls may be able to regulate their aggression, tuning it more sensitively to the specific arousing stimuli. Equally plausible again, however, is the interpretation that parents are likely to intervene and respond differentially to aggression in their boys and girls, even during the first years of life. As we have implied, overt aggression has traditionally been more strongly frowned upon in the behavior of girls. Although the definitive research on the differential socialization of emotions in boys and girls remains to be done, there are many hints and suggestions in the literature that anger and aggression in girls faces a different fate than does hostility in boys. For example, there is some evidence from experimental studies to indicate that sex stereotyping of boys and girls with regard to affect begins at the moment of birth. Condrey and Condrey (1976) found that a crying infant labeled a boy was perceived as angry, whereas the same infant labeled a girl was viewed as frightened or distressed. In a study of mothers' affective reactions to the emotions of their 3–6-month-old infants (Malatesta & Haviland, 1982), mothers commonly responded to boys' anger with a knitted brow (concern), whereas girls' anger was frequently responded to with an angry expression. Mothers show greater difficulty interpreting anger expressions in their preschool-age girls than in their boys and are likely to misinterpret the anger of their girls (Buck, 1975). If anger in girls is clearly not sanctioned, hence redirected and reinterpreted, this is just one of many mechanisms that could suppress their aggressivity and create different patterns of organization of prosocial and antisocial behaviors in boys and girls.

The finding of both greater altruism and aggression among young aggressive boys poses an intriguing question: If at an early age aggressive boys are more sensitive to another's distress, why do they appear to become less sensitive as they get older? Feshbach and Feshbach (1969) demonstrated such a shift, reporting that aggression is positively associated with empathy in 4–5-year-old boys but is negatively associated with empathy at 6–7 years of age. Other evidence shows that older aggressive boys are less, rather than more, altruistic.

One can speculate about factors that may be important: (1) Others notice and frequently respond with hostility to the greater aggression of aggressive boys, but tend to ignore their greater altruism, and (2) aggressive boys, partly as a consequence of greater hostility displayed by others toward them, develop negative images of others, resulting in reduced likelihood of prosocial responding. In line with this possibility are the findings by Dodge (1980) (see also Chapter 11) that aggressive boys are more often the objects of aggression and that there is a greater disposition by aggressive boys to attribute negative intent to others.

The complex findings on continuities, patterning, and styles of aggression and altruism in toddler-age children appear to reflect coherent underlying organizations of behavior. Current research constitutes a step toward the systematic delineation of these early behavioral patterns.

Acknowledgement

This chapter summarizes research from different projects conducted at the Laboratory of Developmental Psychology, NIMH. Authors are listed in alphabetical order.

References

Barnett, M. A., & Bryan, J. H. (1974). Effects of competition with outcome feedback on children's helping behavior. *Developmental Psychology, 10*: 838–842.

Barnett, M. A., King, L. M., & Howard, J. A. (1979). Inducing affect about self or other: Effects on generosity in children. *Developmental Psychology, 15*: 164–167.

Barrett, D. E. (1979). A naturalistic study of sex differences in children's aggression. *Merrill-Palmer Quarterly, 25*: 193–203.

Barrett, D. E., & Yarrow, M. R. (1977). Prosocial behavior, social inferential ability, and assertiveness in children. *Child Development, 48*: 475–481.

Bryant, B. K., & Crockenberg, S. B. (1980). Correlates and dimensions of prosocial behavior: A study of female siblings with their mothers. *Child Development, 51*: 529–544.

Buck, R. W. (1975). Nonverbal communication of affect in children. *Journal of Personal and Social Psychology, 31*: 644–653.

Buss, A. H., & Plomin, R. (1975). *A temperament theory of personality development.* New York: Wiley.

Condrey, J. C., & Condrey, S. (1976). Sex differences: A study of the eye of the beholder. *Child Development, 47*: 812–819.

Cummings, E. M., Iannotti, R. J., & Zahn-Waxler, C. (1985). The influence of conflict between adults on the emotions and aggression of young children. *Developmental Psychology, 21*, 3.

Dodge, K. A. (1980). Social cognition and children's aggressive behavior. *Child Development, 51*: 162–170.

Eckerman, C. O., Whatley, J. L., & Kutz, S. L. (1975). Growth of social play with peers during the second year of life. *Developmental Psychology, 11*: 42–49.

Feshbach, N. D., & Feshbach, S. (1969). The relationship between empathy and aggression in two age groups. *Developmental Psychology, 1*: 102–107.

Friedrich, L. K., & Stein, A. H. (1973). Aggressive and prosocial television programs and the natural behavior of preschool children. *Monographs of the Society for Research in Child Development*, 38(4, Serial No. 151).

Goldsmith, H. H., & Campos, J. J. (1982). Toward a theory of infant temperament. In R. N. Emde & R. J. Harmon (Eds.), *The development of attachment and affiliative systems* (pp. 161–185). New York: Plenum.

Harris, M. B., & Siebel, C. E. (1975). Affect, aggression, and altruism. *Developmental Psychology, 11*: 623–627.

Hay, D. F. (1984). Social conflict in early childhood. In G. Whitehurst (Ed.), *The annals of child development* (Vol. 1, pp. 1–44). Greenwich, CT: JAI Press.

Hay, D. F., & Ross, H. S. (1982). The social nature of early conflict. *Child Development, 53*: 105–113.

Isen, A. M., Horn, N., & Rosenhan, D. L. (1973). Effects of success and failure on children's generosity. *Journal of Personal and Social Psychology, 27*: 239–247.

Loeber, R. (1982). The stability of antisocial and delinquent child behavior: A review. *Child Development, 53*: 1431–1446.

Malatesta, C., & Haviland, J. (1982). Learning display rules: The socialization of emotion expression in infancy. *Child Development, 53*: 991–1003.

Moore, B. S., Underwood, B., & Rosenhan, D. L. (1973). Affect and altruism. *Developmental Psychology, 8*: 99–104.

Murphy, L. B. (1937). *Social behavior and child personality*. New York: Columbia University Press.

Mussen, P. H., & Eisenberg-Berg, N. (1977). *Caring, sharing, and helping*. San Francisco: Freeman.

Muste, M. J., & Sharpe, D. F. (1947). Some influential factors in the determination of aggressive behavior in preschool children. *Child Development, 18*: 11–28.

Olweus, D. (1979). Stability and aggressive reaction patterns in males: A review. *Psychology Bulletin, 86*: 852–875.

Olweus, D. (1980). Familial and temperamental determinants of aggressive behavior in adolescent boys: A causal analysis. *Developmental Psychology, 16*: 644–666.

Parke, R. D., & Slaby, R. G. (1983). The development of aggression. In E. H. Hetherington (Ed.), *Carmichael's manual of child psychology* (4th ed., Vol. IV, pp. 547–641). New York: Wiley.

Radke-Yarrow, M., & Zahn-Waxler, C. (1982). Roots, motives, and patterns in children's prosocial behavior. In J. Reykowski, J. Karylowski, D. Bar-Tal, & E. Staub (Eds.), *Origins and maintenance of prosocial behavior* (pp. 155–176). New York: Plenum.

Radke-Yarrow, M., Zahn-Waxler, C., & Chapman, M. (1983). In E. H. Hetherington, (Ed.), *Carmichael's manual of child psychiatry* (4th ed., Vol. IV). New York: Wiley.

Radke-Yarrow, M., Zahn-Waxler, C., Cummings, E. M., Strope, B., & Sebris, S. L. (1981 April). *Continuities and change in the prosocial and aggressive behavior of young children*. Paper presented at the Meeting of the Society for Research in Child Development, Boston.

Rheingold, H. L., Hay, D. F., & West, M. (1976). Sharing in the second year of life. *Child Development, 47*: 1148–1158.

Rosenhan, D. L., Underwood, B., & Moore, B. (1974). Affect moderates self-gratification and altruism. *Journal of Personal and Social Psychology, 30*: 546–552.

Rothbart, M. K., & Derryberry, D. (1981). Development of individual differences in temperament. In M. E. Lamb & A. L. Brown (Eds.), *Advances in child developmental psychology*. Hillsdale, NJ: Erlbaum.

Rushton, J. P., & Littlefield, C. (1979). The effects of age, amount of modeling and a success experience on seven to eleven-year-old children's generosity. *Journal of Moral Education, 9*: 55–56.

Rutherford, E., & Mussen, P. (1968). Generosity in nursery school boys. *Child Development, 39*: 755–765.

Strayer, J. (1980). A naturalistic study of empathic behaviors and their relation to affective states and perspective-taking skills in preschool children. *Child Development, 51*: 815–822.

Thomas, A., Chess, S., & Birch, H. (1968). *Temperament and behavior disorders in children.* New York: New York University Press.

Underwood, B., Froming, W. J., & Moore, B. S. (1977). Mood, attention, and altruism: A search for mediating variables. *Developmental Psychology, 13*: 541–542.

Yarrow, M. R., & Waxler, C. Z. (1976). Dimensions and correlates of prosocial behavior in young children. *Child Development, 47*: 118–125.

Yarrow, M. R., & Waxler, C. Z. (1977). Emergence and functions of prosocial behaviors in young children. In R. D. Parke and G. M. Hetherington (Eds.), *Child psychology: contemporary readings* (pp. 260–263). New York: McGraw-Hill.

Zahn-Waxler, C., Cummings, E. M., McKnew, D., & Radke-Yarrow, M. (1984). Altruism, aggression and social interactions in young children with a manic-depressive parent. *Child Development, 55*: 112–122.

Zahn-Waxler, C., Iannotti, R., & Chapman, M. (1982). Peers and prosocial development. In K. Rubin and H. Ross (Eds.), *Peer relationships and social skills in childhood.* Berlin & New York: Springer-Verlag.

Zahn-Waxler, C., & Radke-Yarrow, M. (1982). The development of altruism: Alternative research strategies. In N. Eisenberg (Ed.), *The development of prosocial behavior*. New York: Academic Press.

Zahn-Waxler, C., Radke-Yarrow, M., & King, R. A. (1979). Child-rearing and children's prosocial initiations toward victims of distress. *Child Development, 50*: 319–330.

7   Aggression and altruism: a personality perspective

Seymour Feshbach and Norma Deitch Feshbach

The properties, antecedents, and relationships of aggression and altruism can be examined from a number of different perspectives, each focusing attention on different relevant parameters and processes. The examination of aggression and altruism from a biological viewpoint is oriented to the role of neurochemical and genetic factors and to possible evolutionary functions of these behaviors. A socialization perspective leads to a consideration of child-rearing patterns, to variations in experiences believed to influence aggression and altruism, and particularly, to reinforcement histories. Related to the socialization perspective is the cultural perspective, the latter emphasizing the cultural norms and rules that regulate appropriate and inappropriate expressions of aggressive and altruistic behaviors.

This chapter assumes still another stance in approaching the question of the development of aggression and altruism – that of the child's personality structure and dynamics. These perspectives are not mutually exclusive – there is interaction between the variables each emphasizes, and an understanding of aggression and altruism and their interrelationship must reflect considerations from all these perspectives. However, the realities of research impose a more constrained and defined approach. In addition, in our judgment, personality-related issues of aggressive and altruistic behaviors are central to an understanding of the development and meaning of these behaviors.

We first address issues concerning the relationship(s) that might be expected between these two behavior domains, as well as the mediating personality processes and antecedent developmental factors implicated in these relationships. Theory and data relevant to one demonstrated mediating process – empathy – are then considered. In this regard, findings derived from our empathy training program are presented and their implication for the development of aggressive and altruistic behaviors discussed. Findings of a recent developmental study bearing on the relationship between aggression and assertiveness are then presented. The degree and

189

pattern of association between aggression and assertion are of special interest because of the theoretical linkages between these two behavioral dimensions, which actually differ sharply in their social and personality implications. These data accentuate the importance of a personality perspective for programs designed to influence the development of aggression and altruism.

The relationship between aggression and altruism

Why is it so often the case that one chooses to address the origins of aggression and altruism rather than any number of possible pairings, such as aggression and anxiety, altruism and autonomy, altruism and competition, or sexuality? Among the considerations that influence the decision to juxtapose aggression and altruism, one may assume that two considerations were important. First, aggression and altruism have been approached theoretically and empirically from both a biological and social perspective. Second, there is an implied contrast and opposition between these two behavior patterns, particularly at the human level. Altruism is the quintessence of prosocial behavior. When used in its most restricted sense, it denotes self-sacrifice. When more broadly applied, it connotes cooperation, generosity, and helping behavior. Fostering altruism is presumably a major objective of socialization. As professionals, many of us are engaged in constructing programs designed to help parents and teachers develop and reinforce altruistic behaviors in children. In brief, altruism is positively valued as a "social good." By contrast, aggression is negatively valued; it connotes destructive and injurious effects and is a behavior to be modified, controlled, and regulated. In a kind of parallel, reciprocal relationship to empathy and prosocial behavior-enhancing efforts, a good deal of current interest has been expressed in the formulation and evaluation of programs aimed at reducing aggressive behaviors and at promoting nonaggressive resolutions of conflict and frustrating situations (Goldstein, Sherman, Gershaw, Sprafkin, & Glick, 1978).

Aggression and altruism are behaviors that have biological and social roots as well as contrasting social evaluations. Are they associated in other ways? Are these two systems functionally and dynamically related so that the child who is disposed to being aggressive is unlikely to be altruistic? Conversely, is the altruistic child unlikely to be a very aggressive child? What are the mechanisms that might link or dissociate altruism and aggression? These questions as to the nature of the relationship give rise to the further question of what the relationship should be. Is altruism necessarily a desirable behavior and aggression undesirable? It is helpful to consider the questions of what is and should be the relationship between aggression and altruism within a personality framework. In particular, it is useful to consider the properties and dynamics of aggressive and altruistic behaviors at different stages of the child's development. Furthermore, in order to evaluate the effects of intervention programs and broader issues of socialization efforts, it is important to determine other personality dimensions to which these behaviors might be linked.

Anecdotal observations at the infrahuman and human level suggest that strong aggressive dispositions and strong altruistic dispositions can characterize the same organism. For example, the African wild dog provides a striking contrast between the savage behavior displayed when attacking prey and the gentle, nurturant behavior extended toward others in its pack. After eating their prey, the pack of wild dogs return to their den and regurgitate, making it possible for the young and other adults that remained behind to share in the bounty. The sick and the crippled, unable to participate in the hunt, are thus sustained by the pack (Wilson, 1975). It is easy to find analogues at the human level – the parent who is nurturant, protective, and self-sacrificing in intrafamily interactions while readily aggressive toward individuals outside the family structure. It may be objected that different species or different objects are involved in these examples. The manifestation of strong aggressive and altruistic behaviors toward the same object is undoubtedly a less probable occurrence than their display toward different objects. However, the point remains that very aggressive and very altruistic response patterns can coexist in the same individual.

In addition, certain forms of aggressive behavior are also altruistic actions. For example, honeybee workers will embed their barbed stings in an intruder that threatens the hive. The honeybee worker will die as a result of the aggressive attacks but, in the process, saves the hive (Sakagami and Akahira, 1960). Again, analogous behavior can be observed at the human level. The kamikaze pilot, in directing his plane at an enemy warship, was simultaneously carrying out a violent yet altruistic act. Samurai traditions, in fact, embody the theme of violence embedded in altruism. By providing examples from varied species, we do not imply that the mechanisms mediating infrahuman aggression and violence are similar to those mediating human aggression and violence. Quite the contrary, it appears to us that the differences between the human and animal mediating processes are far more important than the similarities. Nevertheless, both the animal and human examples serve to illustrate the point that aggression and altruism need not be incompatible and, moreover, that an aggressive act can be an altruistic act.

The empirical literature on the relationship in children between *aggres-*

sion and *altruism* or comparable prosocial behaviors similarly reflects a variety of patterns (S. Feshbach & Weiner, 1982; Radke-Yarrow, Zahn-Waxler, & Chapman, 1984). The age and sex of the sample studied appear to be important factors influencing the degree of association and direction between aggression and various measures of prosocial behavior. In her classic study investigating social behavior in preschool children, Lois Murphy (1937) observed a positive relationship between aggressive and sympathetic behaviors. A positive association between aggression and empathy was noted by N. Feshbach and Feshbach (1969) for preschool and kindergarten boys but not for girls, and Friedrich and Stein (1973) also reported a positive relationship between aggression and prosocial behavior for a similar age group. Yarrow and Waxler (1976), in controlling for degree of social interaction, observed a positive relationship between aggression and prosocial behavior, but only for low aggressive boys.

By contrast, studies carried out with postkindergarten-aged children tend to reflect an inverse relationship between aggression and a cluster of prosocial/altruistic behaviors. The relationship is, however, inconsistent, the data sometimes indicating no association, and ofttimes significant for only one sex. Rutherford and Mussen (1968), Harris and Siebel (1975), and O'Connor, Dollinger, Kennedy, and Pelletier-Smetko (1979), working with elementary-age and older children, all reported negative, if modest, associations between aggression and prosocial behavior.

These findings suggest that at a younger age level the child's aggression may be more a reflection of the child's social interest, activity, and maturity than of hostility. It would appear that self-assertion is an important component of aggression in the young child and that developmental changes in the mode in which self-assertion is expressed may account for the varying relationship observed between aggression and altruism as a function of age. It is also possible that gender-based differences in the freedom to be assertive may contribute to gender-based differences in the relationship between these two behavior domains. At a later point in this chapter, we shall consider similarities and differences in the developmental course of aggression and assertiveness.

Empathy as a mediating process

An important variable hypothesized to mediate between aggression and prosocial behavior is empathy (N. Feshbach & Feshbach, 1969, 1972, 1973). Empathy is not, in itself, an explicit prosocial response, nor does it entail a behavioral transaction, as is the case with acts of generosity, cooperation, or helping. A stimulus person, however, who elicits an empathic response in another individual may feel gratified by the other's expression of empathy. In that sense, empathy can be considered one type of positive social interaction. But the empathic response is not inevitably communicated to the stimulus person. It is an inferred internal response. During the 1970s, the nature of the internal response was the subject of theoretical differences and debate. In an early paper by Feshbach and Roe (1968), empathy was defined as a shared emotional response between observer and stimulus person. Several other investigators during this period used a more cognitive definition of empathy, conceptualizing empathy in terms of role taking, perspective taking, or social comprehension (Borke, 1971; Chandler & Greenspan, 1972; Chandler, Greenspan, & Barenboim, 1973, 1974; Deutsch & Madle, 1975; Shantz, 1975).

While maintaining the affective criterion of empathy, N. Feshbach developed an integrative cognitive–affective model. The affective empathy reaction was postulated to be a function of three component factors: (1) the cognitive ability to discriminate affective cues in others, (2) the more mature cognitive skill entailed in assuming the perspective and role of another person, and (3) emotional responsiveness, that is, the affective ability to experience emotions (N. Feshbach & Roe, 1968; N. Feshbach, 1973, 1975b, 1978; N. Feshbach & N. Kuchenbecker, 1974). This theoretical model should be distinguished from a development model of empathy subsequently formulated by Hoffman (1975, 1978), which also has three components – cognitive, affective, and motivational – and focuses on the empathic response to distress in others. The early debate on the cognitive versus affective approach to empathy has subsided in recent years. There appears to be a general consensus that empathy entails both affective and cognitive elements, the relative role of each varying with the situation and the age and personality of the child.

From a theoretical standpoint, the three-component model of empathic behavior suggests several mechanisms that should result in lower aggression and greater prosocial behavior in the empathic child as compared with the child who manifests little empathy. The ability to discriminate and label the feelings of others is a prerequisite to taking into account the others' needs when responding to social conflicts. Furthermore, the more advanced cognitive skill entailed in examining a conflict situation from the perspective of another person should result in the reduction of misunderstandings, accompanied by a lessening of conflict and aggression and a greater likelihood of cooperative and other prosocial responses. The assumption of a process of this kind underlies the rationale for the many types of therapy, "dialogue," and comparable interpersonal communication procedures that have been applied to the resolution of conflict situations.

The affective component of empathy has a special relationship to the regulation of aggression. Aggressive behavior is a social response that has the defining characteristic of inflicting injury on persons or objects, causing pain and distress. The observation of these noxious consequences should elicit distress responses in an empathic observer even if the observer is the instigator of the aggressive act. The painful consequences of an aggressive act through the vicarious response of empathy should function as inhibitors of the instigator's own aggressive tendencies (N. Feshbach & Feshbach, 1969). An important property of empathic inhibition is that it applies to instrumentally as well as anger-mediated aggressive behavior. Thus, one would predict, on the basis of the affective as well as the cognitive components of empathy, that children high in empathy should manifest less aggression than those low in empathy. In an extension of this analysis, a comparable affective mechanism has been applied to the analysis of distress (Hoffman, 1975, 1977, 1978). The child who experiences empathically shared distress is motivated to reduce these painful distress feelings. One method for reducing empathically induced distress is to alleviate the distress of the other child through an altruistic, helpful response. Consequently, while the empathic child may find other ways of reducing empathic distress, such as avoidance and denial, one would still expect to find a positive relationship between empathy and prosocial behavior.

The data bearing on the relationship between empathy and prosocial behaviors and between empathy and aggression are partially supportive of these theoretical expectations. The special role played by empathy in regulating antisocial behavior and in promoting positive social behavior was explored in a myriad of studies during the 1970s. The pattern of findings concerning the relationship of empathy or some component of empathy to various manifestations of prosocial behavior, such as sharing, cooperation, generosity, and helping, has been less consistent than the obtained inverse relationship noted between empathy and such negative behaviors as aggression and delinquency. The inherent problems in relating social cognitive and empathic skills to social behavior have been well noted by Shantz (1975, 1985) and others. Psychometric limitations of empathy measures and situational limitations of the prosocial behavior are but two factors that attenuate the relationship between empathy and prosocial actions. Overall, the findings reflect either negligible relationships or positive correlations between empathy and some form of prosocial behavior (Radke-Yarrow et al., 1983).

The inverse relationship between empathy and aggression appears to be a more stable phenomenon, particularly for males. N. Feshbach and Feshbach's (1969) findings from an early study indicating that 6- to 8-year-old boys high in aggression were low in empathy have been supported in a number of different studies employing variable measures of empathy and aggression and carried out with similar or older age groups (Huckabay, 1972; Mehrabian & Epstein, 1972; N. Feshbach & Feshbach, 1982). Sometimes a particular component of empathy is evaluated, such as perspective taking (Chandler et al., 1973) or social sensitivity (Rothenberg, 1970). Other times a broader index of empathy such as the Feshbach and Roe (1968) Affective Situation Test, the new Bryant (1982) measure, or the new N. Feshbach (1982) measure is employed. Assessments of aggressiveness include teachers' ratings of aggression, cruelty, and competitiveness (Barnett, Matthews, & Howard, 1979) and delinquency. One study, contrary to the predominant pattern, reports positive correlations between perspective-taking skills and disruptive difficult classroom behavior in elementary school children (Kurdeck, 1978).

The different relationships between empathy/prosocial behavior and empathy/antisocial behavior may be a reflection of the complex structure of empathy. The emotional and cognitive components can vary independently and may affect social interaction and the empathic response in different ways. The emotional component, in particular, appears to be a source of the variability that is frequently observed in this relationship. If the person is emotionally constricted, the empathic response is likely to be flat and devoid of such motivating properties as aggression inhibition (N. Feshbach & Feshbach, 1969) and impetus to generosity (N. Feshbach, 1975). On the other hand, if the person lacks emotional control and differentiation, the empathic response is likely to be excessive and egocentric, obscuring the cognitive aspects of the social interaction and facilitating inappropriate social behavior (N. Feshbach & Feshbach, 1982). Thus, the cognitive component of empathy, a necessary prerequisite for effective social and prosocial behavior, may be rendered ineffective by the intensity of the stimulated affect.

Still another factor complicating the association between empathy and prosocial behavior is the general issue of the circumstances under which empathy is likely to be evoked. Even highly empathic individuals are not empathic in all situations. Some situations are ambiguous and the affects experienced by the protagonists may be unclear. Or again, there may be conflicting affective and social cues. Still other factors may reduce empathic responsiveness through interference with role taking and perspective taking. For example, it may be difficult to assume the perspective and adopt the framework of an individual one intensely dislikes or with whom one is in sharp disagreement or with whom one has very little in common. Yet other situational factors may have such affective-laden significance that they may overstimulate or, conversely, even block affective responses. All these situational contingencies reduce the likelihood of an empathic response and of prosocial behaviors that might be mediated by empathy. Thus, the three-component model of empathy – affective discrimination, perspective taking, and affective responsiveness – that provided a basis for examining individual differences in empathy may also suggest a basis for analyzing situational sources of variation in empathic responsiveness. Parenthetically, sources of variation suggested by this model can be directly incorporated into the measurement of empathy, and the model can be used as a basis for comparing and analyzing different measures.

In summary, empathy and prosocial behavior, although compatible and synchronous, are not automatically or inevitably linked. The inverse relationship hypothesized between empathy and aggression is more consistently obtained. Nevertheless, empathy appears to be one important ingredient of prosocial development. It is a process that facilitates and sustains positive social orientation and responses in a wide variety of conditions and contexts.

Empathy training and its effects

The data indicating that empathy and aggression are inversely related in the elementary school-age child as well as evidence of weaker but nonetheless positive associations between empathy and prosocial behavior encouraged us to design a training program for elementary school-age children that would enhance the empathic responsiveness of children. The theoretical rationale for this program was based on (1) the linkages proposed between empathy and the regulation of aggression and between empathy and positive social actions, and (2) N. Feshbach's three-component model. Each of the three components – discrimination of affect, role taking and perspective taking, and affective responsiveness – provided the basis for the training exercises that were developed. The exercises were addressed to the enhancement of these cognitive and affective dimensions and did not directly entail training in the control of aggression, response alternatives to aggression, or prosocial behaviors. From a theoretical standpoint, we were interested in determining whether increasing the child's capacity to discriminate affect, to assume the perspective of others, and to experience affect (that is, by strengthening the components of empathy) could alter aggressive and prosocial behaviors.

As a secondary note, we also believe there were ethical advantages in the selection of empathy training as the route to decreasing aggression and promoting prosocial behaviors. The implementation of a training program to achieve these objectives entails ethical as well as theoretical and methodological issues. Direct modification of a social response involves a moral evaluation of that response. Questions and dilemmas regarding moral judgments are minimal when behaviors are extreme and fall within the clinical or criminal range. However, when one is dealing with behaviors that are less extreme, even when they entail problems, evaluative issues and evaluative questions become relevant.

Our personal goal was to reduce the incidence of aggressive behavior in the schools, in addition to fostering cooperative behaviors and generosity. Yet some would take issue with these goals. There were graduate students on our own project who felt that aggression can be an appropriate and adaptive response to classroom and school discrimination. It must also be acknowledged that there are many who would place a greater value on competition and on self-seeking and self-actualization as opposed to other-person-oriented behaviors. One can eschew, to some extent, troublesome ethical questions entailed in directly modifying aggressive and prosocial behaviors through an empathy training program focusing on the enhancement of consensually valued affective and cognitive competencies that theoretically mediate these behaviors.

Before implementing the empathy training study proper, a pilot study was carried out in which the effects of an empathy training curriculum that focused on cognitive factors were compared with those of a curriculum that entailed the integration of cognitive and affective elements. The cognitive-affective training procedure was more successful in engaging the children's interest and also in producing behavior change than was the cognitive curriculum. Analyses of the pilot study data indicated that the children in the cognitive-affective training condition displayed a significantly greater decline in aggression than did a control group that had not participated in any training exercises.

In view of these encouraging preliminary findings, the larger-scale empathy training study was undertaken. Since the procedures used in the empathy training program have been extensively described elsewhere (N. Feshbach, 1979, 1980, 1982; N. Feshbach & Feshbach, 1977, 1982), its principal features will be briefly summarized. Third- and fourth-grade children, including a significant number of highly aggressive youngsters (as assessed by teachers and school administrators), were randomly assigned to either an empathy training group, a problem-solving control activity group, or a control group that received the pre- and postexperimental measures. One-third of the 98 pupils in our sample represented various ethnic minority populations. The children in the empathy training and problem-solving control conditions met in small groups consisting of four boys and two girls. The group sessions were held in various locations in the school, other than the children's classroom, and each session lasted about 45 min. Each experimental and control activity group met three times a week for a period extending over 10 weeks.

The empathy training groups participated in activities that focused on the cognitive and affective components of empathy, whereas the exercises for the children in the problem-solving control condition entailed nonsocial content such as discovery science curriculum. A control condition was incorporated into the design, along with a nonparticipating control group, in order to assess the effects of simply removing children displaying aggressive acting out behavior from the classroom and placing them in small group settings for short periods of time. One of the criteria used in selecting the empathy and control exercises was the interest value for the children. We sought to develop a control curriculum that was educationally valuable and interesting (N. Feshbach, Feshbach, Fauvre, & Ballard-Campbell, 1983).

The effects of the experimental intervention were evaluated through pre- and post-teacher, peer, and self-ratings of aggressive and prosocial behaviors. In addition, measures of self-concept, spatial perspective taking, social sensitivity (Rothenberg, 1970), and empathy (N. Feshbach, 1982) were administered along with several ability and achievement tests. Throughout the 10-week training period, the children's classroom teachers completed daily behavior rating forms twice weekly for each child in the study.

The results reflected systematic and statistically significant positive changes in children who participated in the empathy training activities. Following the empathy training experience, children reported a more positive self-concept and displayed greater social sensitivity to feelings than did children in the two control conditions. As in the pilot experiment, the children in the empathy training groups declined in aggression relative to the non-participating controls, but the problem-solving control activity groups also displayed a decline in aggressive behaviors (N. Feshbach & Feshbach, 1982). Apparently, taking these children out of the classroom and providing them with positive small group experiences facilitated a reduction in aggression whether the training experience focused on empathy or on interesting academic content. However, empathy training proved critical in regard to positive shifts in prosocial behaviors. Children in the empathy training condition significantly differed from both control conditions in the increase of incidents of such prosocial behaviors as cooperation, helping, and generosity. Figure 7.1 reflects both a decline in prosocial behaviors in the control groups and an increment in the experimental group. However, the control–experimental difference should be interpreted in relative rather

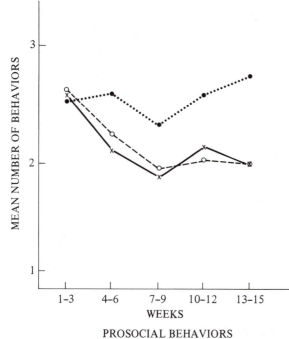

PROSOCIAL BEHAVIORS

Figure 7.1. Prosocial behaviors: (...) empathy training; (———) problem solving; (---) control. The number of weeks includes pre- and post-training week and vacation days.

than absolute terms of an increment vs. decrement, as methodological factors could operate to influence the absolute frequencies, including any tendency of teachers to record fewer behaviors as the study progressed. In the case of prosocial behaviors, merely taking the children out of the classroom was not sufficient. These behaviors were facilitated by specific training in affect identification and understanding, role playing, and emotional expressiveness. The experimental findings indicate that the cognitive/affective model of empathy has empirical value.

Correlates of aggression and prosocial behavior

The correlational findings are especially pertinent to our understanding of the relationship among different social behaviors that were assessed and of the personality context to which aggressive and prosocial behaviors are linked. Several indices of prosocial and aggressive behaviors were utilized – teacher classroom behavior reports averaged by week for each week of

Table 7.1. *Correlates of teacher ratings of aggressive behaviors*

	Boys		Girls	
	Pre	Post	Pre	Post
Teacher rating of prosocial	$-.65^c$	$-.70^c$	$-.73^b$	$-.58^c$
Peer rating of aggression (class play nomination[a])	$.46^c$	$.57^c$	.18	$.47^c$
Peer rating of prosocial (class play nomination[a])	$-.46^c$	$-.45^c$	$-.24$	$-.46^c$
Self-rating of aggression	$.49^c$	$.40^c$	.11	.26
Self-rating of prosocial	.16	.06	$-.20$	.00
Self-concept	$.31^b$	$.33^c$	$-.11$	$-.08$
Wisc-R comprehension	.02	$-.32^b$	.13	.01
Wisc-R vocabulary	.02	$-.10$	.13	.19
TAT Agg. imagery	.14	$.34^c$	$-.21$	$-.03$

[a] These ratings are based on frequency of peer nomination for aggressive and for prosocial roles in a class play.
[b] $p = .05$ level.
[c] $p = .01$ level.

the training, pre- and post-teacher ratings, and pre- and postpeer and self-ratings. To simplify the presentation, we shall focus on the correlates of the teacher ratings of aggression and prosocial behavior, while noting deviations from the correlation pattern yielded by other measures. Also, the correlates of empathy are analyzed in greater detail and will be separately presented and discussed.

The relationships obtained with teacher ratings of aggression and of prosocial behavior are summarized, respectively, in Tables 7.1 and 7.2. As can be seen from these data, the meaning and implication of aggressive and prosocial behavior vary with the sex of the child.

Aggression in boys, as evaluated by teachers as well as by peers, tends to be associated with a positive rather than a negative self-image. Interestingly, whereas teacher ratings and boys' self-ratings of aggression were substantially positively correlated, boys' self-rating of aggression tended to be negatively correlated with self-concept ($r = -.23$; $r = -.14$). In greater accordance with expectation, teacher and peer ratings of aggression are inversely related to indices of boys' intelligence. The correlates of prosocial behavior in boys reflect a comparable pattern, with the direction of the relationships reversed. Prosocial behavior in boys is associated with a negative self-image but is positively correlated with indices of intelligence.

For girls, the correlations between the aggression ratings and the self-

Table 7.2. *Correlates of teacher ratings of prosocial behaviors*

	Boys		Girls	
	Pre	Post	Pre	Post
Teacher rating of aggressive behavior	$-.65^c$	$-.70^c$	$-.73^c$	$-.58^c$
Peer rating of aggression (class play nomination[a])	$-.33^b$	$-.40^c$	.04	$-.02$
Peer rating of prosocial (class play nomination[a])	$.60^c$	$.30^b$	.16	$.55^c$
Self-rating of aggression	$-.22$	$-.36^c$	$-.29^b$	$-.18$
Self-rating of prosocial	.07	$.25^b$	.23	$.33^b$
Self-concept	$-.33^b$	$-.26^b$	.22	$.31^b$
Wisc-R comprehension	$-.12$	$.45^c$	.17	.20
Wisc-R vocabulary	$-.04$	$.26^b$	$-.22$	$-.05$

[a] These ratings are based on frequency of peer nominations for aggressions and for prosocial roles in a class play.
[b] $p = .05$ level.
[c] $p = .01$ level.

evaluation and the cognitive measures were negligible. However, ratings of prosocial behavior in girls tended to be associated with a positive self-concept and inversely related to indices of cognitive ability. The gender-based differences in the cognitive correlates of prosocial behavior are particularly evident for peer ratings of prosocial behavior. For boys, prosocial behavior as assessed by peers consistently correlated positively with indices of intelligence (WISC-R Comp: $r = .36$, $r = .33$; WISC-R Voc: $r = .33$, $r = .24$). For girls, peer prosocial ratings are significantly negatively correlated with the vocabulary measure ($r = -.45$, $r = -.35$) and unrelated to the comprehension measure.

In general, teacher and peer ratings reflect similar patterns for each sex. It is possible that teachers and peers share stereotypes that are unrelated to the children's actual behavior. However, there is substantial evidence that these ratings are indicative of behavioral differences in aggression, especially for boys (Eron, Walder, & Lefkowitz, 1971; S. Feshbach, 1970). In a subsequent field study we found these measures to correlate significantly with aggressive behaviors as assessed in a 6-min. observation situation (N. Feshbach and Feshbach, 1982).

Correlates of empathy

The gender-based differences noted in the correlates of aggressive and prosocial behavior are particularly marked when the relationships with empathy are analyzed. Since the method of assessment of empathy affected the pattern of empathy correlations, a description of the empathy measure is helpful. The Feshbach–Roe measure had been devised for a younger population and at an earlier time, so a new empathy measure was developed and was available for use at the conclusion of the training program. The measure consists of a series of 2- to 2½-min. videotapes showing real children involved in common childhood situations related to the experience of particular emotions. Each videotape showed a story character within an affect-laden situation where his or her immediate facial, postural, behavioral, and verbal emotional reactions were displayed. The content for these videotapes was obtained from interviews with 240 boys and girls varying in age and in social class, economic, and ethnic backgrounds (N. Feshbach & Hoffman, 1978).

Two videotapes illustrate children experiencing each of the following five emotions: pride (winning a race, retrieving a lost kite), happiness (receiving a new bicycle; making ice cream sundaes), anger (being pushed out of line; having a coin counting activity disrupted and one's coins scattered), fear (outside noise suggesting an intruder; concern over falling from a climbing apparatus), or sadness (lost dog; moving from one's neighborhood). The emotions of pride and happiness were designated euphoric empathy; the emotions of anger, fear, and sadness were categorized dysphoric. Separate sets of 10 audiovisual tapes were shown to boys and girls with story characters of the same sex as the subjects. In general, each videotaped story built up to an emotionally intense climax. At the end of each tape, the subject was asked to indicate what he or she was feeling and to rate the intensity of that feeling on a scale from zero to nine.

The empathy score is a statistic based on the degree to which the child's emotional response to each of the 10 videotapes corresponds to the affect experienced by the stimulus child. There were two ways in which this statistic, providing an index of empathy, was calculated. The first procedure relied on a factor analytic model of emotions developed by Davitz (1969). In this case, the empathy score is a function of the extent to which the emotion reported by the child approaches that for the emotion depicted in the videotape. This method is essentially a matching procedure, comparable to that used in earlier studies, with the additional property of providing an empirical basis for determining the degree of affective match. An alternative index of empathy incorporated intensity of the affective response as a multiplicative factor.

These two alternative scoring methods strongly influence the relationships reflected in the data between empathy and other dimensions of personality. Overall, girls respond more empathically than boys. This difference is quite modest and holds primarily for the euphoric affective stimuli of happiness and pride. However, the correlations between euphoric and dysphoric empathy and the various cognitive and social behavior measures were strikingly different for the two sexes.

In examining the results derived from the first affective match measure that recorded how closely the subject child's emotional state matched that of the story character child, we found that for boys the correlations of empathy, when based on affective match alone, were strongly cognitive in nature. Empathy in boys is positively associated with competencies in vocabulary, reading skills, comprehension, spatial perspective-taking, and role-taking skills, with considerable overlap in the correlates of euphoric and dysphoric empathy. Less pronounced are positive associations with anxiety over aggression and negative associations with teacher and peer ratings of aggression.

By contrast, empathy in girls is associated with a positive self-concept, with teacher, peer, and self-ratings of prosocial behavior, and is negatively associated with teacher, peer, and self-ratings of antisocial behavior. This sex difference obtains regardless of the particular affect experienced. These findings showing sex differences in correlation with empathy and personal attributes – that is, an association for boys with cognitive competence and low aggression and for girls with positive self-concept and prosocial behavior – based on an index of empathy in which the intensity of the child's affective response was not considered.

When empathy is scored so that the intensity of the child's feeling is given substantial weight, a different picture emerges. This picture varies substantially with the sex of the child and also with the euphoric or dysphoric nature of the affect. That is, the correlates of empathy are influenced by three interacting factors: the sex of the child, the euphoric or dysphoric nature of the vicariously experienced affect (whether happiness and pride or sadness, fear, and anger), and the intensity of the child's affective experience (whether the degree of reported affect is taken into account as well as the affective match). To explicate this interaction, it is helpful to examine the findings separately for each sex.

As Table 7.3 indicates, the interaction of these three factors is quite dramatic for boys. With the introduction of the intensity of the child's affective report as a major component of the empathy score, the personality and social behavior correlates of euphoric and dysphoric empathy change, but in very different ways for boys and girls. Boys who report intense dysphoric feelings when viewing children in dysphoric situations of sadness, fear, or anger are more likely to display helping behaviors, to perceive themselves as helpful, to display low aggression, to be anxious over aggres-

Table 7.3. Correlates of empathy in boys as related to scoring index and valence of affect[a]

	Euphoric empathy		Dysphoric empathy	
	Affective match	Affective match × intensity	Affective match	Affective match × intensity
Affective match Vocabulary Role-taking skills Field independent		Low prosocial behavior Antisocial Aggressive Aggression anxiety Poor self-concept	Vocabulary Reading competence Social comprehension Spatial-perspective Role-taking skills Prosocial behavior	Social sensitivity Helping Low aggressive Aggression anxiety

[a] All correlates listed are significant at $p = .05$ level.

sion, and to be sensitive to the feelings and motives of others. On the other hand, the correlations obtained for boys who report intense euphoric feelings when viewing children in euphoric situations of happiness and pride convey a sharply different image. Boys who report strong euphoric feelings are rated by their teachers as antisocial and by their peers and themselves as aggressive. In addition, these children are rated low in prosocial behaviors, and they tend to have a poor self-concept and to experience considerable anxiety in regard to aggression. It is clear that those boys who empathize strongly in dysphoric situations are different individuals from those who empathize strongly in euphoric situations, this difference being reflected in the lack of a correlation between these two indices.

What has happened? The introduction of the affect intensity dimension seems to produce a qualitative change in the meaning of the empathic response. When the first empathy index was used, an index that is essentially a match between the particular affect experienced by the child and that of the stimulus observed, without regard to the intensity of the reported affect, empathy in boys is related to a wide range of cognitive skills. This configuration is not dissimilar for euphoric and dysphoric empathy. With the introduction of an intensity factor, social behaviors are now correlated with empathy. Furthermore, the correlations differ for euphoric and dysphoric empathy. (Note that the two scoring methods of empathy–affective match and affective match × intensity are uncorrelated.)

These data suggest that empathy in boys does not have a singular meaning. Its significance depends on the intensity of the empathic response and on whether the boy is empathizing with an euphoric or dysphoric affective situation. Empathy, a term that generally carries positive connotations, is found to be associated with negative attributes for boys who respond with intense empathy when seeing others in situations of happiness and pride. This intricate pattern of the meaning of empathy in boys does not hold true for girls. Empathy in girls is associated with a positive self-concept, with prosocial behavior, and with social understanding and is inversely related to aggression and antisocial behaviors. Girls' personal and social correlates of empathy are fairly consistent for both euphoric and dysphoric empathy regardless of whether affective intensity is measured (Table 7.4).

Why should the correlates of empathy be influenced by the sex of the child, the valence of the vicariously experienced affect, and whether the reported intensity of the affect is weighted heavily, as well as the affective match itself? It may be that the critical factors have to do with control and with boundaries – control over emotional response and boundaries between self and environment. Constructive empathy demands separation between self and object. The mature vicarious experience of affect should not reflect

Table 7.4. *Correlates of empathy in girls as related to scoring index and value of affect*[a]

Euphoric empathy		Dysphoric empathy	
Affective match	Affective match × intensity	Affective match	Affective match × intensity
Positive self-concept	Positive self-concept	Positive self-concept	
	Prosocial behavior	Prosocial behavior	Prosocial behavior
Low aggressive		Low aggressive	Low aggressive

[a] All correlates listed are significant at $p = .05$ level.

the merging of observer and object but should derive from the observer's ability to assume the perspective and share the feeling of the object. Intense empathic responsiveness may indicate a blurring of the bounds between the self and others. Moreover, the experience of strong positive affect may override cognitive controls and lead to impulsive behaviors. In the case of boys reacting to an intense emotion, aggression may represent an accessible outlet. This interpretation does not entirely account for the correlational differences found between euphoric and dysphoric empathy.

The capacity of boys to empathize with individuals who are experiencing sadness, anger, or fear, intensely or not, is generally predictive of positive personal and interpersonal attributes. Apparently, the psychological consequences ensuing from sharing another's distress are different from those experienced in sharing another's pleasure. Experiencing another's pain may be very uncomfortable and may motivate one to reduce that discomfort by being helpful and mitigating the other's distress. This motivational sequence may function to control the possible flood of distress feelings (Hoffman, 1977). By contrast, experiencing the other's pleasure does not seem to have clear motivational consequences for boys and therefore may not provide restraints against excessive emotional release. A lack of emotional control could well be manifested in boisterousness, hyperactivity, aggressiveness, and other egocentric behaviors.

The variations observed in the correlates of empathy indicate that, under certain circumstances, a shared affective response can result in negative social behaviors. Although the data indicate that the disruptive effects of an intense empathic response are restricted to euphoric empathy for boys, theoretically there are situations in which intense dysphoric empathy can be dysfunctional as well. Altruistic and generous behaviors elicited in response to empathic distress can, under some circumstances and from certain frames of reference, be excessive. Can an adult or child who is deeply distressed by the plight of another give too much in the way of succorance and material aid? Should one share one's necessities as one is supposed to share one's wealth? How much wealth is it appropriate to share? To use a more concrete example, should a child deliberately lose or withdraw from a race in order to prevent a peer from suffering the pain of defeat? Empathic distress in the process of fostering altruistic and related prosocial responses, and restraining aggressive tendencies, could also serve to inhibit self-assertive tendencies that are acknowledged to be legitimate and healthy. This is particularly likely to occur when assertion is psychologically equated with selfishness or with aggression.

Assertion, then, is a personality dimension that needs to be taken cognizance of in delineating the dynamics of altruistic and aggressive behaviors, and assessing the psychological meaning and adjustive significance of these behaviors. Toward this end, it will be helpful to review the findings of a developmental study investigating the relationship between aggression and assertion.

Assertion and aggression

Asserting one's rights and expressing one's competence may lead to another person's failure, loss, and even envy. Simply because self-assertion in this sense can hurt someone else, it need not be equivalent to aggression – either hostile or instrumental. Nevertheless, a functional link between assertion and aggression was proposed by psychoanalytic ego psychology theorists (Hartmann, Kris, & Lowenstein, 1949), who suggested that assertion and aggression develop from a common fundamental source. In this view the energy behind assertive and problem-solving behaviors derives from aggressive drive energy, neutralized and sublimated though it may be. However, both an empirical and theoretical distinction can be made between these two behavior dimensions.

Early research in assertion did not adequately distinguish between assertion and aggression and considered both classes of behavior together in the construct of ascendance. Observational studies of assertion and aggression in preschool children yielded significant positive correlations between ascendance and self-confidence (Jack, 1934; Page, 1936) and ascendance and competition (Jack, 1934). The adaptive, coping quality of assertive behavior was also recognized by early researchers (Murphy, 1937) whose hypothesis that assertive children would exhibit more prosocial behavior has been confirmed by recent research (Barrett & Yarrow, 1977).

To clarify the relationship between assertion and aggression further,

assessments were made of assertion and aggression at two grade levels –
kindergarten (17 boys and 17 girls) and third grade (25 boys and 27 girls)
(S. Feshbach and McCarthy, in preparation). The children in this study
came from relatively affluent middle-class backgrounds. Three primary
methods were used in obtaining measures of assertion and aggression: (1)
teacher ratings, (2) children's self-reports, and (3) behaviors as observed
in a group task. The task, designed to be interesting and appropriate for
both age groups, consisted of a semistructured interaction in which a group
of these children were asked to plan and construct a playground using
miniature playground equipment. The children's behaviors were scored by
two observers using a modified Bales (1970) system for classifying behavior
in group situations. Interobserver reliability of 85% was maintained over
the course of the study. A composite assertion score was created by combining three of the Bales scoring categories: "gives suggestions," "gives
opinion," and "gives information." The group task elicited more assertive
than aggressive behavior. Physical aggression rarely occurred. "Seems unfriendly" was the only aggressive behavioral category that was scored.
Fantasy aggression, a category not included by Bales, was also assessed.

There are a number of questions to which the data set yielded by the
several measures of assertion and aggression at two age levels is relevant.
The primary question with which we are concerned is the relationship
between aggression and assertion. In examining this relationship, we are
provided with still another personality perspective on the functional significance of aggression; that is, the extent to which aggressive behaviors
may entail assertive elements and the possible changes in this relationship
with increasing maturity of the child. Before addressing this question, it is
pertinent to consider the consistency of aggressive behaviors and of assertive behaviors; that is, within the constraints of the particular measuring
procedure used, it is relevant to determine whether the different measures
of aggression and of assertion are concerned with discrete behaviors or
whether they are tapping a more generalized behavioral attribute or
disposition.

Consistency of assertion and of aggression

The consistency of assertion and aggression across the three major measurement situations – interaction behaviors, teacher ratings, and self-report
– was assessed by means of Pearson correlations between measures of the
same construct. The data for the measures of assertion are presented
in Table 7.5. Significant positive associations are found at both the kindergarten ($r = .56$; $p < .001$) and third-grade levels ($r = .32$; $p < .05$)

Table 7.5. *Correlations between measures of assertion*

	Group task assertion and teacher rating of assertion		Group task assertion and self-report of assertion		Teacher rating of assertion and self-report of assertion	
	r	p<	r	p<	r	p<
Kindergarten	.59	.001	.37	.06	.30	.09
Third grade	.32	.04	.03	.86	− .15	.28
Boys	.43	.02	.34	.06	.14	.38
Girls	− .03	.85	.02	.91	.11	.49
All	.18	.13	.13	.27	.07	.55
Kindergarten girls	.28	.35	.79	.001	.31	.08
Kindergarten boys	.74	.002	.49	.07	.42	.09
Third-grade girls	.18	.38	− .37	.86	− .07	.72
Third-grade boys	.54	.02	.13	.63	− .16	.44

Table 7.6. *Correlations between measures of aggression*

	Group task aggression and teacher rating of aggression		Group task aggression and self-report of aggression		Teacher rating of aggression and self-report of aggression	
	r	p<	r	p<	r	p<
Kindergarten	.13	.52	.09	.67	.58	.001
Third grade	.28	.07	.29	.07	.35	.01
Boys	.29	.12	.60	.001	.43	.004
Girls	.33	.04	− .004	.98	.32	.04
All	.21	.08	.27	.02	.43	.001
Kindergarten girls	.41	.17	.22	.47	.46	.07
Kindergarten boys	.15	.61	.01	.97	.68	.002
Third-grade girls	.35	.08	− .08	.69	.26	.19
Third-grade boys	.35	.17	.69	.002	.26	.21

between the group task interaction behaviors and teacher ratings. When analyzed by sex, the correlation remains significant for boys only ($r = .43$; $p < .02$). Self-reports of assertive behavior did not correlate significantly with teacher ratings of assertion for any group, and self-reports correlated significantly with assertion in the group task for kindergarten girls only ($r = .79$; $p < .001$).

The data bearing on the consistency of aggression are presented in Table 7.6. The correlation between teacher ratings of aggression and aggressive behavior observed during the group task is significant only for girls (r = .33; p < .04) but approaches significance for third-graders as a group (r = .28; p < .07). Children's self-reports of aggression correlate significantly with teacher ratings of aggression for all children combined (r = .43; p < .001), for third-graders (r = .58; p < .001), for boys (r = .43; p < .01), and for girls (r = .32; p < .05). Self-reports of aggression and aggression observed during the group task were significantly correlated across all subjects (r = .27; p < .02) and for boys (r = .60; p < .001) and approached significance for third-graders (r = .29; p < .06).

Correlation between aggression and assertion

The data that bear most directly on the question of central interest to us are the correlations between aggression and assertion. How closely associated are these two domains? Are there developmental changes in the degree of association? Are there gender-based differences in the relationship between these two social behaviors? If we were to regulate and control aggression through empathy training, would we unintentionally inhibit correlated assertive behaviors?

These questions are of special interest because aggression is negatively valued and assertion is positively valued. In addition, these data may help in the formulation of a developmental personality model linking aggression, assertion, empathy, and altruism.

The correlations for aggression and assertion by age and sex are presented in Table 7.7. The self-report measures are unrelated, indicating that the children discriminate between their aggressive and assertive reactions. A very different pattern is reflected for teacher ratings and behaviors observed during the group task. There is substantial evidence of a significant association between aggression and assertion, with the important exception of third-grade boys. While for the kindergarten-age child the assertive boy is very likely to be the aggressive boy, by the third grade the relationship between these two social behaviors only approaches statistical significance for the boys' group task behaviors and essentially disappears for the teacher ratings of boys. It appears, then, that some elements of aggressive behavior may have a positive functional significance for the 5-year-old in that these may facilitate or reflect the child's efforts at self-assertion and autonomy. But there are more socially effective alternatives to aggression as a means of self-assertion. Presumably, part of the task of socialization, by parents, teachers, and peers, is to foster these alternatives.

The decrease in the relationship between assertion and aggression observed between kindergarten and third-grade boys is consistent with what

Table 7.7. *Pearson correlations between assertion and aggression by age and sex*

Group	Group task r, p	Teacher ratings r, p	Self-report r, p
Kindergarten			
Overall	.36 $p<.06$	.60 $p<.001$	−.19 $p>.10$
Boys	.67 $p<.01$	.65 $p<.01$	−.04 $p>.10$
Girls	.46 $p<.11$	.53 $p<.03$	−.45 $p<.10$
Third grade			
Overall	.41 $p<.01$	.40 $p<.01$	−.03 $p>.10$
Boys	.42 $p<.09$	.19 $p>.10$	−.03 $p>.10$
Girls	.40 $p<.04$	.57 $p<.01$	−.11 $p>.10$
Boys — All	.53 $p<.002$	.38 $p<.012$	−.02 $p>.10$
Girls — All	.34 $p<.04$	.55 $p<.001$	−.10 $p>.10$
All subjects	.42 $p<.001$	.49 $p<.001$	−.10 $p>.10$

one would expect on the basis of the child's increasing cognitive and response differentiation with greater maturity. Why this differentiation does not appear to take place for girls is an intriguing question. It may be that teachers tend to view assertive behavior by girls as a reflection of aggression while perceiving boys' assertive behavior in a more positive light (Freundl, 1977). Thus, the correlation for boys between aggression and assertion in the group task situation, while not significant because of the smaller n, is about equal to that found for girls in that same situation. The fact that teachers see girls as less assertive than boys (despite behavioral evidence indicating that this is not the case) is consistent with the hypothesis that the teachers tend to devalue assertion in girls. One is reminded of studies of teacher stereotypes indicating that assertive girls are perceived as less bright and more aggressive than nonassertive boys (N. Feshbach and Beigel, 1968). Because of possible resistance to girls' efforts at self-assertion, the additional motivation supplied by aggression may help overcome this hypothesized resistance. Also, girls' assertive behaviors may be met with resentment and aggression; the assertive girl then responds aggressively to the unfriendly reception to her advice giving, voicing of convictions, and other assertive behavior.

Overview

Approaching the development of aggression and of altruism from a personality perspective inevitably commits one to a complex model of the antecedents and dynamics of these behavior domains, because personality is multifaceted and because the components of personality are interactive and interrelated. And the complexity of personality is reflected in the correlates of and relationships among prosocial behavior, empathy, aggression and assertion. The personality perspective that has been taken assumes that the development of altruism and aggression is influenced not only by the reinforcement and modeling of specific altruistic and aggressive behaviors but also by the child's development level and other personality attributes that may function as mediating factors (e.g., self-structure, cognitive competence, affective control). The correlational findings are consistent with this conception.

The data further indicate that the relationship of altruism and aggression to these other personality attributes is strongly influenced by the sex of the child. While there is considerable overlap between the sexes in the correlates of altruism and aggression, the personality organization of the altruistic (prosocial) boy differs in a number of important respects from that of the altruistic girl, as does that of the aggressive boy from the aggressive girl. In general, cognitive competencies appear to have a greater role in boys' prosocial and aggressive behaviors. The relationship of these attributes to the child's self-concept also differs between boys and girls. And there are sex differences in how these attributes are correlated with empathic and assertive dispositions.

For boys we find that prosocial behaviors are linked to empathy, to cognitive skills, and to a low self-concept, whereas for girls the pattern is prosocial behaviors, empathy, and a positive self-concept. This is not to say that the development of altruistic behaviors in boys necessarily implies the development of a poor self-image. However, some of the factors that may contribute to a teacher's perception that a boy is high in prosocial behavior (e.g., excessive conformity) may also result in a low self-image, possibly reinforced by feedback from peers. The same behaviors in girls may be perceived by peers as well as teachers as normative, and experienced by girls as egosyntonic and self-enhancing, consistent with sex-role stereotypes of girls' behavior. It should be emphasized, however, that boys and girls also share common antecedents of altruistic behavior. Thus the empathy training program resulted in a significant enhancement of prosocial behaviors both in boys and in girls.

Consistent with the constellation of prosocial correlates, the less cognitively skilled boy and the boy with higher self-esteem are likely to be aggressive. Possibly, these are the more physically powerful boys who engage in successful and instrumental aggressive behavior and whose prowess may, in fact, be valued by their peers (and not only by children). The younger kindergarten-age boy who is aggressive is also likely to be assertive. For girls, aggression appears to be unrelated to cognitive competence and self-concept. There are some significant findings indicating that girls who manifest aggressive antisocial tendencies are low in empathy. Assertion for girls, as in boys, is associated with tendencies toward aggressive response. For girls, this relationship holds for third-graders as well as for kindergarten children, the sex difference in the correlations at third grade becoming manifest in the teacher ratings.

Evidence cited from other studies indicated that assertion in young children is associated with positive social behavior. There is also evidence that aggression in preschool and kindergarten-age children is correlated with empathy and sympathetic behaviors. Given the relationship between aggression and assertion observed in the present investigation, a common factor is suggested (e.g., activity level, social involvement) that fosters both altruistic and aggressive behaviors as well as empathy and assertion in the young child. For the older child, altruism and aggression diverge. It may well be that the meaning of aggression changes between preschool and the later elementary school years, reflecting greater hostility and antisocial properties when manifested in the older as compared with the younger child. There may also be age differences in the prosocial correlates of assertion. Very few data have been reported on how assertion relates to altruistic behavior in older children and adolescents.

Just as the meaning of aggression may vary with circumstances and age, so the meaning of altruistic prosocial behavior may vary as well. Altruistic behaviors that reflect conformity probably have different functional properties from those that arise out of feelings of generosity or empathy. The significance of an empathic response for boys, particularly, varies with the intensity and nature of the affect involved. Intense dysphoric empathy is associated with low aggressive and helping behaviors while intense euphoric empathy is related to aggression and to a lack of prosocial behaviors. Where intense affect is involved in boys' empathic response, the relationship to cognitive competencies becomes minimal and the behavioral correlates vary as a function of the nature of the affect.

One might speculate that a mediating process determining the relationship between empathy and particular social behaviors is the capacity to maintain a distinct boundary between the self and other while still sharing the affect of the other. There are very likely developmental as well as individual and possibly sex-based differences in this regard, with the degree of self–other discrimination and boundary articulation increasing as the child matures. The developing self also enters into the development of assertive behaviors, and of defensive and retaliatory aggressive reactions. Concepts such as self and boundaries between self and other are admittedly amorphous and difficult to assess. Yet the emerging self has important functional properties that are, for the most part, not displayed by infra-human species and that cannot readily be represented in biological terms. Adding these properties to those linking such higher-order competencies as language, attribution, and role taking to aggression and altruism provides compelling evidence that there are fundamental aspects of human aggression and altruism that can only be accounted for in human terms.

References

Bales, R. (1970). *Personality and interpersonal behavior*. New York: Holt, Rinehart & Winston.

Barnett, M. A., Matthews, K. A., & Howard, J. A. (1979). Relationship between competitiveness and empathy in 6- and 7-year-olds. *Developmental Psychology, 15*, 221–222.

Barrett, D. E., & Yarrow, M. R., (1977). Prosocial behavior, social inferential ability and assertiveness in children. *Child Development, 48*, 475–481.

Borke, H. (1971). Interpersonal perception of young children: Egocentrism or empathy. *Developmental Psychology, 5*(2), 263–269.

Bryant, B. K. (1982). An index of empathy for children and adolescents. *Child Development, 53*, 413–425.

Chandler, M. J., & Greenspan, S. (1972). Ersatz egocentrism: A reply to H. Borke. *Developmental Psychology, 7*(2), 104–106.

Chandler, M. J., Greenspan, S., & Barenboim, C. (1973). Judgements of intentionality in response to videotaped and verbally presented moral dilemmas: The medium is the message. *Child Development, 44*, 315–320.

Chandler, M. J., Greenspan, S., & Barenboim, C. (1974). The assessment and training of role-taking and referential communication skills in institutionalized emotionally disturbed children. *Developmental Psychology, 10*(4), 546–553.

Davitz, J. R. (1969). *The language of emotion.* New York: Academic Press.

Deutsch, F., & Madle, R. (1975). Empathy: Historic and current conceptualizations, measurement, and a cognitive theoretical perspective. *Human Development, 18*, 267–287.

Eron, L. D., Walder, L. O., & Lefkowitz, M. M. (1971). *Learning of aggression in children.* Boston: Little, Brown.

Feshbach, N. (1969). Sex differences in children's modes of aggressive responses toward outsiders. *Merrill-Palmer Quarterly, 15*, 249–258.

Feshbach, N. D. (1973, August). Empathy: An interpersonal process. In W. Hartup (Chair), *Social understanding in children and adults: Perspectives on social cognition.* Presented at the meeting of the American Psychological Association, Montreal.

Feshbach, N. D. (1975a). The relationship of child-rearing factors to children's aggression, empathy, and related positive and negative behaviors. In J. deWit & W. W. Hartup (Eds.), *Determinants and origins of aggressive behavior* (pp. 427–436). The Hague, Mouton.

Feshbach, N. D. (1975b). Empathy in children: Some theoretical and empirical considerations. *Counseling Psychologist, 5*(2), 25–30.

Feshbach, N. D. (1978). Studies of empathic behavior in children. In B. A. Maher (Ed.), *Progress in experimental personality research* (Vol. 8, pp. 1–47). New York: Academic Press.

Feshbach, N. D. (1979). Empathy training: A field study in affective education. In S. Feshbach & A. Fraczek (Eds.), *Aggression and behavior change: Biological and social processes* (pp. 234–249). New York: Praeger.

Feshbach, N. D. (1980, May 5–9). *The psychology of empathy and the empathy of psychology.* Presented at the 60th annual meeting of the Western Psychological Association, Honolulu.

Feshbach, N. D. (1982). Sex differences in empathy and social behavior in children. In N. Eisenberg (Ed.), *The development of prosocial behavior.* New York: Academic Press.

Feshbach, N., & Beigel, A. (1968). A note on the use of the semantic differential in measuring teacher personality and values. *Educational and Psychological Measurement, 28*, 923–929.

Feshbach, N. D., & Feshbach, S. (1969). The relationship between empathy and aggression in two age groups. *Developmental Psychology, 1*, 102–107.

Feshbach, N. [D.], & Feshbach, S. (1982). Empathy training and the regulation of aggression: Potentialities and limitations: *Academic Psychology Bulletin, 4*(3), 399–413.

Feshbach, N. [D.], Feshbach, S., Fauvre, M., & Ballard-Campbell, M. (1983). *Learning to care: A curriculum for affective and social development.* Glenview: Scott, Foresman.

Feshbach, N. [D.], & Hoffman, M. (1978, April). *Sex differences in children's reports of emotion-arousing situations.* Paper presented in Diane McGuiness (Chair), *Sex differences: Commotion, motion or emotion: Psychological gender differences.* Symposium presented at Western Psychological Association Meetings, San Francisco.

Feshbach, N. [D.], & Kuchenbecker, N. (1974, September). A three component model of empathy. In R. Iannotti (Chair), *The concept of empathy: Bond between cognition and social behavior*. Presented at the 82nd Annual Conference of the American Psychological Association, New Orleans.

Feshbach, N. [D.], & Roe, K. (1968). Empathy in six- and seven-year-olds. *Child Development, 39*, 133–145.

Feshbach, S. (1970). *Aggression*. In P. Mussen (Ed.), *Carmichael's manual of child psychology* (Vol. II, pp. 159–259). New York: Wiley.

Feshbach, S., & Feshbach, N. [D.] (1972, February). *Cognitive processes in the self-regulation of children's aggression*. Presented at the conference on developmental aspects of self-regulation, La Jolla, CA.

Feshbach, S., & Feshbach, N. D. (1977). *Effects of fantasy and empathy training on aggression*. National Science Foundation grant No. BNS76–01261. Los Angeles: University of California.

Feshbach, S., & Weiner, B. (1982). *Personality*. Lexington: Heath.

Freundl, P. C. When is assertion aggressive? Unpublished doctoral dissertation, University of California, Los Angeles, 1977.

Friedrich, L. K., & Stein, A. H. (1973). Aggressive and prosocial television programs and the natural behavior of preschool children. *Monographs of the Society for Research in Child Development, 38* (4, Serial. No. 151).

Goldstein, A. P., Sherman, M., Gershaw, N. J., Sprafkin, R. P., & Glick, B. (1978). Training aggressive adolescents in prosocial behavior, *Journal of Youth and Adolescence, 7*(1), 73–92, 1978.

Harris, M. B., & Siebel, C. E. (1975). Affect, aggression, and altruism. *Developmental Psychology, 11*, 623–627.

Hartmann, H., Kris, E., & Lowenstein, R. (1949). Notes on the theory of aggression. In A. Freud (Ed.), *The psychoanalytic study of the child* (vol. 3, pp. 9–36). New York: International Universities Press.

Hoffman, M. L. (1975). Developmental synthesis of affect and cognition and its implications for altruistic motivation. *Developmental Psychology, 11*, 605–622.

Hoffman, M. L. (1977). Sex differences in empathy. *Psychological Bulletin, 84*, 712–722.

Hoffman, M. [L.] (1978). Empathy: Its development and prosocial implications. In C. B. Keasey (Ed.), *The Nebraska symposium on motivation, 1977: Social cognitive development*. Lincoln: University of Nebraska Press.

Huckabay, L. M. A developmental study of the relationship of negative moral-social behaviors to empathy to positive social behaviors and to cognitive moral judgment. *Science & direct patient care* II, 5th Avenue Nurse Scientist Conference Proceedings, Denver, Colorado, 1972.

Jack, L. (1934). An experimental study of ascendant behavior in preschool children. In G. D. Stoddard (Ed.), *Behavior of the preschool child. University of Iowa Studies*: Studies in Child Welfare; 9, No. 3.

Kurdek, L. A. (1978). Relationship between cognitive perspective-taking and teachers' ratings of children's classroom behavior in grades one through four. *Journal of Genetic Psychology, 132*, 21–27.

Mehrabian, A., & Epstein, N. (1972). A measure of emotional empathy. *Journal of Personality, 40*(4), 525–543.

Murphy, L. B. (1937). *Social behavior and child personality*. New York: Columbia University Press.

O'Connor, M., Dollinger, S., Kennedy, S., & Pelletier-Smetko, P. (1979). Prosocial behavior and psychopathology in emotionally disturbed boys. *American Journal of Orthopsychiatry, 49*, 301–310.

Page, M. L. (1936). The experimental modification of ascendant behavior in preschool children. *University of Iowa Studies: Studies in Child Welfare, 12*, No. 3.

Radke-Yarrow, M. R., Zahn-Waxler, C., & Chapman, M. (1983). Children's prosocial dispositions and behavior. In P. H. Mussen (Ed.), *Carmichael's manual of child psychology* (vol. IV, pp. 469–546). (4th ed.). New York: Wiley.

Rothenberg, B. B. (1970). Child's social sensitivity and the relationship to interpersonal competence, intrapersonal comfort and intellectual level. *Developmental Psychology, 2*(3), 335–350.

Rutherford, E., & Mussen, P. (1968). Generosity in nursery school boys. *Child Development, 39*, 755–765.

Sakagami, S. F., & Akahira, Y. (1960). Studies on the Japanese honeybee, *Api cerand cerona* Fabricius: 8, two opposing adaptations in the post-stinging behavior of honeybees. *Evolution, 14*(1), 29–40.

Shantz, C. U. (1975). The development of social cognition. In E. M. Hetherington (Ed.), *Review of child development research* (vol. 5). Chicago: University of Chicago Press.

Shantz, C. U. (1985). Social cognition. In P. H. Mussen (Ed.), *Carmichael's manual of child psychology* (4th ed., pp. 495–555). New York: Wiley.

Wilson, E. O. (1975). *Sociobiology: The new synthesis*. Cambridge, MA.: Harvard University Press.

Yarrow, M. R., & Waxler, C. Z. (1976). Dimensions and correlates of prosocial behavior in young children. *Child Development, 47*, 118–125.

8   The socialization of prosocial behavior: theory and reality

Joan E. Grusec and Theodore Dix

In this chapter we shall be concerned with two aspects of the socialization process. First, we shall discuss psychological theory and research designed to establish the most effective ways of training children to adapt to the values and demands of society, and second, we shall then consider research concerned with the actual behavior of parents who have the responsibility of instilling these values in their children. The question of interest is the extent to which psychological theory and parent behavior are similar. Do parents behave the way psychologists say they should? If not, why not? To anticipate, the concordance between psychological dictate and parent behavior is not always perfect, and we shall speculate about why this is so.

Theories of child-rearing

One of the chief tasks parents face is transmitting to their offspring information about socially acceptable ways of behaving and motivating them to behave in accord with this information even in the absence of surveillance. For a psychologist attempting to understand the socialization process, then, the challenge is to find out how societal values are internalized, that is, how children come to adopt them as their own. Throughout the history of psychological thought and theorizing, a number of suggestions have been offered. For Freud, socialization came about as the result of resolution of the Oedipal conflict, in which the child identified with the threatening parent as a way of reducing anxiety about the possibility of castration. By identifying with, or incorporating, the beliefs and attitudes of the feared aggressor, the child became a socialized member of society. Other forms of identification have also been postulated as sources of the internalization of moral attitudes and beliefs (see, e.g., Mowrer, 1960; Sears, 1957). In addition, variants of social learning theory have been proposed to deal with the problem. Children have been thought to behave

218

as their parents wish in order to avoid the conditioned anxiety produced by the temptation to deviate (e.g., Solomon, Turner, & Lessac, 1968). Bandura (1977) proposed that individuals establish standards of achievement for themselves through observing the standards of others and being differentially reinforced for adopting these standards. Adherence to these standards produces self-reinforcement, while their violation leads to self-punishment. In this way, then, behavior is maintained independent of external surveillance and coercion.

One very influential theory has been proposed by Hoffman (1970, 1975, 1982). He argues that different techniques of child-rearing will be differentially effective because of the impact they have on children's emotions and thoughts. Children whose parents use power assertive techniques of discipline (punishment) will not internalize societal standards because there is no need for them to behave prosocially in the absence of concrete threats of punishment by the parent. Furthermore, power assertion arouses hostility, which is detrimental to a desire to conform. Reasoning, on the other hand, particularly what Hoffman labels "other-oriented induction," facilitates the internalization of parental demands. Other-oriented induction makes the child aware of the effects of his or her behavior on others; the knowledge of these effects cannot be escaped, even in the absence of the socializing agent.

Attribution theory and internalization

Recently, attribution theory has been used in an attempt to understand the complexities of the socialization process (Dienstbier, Hillman, Lehnhoff, Hillman, & Valkenaar, 1975; Lepper, 1983; Walters & Grusec, 1977). Attribution theory suggests that individuals attempt to find reasons for why they have engaged in certain acts and that these reasons affect subsequent behavior. In the area of socialization, this means that the cognitions of the child who is the recipient of certain child-rearing practices will be central in determining the effectiveness of those practices. Children who see their behavior as coerced (as occurring in response to fear of punishment or hope of material reward) will attribute it to external forces and be unlikely to repeat it in the absence of such external force. When behavior is less obviously forced, however, as when a parent uses reasoning to gain compliance, it cannot easily be attributed to external pressure and so must have been the result of an inner desire. Thus it is internalized. Certainly reward and punishment may control behavior effectively in the short term. But performance of that behavior in new situations, and in the absence of adult surveillance is, according to attribution theory, mediated by children's inferences about themselves and about the factors controlling their behavior. Children who come to believe that their prosocial behavior reflects values or dispositions in themselves have internal structures that can generate behavior across settings and without external pressures. By contrast, children who view their prosocial conduct as compliance with external authority, will act prosocially only when they believe external pressures are present. This is the attributional model of socialization.

The approach has two interesting implications. First, if too much pressure is put on a child to conform then behavior will not be internalized. But enough pressure must be placed so that the behavior actually occurs, for if it does not then there is no prosocial act about which to make internal attributions. Moreover, a child who successfully resists a parent's pressure to comply may make attributions that will inhibit the development of prosocial behavior (Lepper, 1983). Second, agents of socialization can affect internalization by the way in which they interpret their children's behavior for them. Parents who accentuate internal reasons will promote internalization, while those who stress external reasons will retard internalization. Even if considerable pressure is used to elicit compliance, the salience of that pressure can be reduced by parental interpretation. A parent who punishes undesirable behavior, for example, but accompanies the punishment with compelling reasons why the behavior is unacceptable may mask the coerciveness of the punishment and induce the formation of internal attributions. Even if a child's conduct is spontaneous or unconstrained, internal attributions may occur only after adults assist the child in recognizing the internal or dispositional implications of that behavior.

Substantial evidence supports the attribution position with respect to compliance and internalization. First, research does demonstrate that external force is related to poor internalization. Lepper (1973), for example, induced children to avoid an attractive toy with either mild or strong commands. When they were observed later during the experimenter's absence, children in the mild pressure condition continued to avoid the forbidden toy more than children in the strong pressure condition. Children who had experienced mild pressure also showed more compliance during a generalization test in a different situation. A negative relationship between external pressure and internalization has been observed, as well, in research showing that children who are given concrete rewards for engaging in enjoyable activities choose those activities less in subsequent free-choice play periods than do children who are given no external incentives. Thus intrinsic motivation for these activities is undermined when external incentives are used (Lepper, Greene, & Nisbett, 1973). Other forms of constraint, such as external surveillance (Lepper & Greene, 1975) and making activities the means to an end (Lepper, Sagotsky, Dafoe, & Greene, 1982) similarly reduce intrinsic motivation. Research on parent socialization techniques likewise suggests that external power retards internalization. Hoffman (1970) reviewed a large number of studies showing that parents who rely on coercive discipline practices tend to have children who score poorly on a variety of measures of moral internalization.

As the attribution position might predict, different types of external pressure have somewhat different effects on children's behavior. Social rewards and punishments do not appear to undermine internalization in the same way that concrete contingencies do. C. L. Smith, Gelfand, Hartmann, and Partlow (1979) found that children scolded or praised for sharing did not refer to external factors in explaining their behavior, whereas children given material consequences did. In addition, when verbal reinforcement is given for engaging in an activity, subsequent intrinsic interest in that activity can actually increase, in sharp contrast to reductions in intrinsic motivation observed when material rewards are used (Deci, 1971; Anderson, Manoogian, & Reznick, 1976). Other research suggests that when rewards are seen as providing information about the adequacy of performance, rather than as the cause for engaging in an activity, they do not have a negative impact on intrinsic motivation (Pallak, Costomiris, Sroka, & Pittman, 1982). Thus subtle rewards, or those related to performance, do not have the same adverse effects that powerful, motivationally relevant rewards have.

The second source of support for the attribution position comes from research in which children are asked to supply reasons for why they, or other individuals, have engaged in particular acts. These reasons differ, depending on the salience of external pressures for inducing behavior. Moreover, the kinds of reasons offered are of the type predicted by attribution theory. By about 7 years of age, for example, children begin to think that engaging in freely chosen activities reflects personal desires and dispositions more than does engaging in activities because of adult commands or hope of gaining material rewards. Thus Dix and Grusec (1983) asked children to make attributions about the altruistic behavior of children in stories in which helping either (1) was spontaneous, (2) resulted from the observation of a model, or (3) was done in response to threats of punishment from an adult. In the latter case, children attributed altruism to a desire to please the adult. Altruism that was spontaneous or that occurred after exposure to an altruistic model, on the other hand, was attributed to a personal disposition of helpfulness. Costanzo, Grumet, and Brehm (1974), Karniol and Ross (1976), and M. C. Smith (1975) also demonstrated that children distinguish between spontaneous acts and those induced by external pressure. When behavior, rather than verbal judgment, is used as the dependent measure, the effect appears to emerge even earlier than the age of seven (Wells & Shultz, 1980).

A third source of support comes from studies in which adults provide children with attributions for their behavior, rather than relying on the spontaneous occurrence of such activity in the actors themselves. These studies have demonstrated that behavior attributed to stable, internal dispositions (internal attributions) generalizes more and is more independent of immediate external controls than is behavior attributed to external factors (external attributions). Grusec, Kuczynski, Rushton and Simutis (1978), for example, persuaded children to share prizes they had won with needy children. The persuasion took one of two forms: either the children observed an adult model engage in such sharing, or they were directed to share. Presumably the latter was a more coercive manipulation than the former. Subjects (all of whom had donated) were then told that they had donated either because they felt it was expected (an external reason) or because they were the kind of people who liked to help others (an internal reason). When the actual cause of the child's sharing was ambiguous, that is, in the modeling condition, children exposed to internal attributions shared more when they were alone both immediately and two weeks later than did children exposed to external attributions. In both modeling and direct-instruction conditions, internal attributions elicited more sharing than did external attributions during a generalization test.

In a second study, Grusec and Redler (1980) found that 7- and 8-year-olds exposed to internal attributions for sharing tended to share more on a variety of tests of generalized altruism than did children exposed to social reinforcement, although no difference between attribution and reinforcement were evident on a test of immediate and specific sharing. Dienstbier et al. (1975) had an adult tell children that they (the children) felt badly following transgression either because they had been caught (an external reason) or because they knew they had done something wrong (an internal reason). Subsequent transgression was lower among the children given internal explanations than among those given external explanations. These studies and others (Davison, Tsujimoto, & Glaros, 1973; Dweck, 1975; Jensen & Moore, 1977; Kiesler, Nisbett, & Zanna, 1969; Miller, Brickman, & Bolen, 1975) indicate that internal attributions do lead to greater stability and generalization of behavior than do external attributions.

A final set of studies that provides evidence for the attribution position consists of investigations indicating that reasoning that focuses on internal causes for children's behavior can promote internalization. Clearly the studies just cited demonstrate that statements about children's behavior that stress internal dispositions increase the stability and generality of that behavior. Statements about other kinds of internal causes are also effective. Thus parents may explain the intrinsic importance of just and altruistic conduct and the natural outcomes for others of aggression or selfishness. Correlational studies of parents and their children provide support for the importance of this kind of reasoning within the family. As noted earlier, Hoffman (1970, 1975) cites numerous studies that have examined parental factors related to moral internalization; he concludes that parents who explain to children the impact their behavior has on others, that is, who use "other-oriented induction," tend to have offspring who score well on measures of moral internalization. These children show greater empathy, more concern for others, more principled explanations for behavior, and more guilt after transgression than do those whose parents use little reasoning. Laboratory studies, as well, indicate that reasoning about internal causes (e.g., children should not play with certain toys because the experimenter does not have any more like them and is afraid they might become worn-out or broken) increases conformity and internalization (Cheyne & Walters, 1969; Parke, 1969).

Reasoning that frames children's behavior in terms of external causes should, of course, retard internalization. Thus parents whose verbal interchanges stress compliance, saying "because I said so" or "because if you don't you'll get into trouble," should increase external attributions. It should be noted, however, that even reasoning which does not refer to external pressure can, under certain conditions, interfere with the making of internal attributions. Dix and Grusec (1983) found this to be the case. As noted earlier, we asked children to make attributions about the altruistic behavior of individuals in stories in which helping was either spontaneous or induced through observation of a model or with threats of punishment. In addition, mothers in our stories sometimes reasoned briefly about the need for helping and sometimes did not. For females these reasoning statements, when paired with power assertion, made attributions more internal than when power assertion was used alone, just as would be predicted from the attribution position. However, for females reasoning actually decreased internal attributions when it was paired with spontaneous helping. It appears that even when the content of reasoning concerns internal causes, it can increase external attribution by communicating parents' preferences for children's behavior. When parents are using no explicit pressures, their reasoning can be viewed as implicit pressure. This relationship, as we indicated, held only for girls. For boys, reasoning had no effect in our experimental situation. This finding of sex differences in responsivity to reasoning does tie in with other studies indicating that females are more responsive to inductive reasoning (Kuczynski, 1982) and that they are more empathic (Hoffman, 1975, 1977), although the findings of sex differences in empathy are somewhat equivocal (Radke-Yarrow, Zahn-Waxler, & Chapman, 1983).

Maternal socialization practices

From the preceding analysis of the socialization process, we gain some idea of those practices that might ensure internalization of societal values. The attribution approach has a number of implications for how parents might promote internalization. It suggests that they should avoid the use of material rewards or punishments, emphasizing instead those of a social nature. Under these conditions, internal attributions may be more easily made. Research suggests, however, that direct attribution of positive dispositions should be an even more effective way to promote the generalization of prosocial behavior (recall the findings reported by Grusec and Redler, 1980). Reasoning, possibly paired with more coercive techniques designed to achieve compliance, should be useful. In this section of the paper we shall address the issue of what it is that parents actually do, in everyday life, in their attempt to train acceptable behavior. Do they behave as attribution theory suggests they should? Are some techniques of socialization used more frequently then others? If such is the case one would wish to ascertain why. Do parents employ practices that have received little or no attention in theory or research, and what would an attributional model say about the potential effectiveness of these techniques?

We have gathered data on maternal socialization techniques using two methodological approaches. The first is similar to that employed by Radke-Yarrow and Zahn-Waxler (see, e.g., Zahn-Waxler & Radke-Yarrow, 1982) and first developed by Goodenough (1931). Mothers were trained in both group and individuals sessions to record the altruistic behavior of their children and the reactions that that behavior elicited. We asked them to note all instances of altruism by their children (helping, sharing, giving, defending, comforting, making reparation, encouraging, and showing affection, concern, or consideration) and all situations in which altruism should have occurred but did not. They were asked to write a description of what happened in each of these situations as soon after its occurrence as possible. Data were gathered for approximately 4 weeks by the mothers of 11 boys and 11 girls who were 4 years old and 10 boys and 10 girls who were 7 years old. The children were middle class and Caucasian, and most had mothers who were not employed outside the home.

Reliability of maternal reports was assessed in two ways. After intensive training at identifying and recording altruism and its consequences each mother was shown, individually, a 20-minute videotape of an "average" day in the life of a family. There were 12 altruism-related events embedded in the tape. They were then asked to identify every instance of altruism as they saw it. As well, mothers were visited by a research technician part way through the data-collection period. They were instructed to make two requests for altruism of their child, and the mother and the research technician then made independent written descriptions of the event. In the case of the videotape, mothers correctly identified an average of 96% of the relevant events. Interobserver agreement between the mother and the research assistant for various reactions to altruism ranged from 75 to 100%. Reliability of coding of material from maternal reports was also assessed, and here intercoder agreement ranged from 82 to 96% for each response category.

The second methodology used to assess maternal socialization practices has been a more structured one. In two studies (Grusec, Dix, & Mills, 1982; Dix, Ruble, Grusec, & Nixon, 1982), we read short stories to mothers that depicted prosocial acts and/or various kinds of misdeeds. Examples of these stories included scenarios in which a child helped a neighbor pick up pieces of his newspaper that had been blown all around his yard, a child took the last piece of cake without asking if others wanted it, and a child aggressed physically against another person. Mothers were asked to role play that it was their own child who had engaged in the act and to say how they would respond by describing exactly what they would say and do and how they would feel. Thus, one mother reported in the case of aggression that she would be disappointed in her child, would explain to him that physical assault is wrong, and would punish him by confining him to his room. In addition, in the study by Dix et al., mothers were asked to make various judgments about reasons for the behavior of the child in the story. For example, they were asked to say whether or not the behavior was a function of some disposition in the child, a response to temporary external events (e.g., fatigue), or a reflection of lack of knowledge of appropriate behavior (in the case of misdeeds). In this way we hoped to look at some of the attributions possibly mediating their socialization practices. The mothers who responded in these studies had children ranging in age from 4 to 12 years, specifically, 4, 8, and 12 years for Dix et al., and 8 years for Grusec et al. Intercoder agreement on various categories of maternal response ranged from 82 to 86%.

Compared with the first, this second methodology is more removed from actual day-to-day parent–child interaction. Sometimes mothers may be asked to react to behavior that their child might never display, and in this

Table 8.1. *Percentage of responses to spontaneous altruism*

Responses	Home observation	Dix et al.
Acknowledge, thank, etc.	18	1
Social approval (smile, hug, warm appreciation)	15	11
Praise the act	14	70
Ignore	13	4
Attribution	4	4
Material reward	<1	1

case their efforts to imagine what they might do are strained. To the extent that findings from the two approaches are similar, however, faith can be placed in each one as yielding a reasonably accurate picture of socialization practices. The structured approach also has advantages. It enables us to manipulate various dimensions of children's behavior to assess the effects of a variety of variables on maternal intervention. Waiting for specific behavior to occur in the natural course of daily interaction can be inefficient.

Reactions to altruism

Responses to naturally occurring altruism were collected in two studies – the home observation study and that of Dix et al. A summary of these data is presented in Table 8.1. Since there were few differences between mothers as a function of the age and sex of their children, the data were combined over these variables in Table 8.1 as well as the subsequent table. Aside from differences in the methodologies used to collect data, other distinctions between these two studies should be noted. In the home observation study any responses mothers saw their children receive were reported (e.g., smiles from siblings, praise from a neighbor), while in the role playing or interview studies they reported only their own responses. In the home observations there were many reports of simple acknowledgment of an altruistic act (e.g., "Thanks"). Mothers rarely reported these types of reactions when they were interviewed.

Mothers' responses were divided into six categories: social approval (smiles, hugs, statements of warm appreciation); praise of the act (e.g., "That was a nice thing you did"); acknowledgment and thanks; attribution of positive characteristics to the child ("What a helpful person you are"); ignoring; and material rewards. Some aspects of Table 8.1 should be noted. First, attributions of helpfulness are rarely employed (4% in both studies).

Given some of the findings reported earlier in this paper about the effectiveness of such labeling (e.g., Grusec et al., 1978; Grusec & Redler, 1980), the failure of socializing agents to use it is noteworthy. Second, while dispositional statements are infrequent, social approval, praise, and acknowledgment appear to be the responses of choice, with virtually no indication that mothers (or others in the child's environment) have any tendency to respond to prosocial acts with material reinforcement. Recall that the attributional model suggests material reinforcement may be detrimental to the development of altruism. It is interesting to note that agents of socialization behave as though they have some awareness of this in their interactions with children. The heavy reliance on social reinforcement is another matter. Although effective, our studies suggest that it is less effective in promoting altruism than attributional statements (Grusec & Redler, 1980). The reluctance of mothers and others to use attributional statements is an issue for future research, since they appear not to be using a technique that laboratory studies tell us should be particularly important.

Data from the home observation study enabled us to assess the degree of altruism in which each child engaged, as well as reactions experienced. The average number of spontaneous altruistic acts that children displayed per day was .82 for 4-year-olds and .48 for 7-year-olds. (The number for older children is less because these children were in school and therefore less frequently observed by their mothers.) We assessed the correlation between the use of a particular response to the occurrence of altruism and the amount of altruism a child displayed. We found no relationship between level of altruism and reported usage of any intervention.

What was striking was the uniformity of responses to altruism for all agents of socialization. Thus virtually all children, regardless of how altruistic they were, usually received the same response – some form of acknowledgment, social approval, and/or praise for their behavior. This uniformity of response is in keeping with studies which have found that mothers also tend to be uniform in the way in which they respond to negative behaviors. Grusec and Kuczynski (1980), for example, found that mothers responded in different ways to different kinds of misdemeanors, and that uniformity of responding was greater across a given misdeed than it was within a given mother. Using a home observation technique similar to ours, Zahn-Waxler and Chapman (1982) also found that different classes of misdeeds elicit different discipline techniques. In addition, Nucci and Turiel (1978) observed that nursery school teachers react differently to violations of morality (e.g., physical aggression, failure to be altruistic) than to violations of social conventions (e.g., following school rules). The findings of the home observation study and the study of Dix et al. indicate that this homogeneity of responding holds in the domain of prosocial behavior as well, although our theoretical analysis of socialization does not dictate that parental responses should be so intimately tied to the nature of the behavior being addressed. Why agents of socialization should be so restricted in their usage of intervention procedures as a function of the class of behavior with which they are dealing is an issue we shall discuss in the last section of this paper.

Reactions to the failure to be altruistic

Responses to the failure to be altruistic, e.g., not showing concern for someone who is injured or distressed, not helping someone who clearly needs help, and failing to share have been assessed in three investigations – the home observation study, Grusec et al., and Dix et al. These responses were coded into six categories: moral exhortation (statements about rules and expectations or reasons why a particular behavior is bad, e.g., "It's not your house," "You could put someone's eye out"); direct instruction or forcing the child to behave properly; scolding (verbal punishment, e.g., "That was selfish"); ignoring; empathy training (directing the child's attention to the feelings of others); and physical or material punishment. Empathy training was assessed because it is considered to play such an important part in the development of altruism (e.g., Hoffman, 1975), even though it does not have a specifically defined role in the attributional approach. The percentage of various disciplinary responses in these three studies can be seen in Table 8.2. It should be noted that very few – only 55 – incidents of failure to show altruism were reported in the home observation study, so any conclusions drawn from that study can only be tentative. Nevertheless, the similarities among the three studies are striking. If one looks at the rank ordering of frequency of usage of the various interventions, for example, they are quite similar across the three investigations.

It is evident from Table 8.2 that socializing agents rely to a great extent on moral exhortation in their attempts to deal with failures to be prosocial. We coded in this category any attempts at persuasion and statements of reasons for why one should be prosocial but excluded empathy training, which focused on the feelings of others. Second, punishment, which included withdrawal of privileges or material items, physical punishment, and isolation, was rarely used in attempting to deal with failures to be prosocial – the only form of power assertion reported involved direct instruction or forcing a child to engage in desirable behavior. Social disapproval was frequently used – again, attribution theory suggests that this

Table 8.2. *Percentage of responses to failure to be altruistic and antisocial behavior*

Responses	Failure to be altruistic			Antisocial act		
	Home obs.	Dix et al.	Grusec et al.	Home obs.	Dix et al.	Grusec et al.
Moral exhortation	31	34	27	20	35	34
Direct instruction, forced appropriate behavior	25	9	19	35	23	14
Scolding	16	17	9	10	9	4
No response	11	5	8	13	1	4
Empathy training	5	12	11	3	5	5
Punishment	0	4	3	10	10	16

is more likely to produce internal attributions about behavior than is physical punishment, withdrawal of material rewards and privileges, or isolation.

Because failures to be altruistic were infrequent, we could not relate parental training for lack of altruism to amount of spontaneous altruism. It is interesting to note, however, that parental responding was relatively circumscribed. Thus, punishment was very rarely used, either alone or in combination with reasoning. Some investigators, although not specifically attribution theorists, have underlined the importance of empathy training in the promotion of concern for others (e.g., Hoffman, 1975). But our parents were reluctant to use this technique: Apparently it is not a response that comes naturally in the real world.

Reactions to antisocial acts

Much socialization focuses on the commission of antisocial acts – physical aggression, lying, stealing, cheating, disobedience – rather than on the failure to initiate prosocial acts. Theories of socialization, including attribution theory, make no distinction between these classes of behavior but, as will soon become apparent, agents of socialization do. Responses to antisocial acts, defined as active participation in undesirable behavior, are presented in the second half of Table 8.2. Maternal reactions to antisocial acts were studied in both the Dix et al. and Grusec et al. studies. We classified failures to comply with requests for altruism as antisocial acts in the home observation study. Children in that study were no doubt displaying other misdeeds, but we did not ask mothers to report on them because our pretesting indicated this would make their reporting task too demanding.

Parallels across the three studies for misconduct are generally as striking as those for altruism and the failure to be altruistic. It is clear that parents do use a great deal of moral exhortation in dealing with antisocial acts, but that they are, in fact, reluctant to use empathy training. Second, while power assertion in the form of withdrawal of privileges and material rewards, physical punishment, and isolation was rarely used when children failed to be prosocial, it was used to a moderate degree in dealing with antisocial acts. It was, however, never used alone, but in combination with reasoning. Direct instruction or forced appropriate behavior was used frequently for the commission of antisocial acts, and Dix et al. found that the use of one or the other of these increased significantly with age for antisocial behavior.

Failure to be altruistic and misdeeds compared

Comparisons of discipline interventions used across the two classes of misdeed presented in Table 8.2 are instructive. We shall describe the Grusec et al. study in detail with respect to this comparison since it was specifically designed to compare maternal reactions to antisocial behavior with maternal reactions to failure to be prosocial. The findings of this study, however, parallel those of the other studies summarized in Table 8.2. Grusec et al. read mothers two types of stories – stories about misdeeds that were antisocial and stories about misdeeds that involved failure to engage in prosocial behavior. We had previously attempted to equate these stories in terms of how serious the misdemeanors were perceived to be. We also manipulated severity of misdeed within each type of misdeed, as well as whether the victim of the misdeed was another child, the mother, or a neighbor. The attempt to equate for perceived severity was not entirely successful. While the two types of misdeeds were seen as equally serious when the victim was a peer, parallel misdeeds directed against adults were seen as more serious when the misdeed was antisocial rather than the failure to be prosocial. Nevertheless, the results with respect to discipline held regardless of the victim of the misdeed, so that they do not appear simply to reflect differences in perceived severity. Analysis of mothers' reported discipline techniques indicated that, for girls, they used significantly more empathy training for the omission of altruism than the commission of antisocial acts. As well, they were significantly more likely to use material and physical punishment for antisocial behavior than for failures to be prosocial by either boys or girls.

Summary

In response to the questions posed about the nature of parental training techniques at the beginning of this section, we can draw several conclusions. Children who engage in spontaneous altruism receive a great deal of social reinforcement but little in the way of character attributions or material reinforcement. Failures to be altruistic are met with reasoning, although not much that is empathically oriented in nature. The only type of punishment that occurs is social disapproval. By contrast, agents of socialization respond to antisocial acts such as aggression, dishonesty, and disobedience with reasoning (but not empathically oriented reasoning) and with physical punishment or punishment in the form of withdrawal of rewards and privileges or social isolation. The two are used in combination, however, with punishment never used alone. Finally, parents do not appear to use techniques that have not received some attention by psychological researchers and theoreticians.

Determinants of maternal socialization practices

Our attributional analysis of the development of moral behavior suggests certain parenting practices should be particularly effective in inducing acceptable behavior. Our survey of actual parenting practices, using both naturalistic-observational and role-playing methodologies, indicates that mothers generally act in accord with the dictates of an attributional model. They employ a great deal of reasoning, they avoid material reward for altruism and punishment for failure to be altruistic. When they punish antisocial acts they pair the punishment with reasoning. However, mothers are not using all the discipline techniques they might – for example, empathy training and the attribution of prosocial characteristics are infrequently employed. Moreover, the specificity of maternal behavior relative to particular acts displayed by the child is a compelling feature of much of our data. Mothers select from their repertoire of interventions certain ones as a function of the behavior to which they are responding. Rather than see a great deal of consistency in the way one mother reacts to her child we see, instead, that mothers respond consistently to a particular misdemeanor and that a given mother uses a wide variety of interventions, tailoring them to specific misdeeds.

These findings suggest that, in order to achieve a more complete understanding of the growth of moral behavior, we must have an understanding of what variables affect the behavior of agents of socialization, as well as those that affect the behavior of the objects of socialization. Some idea of how and why adults behave as they do should, in the final analysis, aid us in understanding the level and kind of moral achievements of their children.

We shall focus on two aspects of maternal behavior. The first has to do with the specific goals adults have for the socialization of behavior. To the extent that their aim is different for different classes of behavior one should expect them to rely on different socialization techniques. The second aspect has to do with the impact of different behaviors on the feelings and thoughts of adults. If some child acts arouse more anger than others, or lead adults to make different attributions about their causation, then this could lead to different adult responses.

Consider first the suggestion that parent goals may differ for different behavior. Most theories of socialization assume the goal of parenting is successful internalization of societal values and beliefs. That is, they assume that behavior must be suppressed even in the absence of external surveillance. Yet there may be occasions on which adults are quite happy merely to produce children who conform in their presence. Responding to requests for help, the assumption of responsibility for certain household chores, and playing a stereo quietly need not be internalized. They are required only in the presence of the controlling agent. Some data support the idea that these different goals are associated with different parent practices. Kuczynski (1984) has demonstrated that mothers use different techniques depending on whether they are trying to influence a child in their presence or in their absence. In the former case they use power assertion, while in the latter they are more inclined to reason. Parents of lower socioeconomic status are more likely to be power assertive and controlling while those of higher socioeconomic status are more likely to reason (Hess, 1970). While a number of reasons have been offered for this observation it could well reflect differing goals of socialization for these two groups. Internalization has been suggested to be a middle-class concept, necessary where people are assigned responsibility and must often function independent of scrutiny by others, while in lower-class society surveillance is more often the rule (Hoffman, 1970). To achieve internalization, then, the middle classes may rely to a greater extent on reasoning, while greater use of power assertion achieves the lower-class goal of suppression in the presence of surveillance.

Different goals may reveal themselves in differential treatment of antisocial acts such as aggression and the failure to be prosocial. Recall that we found mothers were more likely to use punishment in response to the commission of antisocial behavior. Our society has different attitudes to these two classes of misdeed and the behavior of our mothers may well reflect these attitudes. Antisocial acts, such as stealing, lying, cheating, and committing physical aggression, involve the violation of explicit and mandatory standards. They are never sanctioned and they are never optional. The failure to be altruistic, in contrast, involves the violation of preferred but not mandatory standards. Sharing, helping, and comforting are praiseworthy but are not explicitly required. If the goal in the case of antisocial acts is swift and uniform suppression mothers may attempt to accomplish this though the use of punishment. Where there is apparent choice, altruism can be encouraged through moral exhortation and sensitizing the child to the feeling of others. In the end, however, the child can make a choice.

Other maternal goals that might affect selection of discipline techniques include a consideration of the relative desirability of different motivating techniques. Our mothers did not rely to any great extent on empathy training, a procedure that, in the end, motivates through the arousal of vicarious discomfort. Perhaps they were unwilling to use too much emotional arousal out of concern for the ultimate well-being of their children. Similarly, if dispositional attributions are perceived by mothers to modify self-perceptions, they may avoid them in an attempt to achieve "better adjustment" in their children. Perhaps mothers avoid telling their children they are good or generous so as not to make them conceited.

Now we turn to the suggestion that different misdeeds have inherent properties to arouse differing emotions and thoughts. Zahn-Waxler and Chapman (1982), for example, suggest that when young children harm objects and show lack of impulse control (e.g., color the sofa with magic markers or spit in their milk) these acts naturally arouse more anger in their mothers than do physical or psychological harm to others. They indicate that this may be the variable mediating different discipline techniques in the two cases – in the former, punishment, and in the latter, reasoning and "dramatic enactments of distress" (surely a form of empathy training). Grusec et al. found that mothers were more upset by antisocial acts than by the failure to be prosocial, even when the two classes of misdeed were rated as equal in severity. Again, this difference in anger could have helped mediate the different responses they made. When angrier, they used more punishment. More serious acts also produced more anger, and this anger may have been responsible for producing differences we also observed in amount of intervention, particularly in the form of increased forced appropriate behavior for all serious misdeeds, and increased punishment for serious antisocial acts.

When children misbehave, as well as engage in good behavior, these acts have an impact on the thoughts as well as the emotions of mothers. We have measured the effects of different acts on some of these thoughts

(Dix et al., 1982). Although the specific relationships between thought and discipline intervention have yet to be worked out, some of the observed child behavior–mother attribution relationships provided material for interesting speculation. For example, as children grow older, their behavior (both good and bad) is more likely to be attributed to stable dispositions and to be seen as intentional and under their own control. In addition, mothers become more upset when their children misbehave as a function of the child's increasing age, with the correlation between amount of affect and dispositional attribution being positive and significant. To the extent that a mother's anger or upset is transmitted to her child, one would expect that mothers who attribute their children's misdeeds to dispositions and who see them as intentional would discipline them in a more emotional way. We find find that expressions of disappointment and hurt increased with age and that empathy training decreased with age (both effects were statistically significant), a suggestion that as mothers become more angry and more convinced that they are dealing with entrenched behavior they are less willing to train sensitivity for the feelings of others and more willing to criticize.

These are but a few of the variables that need to be included in a theory that focuses on determinants of adult socialization behavior. Other characteristics of children's misdemeanors also come to mind as having a limiting effect on adult reactions. Some forms of discipline may aggravate the very behavior they are intended to suppress. Hitting a child for physical aggression, yelling at a crying child, and labeling a child as deceitful for lying may all exacerbate the behavior one intends to eliminate, and agents of socialization may be sensitive to these relationships. Such variables must all be considered before we can have a complete understanding of the socialization process.

Implications for the development of altruism and aggression

In this chapter we have suggested that parent behavior and socialization practices are mediated by the nature of the behavior to which parents are responding. For example, our data suggest that the failure to be altruistic and antisocial behavior (e.g., aggression) are socialized differently. We have suggested that these different reactions may be mediated by different goals for the two classes of behavior, and different affect and cognitions that they produce in agents of socialization.

What are the implications of this position for an understanding of the origins of altruism and aggression? One possibility is that parents are behaving optimally, and that the natural selectivity they display is functional.

Perhaps, for example, we ought to look more carefully at some of the side effects of techniques that appear from our theory and research to be so effective. Perhaps too much empathy or too many appeals to dispositional attributions are harmful. But it is also possible that children are not being socialized in the best possible way. One wonders if greater use of empathy training might not produce individuals with more sensitivity to the plight of others and greater awareness of the impact of their antisocial behavior on the world around them. Perhaps a willingness to use punishment when dealing with failures to be prosocial would produce more altruism. If, indeed, concern for others is seen as a desirable goal of socialization, then a firmer stance may be necessary to achieve this goal. When we know why parents behave as they do and understand the implications of this for the social development of their children, we shall have advanced in our knowledge of the development of altruism and antisocial behavior.

References

Anderson, R., Manoogian, S., & Resnick, J. (1976). The undermining and enhancing of intrinsic motivation in preschool children. *Journal of Personality and Social Psychology*, *5*, 915–922.

Bandura, A. (1977). *Social learning theory*. Englewood Cliffs, NJ: Prentice-Hall.

Cheyne, J.A., & Walters, R.H. (1969). Intensity of punishment, timing of punishment, and cognitive structure as determinants of response inhibition. *Journal of Experimental Child Psychology*, *7*, 231–244.

Costanzo, P., Grumet, J., & Brehm, S. (1974). The effects of choice and source of constraint on children's attribution of preference. *Journal of Experimental Social Psychology*, *10*, 352–364.

Davison, G.C., Tsujimoto, R., & Glaros, A. (1973). Attribution and the maintenance of behavior change in falling asleep. *Journal of Abnormal Psychology*, *82*, 124–133.

Deci, E.L. (1971). Effects of externally mediated rewards on intrinsic motivation. *Journal of Personality and Social Psychology*, *18*, 105–115.

Dienstbier, R.A., Hillman, D., Lehnhoff, J., Hillman, J., & Valkenaar, M.C. (1975). An emotion-attribution approach to moral behavior: Interfacing cognitive and avoidance theories of moral development. *Psychological Review*, *82*, 299–315.

Dix, T., & Grusec, J.E. (1983). Parent influence techniques: An attributional analysis. *Child Development*, *54*, 645–652.

Dix, T., Ruble, D.N., Grusec, J.E., & Nixon, S. (1982). *Parents' beliefs about the causes and development of children's behavior*. Unpublished manuscript.

Dweck, C.S. (1975). The role of expectations and attributions in the alleviation of learned helplessness. *Journal of Personality and Social Psychology*, *31*, 674–685.

Goodenough, F.L. (1931). *Anger in young children*. Minneapolis: University of Minnesota Press.

Grusec, J.E., Dix, T., & Mills, R. (1982). The effects of type, severity and victim of children's transgressions on maternal discipline. *Canadian Journal of Behavioural Science*, *14*, 276–289.

Grusec, J.E., & Kuczynski, L. (1980). Direction of effect in socialization: A comparison of the parent vs. the child's behavior as determinants of disciplinary techniques. *Developmental Psychology, 6*, 1–9.

Grusec, J.E., Kuczynski, L., Rushton, J.P., & Simutis, Z.M. (1978). Modeling, direct instruction, and attributions: Effects on altruism. *Developmental Psychology, 14*, 51–57.

Grusec, J.E., & Redler, E. (1980). Attribution, reinforcement, and altruism. *Developmental Psychology, 16*, 525–534.

Hess, R.D. (1970). Social class and ethnic influences upon socialization. In P.H. Mussen (Ed.), *Carmichael's manual of child psychology* (Vol. 2, pp. 457–557). New York: Wiley.

Hoffman, M.L. (1970). Moral development. In P.H. Mussen (Ed.), *Carmichael's manual of child psychology* (Vol. 2). New York: Wiley.

Hoffman, M.L. (1975). Sex differences in moral internalization. *Journal of Personality and Social Psychology, 32*, 720 729.

Hoffman, M.L. (1977). Empathy, its development and prosocial implications. In C. Keasey (Ed.), *Nebraska Symposium on Motivation* (Vol. 25). Lincoln: University of Nebraska Press.

Jensen, R.E., & Moore, S.G. (1977). The effect of attribute statements on cooperativeness and competitiveness in school-age boys. *Child Development, 48*, 305–307.

Karniol, R., & Ross, M. (1976). The development of causal attributions in social perception. *Journal of Personality and Social Psychology, 34*, 455–464.

Kiesler, C.A., Nisbett, R.E., & Zanna, M.P. (1969). On inferring one's beliefs from one's behavior. *Journal of Personality and Social Psychology, 11*, 321–327.

Kuczynski, L. (1982). Intensity and orientation of reasoning: Motivational determinants of children's compliance with verbal rationales. *Journal of Experimental Child Psychology, 34*, 357–370.

Kuczynski, L. (1985). Socialization goals and mother–child interaction: Strategies for short term and long term compliance. *Developmental Psychology, 20*, 1061–1073.

Lepper, M.R. (1973). Dissonance, self-perception, and honesty in children. *Journal of Personality and Social Psychology, 25*, 65–74.

Lepper, M.R. (1983). Social control processes, attributions of motivation, and the internalization of social values. In E. T. Higgins, D. N. Ruble, & W. W. Hartup, (Eds.), *Social cognition and social development: A sociocultural perspective* (pp. 294–330). New York: Cambridge University Press.

Lepper, M.R., & Greene, D. (1975). Turning play into work: Effects of adult surveillance and extrinsic rewards on children's intrinsic motivation. *Journal of Personality and Social Psychology, 31*, 479–486.

Lepper, M. R., Greene, D., & Nisbett, R. (1973). Undermining children's intrinsic interest with extrinsic reward: A test of the overjustification hypothesis. *Journal of Personality and Social Psychology, 28*, 129–137.

Lepper, M.R., Sagotsky, G., Dafoe, J., & Greene, D. (1982). Consequences of superfluous social constraints: Effects on young children's social inferences and subsequent intrinsic interest. *Journal of Personality and Social Psychology, 42*, 51–65.

Miller, R.L., Brickman, P., & Bolen, D. (1975). Attribution vs. persuasion as a means for modifying behavior. *Journal of Personality and Social Psychology, 31*, 430–441.

Mowrer, O.H. (1960). *Learning theory and the symbolic processes*. New York: Wiley.

Nucci, L.P., & Turiel, E. (1978). Social interaction and the development of social concepts in preschool children. *Child Development, 49*, 400–407.

Pallak, S.R., Costomiris, S., Sroka, S., & Pittman, T.S. (1982). School experience, reward characteristics, and intrinsic motivation. *Child Development, 53*, 1382–1391.

Parke, R. (1969). Effectiveness of punishment as an interaction of intensity, timing, agent nurturance, and cognitive structuring. *Child Development, 40*, 213–235.

Parke, R. (1974). Rules, roles, and resistance to deviation: Recent advances in punishment, discipline, and self-control. In A. Pick (Ed.), *Minnesota symposium on child psychology* (vol. 8). Minneapolis: University of Minnesota Press.

Radke-Yarrow, M., Zahn-Waxler, C., & Chapman, M. (1983). Children's prosocial dispositions and behavior. In P. H. Mussen (Ed.), *Carmichael's manual of child psychology* (4th ed., vol. IV). New York: Wiley.

Sears, R.R. (1957). Identification as a form of behavioral development. In D.B. Harris (Ed.), *The concept of development* (pp. 149–161). Minneapolis: University of Minnesota Press.

Smith, C.L., Gelfand, D.M., Hartmann, D.P., & Partlow, M. (1979). Children's causal attributions regarding help giving. *Child Development, 50,* 203–210.

Smith, M.C. (1975). Children's use of the multiple sufficient cause schema in social perception. *Journal of Personality and Social Psychology, 32,* 737–747.

Solomon, R.L., Turner, L.H., & Lessac, M.S. (1968). Some effects of delay of punishment on resistance to temptation in dogs. *Journal of Personality and Social Psychology, 8,* 233–238.

Walters, G.C., & Grusec, J.E. (1977). *Punishment.* San Francisco: Freeman.

Wells, E., & Shultz, T.R. (1980). Developmental distinctions between behavior and judgment in the operation of the discounting principle. *Child Development, 51,* 307–310.

Zahn-Waxler, C., & Chapman, M. (1982). Immediate antecedents of caretakers' methods of discipline. *Child Psychiatry and Human Development, 12,* 179–192.

Zahn-Waxler, C., & Radke-Yarrow, M. (1982). The development of altruism: Alternative research strategies. In N. Eisenberg (Ed.), *The development of prosocial behavior.* New York: Academic Press.

9   Social–interactional patterns in families of abused and nonabused children

John B. Reid

Although estimates of incidence differ widely from study to study and across years over the past two decades (Gil, 1970; Kempe, 1973; Gelles, 1979), it is clear that serious physical abuse of children is a widespread problem in this country. Regardless of the wide variety of estimates available, child abuse rates are alarmingly high. During 1980, nearly 800,000 reports of child maltreatment were documented in this country (*National Analysis of Official Child Neglect and Abuse Reporting*, 1981); in addition, the same study revealed more than 400 documented fatalities.

Although these figures may seem startling for a highly educated, affluent, youth-oriented nation like ours, such data only scratch the surface of parental violence toward children. As argued by Parke and Lewis (1981), official estimates undoubtedly underestimate the extent of actual parental abusiveness. A number of interview and survey studies indicate that it is indeed normative for parents to employ physical coercion and physical assault in managing their children. Stark and McEvoy (1970) estimated that more than 90% of parents either consistently use or occasionally resort to spanking or other types of physical punishment. On the basis of a recent and careful self-report study using a national probability sample, Gelles (1979) estimated that between 275,00 and 750,000 children were beaten by their parents in 1975 and that nearly 50,000 children were threatened with a deadly weapon by their parents during the same 1-year period. In an analysis of daily self-report data collected from nonabusive, nondistressed parents of preadolescent children over a period of 2 to 3 weeks, Reid (1983) found that, on the average, the parents spanked their children once every 2 weeks and that, given a parent who reacted to a problem of child behavior, the probability that the parental reaction would be spanking or physically assaultive behavior was about .03.

Family interaction and discipline

On the basis of these and similar data, we have proposed that child abuse can best be understood in terms of probabilities (e.g., Reid, Taplin, &

238

Lorber, 1981; Reid, Patterson, & Loeber, 1982). Given that most parents in this country subscribe to the use of physical coercion as a useful and legitimate discipline technique for some situations, and given that any particular child is involved in literally thousands of potential discipline confrontations with his or her parents/caretakers over the course of development (Fawl, 1963; Minton, Kagan, & Levine, 1971; Forehand, King, Peed, & Yoder, 1975; Reid, 1978), there is a certain probability that any youngster will be physically injured by his or her parents. The probability of abuse is assumed to be a function of (1) the rate or number of discipline confrontations, and (2) the degree to which any given discipline confrontation can be solved quickly, without resort to physical aggression by the parent. Obviously, the number of discipline confrontations, the likelihood that the child will respond quickly to parental discipline, and the probability that the parent will use judicious and effective discipline techniques are all interrelated and are affected in turn by a myriad of parent and child trait and state variables, family interaction variables, and situational variables in which the parent–child interaction is embedded. The idea is that the more often any parent engages in discipline confrontations, the more likely that some such confrontations will be physical. Also, the more often parents resort to physical discipline techniques in resolving problems with their children, the more likely it is that physical discipline will escalate into an assault. Since most parents are physically superior to their children, any physical assault has the potential of serious injury to the child.

Such terms as "child abuser," "child-abusive parent," and "child-abusive family" tend to elicit images of rather consistent and intense patterns of individual or family brutality. Although it is the case that abusive parents have a definite bias to view their children's behavior as aversive and deviant (e.g., Mash, Johnson, & Kovitz, 1983) and that numerous studies have found higher rates of aggressive interchanges in the homes of child abusive families than in control families (e.g., Burgess & Conger, 1978; Reid, Taplin, & Lorber, 1981; Reid, Gaines, & Green, 1983), these same studies have found that the overwhelming majority of moment-by-moment interchanges between parent and child are similar in abusive and nonabusive families. In a study recently completed by Reid (1983), about 95% of the moment-by-moment parent–child interactions observed in the homes of both seriously abusive and nonabusive control families were positive or neutral. In only about 5% of the interchanges was there evidence of anger, conflict, or confrontation. Thus, even in seriously abusive families, parents and their children get along most of the time. The remainder of this chapter focuses on the 5 to 10% of transactions between parents and their children that are most likely to lead to abusive episodes – that is, aversive interchanges in general and discipline confrontations in particular.

Some of the earliest clinical observations of child-abusive families suggested that most parents who abuse their children are extremely ineffective and inconsistent in their use of discipline (Young, 1964; Elmer & Gregg, 1967). Using a systematic home observational procedure, Reid et al. (1981) found that, on an event-by-event basis, abusive mothers were significantly less successful than nonabusive mothers in their attempts to bring about an immediate termination of problem behaviors of their children. In that study, abusive mothers were effective in 46% of their discipline attempts; nonabusive parents with child management problems were successful 65% of the time, and nondistressed control mothers were successful on 86% of their attempts. Whereas the nondistressed mother has every reason to be confident in her ability to get her child to mind, in that nearly nine out of ten of her discipline attempts are immediately successful, the abusive mother has no reason to enjoy such confidence. Her attempts at discipline lead to maximum uncertainty: half the time they work, half the time they don't. Not only do abusive parents experience difficulty in resolving discipline situations, but there is a growing body of evidence indicating that most child-abusive episodes represent direct escalations of discipline confrontations (e.g., Gil, 1969, 1970; Thomson, Paget, Bates, Mesch & Putnam, 1971; Kadushin & Martin, 1981; Herrenkohl, Herrenkohl, & Egolf, 1983).

Relationship between abusive behavior by the parent and the behavioral characteristics of the child

It has often been assumed that one parent in a given abusive family is generally the perpetrator of abuse and that that parent directs his or her abuse toward a child who is "perceived" to be somehow different from the other siblings (e.g., Zalba, 1971). In addition, a number of laboratory studies strongly suggest that abusive parents have a remarkably consistent and negative bias in their perceptions and attributions of their children's behavior (e.g., Lorber, Reid, Felton, & Caesar, 1982; Mash, Johnson, & Kovitz, 1983). These ideas of specificity of perpetrator and victim in abusive families may have been oversold. Reid and Kavanagh (unpublished manuscript) conducted an analysis of the rates of aversive/aggressive behavior displayed by individual parents in the homes of 21 child-abusive families. A comparison of observation data for the parents labeled as actual perpetrators with those who were not showed nearly identical rates of aversive behaviors.

Although the direction of effects is not yet clear, a growing body of evidence suggests that the negative sets that characterize abusive parents' perceptions of their children may be determined in part by the fact that their children are harder to manage. Several investigators have found a relationship between low birth weight and the likelihood of child abuse (Elmer & Gregg, 1967; Klein & Stern, 1971). Other studies have reported that abused children have a higher incidence of mental retardation (e.g., Elmer & Gregg, 1967; Sandgrun, Gaines, & Green, 1975), physical handicaps (Johnson & Morse, 1968; Gil, 1970), hyperactivity (Friedman, 1972; Green, Gaines, & Sandgrun, 1974), and behavioral abnormalities (Gil, 1970). It should be noted, however, that in many such studies, it was not determined whether behavioral or mental abnormalities were precursors or results of the abusive process.

A number of recent home observational studies comparing class samples of nondistressed and child-abusive families strongly suggest that parents who physically abuse or fear that they will physically abuse their children experience more misbehavior from their children than do those parents who report no problems along the lines of child management. Burgess and Conger (1977) found more fighting and conflict among siblings in families characterized by physical child abuse than in either nondistressed families or families characterized as neglectful.

Reid et al. (1981, 1982) conducted observational studies in the homes of families at risk of child abuse ($n = 27$), families referred for treatment because of one or more oppositional children ($n = 61$), and nondistressed control families ($n = 27$). The groups of families participating in our studies were comparable on a number of demographic factors. Approximately one-third of the families had no resident father; and the average age of the target child was 8.6 years. The parents' mean educational level was 11th grade, and their mean occupational level was clerk or blue collar.

The Family Interaction Coding System (FICS) used in these and other studies conducted at our center was initially developed during the 1960s (Reid, 1967); it was continuously refined and evaluated during the 1970s (e.g., Reid, 1970, 1978; Taplin & Reid, 1973; Jones, Reid, & Patterson, 1975). The coding system has been used extensively for the evaluation of levels of aggression displayed by children and their families in the home setting (e.g., Patterson & Reid, 1973; Patterson, 1974, 1982; Weinrott, Bauske, & Patterson, 1979; Reid, Taplin, & Lorber, 1981; Reid, Patterson, & Loeber, 1982). In these studies, the instrument has demonstrated consistent usefulness in discriminating between (1) children referred for antisocial conduct and matched control youngsters; and (2) parents of socially aggressive youngsters and parents of nonaggressive youngsters. Studies have also been carried out (summarized in Reid, 1978) demonstrating substantial interobserver and test–retest reliability of the FICS as well as

Table 9.1. *FICS code categories grouped by composites*[a]

Aversives (TAB)	Neutral (NEU)	Positive (POS)
Command negative[b]	Command	Approval
Dependency	Cry	Attention
Destroy	No response	Compliance
Disapproval	Receive	Indulge
High rate	Self-stimulation	Laugh
Humiliate[b]		Normative
Ignore		Physical positive
Negativism		Play
Noncompliance		Talk
Physical negative[b]		Touch
Tease		Work
Whine		
Yell[b]		

[a]Based on Likert scale ratings of the aversiveness of the mothers' sons' behavior. The sons ranged in age from 3 to 12 years, mean age 8.5 years. TAB category is composed of behaviors rated "somewhat annoying" to "extremely annoying"; POS category is composed of behaviors rated "somewhat pleasant" to "extremely pleasant"; the remaining behaviors make up the NEU composite.
[b]These four categories make up the abuse cluster (AC).
Source: Hoffman (1983).

strong and positive correlations with other measures of child aggression. A recent study by Weinrott (1982) compared the FICS with three other observational systems currently in use and found substantial convergent and divergent validity.

This coding system was designed to provide a sequential account of family interaction in the home. During an observation period, each member of the family serves as the focal subject for at least two 5-min periods. All behaviors of the focal subject and all the reactions and interactions from other family members to the focal subject are coded at 6-second intervals using 29 defined behavioral categories (see Table 9.1). Thirteen of these categories define aversive behaviors (e.g., hit, threat, tease, and cry). The remaining categories cover prosocial and neutral behaviors such as play, talk, laugh, comply, and work.

The observational data can be summarized to provide rate-per-minute scores for individual or groups of behaviors. It can provide estimates of the duration of behavior and can be analyzed sequentially to determine the conditional relationships of behaviors among interactants. The most commonly used rate-per-minute score has been total aversive behavior (TAB), which is the aggregate rate per minute of all 13 aversive behaviors for a given subject. The most commonly used sequential scores have been conditional probabilities, such as the probability that an aversive behavior by a child is immediately followed by a positive or aversive behavior by another family member. Studies summarized by Reid (1978) and Patterson (1982) have shown the TAB score, and a variety of sequential scores, to discriminate mothers and children reliably in aggressive families from normal controls.

The study conducted by Reid et al. (1981) found that the youngsters in the high-risk-for-abuse families displayed higher moment-by-moment rates of both highly aversive behaviors, such as hitting and threatening others, and mildly obnoxious behaviors, such as whining and teasing, than did their counterparts in either the nondistressed families or the families with oppositional children. In accord with the home observational data in this study, parents in the high-risk group reported significantly more discipline problems on a daily basis than did parents in the other two groups. Such between-group differences support the notion that parents characterized as being abusive or potentially abusive are confronted with significantly more aversive child behaviors on a daily basis than are parents who are not so classified.

Correlational analyses carried out within groups of nondistressed families, abusive families, and families with oppositional children clearly show that, as a general rule, the more aversive behavior shown by the child, the greater the likelihood that the parents would demonstrate higher rates of aversive behavior (Reid et al., 1982). Correlations between the rate of aversive behavior for children and that for their parents ranged from .24 to .65 in three groups. Within the child-abusive sample, a further finding was quite disturbing. The correlation between the rates of children's aversive behavior and the rates at which their parents were observed to hit them in the home setting was .53 for mothers and .74 for fathers. Regardless of the causal direction, such findings strongly suggest that the more aversive the child, the higher the risk of abusive behavior by the parents.

The characteristics of parents related to abusiveness toward their children

There is a growing body of indirect, as well as direct, evidence that the degree to which parents are abusive to their own children is related to their own level of irritability on a moment-by-moment level as well as the degree to which they are under stress in their daily lives. Marital conflict has been found in a number of studies to be associated with child abuse (e.g., Green, 1976; Reid, Taplin, & Lorber, 1981; Straus, 1980). Along the same lines, relationships between child abuse and situational or financial stress on the family have been reported in a number of studies (e.g., Garbarino, 1976; Justice & Duncan, 1976; Egleland, B., & Brunnquell, D., unpublished observations). Emotional problems of parents who are not child abusive, such as depression, have also been found to be associated with a decreased ability to handle discipline situations (Patterson, 1982). Finally, Wahler and associates (e.g., Wahler, Berland, Coe, & Leske, 1976; Wahler, Leske, & Rogers, 1979) found that families with severe child management problems compared with nondistressed controls had fewer self-rated positive contacts with people in the community and more negative contacts, and that the negative contacts were more typically initiated from outside the family. Thus, there is a good deal of evidence to suggest that predictors and indicators of parental irritability and unhappiness tend to be disproportionately prevalent in child-abusive homes.

Although data have been presented to show that the vast majority of moment-to-moment transactions between parents and children, even in abusive families, are neutral or positive, the mothers who were at risk for child abuse demonstrated more than twice the rate of total aversive behavior per minute compared with their nondistressed counterparts (Reid et al., 1981). The trend was similar for fathers but was not statistically reliable. For the most serious of the aversive behaviors included in the observational system (i.e., Physical Negative behavior and Command Negatives – Hits and Threats), the difference was more striking. The high-risk mothers were observed to demonstrate more than four times the rate of hitting and five times the rate of threats. Again, the trend was similar for the fathers but did not reach statistical significance. In terms of the aversive behavior directed at each other by parents in these families, the parents in the high-risk group were observed to exchange more than 10 times the rate of aversive behaviors than that observed for the nondistressed control parents.

To summarize these observational findings, parents self-referred because they had already lost or feared that they would lose control during discipline situations demonstrated significantly higher rates of aversive, irritable behavior toward their children than did parents who had not experienced such problems; those abusive parents also demonstrated higher rates of what might be called quasiabusive behaviors (i.e., hitting and threatening) on a moment-by-moment basis. Finally, not only do such parents behave more aversively toward their children on a moment-by-moment basis, but in two-parent families, they direct more aversive initiations at each other than do parents in the control groups.

In order to determine whether or not the relationship between moment-by-moment generally aversive behavior by the parents is associated with more serious or quasiabusive behavior by parents, Reid et al. (1982) investigated the relationship between the rates of mildly aversive behavior (i.e., TAB minus hits and threats) by parents and their rates of hitting and threatening. In the nondistressed sample, the correlations between mildly aversive behavior and hitting was .66 for mothers (it was near zero for fathers because only one nondistressed father was observed to hit). The correlation between generally aversive behavior and threatening was .61 for mothers and .33 for fathers. For the child-abusive sample, the correlation between generally aversive behavior and hitting was .59 for mothers and .78 for fathers; the relationships between aversive behavior and rate of threats was .62 for mothers and .68 for fathers.

Of particular interest in that study was an additional finding. The correlation between the rate of hitting and the rate of threatening for mothers in the abusive group was .81; for fathers, .86. By contrast, in the nondistressed group, the comparable figures were .66 for mothers and .08 for fathers – recall that fathers in the nondistressed group did not show hitting.

These data may be of some importance in understanding child-abusive behavior by parents. First, the data strongly suggest that, regardless of whether the behavior of nondistressed or abusive families is considered, those parents who direct more aversive comments toward their children or who express their anger more openly, as evidenced by yelling, disapproval, humiliation, and so forth, are more likely to demonstrate either quasiabusive or full-blown abusive behaviors toward their youngsters. Thus, any treatment program or prevention program aimed at child abuse or abusive punishment practices by parents should focus in significant part on teaching parents to reduce low-level aversive behaviors toward their youngsters as well as focusing on the more obvious problems of beatings and abusive spankings. The practical implication of these findings is that, given further research, it may be possible to assess the risk of child abuse in families by measurement of low-level aversive behavior demonstrated by parents toward their children. The advantage of such an assessment focus is obvious. Whereas persons under investigation for child abuse will most certainly be hesitant to reveal highly abusive child management practices such as spanking, slapping, hitting with objects, or kicking, they are not nearly as likely to conceal moment-by-moment disapprovals, teasing, or ignoring of their children. Composites of such mildly aversive behavior are associated significantly with the incidence of the quasiabusive or seriously abusive behaviors (Reid et al., 1982).

Both systematic parent self-report data and systematic observer impression data are in accord with the observation data summarized above in demonstrating a relationship between child abuse and aversive behavior by parents on a day-to-day basis. A study was recently completed at our center, consisting of 21 chronic and serious child-abusive families and 21 nonabusive control families whose demographic characteristics were highly similar to those studied by Reid et al (1981, 1982). In this investigation, Reid (1983) asked parents on a daily basis specifically how many times they punished their children and what types of punishment they employed. Parents in the child-abusive families reported spanking their children approximately once every 3 days; parents in the nonabusive families reported spanking their children on the average of once every 10 days. A finer analysis of the parent self-report data on spanking revealed that when spanking on the bottom with an open hand was separated from other and potentially more serious types of hitting (e.g., slapping in the face, kicking, pushing, biting), the abusive and nonabusive parents did not differ in the rate of conventional spanking, but that the excess of physical discipline reported by the child-abusive parents was accounted for by their extensive use of the more serious and abusive types of physical force. Incidentally, aside from the abusive parents' greater dependence on physical coercion in discipline situations, it was also found that the abusive parents reported significantly less use of playful teasing and humor than did nonabusive parents in dealing with discipline confrontations. Although teasing is generally rated aversive by parents (Hoffman, 1975), its specific use in dealing with discipline confrontations may be useful.

In the same study (Reid, 1983), an observer-impressions instrument (Reid, Bauske, & Brummett, 1981) was completed by observers immediately after home observations were carried out. An analysis of the responses of these observers indicated that abusive parents gave the impression of enjoying their children significantly less than did the nonabusive control parents. Observers also reported getting the impression that there was a fight or a hassle in the family before they appeared for the observation significantly more often in the abusive than the nonabusive families. Finally, the observers recorded significantly more impressions for the families in the abusive group that the child was afraid of his or her parents.

We employed one new instrument in this recent study of child-abusive families. Each day during the initial assessment period, parents in both groups were given "discipline report forms" to be filled out for each weekday. On this form, the parent indicated the most significant discipline confrontation for each day. In addition to describing the incident, the parent filled out several items describing the incident. One such item was a rating of how angry the parent felt. Parents in the abusive group reported feeling significantly more anger per discipline confrontation than did parents in the nonabusive group.

Taken together, these various data provided by various agents strongly suggest that child-abusive behavior is not a phenomenon that erupts unexpectedly because of strong situational stress, a momentary emotional upset, or momentary lacunae in the superegos of parents. Rather, child-abusive behavior is most common by parents who are most often aversive, irritated, and possibly frustrated in dealing with discipline confrontations. In the opinion of this writer, child abuse in such families is inevitable, if not always detected. For a parent who reports spanking his or her child on the average of once every three days (and spanking for that parent typically means something more serious than spanking on the bottom with an open hand), who makes a practice of using threats in his or her attempts to control the behavior of their children, it is simply a matter of time before a discipline confrontation will escalate into violence.

The topography of parents' aversive behavior toward their children

As indicated earlier in this paper, more than 90% of the moment-by-moment interactions between parents and their children, even in serious and chronic child-abusive families, are either positive or neutral. The 5 to 10% of parent–child interactions that are not positive or neutral, however, can vary from mildly aversive to physically abusive in nature. Over the last few years, members of our group at the Oregon Social Learning Center have become increasingly interested in the inter-relationships among frequency, rate, duration, and intensity of negative interchanges between children and their parents. In the section that follows, some preliminary findings will be presented, as well as their implications for assessment, prevention, and treatment endeavors in the area of child abuse.

It is our position that child-abusive behavior is a direct function of (1) the number, frequency, or rate of aversive interactions between parent and child; and (2) the ability of the parent and child to quickly terminate such aversive interchanges when they occur – the duration of aversive interchanges (e.g., Reid et al., 1981, 1982). Some data have already been presented in this chapter in support of the following ideas. First, parents in child-abusive families demonstrate significantly higher rates of both mildly aversive and highly aversive interactions with their children (e.g., hitting, threatening, and yelling) than do parents in nonabusive families. Second, within samples of abusive and nonabusive families, there is a significant relationship between the number of low-level aversive interchanges and the rate of highly aversive interchanges between parents and children. There is even some preliminary evidence to suggest that the relationship between the frequency of mildly aversive parent behaviors and abusive behavior by parents is exponential. In an analysis reported by Reid et al. (1982), a correlation of .67 was found between mothers' observed rates of total aversive behavior and the ratios of hits and threats to less aversive behaviors that made up those scores. The implications of such findings are important for those of us who have an interest in prevention/intervention activities in the area of child abuse. This density–intensity relationship strongly suggests that any intervention activities designed to reduce the risk of parental violence toward their children must focus intensively on a reduction of the general, day-to-day negative interactions between high-risk parents and their children. If, in fact, the relationship between general aversive behavior by parents and highly abusive behavior is exponential, then significant reductions in actual abusiveness can be expected when general levels of aversive parent behavior are reduced.

In order to better understand the occurrence of aversive behavior in the course of day-to-day parent–child social exchanges, we have begun to examine the patterning or positioning of both mildly and highly aversive parent behaviors during quasinatural parent–child interaction observed in the home setting.

The following analyses represent our first attempts to conduct descriptive and sequential analyses of the microsocial aversive behavior of child-abusive parents. These analyses used observational data collected in the homes of 48 nondistressed families; 53 families referred because of child management problems, but for whom no child abuse was indicated nor suspected; and 28 high-risk, abusive families. The groups were formed from the subjects who participated in the studies conducted by Reid et al. (1981, 1982) and Reid (1983). There were no significant group differences in family size, proportion of single-parent families, family income, or age of target child. The average age of the referred children in the three groups was 8.4 years, with a range of 3 to 13 years. In this preliminary set of analyses, we focused on mothers' behavior; depending on the group, 30 to 40% of the families were single-parent families with no resident father.

The purpose of the first set of analyses was to examine the rates of generally aversive behavior for the three groups of mothers, and to examine the relationship between abusive and mildly aversive maternal behavior for the three groups. As can be seen in Table 9.2, abusive mothers demonstrate nearly twice the rate of aversive behavior as do nonabusive families with management problems, and nearly four times the rate of aversive behavior as do their counterparts in nondistressed families. If only the most

Table 9.2. *Mean rates at which mothers were observed to emit generally aversive and highly aversive behaviors in the home setting*

Measure	Group 1[a]	Group 2[b]	Group 3[c]	Differences between group means
Total aversive behavior per minute[d]	.12	.38	.75	Group 1 < 2; $p < .10$ Group 2 < 3; $p < .05$ Group 1 < 3; $p < .01$
Total abusive behavior per minute[e]	.003	.02	.08	Group 1 < 2; $p < .15$ Group 2 < 3; $p < .01$ Group 1 < 3; $p < .01$
Proportion of all aversive behavior that was abusive[f]	.01	.05	.11	Group 1 < 2; $p < .10$ Group 2 < 3; $p < .05$ Group 1 < 3; $p < .01$

[a]Nondistressed ($n = 48$).
[b]Referred for child management problems; no known child abuse ($n = 53$).
[c]Referred for child-management problems; admitted to child-abusive behavior.
[d]Including FICS behaviors: command, disapprove, high rate, negative, tease, whine, threat, destructive, humiliate, ignore, noncomply, hit, yell.
[e]Including FICS behaviors: threat, humiliate, hit, yell.
[f]Total abusive behaviors divided by total aversive behaviors.
Source: Reid and Arkis (unpublished observations).

abusive of the aversive parent behaviors are considered (threatening, humiliating, yelling, and hitting), abusive mothers demonstrate four times the rate of quasiabusive behavior as do their counterparts in families with child management problems but no child abuse; and about 20 times the rate of such highly aversive behaviors as do nondistressed mothers. Finally, the ratio of abusive to less abusive behaviors demonstrated by the three groups of mothers is also of interest. On the average, only 2% of the aversive behavior demonstrated by nondistressed mothers is of a highly aversive or abusive type; 5% of aversive behavior by distressed but nonabusive mothers is abusive; and 10% of aversive behavior demonstrated by child-abusive mothers is abusive in nature. Putting these numbers together, one can conclude, not only that abusive mothers are three, nearly four, times as likely to engage in aversive interchanges with their children, but, given an aversive interchange, the likelihood that an abusive parent will engage in quasiabusive child-directed behaviors is five times that of the nondistressed parent. It is not surprising that such parents occasionally injure their children.

A second set of analyses was carried out in order to get a preliminary impression of the distribution of aversive events over the course of parent–

Table 9.3. *Length of aversive episodes by mothers: relationship to abusive behavior*

Length of episode (sec)	Nondistressed mothers (*n* = 48)	Mothers with child management problems, no evidence of child abuse (*n* = 53)	High risk, child abusive (*n* = 28)
1–11	.97 (.83)[a]	.92 (.76)[a]	.95 (.83)[a]
12–23	.03	.05	.04
> 23	.002[b]	.03	.01

[a]Numbers in parentheses indicate mean proportion of aversive episodes consisting of one aversive behavior only.
[b]The mean proportion for nondistressed mothers was significantly less than that for mothers in either of the other groups (*p* < .001).
Source: Reid and Kavanagh (unpublished observations).

child interaction. One question of general interest was the extent to which aversive behaviors by mothers were demonstrated as single, brief events or as extended aversive chains or bursts of aversive events. In addition, we were interested in whether the distributions of aversive behavior varied as a function of whether parents were abusive or nondistressed. The results of this analysis are shown in Table 9.3. The vast majority of aversive episodes by mothers, regardless of group membership, consisted of one aversive maternal behavior, and over 90% of the aversive episodes for mothers in each of the three groups lasted 11 seconds or less. On the average, between 3 and 5% of the aversive episodes for mothers in the three groups lasted 12 to 23 sec. Thus, regardless of group membership, nearly all aversive episodes demonstrated by mothers were of extremely short duration. Examination of those episodes lasting more than 23 sec suggests that, for nondistressed parents, episodes of this length are extremely rare (less than .2% of their episodes). For both the distressed and abusive mothers, significantly higher percentages of their aversive episodes lasted for more than 23 seconds. Recall that at the beginning of this chapter it was argued that one factor determining parental abusiveness is the ability of the parent to quickly terminate abusive or aversive episodes once they begin. These data suggest that those parents who have difficulties handling discipline with their children tend to engage in significantly more extended aversive chains than do parents who do not complain of such problems.

The next obvious question is the extent to which the more serious or abusive of parental aversive behaviors tend to occur in chains of longer

Table 9.4. *Mean proportions of discrete aversive and abusive behaviors in each episode length*[ab]

Length of episode (sec)	Nondistressed mothers (n = 48)	Mothers with child management problems, no evidence of child abuse (n = 53)	High-risk, child abusive (n = 28)
1–11	.12	.10	.14
12–23	.17	.20	.24
> 23	.23	.39	.35

[a]Threaten, yell, humiliate, or hit.
[b]There was a significant effect for length of episode ($p < .01$); and the groups–times–episode interaction approached significance ($p < .18$), with normal mothers being less abusive during longer episodes.
Source: Reid and Kavanagh (unpublished observations).

duration. Our model predicts that more serious aversive behaviors should occur in those aversive parent-child interactions which are not quickly terminated. The relevant data are shown in Table 9.4. As can be seen in Table 9.3, between 10% and 14% of the aversive behaviors demonstrated by mothers during short episodes are potentially abusive in nature (threatening, yelling, humiliating, or hitting). Within aversive episodes of intermediate length (12 to 23 sec), the proportion of potentially serious aversive behaviors increases markedly for mothers in the three groups (i.e., to between 17 and 24%). For the longest episodes (more than 23 sec), the proportions of serious behaviors increase again, most markedly for the distressed and abusive mothers. These data are clearly in accord with the notion that the longer an aversive interaction between parent and child persists, the more likely it is that the parent will engage in seriously abusive behavior toward the child.

These data can also be interpreted in a reasonably optimistic manner by those of us who are also interested in developing intervention procedures for parents who are at high risk for abusing their children. First, abusive parents are similar to nonabusive parents in that the vast majority of their interactions with their children are neutral or positive in nature (neutral and positive composites were combined, not analyzed separately). It is during extended aversive interactions (which comprise less than 5% of their aversive episodes and less than .2% of their total interactions with their children) that they appear to behave differently than normal parents. That is when they have a high likelihood of demonstrating seriously abusive behavior toward their children. Put in more clinical or common-sense terms, these data suggest that abusive parents are at risk on a moment-by-moment basis during those times when they become involved in extended aversive episodes (probably concerning discipline) with their children. Although these episodes are really quite rare in comparison with all the moment-by-moment social exchanges they have with their children, they are extremely dangerous when they do happen: looking at Table 9.3, nearly 40% of such interactions lead to a potentially abusive behavior by the parent.

The clinical implication of such data, given that they crossvalidate in future studies, is the need for particular clinical emphasis on teaching parents quick methods for terminating discipline confrontations when they occur. Rather than teaching parents to talk and lecture or explain to the young child when they discover transgressions, it is probably the case that they should rely on discipline techniques which quickly terminate their interaction with the child in a manner which gives the parents a feeling of success (e.g., immediate time-out). Substantial effort has been expended at our center to develop and assess methods to teach parents to deal with discipline problems more quickly and effectively (e.g., Patterson, 1974a, 1974b; Patterson, Chamberlain, & Reid, 1982; Patterson & Reid, 1975; Patterson, Reid, Jones, & Conger, 1975). Some preliminary work reported by Reid et al. (1982), Reid and Kavanagh (unpublished manuscript), and Wolf (1983) suggests that teaching parents such procedures to terminate discipline conflicts is both possible and effective in reducing the parents' rate of aversive behavior directed toward their children.

A final comment

Most of the data presented in this chapter are quite preliminary in nature and need to be crossvalidated. Nevertheless, such data suggest that the direct and fine-grained observation of family interaction provides a potentially powerful technology for the investigation of important exchanges that occur between parents and their children. Although it is understandable that observational studies of families of abusive parents or aggressive youngsters have focused initially on aversive exchanges, it must be kept in mind that such interactions represent but a small fraction of the microsocial fabric of these families. We have yet to employ this technology systematically in the investigation of positive interactions within the family. As other chapters in this volume make clear, further scientific effort must be expended on the investigation of the development and exchange of positive or altruistic behavior by children and their families.

In the case of child abuse, we are beginning to accumulate specific information that may lay the groundwork for effectively teaching families not to hurt or threaten their children, but more specific information is needed on which to devise techniques to help such families develop more positive modes of interaction. There is no reason why the techniques described in this chapter cannot be modified to study the positive side of family life.

References

Burgess, R. L., & Conger, R. D. (1977). Family interaction patterns related to child abuse and neglect: Some preliminary findings. *Child Abuse and Neglect: The International Journal, 1*, 269–277.

Burgess, R. L., & Conger, R. D. (1978). Family interaction in abusive, neglectful, and normal families. *Child Development, 49*, 1163–1173.

Elmer, I. E., & Gregg, G. S. (1967). Developmental characteristics of abused children. *Pediatrics, 40*, 596–602.

Fawl, C. L. (1963). Disturbances experienced by children in their natural habitats. In R. G. Barker (Ed.), *The stream of behavior*, (pp. 99–126). New York: Appleton-Century-Crofts.

Forehand, R., King, H. E., Peed, S., & Yoder, P. (1975). Mother–child interactions: Comparison of a noncompliant clinic group and a nonclinic group. *Behavior Research and Therapy, 13*, 79–84.

Friedman, S. B. (1972). The need for intensive follow-up of abused children. In C. H. Kempe & R. E. Helfer (Eds.), *Helping the battered child and his family*. Philadelphia: Lippincott.

Garbarino, J. (1976). Some ecological correlates of child abuse: The impact of socioeconomic stress on mothers. *Child Development, 47*, 178–185.

Gelles, R. J. (1979). *Family Violence*. Beverly Hills, CA: Sage.

Gil, .D. G. (1969). Physical abuse of children: Findings and implications of a nationwide survey. *Pediatrics, 44*, 857–865.

Gil, D. G. (1970). *Violence against children: Physical child abuse in the United States*. Cambridge, MA: Harvard University Press.

Green, A. (1976). A psychodynamic approach to the study and treatment of child-abusing parents. *Journal of Child Psychiatry, 15*, 414–429.

Green, A. H., Gaines, R. W., & Sandgrun, A. (1974). Child abuse: Pathological syndrome of family interaction. *American Journal of Psychiatry, 131*, 882–886.

Herrenkohl, R. C., Herrenkohl, E. C., & Egolf, B. P. (1983). Circumstances surrounding the occurrence of child maltreatment. *Journal of Consulting and Clinical Psychology, 51*, 424–431.

Hoffman, M. L. (1975). Moral internalization, parental power and the nature of parent-child interaction. *Developmental Psychology, 11*, 228–239.

Johnson, B., & Morse, A. H. (1968). Injured children and their parents. *Children, 15*, 147–152.

Justice, B., & Duncan, D. F. (1976). Life crisis as a precursor to child abuse. *Public Health Reports, 91*, 110–115.

Kadushin, A., & Martin, J. (1981). *Child abuse: An interactional event*. New York: Columbia University Press.

Kempe, C. H. (1973). A practical approach to the protection of the abused child and rehabilitation of the abusing parent. *Pediatrics, 51*, 804–812.

Klein, M., & Stern, L. (1971). Low birth weight and the battered child syndrome. *American Journal of the Disabled Child, 122*, 15–18.

Light, R. J. (1973). Abused and neglected children in America: A study of alternative policies. *Harvard Educational Review, 43*, 556–598.

Lorber, R., Reid, J. B., Felton, D., & Caesar, R. (1982, November). *Behavioral tracking skills of child abuse parents and their relationships to family violence.* Paper presented at the meeting of the Association for the Advancement of Behavior Therapy, Los Angeles, CA.

Mash, E. J., Johnson, C., & Kovitz, K. (1983). A comparison of the mother-child interactions of physically abused and non-abused children during play and task situations. *Journal of Clinical Child Psychology, 12*, 337–346.

Minton, C., Kagan, J., & Levine, J. A. (1971). Maternal control and obedience in the two-year-old child. *Child Development, 42*, 1973–1984.

National Analysis of Official Child Neglect and Abuse Reporting: Annual Report, 1980. (1981). Denver, CO: The American Humane Association Child Protection Division.

Parke, R. D., & Lewis, N. G. (1981). The family in context: A multilevel interactional analysis of child abuse. In R. W. Henderson (Ed.), *Parent–child interaction – Theory, research, prospects.* New York: Academic Press.

Patterson, G. R. (1974a). Interventions for boys with conduct problems: Multiple settings, treatments, and criteria. *Journal of Consulting and Clinical Psychology, 42*, 471–481.

Patterson, G. R. (1974b). Retraining of aggressive boys by their parents. Review of recent literature and follow-up evaluation. In F. Lowey (Ed.), Symposium on the severely disturbed preschool child, *Canadian Psychiatric Association Journal, 19*, 142–149.

Patterson, G. R. (1982). *Coercive family process.* Eugene, OR: Castalia.

Patterson, G. R., Chamberlain, P., & Reid, J. B. (1982). A comparative evaluation of parent training procedures. *Behavior Therapy, 13*, 638–650.

Patterson, G. R., & Reid, J. B. (1973). Intervention for families of aggressive boys: A replication study. *Behavior Research and Therapy, 11*, 383–394.

Patterson, G. R., Reid, J. B., Jones, R. R., & Conger, R. E. (1975). *A social learning approach to family intervention: Families with aggressive children* (vol. 1). Eugene, OR: Castalia.

Reid, J. B. (Ed.) (1978). *A social learning approach to family intervention: Vol. 2. Observation in home settings.* Eugene, OR: Castalia.

Reid, J. B. (1983). *Final Report: Child Abuse: Developmental Factors and Treatment.* Grant No. 7 ROI MH 37938, NIMH, USPHS.

Reid, J. B., Patterson, G. R., & Loeber, R. (1982). The abused child: Victim, instigator, or innocent bystander? In D. J. Bernstein (Ed.), *Response structure and organization* (pp. 47–68). Lincoln, NB: University of Nebraska Press.

Reid, J. B., Taplin, P. S., & Lorber, R. (1981). A social interactional approach to the treatment of abusive families. In R. Stuart (Ed.), *Violent behavior: Social learning approaches to prediction, management, and treatment* (pp. 83–101). New York, Brunner/Mazel.

Sandgrun, R. W., Gaines, R. W., & Green, A. H. (1975). Child abuse and mental retardation: A problem of cause and effect. *Journal of Mental Deficiency, 19*, 327.

Stark, R., & McEvoy, J. (1970). Middle class violence. *Psychology Today, 4*, 52–65.

Straus, M. A. (1980). Social stress and marital violence in a national sample of American families. In F. Wright, C. Bain, & R. W. Rieber (Eds.), *Forensic psychology and psychiatry. Annals of the New York Academy of Science, 347.*

Thomson, E. M., Paget, N. W., Bates, D. W., Mesch, M., & Putnam, T. I. (1971). *Child abuse: A community challenge.* East Aurora, NY: Henry Stewart and Children's Aid and Society for the Prevention of Cruelty to Children.

Wahler, R. G., Berland, R. M., Coe, T. D., & Leske, G. (1976). *Social systems analysis: Implementing an alternative behavioral model*. Paper presented at the Ecological Perspectives in Behavior Analysis Conference, Lawrence, KS.

Wahler, R. G., Leske, G., & Rogers, E. S. (1979). The insular family: A deviance support mechanism for oppositional children. In L. A. Hamerlynck (Ed.), *Behavioral systems for the developmentally disabled: I. School and family environments* (pp. 137–174). New York: Brunner/Mazel.

Weinrott, M. R., Reid, J. B., Bauske, W., & Brummett, B. (1981). Supplementing naturalistic observation with observer impressions. *Behavioral Assessment, 3*, 151–159.

Wolf, D. A. (1983, June). *Child abuse prevention with at-risk parents and children*. Paper presented at the Vermont Conference on Prevention, Burlington, VT.

Young, L. (1964). *A study of child abuse and neglect*. Princeton: McGraw-Hill.

Zalba, S. R. (1971). Battered children. *Transaction, 8*, 58–61.

10 Naturalistic observation of cooperation, helping, and sharing and their associations with empathy and affect

Robert F. Marcus

Cooperation, helping, and sharing have been the focus of many reviews of prosocial behaviors (Staub, 1978, 1979; Bryan, 1975, Rushton, 1980; Radke-Yarrow, Zahn-Waxler, & Chapman, 1983). These behaviors have been studied both with the use of tasks designed to measure such interactions in laboratory settings and through direct observation in naturalistic settings. The question of whether such behaviors have been found to increase with the age and experience of the individuals studied has great significance, since cooperation, helping, and sharing are highly prized and their development has been viewed as a major goal of socialization (Rushton, 1980). However, generalizations about developmental trends based on existing data have been difficult to make. A recent extensive review of frequencies of these behaviors as related to age fails to document a unidirectional trend with age (Radke-Yarrow et al., 1983). These investigators state that there "are increases, no changes, and decreases depending on the prosocial behavior, the research methods, and the ages studied" (p. 42).

One way to proceed toward disentangling and clarifying the developmental and correlational research on the above behaviors done this far, as well as to generate new directions for future research, is to hold the method constant while doing a finer-grained analysis of the concepts and findings from present studies. This chapter examines research in naturalistic settings and, in particular, the findings as they relate to conceptualizations of prosocial behavior. Direct observation in natural settings is taken as a starting point because it is believed this is necessary to avoid the creation of fictional accounts of behavioral development (Baldwin, 1967) and to promote ecologically valid measurement (Bronfenbrenner, 1974). The richness and multifaceted nature of behavior can best be viewed in natural settings and is illustrated through use of current research.

Cooperation, helping, and sharing are sequences of behavior that commonly occur in the normal interaction between children of widely varying ages. They are names given by observers to slices of the stream of behavior that vary from one another in collectively understood ways. Careful examination of such behaviors in natural settings shows that they are remarkably similar in form yet distinguishable by subtle earmarks of attitude and other features. For example, "Child 1 picked up a block and gave it to child 2 and child 2 continued to build a tower." This would be impossible to label as an instance of cooperation, helping, or sharing without more information. Similarly, if we had described this episode as "child 1 angrily slapped child 2's hand with a block and child 2 latched onto it and grabbed it quickly away," we would be reluctant to call this by some prosocial name.

Our language has enabled us to make subtle distinctions with regard to attitude or intention, Wright (1960) quotes Allport and Odbert as saying that there are 17,953 English words to describe as many ways of behaving. The definition of prosocial behavior in natural settings is also complicated by the fact that slicing the stream of behavior in different ways may yield behaviors with different names. Furthermore, decisions about where one begins and ends observation are sometimes quite arbitrary. For example, terminating observation after the first action in episode 1 above would lead to application of the term "helping," whereas if one saw that both were building the tower, the label "cooperation" might be affixed.

At this point one can appreciate how tempting it is to take the observation of cooperation, helping, or sharing into the laboratory where the event can be measured in terms of game strategies, countable chips, prizes, and so forth. One would gain in terms of objectivity and ease of measurement, but the external validity (or generalizability) would be greatly reduced. Still, the trained people-watcher is nagged by the suspicion that in this way the Queen of Hearts, as in the Alice in Wonderland classic, has merely called the prosocial behavior whatever she chooses to call it and the operational definition tail is perhaps wagging the dog. Krebs (1970) suggested that operationalization of prosocial behaviors may merely be an avoidance of more serious considerations about definition. Inconsistency of the developmental findings with regard to the use of laboratory games or tasks to measure cooperation and naturalistic data, and lack of correlation between naturalistic and laboratory findings on many other prosocial behaviors may be one of the consequences of the use of quick and simple measurement (see Radke-Yarrow et al., 1983).

The major theme of this chapter is that prosocial behaviors can best be observed in the settings in which they usually occur, as expressed by real-life participants who act and react to subtle inner promptings and external cues. It is in natural settings that sensitivity or insensitivity to the other's behavior and affect, as well as one's own thoughts and feelings, may combine in complex ways to elicit, sustain, dampen, and eventually terminate the cooperation, helping, or sharing.

The purposes of this chapter are (1) to examine the meaning of the terms of cooperation, helping, and sharing as they appear in common usage; (2) to offer dimensions along which these naturally occurring prosocial behaviors can be analyzed; (3) to examine and analyze definitions of prosocial behavior used in naturalistic observation research; and (4) to suggest how interrelations of cooperation, affect, and empathy can be examined in face-to-face interactions in real-life settings.

Common usage definitions of prosocial behaviors

Why should we bother to look at definitions? There are at least two important reasons for a serious discussion of the definitions of cooperation, helping and sharing in natural settings. First, the definition determines other methodological decisions which must be made. Second, the particular facet of that behavior chosen for study and the criteria you establish will help to determine whether the hypothesized relations are obtained. The methodological issues can best be explained by saying that in the absence of standardized definitions of social behaviors for observational studies (Gellert, 1955; Wright, 1960) the researcher often falls back on precedence and quickly becomes distracted by other important issues of sampling strategy, interrater agreement, size of observation unit, and so forth. However, the definition used will determine whether the variable has face validity, thereby influencing the ease with which interrater agreement is obtained. The definition will determine the size of the unit one may wish to observe. The definition will also determine whether it is one or two children you will need to observe. Second, the definition of a complex behavior such as cooperation requires that in order to establish its presence we must piece together a number of clues about the task or activity, about the verbal and nonverbal components of cooperation and about the context within which it occurs. In observing the situation of two children building a sandcastle, in which one child sculpts the castle while the other fetches sand and water, one may judge that these separate behaviors constitute supplemental actions toward the achievement of a goal. The definition used and the particular research interest might lead us to focus on the smoothness or halting quality of the meshing of the children's behaviors or the attitude of cooperation as revealed in the intensity or type of affect observed. The affect may be seen in facial, vocal, or body clues or the kind of fantasy evident in that play. Such distinctions have been variably attended to both in common understandings about the meanings of those terms and in research definitions.

The example of one boy giving a block points out the need for understanding the common usage of prosocial terms. One observer could conclude that child 1 *helped* because child 1 made it easier for child 2 to construct his bridge. Or, the observer could conclude that it was an instance of *cooperation* because both were working together to build a bridge. One could also say that child 1 *shared* his blocks with child 2 because they were initially in his possession. The behavior is exactly the same, yet our common understanding of the meanings of those terms would require the observer to look carefully at what happened before and after the block exchange and determine whose project the bridge was. Dictionary definitions of those terms help us to determine which of the three kinds of behavior was present by suggesting three questions (*Webster's Ninth New Collegiate Dictionary*, 1984): Who is benefiting? Does a state of need exist for the recipient? Does the giver own the transmitted material? There still may be some instances in which a particular behavior meets the criteria for two kinds of behavior. The researcher may need to make more arbitrary distinctions using a dimension such as duration, but this is not so much a weakness in observational research as a matter of remarkable similarity between those behaviors. These inferences were drawn from the following dictionary definitions:

> *share* – 1: to divide and distribute in shares: (APPORTION – usu. used with *out* or *with* 2a: to partake of, use, experience, occupy, or enjoy with others b: to have in common 3: to grant or give a share in. . . . Syn. SHARE implies that one as the original holder grants to another the partial use, enjoyment, or possession of a thing though it may merely imply a mutual use or possession. . . . (p. 1082)
>
> *help* – 1: to give assistance or support to. . . . 2a: to make pleasant or bearable: Improve, Relieve. . . . b: archaic: Rescue, Save c: to get (oneself) out of difficulty 3a: to be of use to: benefit b: to further the advancement of: promote 4a: to change for the better. . . . Syn. Help, Aid, Assist mean to supply what is needed to accomplish an end. Help carries a strong implication of advance toward an objective. . . . (p. 563)
>
> *co-op-er-ate* – 1: to act or work with another or others: act together 2: to associate with another or others for mutual benefit. (p.288)

Dimensional analysis of cooperation, helping, and sharing

It is relatively rare for researchers to discuss the nature of the definition used in their studies, and there are few aids they might use to evaluate their category systems. Wright (1960) and Lambert (1960) have offered some conceptual dimensions that can be used for such purposes. Wright

(1960) suggests that category systems may require the observer to focus on literally objective phenomena, or the observer may be required to infer that the behavior belongs to a more abstract class of behavior with which it shares common features. It may share in such features as motivational basis, appearance, or function. Kicking, touching, patting, and hand raising are movements, a palpable level requiring little inference, while such behaviors as nurturance, dependency, and altruism require the observer to infer some of the above features. The bases for such inferences are rarely stated by the researcher.

A second distinction that can be made about category systems is whether their definitions are "psychologically specific" and discriminative in the sense that only a single behavior or few behaviors will meet the criterion (Wright, 1960). Alternatively, the category system may be more psychologically general, with many behaviors counting as scoreable instances. For example, a person can physically help another child in many ways but can give a hug in relatively few ways.

Third, Wright (1960) asks whether a category system is taken from the "unplanned network of everyday notions about behavior" or is tied to statements of developed conceptual schemes (p. 125). While some terms such as attachment or egocentrism bring to mind relatively well-developed conceptual schemes, helping or cooperation may derive more from common notions or less well-developed theories.

Lambert (1960) adds two distinctions concerning how the stream of behavior is subdivided and whether the presence or absence of the social behavior alone is determined or other facets are evaluated as well. "Acts" require that the observer focus on the behavior of individuals; these acts may be social because they have social-sounding names, are directed at other people, and are interpreted in terms of the context. "Interacts" require that the observer record the behavior of two individuals (e.g., of one that is antecedent to the behavior of the other). Lambert also refers to quantitative versus qualitative distinctions, although these terms may be misleading. He means that one might record the presence or absence of the social behavior itself or important facets of it such as its duration, kind, complexity, kind of psychomotor involvement, attitude, or affect.

The consideration of dictionary and dimensional analysis is applied to definitions of prosocial behaviors used in naturalistic studies in the following section. This analysis is used to evaluate the findings of developmental trends and frequencies and is finally used to show the importance of these dimensions for further observational research on prosocial behavior, affect, and empathy.

**Empirical studies of cooperation, helping, and sharing
in natural settings**

Relatively few observations have been made of cooperation, helping, and sharing behaviors in natural settings over the past 50 years. The vast majority of studies have been limited to the observation of preschool children in classroom settings during free play situations in which supervising adults are present and where the environment is stimulating. Although one cannot safely generalize to unsupervised, unstructured, unfamiliar situations, homes, or other natural settings, such repeated observations in similar settings provide a control for extraneous influences across many studies despite variations in subjects and methods.

Review of naturalistic observation studies in this chapter is limited to those in which the frequency data are presented along with records of the total time each child was observed. Only those studies in which definitions were given and in which there was an attempt to establish interrater agreement, at an acceptable level, are presented. Tables 10.1, 10.2, and 10.3 present the findings of research studies in which the frequencies have been transformed into a standard per minute figure and the correlations with age are also given when they are reported.

Cooperation

The definitions of cooperation used in the seven studies listed in Table 10.1 are uniform in that they are all psychologically general and include many different kinds of behaviors, which are classified together. That is, there are numerous ways in which children can be seen to (1) dramatize situations of adult life (see definitions by Parten, 1932; Barnes, 1971); (2) play formal games (Parten, 1932; Barnes, 1971; Marcus, Telleen, & Roke, 1979; Roke, 1979); (3) work toward achievement of a common goal (Parten, 1932; Barnes, 1971; Friedrich & Stein, 1973; Strayer, Waring, & Rushton, 1979; Iannotti, 1981); or (4) play in such a way that there is a division of labor in which the efforts of one child supplement the efforts of another (Parten, 1932; Barnes, 1971; Friedrich & Stein, 1973). The relationships among the four subclasses of behavior are unknown, but one might conceivably wish to use them in a standard definition of cooperation.

A common error made in most studies, and a methodological problem of importance, is that cooperation is considered an "act" rather than an "interact." An "act" can be seen by observing one person's behavior while an "interact" must involve observation of the behavior of two people linked

Table 10.1. *Naturalistic studies of cooperation*

	Sample size (*n*)	Ages	Findings
Parten (1932)	34[a]	2 to 4–11	$\bar{x}$ = .16/min. ρ age and cooperation = .67
Barnes (1971)	42	3 to 5	$\bar{x}$ (5-year-olds) = .03/min $\bar{x}$ (3- and 4-year-olds) = .06/min
Iannotti (1985)	52	4 to 5	$\bar{x}$ (males) = .08/min $\bar{x}$ (females) = .09/min *r* age and cooperation = .273 ($p < .05$)
Strayer, Wareing, & Rushton (1979)	26	3 to 5	$\bar{x}$ = .12/min
Friedrich & Stein (1973)	97	3 to 5	$\bar{x}$ (males) = .176/min[b] $\bar{x}$ (females) = .109/min
Marcus, Telleen, & Roke (1979)	32	3 to 5	$\bar{x}$ (3-year-olds) = .60/min $\bar{x}$ (4-year-olds) = .43/min *r* age and cooperation = -.15 (ns)
Roke (1979)	31	3 to 6	$\bar{x}$ = .40/min *r* age and quant. cooperation = .25 (ns) *r* age and complexity of cooperation = .22 (ns) *r* age and duration of cooperation = .35 ($p < .05$)

together in some manner (i.e., they follow sequentially). The studies listed in Table 10.1 view cooperation as an act performed by one individual regardless of the response made by the child with whom he is "cooperating." Observers are asked, for example, to conclude that by watching one child's behavior, say, digging a hole, that this is an instance of division of labor and supplementary behavior. Only if one were to continue to watch and observes a nearby child drop a seed into the hole 3 min later could one safely conclude that a division of labor is organized around the activity of flower planting. While one could observe alternating actions by one child and record this as an instance of cooperation, one should be concerned whether this type of behavior is equivalent to the above in terms of level of organization or complexity. Time-sampling procedures that focus on the actions of one child for a few seconds may tend to overestimate the frequency of cooperation because the action may not be part of a coop-

Table 10.2. *Naturalistic studies of helping*

	Sample size (*n*)	Ages	Findings
Strayer, Wareing, & Rushton (1979)	26	3 to 5	"Helping activities": $\bar{x}$ = .01/min "Comforting": $\bar{x}$ = .0076/min
Iannotti (1985)	52	4 to 5	"Helping": $\bar{x}$ (males) = .02/min $\bar{x}$ (females) = .03/min *r* age and helping = .107 (ns) "Comforting": $\bar{x}$ (males = '< .00 $\bar{x}$ (females) = < .00
Severy & Davis (1971)	55	3 to 5 and 8 to 10	"Psychological" and "Task" helping: $\bar{x}$ (ages 3–5) = .10.min $\bar{x}$ (ages 8–10) = .04/min
Eisenberg & Lennon (1980)	51	4 to 5	"Helping": $\bar{x}$ = .008/min
Yarrow & Waxler (1976)	77	3 to 7½	"Helping": $\bar{x}$ = .16/min *r* nonsignificant with age (*p* < .120)
Murphy (1937)	70		"Sympathy": $\bar{x}$ = < .01/min
Eisenberg-Berg, Cameron, Tryon, & Dodez (1981)	33	4 to 5	"Prosocial behavior" (helping and comforting combined): $\bar{x}$ (males) = .028/min $\bar{x}$ (females) = .015/min $\bar{x}$ (combined) = .022/min
Strayer (1980)	14	4 to 5	"Empathic behavioral response": $\bar{x}$ = .09/min
Stith & Connor (1962)	65	3 to 6	"Help": $\bar{x}$ (38–46 mos.) = .91/min $\bar{x}$ (47–55 mos.) = 1.15/min $\bar{x}$ (56–63 mos.) = 1.25/min $\bar{x}$ (64–75 mos.) = 1.33/min x^2 age. *p* < .05
Whiting & Whiting (1975)	24	3 to 11	"Offers help": $\bar{x}$ = .043/min "Offers support": $\bar{x}$ = .02/min *r* age and offers help and offers support (girls) = .66 (*p* < .01) *r* age and offers help and offers support (boys) = .10 (ns)

Table 10.2 (*cont.*)

	Sample size (*n*)	Ages	Findings
Eisenberg-Berg & Hand (1979)	35	4 to 5	$\bar{x}$ (helping and comforting) = .03/min
			r age and helping/comfort = .26
Krebs & Stirrup (1974)	24	7 to 9	"Altruism" (offers help, offers support and suggests responsibility
			r age and altruism = .25 (ns)

Table 10.3. *Naturalistic studies of sharing*

	Sample size (*n*)	Ages	Findings
Strayer, Wareing, & Rushton (1979)	26	3 to 5	"Sharing and Donating": $\bar{x}$ = .13/min
Ianotti (1985)	52	4 to 5	"Sharing": $\bar{x}$ = .03/min
			r age and sharing = nonsignificant correlation [c]
Eisenberg-Berg, Hand, & Hake (1981)	58	2½ to 4	"Sharing": $\bar{x}$ (younger) = .0124/min
		4 to 5	$\bar{x}$ (older) = .0109/min
Eisenberg-Berg & Lennon (1980)	51	4 to 5	"Sharing": $\bar{x}$ = .003/min
Eisenberg-Berg & Hand (1979)	35	4 to 5	"Sharing": $\bar{x}$ = .02/min
			r age and sharing = .51
Yarrow & Waxler (1976)	77	3 to 7½	"Sharing": *r* nonsignificant between age and sharing ($p < .120$)
Parten (1932)	34	2 to 4–11	"Associate Play" (borrowing and loaning and spontaneous interaction)
			$\bar{x}$ = .23/min
			r age and associate play = .51
Barnes (1971)	42	3 to 5	"Associative Play" (as Parten, 1932)
			$\bar{x}$ (3 and 4-year-olds) = .19/min
			$\bar{x}$ (5-year-olds) = .39/min

erative interplay. Observation of both children's behavior in an event sampling or elaborated time sampling allows for the other's response, which is necessary for correct categorization of cooperation.

There are two kinds of judgments about the act of cooperation which are often made, one by the researcher and one by the observer. The researcher makes the assumption that such disparate acts as building a sandcastle, playing ring-around-the-rosy, playing house, and attempting to get a jar down from a shelf have something in common. This common feature may be alternating behaviors or contributions by both children. One should expect explanation for such aggregation (i.e., combination of separate acts into one major category) or that the components be separated and examined empirically for homogeneity. They may actually develop in different ways, and some may not be developmental at all.

The second, and related, judgment is an inference by the observer concerning the organization of behavior, which must be identified in order to classify it as an instance of cooperation. The definition used by Parten and Barnes best illustrates this inferential process; it requires observers to make inferences about (1) the purpose of the group activity, e.g., to achieve some cooperative goal, make a "material product . . . [or] attain some competitive goal" (Parten, p. 251); (2) the leadership and organization of the group, e.g., group activity is controlled by "one or two members" (Parten, p. 251); and (3) the fit between what the child and the other do, e.g., in a "division of labor . . . taking of roles . . . efforts of one child supplemented by another" (Parten, p. 251). The basis for such inferences is not always clear to observers and would suggest a need for more detailed and specific identification of their empirical referents. This level of inference stands in contrast to other systems requiring a lower level of inferences, such as those that focus on "use of a common object . . . exchange of objects" (Marcus et al., 1979, p. 346).

Another example of the second kind of inference concerns what could be called a cooperative attitude and is therefore close to a qualitative judgment. In reviewing experimental and dictionary definitions of cooperation, placing greatest emphasis on experimental studies, Cook and Stingle (1974) concluded that definitions varied as to whether they focused on behaviors alone, that is, patterns of response "such as a series of choice matching responses, turn taking, or choosing alternatives" or whether they emphasized intention or attitude, such as the "desire to work with another for mutual benefit" (p. 919). The naturalistic definitions reviewed here also used phrases such as "striving" to attain some competitive goal (as in a team collaboration), a "marked sense of belonging . . . to the group" (Parten, p. 251), mutual involvement (Iannotti, 1981).

Distinctions are also made in a few studies in which qualifiers are added to the definitions already used. Friedrich and Stein (1973) used two qualifiers, the "intensity" of involvement and the number of times cooperation persisted across time-sampled units (duration). Roke (1979) included two qualifiers that were evaluated separately: duration or persistence across time units; and complexity, rated as simple to complex.

An important conclusion about developmental change can be reached on the basis of joint consideration of the definitions with the obtained results of the seven studies reviewed here. Positive correlations between cooperation and age can be seen in those studies in which qualitative components have been evaluated. The Parten and Barnes studies, in which the intention or attitude was part of the definition; the Friedrich and Stein study, which incorporated measurement of duration and intensity; the Iannotti inclusion of "mutual involvement"; and the Roke measurement of duration all resulted in measures that correlated positively with age. When the Roke and Marcus et al. studies did not include such aspects in their time sampling category system, they did not show such an increase in cooperation with age.

Additional support for the conclusion that qualitative rather than quantitative dimensions of cooperation are correlated positively with age may be seen in studies using rating scales to evaluate cooperation. Marcus et al. (1979) asked observers and teachers to rate the cooperation of children aged 3 to 5 on a 7-point scale ranging from highly individualistic to highly cooperative. Correlations between teacher and observer ratings and age were all positive and statistically significant. Payne (1980) had teachers rate the cooperative behavior of 41 fourth- through sixth-graders on a 1- to 7-point scale. Teacher ratings of cooperation were found to correlate positively and significantly with age (.32, $p < .05$). Ratings by teachers or observers that allow for judgments to be made about the children's intentions or attitudes permit evaluation of such qualitative dimensions. Cairns and Green (1979) also suggested that time-sampling data reflect a large situational component but that ratings do not and thus may be better suited to detecting individual differences, provided some of the problems with stereotypes or reputations can be eliminated.

Another observation of interest is the relationship between the frequencies and the psychological generality of the definition of cooperation. Those definitions that are more psychologically general and more liberal and inclusive show frequencies in the .40 to .60 per minute range, or, in other words, 24 to 36 per hour (Marcus et al., 1979; Roke, 1979). Cooperation would thus be seen as more common than the remaining studies would indicate (the range was .03 to .176 per minute, or 1.8 to 10.56 per hour). The more conservative estimates were obtained when definitions omitted such general categories as "use of a common object," and "exchange of objects" (as in Marcus et al., 1979, and Roke, 1979).

Helping

Naturalistic studies of helping are presented in Table 10.2. Helping has come to be seen as a response to emotional and nonemotional needs. Helping in response to nonemotional needs takes the form of handing some material goods to the other (e.g., paper, crayons, tools, shovels), supplying information (directions, suggestions) or facilitating the activities of the other (e.g., by fixing the other's toy or holding a bicycle for the other), or the child may request these of a third party. Helping in response to the emotional needs of others, variably known as "psychological helping," "comforting," "support," "altruism," "empathic behavioral interaction," "sympathy," or "nurturance" can be in the form of any of the above responses to nonemotional needs. It may also be in the form of praise, encouragement, smiling, affection, rescuing by removing the cause of distress, protecting or defending by physical or verbal means, or comforting by physical (hugs, pats) or verbal means (expressions of solicitude or warning), or by a more passive looking on. Both forms of helping can be distinguished from cooperation because (1) it is the recipient who benefits more rather than both, and (2) the level of organization of helping behavior is less than in cooperation, since there needn't be the sustained encounter one sees in reciprocal role playing or repeated supplemental actions. As with cooperation, the research on helping behavior derives from commonly held notions rather than theoretically linked constructs.

Both kinds of helping behavior require that one identify the need that cues the helping response, and it is this which poses some problems in naturalistic observation of helping behavior. It is relatively easier to identify distress cues that elicit helping of the emotional kind, but it is much more difficult to identify cues that signal nonemotional needs, both for the observer and for the child. Although it is common for studies of helping in response to emotional needs to be viewed as an "interact" rather than as an "act," only one study reviewed here considers responses to nonemotional needs as an "interact." This is probably true because it is relatively easier to detect preceding and associated distress cues such as crying, anger, and upset of some kind as a cue to helping. The cues to nonemotional helping, such as a toy that isn't working well, a sandcastle that could be built faster if the child had a shovel, are much more subtle. Nonemotional helping is thus likely to be overestimated unless the more subtle cues are specified, since there are also many acts resembling helping that are not in response to need, in addition to those that are. Therefore, the former are questionable as a helping response.

A second issue in naturalistic observation of helping behavior is that observers must not only infer the presence of a need but also infer that helping has indeed taken place. That is, attainment of the other's goal has been facilitated or that mental well-being was achieved (see definitions concerning goal attainment by Yarrow & Waxler, 1976; Strayer et al., 1979; Severy & Davis, 1971; and Iannotti, 1985). Such a high level of inference might be made, thereby establishing that helping has taken place, if the behavior of the helper results in the recipient producing a better product than would otherwise have been produced, the recipient's goals were reached more quickly or efficiently, or the recipient was accepting or pleased with the assistance. The dictionary definition does not allow for help that does not have facilitating effects. To avoid overestimation of helping behavior, it would be useful to clarify the bases for such inferences about facilitation.

Research has focused on many varieties of helping behavior of both kinds but has generally not focused on qualities such as duration, effectiveness, complexity, co-occurring affect, or type of psychomotor involvement. Whiting and Whiting (1975) are an exception in that observers were asked to judge both that there was a need for help and that the helper intended to help the recipient. The observer scored helping or support as having occurred if "the rater judged either the 0 wanted the offered object or that P intended to help 0" (giving help) or that "the intent seems to be to offer emotional support or encouragement" (p. 191). The basis for judging intention is not specified, but one might speculate that observers may have used nonverbal clues (facial, vocal, body) or contextual clues (e.g., help was not solicited) in order to make their judgments.

Definitions in the category systems varied from moderate to low psychological specificity. The most general and inclusive definitions are those that do not enumerate the behaviors that would fit certain criteria but are in the form of general headings such as "helping someone achieve a goal" (Yarrow & Waxler, 1976; Strayer et al., 1979) or "alleviate another's nonemotional needs" (Eisenberg-Berg & Lennon, 1980). Definitions that are slightly more psychologically specific identify "fixing" (Severy & Davis, 1971) or protecting verbally or physically (Murphy, 1937). Yet more specific examples are the giving of food or objects in response to need cues by the other (Whiting & Whiting, 1975) and specification of responses that follow distress cues by the other children (Eisenberg-Berg & Hand, 1981).

Conclusions about observations of helping behavior noted in Table 10.2

may relate to the psychological generality of the definitions used and the frequencies of their occurrence. Stith and Connor (1962) include not only what would usually be considered helping but also such general categories of "giving praise," "giving reward," and "giving affection" with no requirement that they be in response to emotional or nonemotional needs. A label for such behavior might just as well be "positive social behavior" rather than helping specifically, and the frequencies found here were the highest, ranging from .91 per minute in the 3-year-olds and 1.33 in the 6-year-olds. The positive and significant correlation with age could be more a manifestation of what has been seen as an increase in generally rewarding and positive behavior with age rather than an increase in helping behavior per se (see review by Gellert, 1955). The frequencies reported in other studies of nonpsychological helping range from .008 per minute to .16 per minute, or 8 to 10 times lower than Stith and Connor's findings would suggest. Although one might argue that age differences make comparisons difficult, there is little evidence that helping behavior increases between the ages of 3 to 7½ (Yarrow & Waxler, 1976), or 4 to 5 (Eisenberg-Berg & Hand, 1979; Eisenberg-Berg, N., Cameron, E., Tryon, K., & Dodez, R., personal communication, 1981). Severy and Davis (1971) reported a decline in helping behavior in children aged 3 to 5 and 8 to 10, whereas Whiting and Whiting (1975) found a positive correlation with age for girls aged 3 to 11 and Krebs and Stirrup (1974) failed to find increases in helping between the ages of 7 and 9 years.

Psychological helping behavior was found to occur much less frequently than nonpsychological helping and generally appears more uniform in frequency of occurrence. The range is from less than .00 per minute to .09 per minute, with the .09 per minute perhaps being higher because it includes responses to happy feelings as well as distressed ones. Finally, even when both nonemotional and emotional helping are combined, the frequencies do not exceed .10 per minute for all studies other than Stith and Connor.

Sharing

Naturalistic studies of sharing behavior are presented in Table 10.3. Relatively few studies of sharing in natural settings have been conducted. The studies by Parten and Barnes are included because they observed associative play, which occurs when children converse about a common activity, borrow and loan play materials, or do whatever draws their attention. One could say that this psychologically general definition includes sharing ideas about activity, sharing play materials, and sharing an activity. Some of the more recent studies are more psychologically specific because they are limited to instances in which the child gives away or allows another use of an object that was previously in the child's possession (Eisenberg-Berg & Hand, 1979; Iannotti, 1981; Eisenberg-Berg, Hand, & Hake, 1981; Eisenberg-Berg & Lennon, 1980). One definition includes permitting another use of a play area as well (Eisenberg-Berg et al., 1981; Eisenberg-Berg & Lennon, 1980). Only one of the more recent studies includes "verbal offers" as well as actual transfers of objects (Iannotti, 1981). Sharing is correctly seen in all studies as an "act" because it is not necessary to specify the act of the recipient in order to label it correctly as sharing. There is no mention of qualitative dimensions of sharing such as amount, complexity, co-occurring affect, or type of psychomotor involvement. The level of inference one must make is high because observers are asked to infer ownership (possession), and the bases for such inferences are not clear.

When the definitions considered in these studies (see Table 10.3) are examined as they relate to frequencies and correlate with age, the following tentative conclusions may be reached: (1) the more psychologically specific the definition, the lower the frequency of occurrence; and (2) the more psychologically general the definition, the more likely it is that there will be positive correlation with age. The most psychologically specific definitions show frequencies ranging from .003 per minute to .03 per minute (Eisenberg-Berg et al., 1981; Eisenberg-Berg & Lennon, 1980; Iannotti, 1985). The next most general definitions show frequencies of .05 per minute for sharing plus comforting (Yarrow & Waxler, 1976) and .13 per minute for sharing (Strayer, et al., 1979). Finally, the most general and inclusive definitions show frequencies of .19 and .39 per minute (Parten, 1932; Barnes, 1971).

Generally, and with one exception, the studies utilizing more psychologically specific definitions do not find an increase in sharing between the various segments of ages 2 and 7 (Eisenberg-Berg et al., 1981; Iannotti, 1981; Strayer et al., 1979; Yarrow & Waxler, 1976). One of these studies in fact found a decrease in sharing between the age groups 2½ to 4 and 4 to 5 (Eisenberg-Berg et al., 1981). The only exception is noted in a study by Eisenberg-Berg and Hand (1979). In this study, a ρ of .51 between sharing and age was found for 4- to 5-year-olds. However, (1) the positive correlation here was found for spontaneous and unasked-for instances of sharing; and (2) the frequency of sharing was .0195 per minute or 6.5 times as frequent as in the Eisenberg-Berg and Lennon study (1981) and 1.8 times as frequent as the Eisenberg-Berg, Hand and Hake study (1980), suggesting that the samples were different in some unspecified ways; and (3) the definition here excluded the sharing of play areas as in the other two aforementioned studies. Both studies utilizing the most inclusive, psychologically general definitions show increases between the ages of 2 and 5 in associative play (Parten, 1932; Barnes, 1971). Again, when definitions become more psychologically general, they begin to tap into a general sociability or positive social interaction dimension rather than sharing per se, and it is very likely that it is the general rather than the particular social behavior that is increasing. Similarly, Eisenberg-Berg et al. (1981) recently found that "sociability" (neutral and positive social interactions) increases with age between 2½ and 4 to 5 years.

Conclusions and implications for further research

The preceding review of naturalistic studies of prosocial behaviors suggests some interesting general and specific conclusions as well as directions for future research. Studies of cooperation and sharing show evidence of developmental change, but this evidence of increase depends on the definition used in the study. Researchers who hope to identify developmental increments in prosocial behaviors should pay particularly careful attention to qualitative components of those behaviors. Studies of helping behavior do not reliably show such change with age, at least not within the age spans studied thus far. The temptation to regard all prosocial behaviors as undergoing similar developmental change should be avoided at this time. Second, the frequencies of occurrence are also dependent upon the definition used. Third, the degree of inference that must be made from observation, the degree of emphasis on qualitative dimensions, the nature of the act itself as a segment of the stream of behavior, and the varieties or kinds of behavior studied are all highly variable across studies.

The identification of the multifaceted and complex character of cooperation leads to some challenging questions about associations between cooperation and other social and personality variables. Observers of cooperative behaviors in children are able to detect subtle defining criteria such as inferences about the purpose of the activity (common goal), the leadership and organization of the group, and the fit between the behavior of both children. Intention or attitude is observed as "striving" to attain the goal, a "marked sense of belonging," or mutual involvement; qualifiers such as "intensity" of involvement, duration, and complexity of cooperative behavior can be detected by observers. If observers are able to make such distinctions, is it possible that children also make such judgments as they play with one another? Do children make judgments about the quality of their own contribution to cooperation as well as judgments about the contribution of the other child, and do they act accordingly? Specifically, would a child be likely to continue playing in spite of (1) a lack of serious intention or effort by the other child, (2) actions by the other child that fail to enhance the project at hand, or (3) actions that directly frustrate the child's attempt to improve the project? If the duration of cooperative interaction is of such importance, what are some of the motivational and interpersonal determinants of these sustained encounters? It should be possible to examine the verbal and nonverbal components of face-to-face interaction sequences as they relate to duration – one must look at "interacts" rather than "acts." One may investigate the individual differences in the children's ability to "tune in" to the other's experiences (affect, attitude), or in other words empathy, as well as the child's own experiences as they relate to these sequences. To expand further on the implications for future work, research on the interrelation between affect, empathy, and prosocial behavior, including the author's efforts, will now be briefly reviewed.

The development of a theory that would explain the linkages described above with regard to cooperative behavior, affect, and empathy has not progressed far. Among the reasons for this lack of progress has been the failure to conceptualize cooperation as a complex set of acts of varying durations. For theory one must rely on theories of the development of altruistic and moral behavior. These are not entirely adequate since cooperation is not solely for the benefit of the other; nevertheless, such theories are useful because cooperation shares similar features with other prosocial acts. One recently stated theory (Carroll & Rest, 1982) proposes that social sensitivity and affective and cognitive empathy serve as the first component of a fully developed morality. This component is called "recognition and sensitivity." The second component, "moral judgment," involves consideration of ideals and norms related to the situation. "Values and influences," the third component, include devising a plan of action with moral ideals, nonmoral values, goals and pressures in the situation in mind. The last component, "execution and implementation of moral action," includes adjustments in the act in view of impediments plus the organizing and sustaining of behavior to realize the goal. Unfortunately, while the last component seems to call for a motivational basis for sustaining behavior, neither affect nor any other motivational influences are discussed.

A contrasting theoretical model for the development of altruistic behavior, which again is similar but not identical to cooperation, is offered by Hoffman (1975). This model places greatest weight on the empathic and affective motivational basis for altruistic behavior. The theory proposes that vicarious affective responses ("empathic" responses) are present from the beginning of life, and it is the affect generated by empathic sensitivity that motivates altruistic behavior. The cognitive skills of the child (e.g., role taking) continue to develop throughout life and help the child to tailor his or her behavior to the needs of others. Empathy also may become diminished or sharpened depending on the child's life experiences.

Little research evidence has been found to clarify the ways in which empathy and affect serve to facilitate or dampen cooperative interactions between children. The existing research looks primarily at other prosocial behaviors as related to affect or empathy or investigates the associations in an experimental context. It has therefore been difficult to weld a theory together that speaks to the interrelationship of these components. A discussion of literature pertaining to affect, empathy, and prosocial behavior, with special emphasis on cooperative behavior, follows.

A relationship between prosocial behaviors and the positive affect of the child has been found both in naturalistic and in experimental studies. Strayer (1980) investigated the relationship between affective states, empathic responses, and perspective-taking skills among 14 preschool children observed in a preschool setting over a period of 8 weeks. On the basis of Hoffman's theory (1975), it was hypothesized that empathy would be more likely to occur when the ego needs of the child are satisfied; thus the child's affective state would positively (in the case of happy affect) or negatively (in the case of negative affect) influence empathic responses to others. Empathic responses to others included participation in the affect, comforting, help giving, or reinforcing comments in response to another's affect (happy, sad, angry, or hurt). Those children who ranked high in empathy toward others were also those whose predominant affect was happy (rho = .59). Those children who showed predominantly sad affect were found to be lower in empathy toward others. Affective states were unrelated to donation of pennies in an experimental situation, nor were perspective-taking measures correlated with empathy given. The empathy measure reflected a combination of affective responsivity (usually called empathy) plus prosocial behavioral responses; it is not clear which type of response predominated or whether both were the responses to the other child's affect.

Experimental analogues to the Strayer (naturalistic) study have also yielded accumulated evidence over the past 15 years supporting the relationship between transient mood states and prosocial behavior. In a series of studies with elementary school children, from first through fifth grade, children asked to think about happy things were found to be more generous than those asked to recall less pleasant things (Isen, Horn, & Rosenhan, 1973; Moore, Underwood, & Rosenhan, 1973; Rosenhan, Underwood, & Moore, 1974; Underwood, Froming, & Moore, 1977). While these are more transient affect states, there is also some evidence that more enduring positive feelings about oneself (i.e., positive self-esteem) are related to the ability of children to respond to distress in others (Reykowski & Yary-movitz, 1976). It should also be reported that some inconsistencies in the experimental literature have appeared, and the relationship between affect and donation has not been supported in some research (Harris & Siebel, 1975; Cialdini & Kenrick, 1976).

The naturalistic and experimental studies would lead one to speculate that affect may have an important facilitating role in cooperative interactions between children. The cooperative interchange would be likely to persist longer if both children were experiencing positive affect. This hypothesis is based on both the motivating properties of pleasant affect as well as the communication to the other arising from that affect (see Izard, 1978) and signals to the other child that there is pleasure and interest in sustaining the cooperative interaction.

The possible involvement of happy affect in cooperative interactions led to a recent study of cooperation in preschool children (Marcus, 1982). The children were 3 to 6 years of age and were observed in a preschool setting. Graduate students working in pairs were trained to make running records of all verbal and nonverbal behaviors of both children in a cooperative interaction. The recordings began after the rooms were scanned in quadrants in search of interactions that met the definition of cooperation according to Parten (1932). Special features of the cooperative interchanges that were recorded included noting the length of the interchange, reasons for termination, and predominant affect (happy, sad, angry, fearful, neutral) noted in both children (separately). As such data are inherently rich in detail but are time consuming to analyze, only a few findings will be presented at this time. Overall interrater agreement for category of affect (happy, neutral, sad, afraid, angry) was 83% for child 1 and 84% for child 2 throughout all the cooperative episodes. The data consisted of 78 cooperative episodes ranging in length from 2 to 1,500 sec. The following affects were found in at least one child in the dyads: 43% happy, 66% neutral, 3% sad, 2% afraid, 0% angry. Since matching affect in a dyad (e.g., neutral–neutral) was counted as one instance while nonmatching affect (e.g., neutral–happy) was counted twice, the percentages do not add up to 100%. When both children were showing predominantly happy affect, the length of interaction was significantly longer in duration than cooperation episodes with any other affect accompaniment ($p < .01$). This analysis does not distinguish between happy feelings that originate within each child separately and those that "spread" from one to the other through an empathic process; these and other questions pertaining to relationships between affect and cooperation await further research. Perhaps detailed inspection of videotapes of such episodes would prove fruitful in the future.

A second important affective ingredient, suggested by the Strayer (1980) study, is empathy, defined as a vicarious affective response. One study by Marcus, Telleen, and Roke (1979) of 32 preschool children (age x̄ = 47.5 months) evaluated cooperation using both observer and teacher ratings and time-sampled measurements (using a modified Parten, 1932, definition). Empathy was measured using the Feshbach and Roe Affective Situations Test for Empathy (FASTE) (Feshbach & Roe, 1968). This empathy measure correlated with the observer ratings of cooperation ($r = .59$, $p < .01$) and with the separate ratings of two teachers ($r = .48$ and $r = .48$, both $p < .01$). The time-sampled measurement of cooperation was not found to be significantly correlated with the FASTE. A later subanalysis (Marcus & Roke, 1980) of the correlations of the time-sampled measure of cooperation and a breakdown of the FASTE measure into empathy for four separate affects showed that empathy for happy affect was positively and significantly associated with cooperation ($r = .51$, $p < .01$ with age and sex partialed out). A recent replication of this study was completed with refinements made concerning the measurement of empathy (Marcus, Roke, & Bruner, 1983). The sample was a slightly older group of 32 preschool children (age x̄ = 60.7 months). Teacher ratings of cooperation were collected using the same scale used in the study by Marcus, Telleen, & Roke (1979). The FASTE was administered in standard fashion, although the children were videotaped as they responded to the test slides. Ratings were made of the degree of match and intensity of empathic response noted in the children's voices and (separately) faces. The results indicated a positive and significant correlation between the FASTE measure total score and ratings of cooperation ($r = .38$, $p < .05$). When facial empathy and FASTE measures were combined in a multiple regression analysis, the amount of explained variance in cooperation was increased significantly ($p < .05$) by the addition of the facial empathy measure beyond that contributed by the FASTE. However, the two empathy measures should not be viewed as measuring the same thing, since the FASTE measure correlated positively with cooperation while the facial empathy measure correlated negatively. It was suggested that there may be two kinds of empathy being measured and the one may be more cognized (the FASTE), while the other is a less cognized type of empathy. Further research is needed to clarify this issue.

The preceding research findings concern the relationship among affect, empathy, and prosocial behavior, but an analogue can be drawn to the study of aggression, anger, and empathy. Feshbach's (1970) theoretical model concerning responses to situations of aggression instigation includes components of anger and aggressive drive as intervening processes (p. 179).

Anger and an aggressive drive may be separated "although under most circumstances they can be considered equivalents" (p. 179), and "anger responses may be considered to have drive properties in the sense of an energizer of ongoing behavior" (p. 162). The frustration–aggression hypothesis, for example, is reconceptualized as a process by which frustrations produce rage or anger responses and movements that become increasingly focused and directed (p. 208). By contrast, Bandura's (1977) theory places frustration or anger arousal in his model as facilitating but not as a necessary condition for aggression to occur. Recently developed approaches to helping people control aggression focus quite strongly on lessening anger in the face of provocation (Meichenbaum, 1975; Novaco, 1978). Unfortunately, this author has not found a single naturalistic observation study of aggression in which the involvement of angry affect was also observed. Hartup (1974) distinguished between instrumental and hostile aggression and found that hostile aggression does not decline with age, whereas instrumental aggression does. This finding would suggest that affect may continue to be a major energizer of aggressive behavior throughout childhood. Unfortunately, just as we do not know the extent to which angry affect is involved in aggressive behavior, we know little about how an empathic response or an angry counterresponse from another child or adult might moderate the course of angry aggression. It would be possible to see such changes in ongoing sequences of interactions between children.

This brief review of research suggests certain tentative conclusions and avenues for further research. The first is that affect is an important facilitator of prosocial behavior in general and cooperative behavior specifically, although the latter point needs further research support. Second, the research has tended to support the facilitating impact of happy affect in particular upon prosocial responses in general as well as upon cooperative behavior. Positive affect may be influencing the child's readiness to engage in various prosocial behaviors by sensitizing the child to the other's needs, as in the component of moral behavior noted by Carroll and Rest (1982), although the sensitizing is likely to be for positive affect rather than the negative affect one might see in moral dilemmas. Positive affect may also facilitate the child's cooperation by reducing egoistic concerns (as per Hoffman, 1975), or it may be vicariously rewarding to the child to play with another who happily engaged in cooperative interaction with that child. This second explanation is a more hedonistic motivation for prosocial behavior – the child continues because it increases in his or her own happiness. The latter explanation is an indication of the empathic facilitator of prosocial behavior, a "second-hand" experience of happy affect at work. Further research in natural settings investigating the complexity of cooperation, its affective components, its duration, the nature of emotional contagion of the parties regarding affect, and empathic responses to that affect will be informative. A return to research of a more holistic nature rather than a more fragmentary empirical approach is suggested in this consideration of the definition of behavior.

References

Baldwin, A. (1967). *Theories of child development*. New York: Wiley.

Bandura, A. (1977). *Social learning theory*. Englewood Cliffs, NJ: Prentice-Hall.

Barnes, K.E. (1971). Preschool play norms: A replication. *Developmental Psychology, 5*, 99–103.

Bronfenbrenner, V. (1974). Developmental research, public policy and the ecology of childhood. *Child Development, 45*, 1–5.

Bryan, J.H. (1975). Children's cooperation and helping behaviors. In E. M. Hetherington (Ed.), *Reviews of child development research* (Vol. 5, pp. 127–181). Chicago: University of Chicago Press.

Cairns, R.B., & Green, J.A. (1979). How to assess personality and social patterns: Observation or ratings. In R. B. Cairns (Ed.), *The analysis of social interaction* (pp. 209–225). Hillsdale, NJ: Erlbaum.

Carroll, J.L., & Rest, J.R. (1982). Moral development. In B. Wollman (Ed.), *Handbook of developmental psychology* (pp. 434–449). Englewood Cliffs, NJ: Prentice-Hall.

Cialdini, R.B., & Kenrick, D.T. (1976). Altruism as hedonism: A social development perspective on the relationship of negative mood state and helping. *Journal of Personality and Social Psychology, 34*, 907–914.

Coke, J.C., Batson, C.D., & McDavis, K. (1978). Empathic mediation of helping: A two-stage model. *Journal of Personality and Social Psychology, 36* (7), 752–766.

Cook, H., & Stingle, S. (1974). Cooperative behavior in children. *Psychological Bulletin, 81*, 918–933.

Eisenberg-Berg, N., Cameron, E., Tyron, K., & Dodez, R. (1981). Socialization of prosocial behavior in the preschool classroom. *Developmental Psychology, 17*, 773–782.

Eisenberg-Berg, N., & Hand, M. (1979). The relationship of preschooler's reasoning about prosocial moral conflicts to prosocial behavior. *Child Development, 50*, 356–363.

Eisenberg-Berg, N., Hand, M., & Hake, R. (1981). The relationship of preschool children's habitual use of space to prosocial, antisocial, and social behaviors. *Journal of Genetic Psychology, 138*, 111–121.

Eisenberg-Berg, N., & Lennon, R. (1980). Altruism and the assessment of empathy in the preschool years. *Child Development, 51*, 552–557.

Feshbach, N.D., & Roe, K. (1968). Empathy in six- and seven-year-olds. *Child Development, 39*, 133–145.

Feshbach, S. (1970). Aggression. In P. H. Mussen (Ed.), *Carmichael's manual of child psychology* (3rd ed.) (vol. 2, pp. 159–259). New York: Wiley.

Friedrich, L.K., & Stein, A.H. (1973). Aggressive and prosocial television programs and the natural behavior of preschool children. *Monographs of the Society for Research in Child Development, 38*, (4, Serial No. 151).

Gellert, E. (1955). Systematic observation: A method in child study. *Harvard Education Review, 25* (3), 179–195.

Harris, M.B., & Seibel, C.E. (1975). Affect, aggression, and altruism. *Developmental Psychology, 11*, 623–627.

Hartup, W. (1974). Aggression in childhood: Developmental perspectives. *American Psychologist*, 29, 336–341.

Hoffman, M. (1975). Developmental synthesis of affect and cognition and its implications for altruistic motivation. *Developmental Psychology, 11*, 607–622.

Iannotti, R.J. (1985). Naturalistic and structured assessments of prosocial behavior in preschool children: The influence of empathy and perspective taking. *Developmental Psychology, 21*, 46–55.

Isen, A.M., Horn, N., & Rosenhan, D.L. Effects of success and failure on children's generosity. *Journal of Personality and Social Psychology, 27*, 239–247.

Izard, C.E. (1978). On the ontogenesis of emotions and emotion-cognition relationships in infancy. In M. Lewis and L. Rosenblum (Eds.), *The development of affect* (pp. 389–412). New York: Plenum.

Krebs, D. (1970). Altruism: An examination of the concept and a review of the literature. *Psychological Bulletin, 73*, 258–302.

Krebs, D. (1975). Empathy and altruism. *Journal of Personality and Social Psychology, 32*, 1134–1146.

Krebs, D., & Stirrup, B. (1974). Role taking ability and altruistic behavior in elementary school children. *Personality and Social Psychology Bulletin, 1*, 407–409.

Lambert, W.W. (1960). Interpersonal behavior. In P. H. Mussen (Ed.), *Handbook of research methods in child development* (pp. 854–917). New York: Wiley.

Marcus, R.F. (1982). *Cooperation and affect in young children*. Unpublished manuscript.

Marcus, R.F., & Roke, E.J. (1980). *The specificity to empathic response in young children*. Paper presented at the annual convention of the American Psychological Association, Montreal.

Marcus, R.F., Roke, E.J., & Bruner, C. (1983). *Verbal and nonverbal empathy and the prediction of social behavior in young children*. Paper presented at the Annual Convention of the American Psychological Association, Washington, DC.

Marcus, R.F., Telleen, S., & Roke, E.J. (1979). Relation between cooperation and empathy in young children. *Developmental Psychology, 15*, 346–347.

Meichenbaum, D.H. (1975). A self-instructional approach to stress management: A proposal for stress inoculation training. In C. Spielberger and I. Sorason (Eds.), *Stress and anxiety* (Vol. 2, pp. 237–263). New York: Wiley.

Moore, B.S., Underwood, B., & Rosenhan, D.L. Affect and altruism. *Developmental Psychology*, 1973, 8, 99–104.

Murphy, L.B. (1937). *Social behavior and child personality*. New York: Columbia University Press.

Novoco, R. (1978). Anger and coping with stress. In J. Foreyt & D. Rothjen (Eds.), *Cognitive behavior therapy, theory, research and procedures*. New York: Plenum.

Parten, M.B. (1932). Social participation among preschool children. *Journal of Abnormal and Social Psychology, 27*, 243–269.

Payne, F.D. (1980). Children's prosocial conduct in structured situations and as viewed by others: Consistency, convergence, and relationships with person variable. *Child Development, 51*, 1252–1259.

Radke-Yarrow, M., Zahn-Waxler, C., & Chapman, M. (1983). Children's prosocial dispositions and behavior. In P. H. Mussen (Ed.), *Carmichael's manual of child psychology*, (4th ed.) Vol. IV, pp. 469–545). New York: Wiley.

Reykowski, S., & Yarymovitz, M. (1976). *Elicitation of the prosocial orientation*. Unpublished manuscript. Warsaw, Poland: University of Warsaw.

Roke, E.J. (1979). *Parental correlates of cooperative behavior in young children*. Unpublished doctoral dissertation. Baltimore, University of Maryland.

Rosenbaum, D.L., Underwood, B., & Moore, B. (1974). Affect moderates, self-gratification and altruism. *Journal of Personality and Social Psychology, 30*, 546–552.

Rushton, J.P. (1980). *Altruism, socialization and society*. Englewood Cliffs, NJ: Prentice-Hall.

Severy, L.J., & Davis, K.E. (1971). Helping behavior among normal and retarded children. *Child Development, 42*, 1017–1031.

Staub, E. (1978). *Positive social behavior and morality: Social and personal influence* (Vol. 1). New York: Academic Press.

Staub, E. (1979). *Positive social behavior and morality: Socialization and development* (Vol. 2). New York: Academic Press.

Stith, M., & Connor, T. (1962). Dependency and helpfulness in young children. *Child Development, 33*, 15–20.

Strayer, J.A. (1980). Naturalistic study of empathic behaviors and their relation to affective states and perspective-taking skills in preschool children. *Child Development, 51*, 815–822.

Strayer, F.F., Wareing, S., & Rushton, J.P. (1979). Social constraints on naturally occurring preschool altruism. *Ethology and Sociobiology, 1*, 3–11.

Underwood, B., Froming, W.J., & Moore, B.S. (1977). Mood, attention and altruism: A search for mediating variables. *Developmental Psychology, 13*, 541–542.

Webster's Ninth New Collegiate Dictionary. (1984). Springfield, MA: Merriam-Webster.

Whiting, B., & Whiting, J.W.M. (1975). *Children of six cultures*. Cambridge, MA: Harvard University Press.

Wright, H.F. (1960). Observational child study. In P. H. Mussen (Ed.), *Handbook of research methods in child development* (pp. 71–139). New York: Wiley.

Yarrow, M.R., & Waxler, C. (1976). Dimensions and correlates of prosocial behavior in young children. *Child Development, 47*, 118–125.

11 Social information-processing variables in the development of aggression and altruism in children

Kenneth A. Dodge

In spite of a long history of studying children's cognitive processes and an equally long history of studying children's social and aggressive behavior, until recently researchers have largely ignored the study of the relation between cognition and social behavior (cf. Flavell & Ross, 1981). Likewise, Parke and Slaby (1983) recently chastised researchers for failing to view aggressive behavior in its broad ecological context. The goal of this chapter is to integrate the study of aggression with an understanding of children's cognitive and social development. This work may contribute to our understanding of children's social cognitive processes as well as lead to intervention efforts aimed at reducing aggressive behavior and increasing prosocial behavior in children.

This chapter briefly reviews recent research that bears on this problem. While this research covers a broad range of cognitive processes, including social cognitive skills and attributions, it suffers greatly from the lack of a comprehensive theory of the ways in which children process social cues and come to respond behaviorally in a social interaction. The framework for such a theory, in the form of a social information-processing model, is formulated in this chapter. A set of research studies that utilize this model is described in some detail. These studies suggest that children's cognitive processes and social behavior can reciprocally influence each other in a way that can perpetuate deviant aggressive behavior. This hypothesis is supported by an observational study of children's play behavior over time. Finally, the implications of the social information-processing model for future research and clinical efforts are outlined.

The cognition-aggression relationship

Berkowitz (1977) and Novaco (1978) suggested that the key factor in determining whether a person aggresses in a situation is not the situational stimulus itself, but rather the person's interpretation of the stimulus. That

280

is, a provocation stimulus is a cue for an aggressive response only when the person interprets the stimulus as hostile, and not when the person interprets the stimulus as benign. We have found that, given the very same provocation stimulus, children who interpreted the provocation as hostile responded with aggression 77% of the time, whereas children who interpreted the provocation as benign responded with aggression only 24% of the time (Dodge, 1980). How a child perceives a provocation stimulus, then, has dramatic effects on the probability that he or she will respond with aggression.

In addition to the inferences about peers' behavior made by children, it is apparent that social cognitive skills may also be related to prosocial and aggressive behavior. Aggressive behavior has been found to correlate with deficits in cognitive skill in many areas, including the following: self-rehearsal of responses (Kendall, 1977; Meichenbaum & Goodman, 1971), the inhibition of premature social responding (Camp, 1977; Dodge & Frame, 1982; Dodge & Newman, 1981), interpersonal problem solving (Spivack & Shure, 1974), and referential communication (Chandler, Greenspan, & Barenboim, 1974). These studies led Eron (1980) to hypothesize that if aggressive children can learn nonaggressive competent cognitive strategies to solve interpersonal tasks, they will not resort to aggressive behavior. By implication, Eron argues that aggressive behavior may be either a deviant strategy for solving problems or a frustration response following a failure to solve a problem. Bandura (1973) further argues that "socially and verbally unskilled persons, having limited means for handling discord, are likely to become physically aggressive at the slightest provocation" (p. 255). The relation between aggression and social cognitive skills deficits is inherent in this theorizing.

Three cognitive skills have been studied most thoroughly in this context: empathy, role taking, and problem solving. Feshbach (1970) suggested that empathic skills enable a person to understand and experience another's perspective in an aggressive interaction and should therefore lead to reduced aggressive behavior. Studies testing this hypothesis, however, have led to mixed findings (see Chapter 6 in this volume for a review of the literature). Studies of the relation between empathy and prosocial behavior are equally perplexing (see Chapter 6 in this volume and Radke-Yarrow, Zahn-Waxler, & Chapman, 1983, for reviews).

Chandler (1973; Chandler, Greenspan & Barenboim, 1974) studied the relationship between role-taking skills and aggressive behavior and found that delinquent and emotionally disturbed, aggressive boys are relatively deficient in these skills. Also, training in role-taking skills can lead to a decrease in the display of deviant behavior in these boys. On the other hand, Kurdek (1978) found high perspective-taking abilities to be associated with being disruptive and fighting.

The relationship between problem-solving skills and aggressive behavior is equally baffling. Spivack and Shure (1974; Spivack, Platt, & Shure, 1976) found a negative correlation between the skill of generating many solutions to interpersonal problems and aggressive behavior. Dodge (1985) found no such relationship concerning the quantity of solutions generated, whereas Richard and Dodge (1982) found that the quality of solutions to interpersonal problems differentiated aggressive and nonaggressive boys. The solutions generated by aggressive boys tended to be less competent and less likely to lead to success than those of nonaggressive boys.

Resolving these contradictory findings is no small task. Certainly, studies have varied in the methods used to measure skills, the types of aggressive and prosocial behaviors assessed, and the subject populations tested. Differences in these parameters across studies may account for some of the discrepant findings. More thorough discussions of these issues are provided by Krasnor and Rubin (1981) and Shantz (1983). On the whole, these studies suggest that social cognitive processes *are* related to aggressive and prosocial behavior, but the relation, as presently studied, is a weak one; that is, most studies of cognitive processes have accounted for only small portions of the variance in aggressive and prosocial behavior. Perhaps one reason for the generally weak findings is that researchers have studied cognitive skills one at a time, as if one skill, such as role taking, could and should explain *all* aggressive and prosocial behavior.

A related problem has been that some researchers have assumed generalizability of their constructs across tasks and situations. That is, researchers have sometimes measured a cognitive skill in one context (such as in a spatial perspective-taking task) and expected this skill to relate to behavior in a different context (such as peer relations). This assumption is often *not* warranted (Mischel, 1968). An aggressive child does not behave aggressively on all occasions and in all situations, just as a child's level of social cognitive skills varies across tasks (Fisher, 1980; Ford, 1979). Clearly, assessment of the relationship between cognitive processes and aggressive and prosocial behavior must occur within situations. For example, if one is trying to explain a child's aggressive behavior in turn-taking play situations, one should assess that child's cognitive processing in and about turn-taking situations.

Perhaps the most critical indictment of research in this area has been leveled recently by Shantz (1983), who concluded:

In short, there has not been sufficient and detailed theory guiding the research on social-cognitive/behavioral relations. . . . The most frequently investigated position is that advanced social-cognitive abilities (of various kinds) are positively related to the frequency of prosocial behavior and negatively related to the frequency of antisocial behavior. It is unclear . . . why this position is so widely held since social information and understanding, however derived . . . can be used for social good or ill.

A social information-processing model

Research in this area is therefore in search of a comprehensive model of how, and in what manner, cognitive processes may be related to aggressive and prosocial behavior. Such a model must not be so broad as to be untestable, or so situation-specific as to lack utility (Goldfried & d'Zurilla, 1969; McFall, 1982). Rather, the model should specify the requisite cognitive processes involved in most responding to social stimuli and should lead researchers to be able to predict aggressive and prosocial behavior to a highly accurate degree. The model should also describe the cognitive processes, acquired in development, that enable individuals to refrain from aggression. This model should serve several functions. It should organize varied and seemingly unrelated fields of research, contribute to the theoretical understanding of how basic social cognitive processes are involved in aggressive and prosocial behavior, provide conceptual tools for the assessment of social cognitive skill deficits in clinically aggressive children, and provide a theoretical basis for comprehensive intervention programs to increase prosocial behavior and decrease aggression in clinically aggressive children.

Recent investigations have led the author to the formulation of such a comprehensive model (Dodge, 1985). This model is extracted from Flavell's (1974) information-processing conceptions of the stages involved in making social inferences, Goldfried and d'Zurilla's (1969) articulation of a behavioral-analytic approach to interpersonal problem-solving, theories of human information processing and cognitive problem solving (Newell & Simon, 1972; Shiffrin & Schneider, 1977), and recent formulations of social skills (McFall, 1982; McFall & Dodge, 1982). The model is a tool for understanding both skill deficits and biases in cognitive processing. It describes the necessary steps involved in processing social information and responding to social stimuli within a given situation in a competent manner. It is not implied that children consciously follow these steps but that logically these steps must occur.

According to the model (depicted in Fig. 11.1), each social stimulus situation presented to a child can be considered as a task or a problem. A child comes to that situation with a data base (his or her memory store of past stimuli, events, and outcomes) and a set of programmed directives or

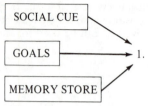

1. Encoding Process
   A. Perception of social cues
   B. Search for cues
   C. Focus (attention to cues)

2. Interpretation Process
   A. Interpretation of memory store, goals, and
      new data
   B. Search for interpretations
   C. Match of data to programmed rule structure

3. Response Search Process
   A. Search for responses
   B. Generation of potential responses

4. Response Decision Process
   A. Assessment of consequences of potential
      responses
   B. Evaluation of adequacy of potential
      responses
   C. Decision of optimal response

5. Enactment Process
   A. Behavioral repertoire search
   B. Emission of response

Figure 11.1. A social information-processing model of competence.

goals. The data base might consist of probability estimates for various behavioral sequences and outcomes based on past experiences. The goal may vary according to the child's needs at the time and as a function of socializing experiences. Renshaw and Asher (1982) cite the example of two children who are playing a board game. The child's goal might be to win the game, to get better at the game, or to enhance the friendship with the peer. These varying goals have implications for that child's behavior during the game and might affect the probability that a child will display aggressive behavior toward the peer. It is also the case that a child's goals may change during the course of an interaction and may actually be created as a function of the interaction.

In any case, in each situation the child receives as input from the environment a set of social cues. That child's behavioral response to those cues occurs as a function of his or her progression through several cognitive steps. Each step is a necessary, but insufficient part of appropriate responding. Failure to perform skillfully at a step will increase the probability of a deviant behavioral response. The steps are sequential in time, meaning that competent responding requires an orderly progression of cognitive steps. This model distinguishes between competent behavior, which is a subjectively judged phenomenon that is a function of both the actor and a rater of the behavior, and specific cognitive steps preceding the behavior (McFall, 1982). The cognitive steps are stages in a child's processing of social information. The steps involve both processing skills, which are objectively measured acquired abilities, and interpretation skills, which are subjectively determined judgments by the child based on probability estimates. Hence, it is possible to assess both skill deficits and cognitive biases at each step of the process. The major theoretical postulation of the model is that the way a child processes social information (as a function of both processing skills and interpretations) can have a great impact on his or her behavioral response. More specifically, it is postulated that behavior occurs as a function of both biases and deficits in the way a child processes social cues.

The first step of social information processing for the child is to encode the social cues in the environment. Obviously, there are many substeps to this process, beginning with the awareness of the existence of cues, as Flavell (1974) points out. The child attends to cues, receives them through sensory processes and then perceives them. Processing skills involved in the accurate encoding of information include rehearsal, chunking, and mnemonic devices to aid storage of information. In order to perform skillfully at this step, the child must be as free as possible from debilitating biases in encoding. For example, when confronted with a provocation by a peer, such as being hit in the back, the child may or may not display skills of adequately and accurately focusing on appropriate cues, such as the peer's facial expression at the time of the event. Debilitating encoding biases are evidenced when the child focuses on a deviant portion of the relevant cues, such as only the outcome he or she has suffered. Of course, the child cannot attend to all cues and must select appropriate cues for attention. Children learn heuristics for efficient means of attending to certain cues. In some cases, the heuristics prove inappropriate, such as when the child focuses only on the outcome of a behavior. "Appropriateness" of a child's heuristics (biases) is determined by both the task and cultural norms. Livesley and Bromley (1973) found that heuristics used by children change as they get older. Younger children attend to specific behaviors and concrete features of their stimulus world, whereas older children begin to attend to generalities and psychological aspects of behavior, including traits, habits, and beliefs of the stimulus person. It is also the case that socializing experiences can have a dramatic impact on the encoding processes of children (Costanzo & Dix, 1983). It is postulated that a breakdown at this step, due to a processing skill deficit or an interpretive bias, could lead to deviant behavior.

The second step is an interpretation process. Once the child has perceived the social cues, he or she must make sense of them. This step is sometimes indistinguishable from the first, in that it may not be possible to discriminate what a child encodes from the meaning applied to the encoded information. Somehow, however, the child makes a meaningful inference. The child may do this by integrating the encoded cues with his or her memory of past events. The child who was hit by a peer may decide whether the peer was trying to be hostile or was acting benignly. He or she may match the encoded stimulus cues with a memory having a programmed rule structure. For example, the rule might be: If the peer laughs after hitting me, then I know he or she meant to hurt me. Research on the bases for children's interpretations of social cues is quite substantial and exists under various names, including social cognition (Shantz, 1975; 1983), person perception (Livesley & Bromley, 1973), attribution theory (Jones & Davis, 1965), role taking (Chandler, 1973), moral judgments (Karniol, 1978), assimilation and accommodation (Piaget, 1928), and representation of schemas (Miller, 1969) and scripts (Shank & Abelson, 1977). This work has described a variety of rule structures that develop during childhood for use in interpretation processes, including the use of covariation information (DiVitto & McArthur, 1978; Kelley, 1967), multiple sufficient and multiple necessary causes (Smith, 1975), and discounting principles (Costanzo, Grumet, & Brehm, 1974). The present model posits directly that skill deficits and attributional biases during the interpretation process increase the probability of deviant behavioral outcomes.

The third step is a response search process. Once the child has interpreted a situation, he or she must search for possible behavioral responses. The skills of generating many and varied behavioral responses to situations are critical to this step of social information processing. According to Kendler (1968), young children are not capable of the spontaneous production of representational responses. Therefore, developmental level may affect the processing of social information and, hence, behavioral responding. The work of Spivack and Shure (1974; Spivack, Platt, & Shure, 1976) suggests that a deficit in the skill of generating many responses to interpersonal problems is related to the display of aggressive behavior. Also important at this step of processing are the types of responses generated. Children learn to apply rule structures at this step of processing in order to generate responses. For example, the child who was hit in the back may apply the following rule: if the peer intends to hurt me, then I have available to me the option of hitting him or her back. Piaget (1932) suggested that young children first apply a different rule during development: If I get hurt, then I can hit back. Previous experiences, responses learned from role models, and skills in brainstorming all contribute to the quality of the responses generated by children. Recently, Richard and Dodge (1982) found that aggressive boys generate less competent responses to several interpersonal problem situations than do nonaggressive socially adjusted boys. In that study, the first responses generated by aggressive boys were judged by independent raters to be as competent as the first responses generated by nonaggressive boys. Subsequent responses generated by aggressive boys, however, were more frequently judged as incompetent and were more frequently aggressive than were those of nonaggressive boys. These data suggest that aggressive boys may have only a single competent behavioral response available to them in several social situations. When an alternate response is called for, their response search skill deficits become obvious, and their behavioral performance deteriorates.

Beyond generating responses, the child somehow chooses an optimal response, which takes place at the next step of social information processing. In choosing a response, the child may use skills of assessing the probable consequences of each generated response so that he or she can evaluate the adequacy of response possibilities. The ability to perform concrete operations in the Piagetian sense is obviously necessary here. These skills involve highly complex cognitive representations and therefore may be a source of difficulty for young children or children who do not delay gratification. It has been hypothesized that the impulsive behavior of some aggressive children reflects a failure to engage in response evaluation processes by those children (Kendall & Wilcox, 1979). Spivack and Shure (1974) called these skills consequential thinking. In a recent study, Dodge (1985) found that aggressive children are deficient in being able to recognize the inadequacy of certain potential responses to hypothetical situations.

In addition to processing skills, interpretive biases are relevant at this step, as is the case when a child judges the probabilities of various outcomes to each possible behavioral response. For example, the child who was hit in the back may decide against choosing a response that involves asking the peer instigator of the stimulus to stop hitting him because he has estimated the likelihood of success with this approach to be very poor. In choosing a behavioral response, a child must take into account both the environmental context in which the behavior is to be displayed, and his or her own behavioral repertoire.

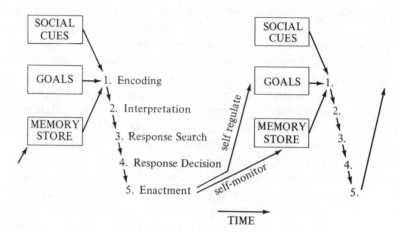

Figure 11.2. Sequential aspects of social information processing.

In the fifth step of processing, the child proceeds to act out a chosen behavioral response, a process called enactment. Verbal and motoric-behavioral skills, acquired over time through practice, are critical here. The child who decides to respond to a peer's provocation with a verbal statement of displeasure and a request to stop the provocation must possess the verbal skills to accomplish this task. A promising method for assessing a child's enactment processes is the role-play procedure employed by McFall (1977) and others in their investigations of assertive behavior in adults. Role-play procedures have also been used with children. For example, Gottman, Gonso, and Rasmussen (1975) asked children to role play how they would go about making a friend. In assessing enactment skills, it is essential to separate enactment processes from response search and decision processes. Otherwise, role-play responses are confounded with these other processes.

The social information processing of a child does not terminate at the time of enactment (see Fig. 11.2). The child must monitor the effects of his or her behavior and regulate it accordingly, in the same way that a ship's captain must alter his or her ship's course according to the nautical signs that are read. As this process involves a new data base and different environmental cues continually, the child begins to repeat the five step process over and over.

The proposed social information processing model is consistent with two classical theories of aggression: social learning theory (Bandura, 1973) and the frustration–aggression hypothesis (Berkowitz, 1962; Dollard, Doob, Miller, Mowrer, & Sears, 1939). It adds to those theories by articulating the cognitive processing mechanisms that often mediate aggressive responding. If aggression is conceptualized as an instrumental response, the child displaying this response may be thought of as processing information in a way that leads him or her to conclude that aggression is warranted, appropriate, or the only available response (Patterson, 1976). If aggression is conceptualized as a hostile response to frustration, the child's inadequate processing of social cues may be thought of as contributing to his or her frustration and to an aggressive response in either of two ways. First, if a child misinterprets, in a hostile direction, the intention of others in provocation situations, he or she may be more likely to become frustrated and to retaliate aggressively (Berkowitz, 1977; Dodge, 1980). Second, if a child is unskilled at processing social cues, he or she may experience social discomfort and aggress as a result of that frustration. With unskilled processing, the slightest provocations can act as instigations to aggression (Allen, 1978; Toch, 1969).

Assumptions of the proposed model

Several assumptions underlie the proposed social information processing model. The first assumption is that processing occurs extremely rapidly and often at a nonconscious level. In this way, the concept of interpersonal responding is similar to a concept in the cognitive literature called automatic information processing (Shiffrin & Schneider, 1977). But processing can also occur at a more controlled level. Controlled processing is a form of problem solving that is most likely to occur in novel situations, when the situation demands an interpersonal response from a child (as in the coercive situations described by Patterson & Cobb, 1971), and when many different responses are possible (Goldfried & d'Zurilla, 1969). A second assumption is that a child's social information-processing skills may vary across situations. For example, a child's response search skills may be deficient in peer group entry situations but not in peer provocation situations, or vice versa. It is therefore hypothesized that deviant or unskilled social information processing should be evidenced by a child only in those situations that lead the child to display deviant behavior. This hypothesis is relevant both to researchers studying social cognitive skills and to clinicians assessing cognitive processing in aggressive children. A third assumption is that the steps of social information processing involve skills that are acquired over time through a learning process. One empirical hypothesis arising out of this assumption is that children may vary in their processing according to their developmental level. A second hypothesis is that if a child is deficient in processing at a certain step, skills involved in that step may be trained.

A fourth assumption of the proposed model is that each step of the response process can be assessed independently. For example, one can assess response search skills by holding the interpretation step constant, that is, by presenting to the child a given interpretation of a social situation. This assumption provides the basis for a number of research studies in which the investigator has used this model to study the role of social information processing in children's aggressive behavior.

Studies of social information processing in aggressive children

Attributional studies

This program of research began with the recognition that aggressive behavior among children occurs in the context of a social interaction and that attention to the social information processing by members of a dyad may be important in understanding the evolution of aggressive behavior patterns in the dyad. We decided to employ the concepts from the social information processing model to achieve an understanding of how some children come to adopt aggressive behavior patterns in their interactions with peers. We hypothesized that aggressive boys engage in deviant antisocial behavior as a function of biases in their interpretations of peers' behavior (at step 2 of the proposed model). Specifically, we hypothesized that, in response to an ambiguous provocation, such as getting hit in the back or having one's toys knocked to the ground by a peer, aggressive boys would be more likely to attribute hostile intentions to the peer perpetrator of the provocation than would nonaggressive boys. It was predicted that the difference between these groups in interpretations of this stimulus would then mediate differences in children's behavioral responses.

To test this hypothesis, we (Dodge, 1980) presented aggressive and nonaggressive boys with ambiguous provocation stimuli in the form of hypothetical stories such as the following:

Imagine that you are standing on the playground playing catch with several other boys. A boy named ———— is holding the ball. You turn your head in the other direction, and the next thing you realize is that the ball has hit you in the back real hard, and it hurts a lot. The other boys are laughing.

These stories were presumed to hold the first step of information processing, that of encoding cues, constant since they were simple and easily understood. We then assessed the boys' interpretations of the intention of the named peer (step 2) by asking them to attribute either a hostile or benign intention to the peer. Finally, we asked the boys to describe what they would do (step 3) in response to the provocation. It was hypothesized that aggressive boys would attribute hostile intentions to the peer more frequently than would nonaggressive boys and that these attributions would mediate differences in generated behavioral responses between the groups.

Both hypotheses were supported. Aggressive boys were 50% more likely than nonaggressive boys to attribute a hostile intention to the peer instigator of the provocation. Aggressive boys were also more likely than nonaggressive boys to say that they would respond to the provocation with some form of retaliatory aggression, and this difference occurred as a direct function of the difference in the interpretations made about the provocation. That is, when boys in either group interpreted the provocation as hostile they responded with aggression, and when they interpreted the provocation as accidental they did not retaliate. Since aggressive boys more frequently made a hostile interpretation, they more frequently retaliated aggressively. When the interpretation was taken into account, the difference between the two groups in their behavioral responses diminished greatly. Attributional differences thus mediated boys' aggressive behavior. While the first study was conducted only with boys, subsequent studies have replicated this finding with girls (Dodge & Tomlin, 1983). These replications have also included assessments of children's attributions during actual interpersonal interactions (Steinberg & Dodge, 1983).

It was also hypothesized in the first study that characteristics of the stimulus person who instigated the provocation, called the target, could have an effect on the interpretations and generated behavioral responses by children. We therefore manipulated the status of the target as aggressive or nonaggressive by using the names of peers who fit our criteria as aggressive or nonaggressive as the peer instigators of the provocations. Indeed, boys were five times more likely to attribute a hostile intention to the aggressive targets than to the nonaggressive targets. Likewise, boys said they would be more likely to retaliate aggressively when the target was an aggressive peer than when he was a nonaggressive peer.

The data reported in these studies strongly support the general hypothesis that the way children interpret and process social information could have profound effects on their behavior in a social interaction. Based on these findings, we proposed a reciprocal influence model of the relationship between attributions of hostility and aggressive behavior among children (see Fig. 11.3). According to this model, when confronted with an ambiguous provocation by a peer, such as getting pushed in the back or having one's puzzle knocked to the ground, aggressive children are biased in the direction of presuming that the peer is acting with hostile intent. When they view the peer as acting in a hostile way toward them, they are inclined to retaliate with what they feel is justified aggression. In this way, an

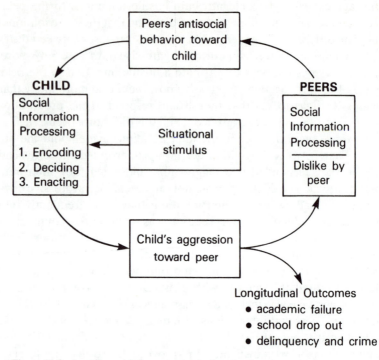

Figure 11.3. A reciprocal influence model of aggression.

ambiguous, possibly accidental act by a peer has led to an intentional, aggressive act by the aggressive child. If we consider the course of this hypothetical peer interaction, we realize that the peer is now the recipient of an aggressive provocation that seems to that peer to be unwarranted. The peer processes this information as evidence of the aggressive child's hostility. The peer views the child as being inappropriate and "out of touch" socially. The peer comes to dislike the other child and to treat the other child in antisocial ways. Of course, these antisocial behaviors are interpreted by the aggressive child as support for his or her belief that peers are hostile. These behaviors also make this child "perceptually ready" (Brunner, 1957) to attribute hostile intent to the peer the next time that an ambiguous provocation occurs. Subsequent ambiguous provocations are inevitable among active children who engage in a lot of rough and tumble play. Over time, both the child and the peers may develop attributional biases toward each other which exacerbate the hostility between them. The aggressive responses by a child to a provocation may eventually become "automatic" and immediate. This child becomes habitually aggressive and is at risk for a variety of antisocial outcomes, including juvenile delinquency and becoming a school dropout (Kuperschmidt, 1983).

The process described is a classic vicious cycle between hostile attributions and aggressive behavior. In many ways, it resembles the coercive interactions between mothers and aggressive children observed by Patterson (1976) and Reid (Chapter 9) and the escalating aggressive control patterns between mothers and toddlers observed by Bates (1980). The process depicted in the figure describes *peer* interactions however, and may explain how peer social rejection is related to attributional biases and aggression.

Although the proposed reciprocal influence model is highly speculative and difficult to test, several specific predictions are implied in this model. First, the model predicts that a high proportion of aggressive behaviors occur during ambiguous situations. Second, the model predicts a positive correlation between the frequency with which a child aggresses against peers and the frequency with which that child is the target of aggression by peers. This prediction is not intuitively obvious, since aggressive boys are often thought of as bullies who dominate peers. The model predicts more than a correlation, however. It predicts reciprocal causation. Specifically, it is predicted that the child who aggresses against peers in the early moments of interaction with peers will be the one who is the target of peers' aggression in later interactions. Finally, the model predicts that the child who is the target of aggression in early peer interactions will be relatively likely to display high rates of aggression in later interactions.

An observational study

These four predictions were tested in a short-term longitudinal study of peer interactions. While another purpose of the study was to observe the development of peer friendships and status over time (cf. Dodge, 1983), this study also allowed us to observe patterns of aggressive behavior over time. Six play groups were assembled, each with eight previously unacquainted 7-year-old boys. Boys were brought together for an hour a day for eight days over a 2-week period and were allowed to play freely in a large room stocked with toys. Observers sitting behind a one-way mirror noted the occurrence of each act of verbal and physical aggression, and coded the initiator and recipient of each act. Verbal aggressive acts were hostile statements to peers, and included threats, insults, and contentious statements. Physical aggressive acts were defined as assaultive behavior intended to harm or hurt a peer. Observers also coded the circumstance in which each aggressive act occurred. At the end of the eighth session, each of the boys was privately interviewed in order to solicit peer nominations for aggression. Groups of aggressive, average, and nonaggressive boys were formed by these peer nominations. The previously displayed patterns of aggressive behavior among these boys were then examined to test the hypotheses under study.

The first hypothesis concerned the circumstances in which aggressive behavior occurs. It was predicted that ambiguous interactions involving a high level of activity would form the settings in which much aggressive behavior occurred. This hypothesis was based on the rationale that these settings would be most likely to lead to misinterpretations of peers' intentions. The procedure used to test this hypothesis was one of comparing conditional probabilities (Bakeman, 1978). The conditional probability of an aggressive behavior occurring just following a particular behavior category was compared to the unconditional, or base rate, probability of an aggressive behavior. These comparisons were made by z-score tests (Schlundt, 1982). Several circumstances were found to increase dramatically the probability that an aggressive behavior would occur immediately afterward, or within several "lags" of behaviors. These aggression-inducing circumstances included instances of rough-and-tumble play among peers, possession of a peer's toy object by a child, norm-setting or bossy statements by a child to a peer, and previous aggressive behaviors. The first three of these circumstances are indeed ones in which a child could easily misconstrue the meaning of the interaction or the intentions of the peer. These findings also provide support for the model's hypothesis that aggressive behavior is reciprocated in children's social interactions. When one child aggresses against a peer, the peer has a greater than base rate probability of retaliating with counteraggression.

The second hypothesis was that children who display high frequencies of aggressive behavior will be the targets of high frequencies of aggression by peers. This hypothesis was supported by two statistical analyses. First, the aggressive group of boys, as nominated by peers, was found to display aggression and to be the target of peers' aggression more frequently than were the average or nonaggressive groups (Table 11.1). Second, a positive correlation ($r = .41, p < .01$) was found between the frequency with which a boy initiated aggression and the frequency with which he was the target of peer aggression. Indeed, the attributional bias among aggressive boys and the bias among peers toward aggressive boys which have been described in previous studies were found in this study to have a behavioral basis, or at least a behavioral correlate: boys who aggress are likely to be the target of peers' aggression.

The third hypothesis was that the child who frequently aggresses against

Table 11.1. *The relationship between aggressive behavior and being the target of peer aggression*

Subjects	Aggressive acts initiated (Agg-I)	Aggressive acts received (Agg-R)	Percentage difference
Aggressive boys (*n* = 12)	32.6	22.8	+43
Average boys (*n* = 24)	19.6	20.4	− 4
Nonaggressive boys (*n* = 12)	9.2	11.8	−22

Note: Scores represent group mean frequencies summed over eight sessions. Correlation between Agg-I and Agg-R = .41; *p* < .01. Prediction of Agg-I in session 2 from Agg-I in session 1 is enhanced by Agg-R in session 1: R square change = .03; *p* < .01. Prediction of Agg-R in session 2 from Agg-R in session 1 is enhanced by Agg-I in session 1: R square change = .02; *p* < .02.

peers in one session will be the target of a great deal of peer aggression in later interactions. This hypothesis was tested by regression equations in which the frequency with which a child was the target of aggression in one session was predicted from the frequency of that child's display of aggression in the preceding session. Indeed, this hypothesis was supported: the frequency with which a boy was the target of aggression in session two could be predicted from the frequency of that boy's aggression in session one, even when the frequency with which the same boy was the target of aggression in session one was partialed out (*p* < .01). Likewise, the fourth hypothesis was supported by similar analyses. The frequency of a boy's aggression in session two could be predicted from the frequency with which that boy was the target of aggression in session one, even when the frequency of that boy's aggression in session one was partialed out.

It is also not surprising in this study that the boys who displayed high frequencies of aggressive behavior toward peers in early interactions had a high probability of becoming disliked by peers (Dodge, 1983). The relation between aggression and children's sociometric status has been a matter of controversy in the past (Olweus, 1977). This study and others (e.g., Coie, Dodge, & Coppotelli, 1982) clarify this relation by demonstrating that, while aggression is not at all correlated with liking by peers (*r* = − .02), it is highly positively correlated (.72) with disliking by peers. This paradoxical finding is explained by the fact that measures of the strength of liking by peers and disliking by peers are only moderately negatively correlated (*r* = − .29).

While the observational study reported here does not identify the origins of boys' aggression, it does support a reciprocal influence model of the maintenance and exacerbation of aggression patterns among boys. Boys who aggress against peers will later become the targets of peer aggression, and vice-versa. These boys will become rejected by peers who will then treat them in antisocial ways. The antisocial treatment will serve to perpetuate and exacerbate the reciprocal aggression.

The experimental studies described earlier, which grew out of the social information processing framework, support the hypothesis that biased attributions may be a mediating link in this reciprocal pattern. The implication of this work is that biased attributional processes and aggressive behavior patterns may reinforce each other in such a way as to perpetuate and strengthen their interrelationship. Change in such a system may be difficult to achieve. Indeed, Campbell and Yarrow (1961) found that even when behavior patterns in a child changed over time, the child's assessment by peers did not change as quickly. The present data suggest that if the negative peer assessments continue, they could serve to reinstigate aggressive behavior in a child.

Implications of the social information-processing framework

The social information processing model that has been described in this chapter has several implications for future research and clinical efforts by those interested in aggressive and prosocial behavior in children. An outcome of this work will undoubtedly be the modification of the model, as future studies suggest either different cognitive processes or a different pattern of the relationship between cognitive processing and social behavior.

One major implication of the social information processing approach is that it ought to be possible to make highly accurate predictions of behavior within specific social situations through the combined assessment of processing at every step of social information processing. The precise relationship between a set of social information processing skills and behavioral performance is not yet clear, but could be evaluated by the use of multiple regression techniques. It is hypothesized that assessment of each of the five steps of processing provides unique information for the prediction of behavior, but it is not yet known whether certain steps are more critical than others in discriminating between competent and deviant behavior. It is also probable that certain steps are more critical in some situations than in others. For example, in initiating play with peers, the encoding step may be relatively simple and nondiscriminating or nonpredictive of behavior, while in ambiguous provocation situations it may be critical. The reverse may be true for the response search step. The conceptual framework described in this chapter provides an empirical method for assessing these kinds of predictions. The proposed empirical work would involve the assessment of social information processing at every step of the model and the prediction of behavior within a situation through multiple regression techniques.

Whereas developmental studies of the individual cognitive skills described in this chapter have been conducted for many years (such as skills of role taking), very little developmental information exists concerning children's acquisition of the whole process, including the realization of the need for such a process, the appropriate sequencing of information-processing steps, and the ability to relate one step of processing to the next step. The proposed model provides a framework for the empirical investigation of these aspects of children's social cognitive development.

Another major implication of this work is that successful intervention with an aggressive child may be very difficult to achieve, once the reciprocal influence patterns have been developed. Prevention of these patterns, or interruption in early stages, may be a more reasonable path to follow. The model described in this chapter provides clinicians with a conceptual framework for the assessment and training of social cognitive skills in deviant, aggressive children who are in the early stages of their development. According to this framework, depicted in Figure 11.4, assessment of social information processing biases and skills deficits should occur in two steps. In the first step, the clinician must determine those social situations that lead the child client to behave in deviant aggressive ways. The clinician may do this by a combination of observations and interviews with the child and significant others. The pool of all social situations that confront a child is large and diverse, and may vary according to the age, gender, and culture of the child. Goldfried and d'Zurilla (1969) and Freedman, Rosenthal, Donahoe, Schlundt, and McFall (1978) described methods for developing taxonomies of critical social situations. Very little systematic research has been conducted in this area with young children, however. The clinician must determine the pool of social situations for the child; after the pool of situations has been generated, and a list of problematic situations within that pool has been determined, the clinician then must assess the child's skills and biases at each step of social information processing within each of the problematic situations, in order to identify specific areas of deficits and biases. The result of this two-step assessment procedure is a profile of the child's social information processing skills and patterns. Once this profile has been determined, the clinician can attempt to train the child in critical social skills and to alter deviant biases on the child's part. Theoretically, this training could interrupt the developing problematic cycle and

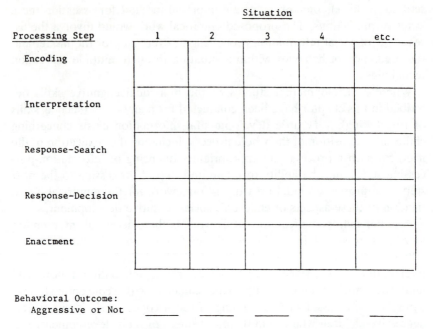

Figure 11.4. Profiling children's social information-processing biases and deficits.

lead to increased social competence and reduced aggressive behavior in the child client. While this possibility is an exciting implication of this perspective, caution must be expressed because this is an untested assertion.

Summary

This chapter reviewed a number of studies relating cognitive processes, including empathy, attributions, and problem-solving skills, to children's aggressive and prosocial behavior. It was found that in the bulk of these studies, cognitive processes provide only weak predictions of social behavior, possibly because the studies lack a comprehensive theoretical framework which describes the manner in which cognitive processes ought to be related to behavioral performance. We have borrowed from the human information-processing and cognitive development literatures to propose such a framework. This model was described in detail, and several studies employing this model were reviewed. Finally, we suggested several ways in which the proposed conceptual framework could guide future empirical research and clinical efforts to promote prosocial development and to inhibit aggressive responding in children.

The social information-processing model has been applied in this chapter to the study of children's interpersonal aggressive behavior. It may also provide a useful framework for studying other areas of human social functioning, however. McFall and Dodge (1982) proposed a similar approach to the study of assertive behavior in adults, heterosocial relations, and children's peer relations. While there are limits to the utility of this framework for the study of human social behavior, at this point we are still exploring the potential of this approach.

Acknowledgements

Support for this research was provided by NIMH grant MH37062, and grants from the Spencer Foundation and the Foundation for Child Development. The author would like to thank Richard M. McFall for his comments on a draft of this paper and for his support throughout the conduct of this research.

References

Allen, J. (1978). *Assault with a deadly weapon: The autobiography of a street criminal*. New York: McGraw-Hill.

Bakeman, R. (1978). Untangling streams of behavior: Sequential analyses of observation data. In G. P. Sackett (Ed.), *Observing behavior: Vol II: Data collection and analysis methods* (pp. 63–78). Baltimore: University Park Press.

Bandura, A. (1973). *Aggression: A social learning analysis*. Englewood Cliffs, NJ: Prentice-Hall.

Bates, J. E. (1980). The concept of difficult temperament. *Merrill-Palmer Quarterly, 26*, 299–319.

Berkowitz, L. (1962). *Aggression: A social psychological analysis*. New York: McGraw-Hill.

Berkowitz, L. (1977). Situational and personal conditions governing reactions to aggressive cues. In D. Magnussen and N. S. Endler (Eds.), *Personality at the crossroads: Current issues in interactional psychology*. Hillsdale, NJ: Erlbaum.

Bruner, J. S. (1957). On perceptual readiness. *Psychological Review, 64*, 123–152.

Camp, B. (1977). Verbal mediation in young aggressive boys. *Journal of Abnormal Psychology, 86*, 145–153.

Campbell, J. D. & Yarrow, M. R. (1961). Perceptual and behavioral correlates of social effectiveness. *Sociometry, 24*, 1–20.

Chandler, M. J. (1973). Egocentrism and antisocial behavior: The assessment and training of social perspective-taking skills. *Developmental Psychology, 9*, 326–337.

Chandler, M. J., Greenspan, S., & Barenboim, C. (1974). Assessment and training of role-taking and referential communication skills in institutionalized emotionally disturbed children. *Developmental Psychology, 10*, 546–553.

Coie, J. D., Dodge, K. A., & Coppotelli, H. (1982). Dimensions and types of social status: A cross-age perspective. *Developmental Psychology, 18*, 557–570.

Costanzo, P. R., & Dix, T. H. (1983). Beyond the information processed: Socialization in the development of attributional processes. In E. T. Higgins, D. N. Ruble, & W. W.

Hartup (Eds.), *Social cognition and social development* (pp. 63–81). Cambridge: Cambridge University Press.

Costanzo, P. R., Grumet, J. F., & Brehm, S. S. (1974). The effects of choice and source of constraint on children's attributions of preference. *Journal of Experimental Social Psychology, 10*, 352–364.

DiVitto, B., & McArthur, L. Z. (1978). Developmental differences in the use of distinctiveness, consensus, and consistency information for making causal attributions. *Developmental Psychology, 14*, 474–482.

Dodge, K. A. (1980). Social cognition and children's aggressive behavior. *Child Development, 51*, 162–170.

Dodge, K. A. (1983). Behavioral antecedents of peer social rejection and isolation. *Child Development, 54*, 1386–1399.

Dodge, K. A. (1985). A social informational processing model of social competence in children. In M. Perlmutter (Ed.), *Minnesota Symposium in Child Psychology* (pp. 77–125). Hillsdale, NJ: Erlbaum.

Dodge, K. A., & Frame, C. M. (1982). Social cognitive biases and deficits in aggressive boys. *Child Development, 53*, 620–635.

Dodge, K. A., & Newman, J. P. (1981). Biased decision-making processes in aggressive boys. *Journal of Abnormal Psychology, 90*, 375–379.

Dodge, K. A., & Tomlin, A. (1983). *The role of cue-utilization in attributional biases among aggressive children.* Unpublished manuscript, Indiana University.

Dollard, J., Doob, C. W., Miller, N. E., Mowrer, O. H., & Sears, R. R. (1939). *Frustration and aggression.* New Haven: Yale University Press.

Eron, L. D. (1980). Prescription for reduction of aggression. *American Psychologist, 35*, 224–252.

Feshbach, S. (1970). Aggression. In P. Mussen (Ed.), *Carmichael's manual of child psychology.* New York: Wiley.

Fisher, K. W. (1980). A theory of cognitive development: The control and construction of hierarchies of skills. *Psychological Review, 87*, 447–531.

Flavell, J. H. (1974). The development of inferences about others. In T. Mischel (Ed.), *Understanding other persons.* Totowa, NJ: Rowman and Littlefield.

Flavell, J. H., & Ross, L. (Eds.) (1981). *Social cognitive development: Frontiers and possible futures.* Cambridge: Cambridge University Press.

Ford, M. E. (1979). The construct validity of egocentrism. *Psychological Bulletin, 86*, 1169–1188.

Freedman, B. J., Rosenthal, L., Donahoe, C. P., Jr., Schlundt, D. G., and McFall, R. M. (1978). A social-behavioral analysis of skill deficits in delinquent and nondelinquent adolescent boys. *Journal of Consulting and Clinical Psychology, 46*, 1448–1462.

Goldfried, M. R., & d'Zurilla, T. J. (1969). A behavior-analytic model for assessing competence. In C. D. Spielberger (Ed.), *Current topics in clinical and community psychology* (Vol. 1). New York: Academic Press.

Gottman, J. M., Gonso, J., & Rasmussen, B. (1975). Social interaction, social competence, and friendship in children. *Child Development, 46*, 709–718.

Jones, E. E., & Davis, K. E. (1965). From acts to dispositions: The attribution process in person perception. In L. Berkowitz (Ed.), *Advances in experimental social psychology* (Vol. 2). New York: Academic Press.

Karniol, R. (1978). Children's use of intention cues in evaluation behavior. *Psychological Bulletin, 85*, 76–85.

Kelley, H. H. (1967). Attribution theory in social psychology. In D. Levine (Ed.), *The Nebraska symposium on motivation.* Lincoln: University of Nebraska Press.

Kendall, P. C. (1977). On the efficacious use of verbal self-instructional procedures with children. *Cognitive Therapy and Research, 1,* 331–341.

Kendall, P. C., & Wilcox, L. E. (1979). Self-control in children: Development of a rating scale. *Journal of Consulting and Clinical Psychology, 47,* 1020–1029.

Kendler, T. S. (1968). Development of mediating responses in children. In J. C. Wright & J. Kagan (Eds.), Basic cognitive processes in children. *Monograph of the Society for Research in Child Development, 28,* 33–51.

Krasnor, L., & Rubin, K. (1981). The assessment of social problem-solving skills in young children. In T. Merluzzi, C. Glass, & M. Genest (Eds.), *Cognitive assessment.* New York: Guilford.

Kuperschmidt, J. (1983). *Predicting delinquency and academic problems from childhood peer status.* Paper presented as part of a symposium on strategies for identifying children at social risk (J. Coie, Chair). Biennial meeting of the Society for Research in Child Development, Detroit.

Kurdek, L. (1978). Relationship between cognitive perspective-taking and teachers' rating of children's classroom behavior in grades one through four. *Journal of Genetic Psychology, 132,* 21–27.

Livesley, W. J., & Bromley, D. B. (1973). *Person perception in childhood and adolescence.* London: Wiley.

McFall, R. M. (1977). Analogue methods in behavioral assessment: Issues and prospects. In J. D. Cone & R. P. Hawkins (Eds.), *Behavioral assessment: New directions in clinical psychology* (pp. 152–177). New York: Brunner Mazel.

McFall, R. M. (1982). A review and reformulation of the concept of social skills. *Behavioral Assessment, 4,* 1–33.

McFall, R. M., & Dodge, K. A. (1982). Self-management and interpersonal skills learning. In P. Károly & F. H. Kanfer (Eds.), *Self-management and behavior change* (pp. 353–392). New York: Pergamon.

Meichenbaum, D. H., & Goodman, J. (1971). Training impulsive children to talk to themselves: A means of developing self-control. *Journal of Abnormal Psychology, 77,* 115–126.

Miller, G. A. (1969). The organization of lexical memory: Are word associations sufficient? In G. A. Talland & N. C. Waugh (Eds.), *The pathology of memory.* New York: Academic Press.

Mischel, W. (1968). *Personality and assessment.* New York: Wiley.

Newell, A., & Simon, H. (1972). *Human problem solving.* Englewood Cliffs, NJ: Prentice-Hall.

Novaco, R. W. (1978). Anger and coping with stress: Cognitive-behavioral interventions. In J. P. Foreyt & D. P. Rathjen (Eds.), *Cognitive behavioral therapy.* New York: Plenum.

Olweus, D. (1977). Aggression and peer acceptance in adolescent boys: Two short-term longitudinal studies of ratings. *Child Development, 48,* 1301–1313.

Parke, R. D., & Slaby, R. G. (1983). The development of aggression. In P. H. Mussen (Ed.), *Handbook of child psychology* (4th ed.) (Vol. IV, pp. 547–642) (E. M. Hetherington, Vol. Ed.). New York: Wiley.

Patterson, G. R. (1976). The aggressive child: Victim and architect in a coercive system. In E. J. Mash, L. A. Hamerlynck, & L. C. Handy (Eds.), *Behavior modification in families.* New York: Brunner Mazel.

Patterson, G. R., & Cobb, J. A. (1971). A dyadic analysis of aggressive behaviors. In J. P. Hill (Ed.), *Minnesota symposium of child psychology* (Vol. 5). Minneapolis: University of Minnesota Press.

Piaget, J. (1928). *Judgment and reasoning in the child.* New York: Harcourt, Brace.

Piaget, J. (1932). *The moral judgment of the child.* London: Kegan Paul.

Radke-Yarrow, M., Zahn-Waxler, C., & Chapman, M. (1983). The development of prosocial behavior. In P. Mussen (Ed.) *Handbook of child psychology* (4th ed.) (Vol. IV, pp. 469–546) (E. M. Hetherington, Vol. Ed.). New York: Wiley.

Renshaw, P. D., & Asher, S. R. (1982). Social competence and peer status: The distinction between goals and strategies. In K. H. Rubin & H. S. Ross (Eds.), *Peer relationships and social skills in childhood.* New York: Springer-Verlag.

Richard, B. A., & Dodge, K. A. (1982). Social maladjustment and problem-solving in school-aged children. *Journal of Consulting and Clinical Psychology, 50*, 226–233.

Schlundt, D. G. (1982). Two PASCAL programs for managing observational data bases and for performing multivariate information analysis and log-linear contingency table analysis of sequential and nonsequential data. *Behavior Research Methods and Instrumentation, 14*, 351–352.

Shank, R. C., & Abelson, R. (1977). *Scripts, plans, goals and understanding.* Hillsdale, NJ: Erlbaum.

Shantz, C. U. (1975). The development of social cognition. In E. M. Hetherington (Ed.), *Review of child development research* (Vol. 5). Chicago: University of Chicago Press.

Shantz, C. U. (1983). Social cognition. In J. H. Flavell & E. M. Markman (Eds.), *Cognitive development*, a volume in P. H. Mussen (Ed.), *Handbook of child psychology* (4th ed.). New York: Wiley.

Shiffrin, R. M., & Schneider, W. (1977). Controlled and automatic information processing: II. Perceptual learning, automatic attending, and a general theory. *Psychological Review, 84*, 127–188.

Smith, M. C. (1975). Children's use of the multiple sufficient cause schema in social perception. *Journal of Personality and Social Psychology, 32*, 737–747.

Spivack, G., Platt, J. J., & Shure, M. B. (1976). *The problem-solving approach to adjustment: A guide to research and intervention.* San Francisco: Jossey-Bass.

Spivack, G., & Shure, M. B. (1974). *Social adjustment of young children: A cognitive approach to solving real-life problems.* San Francisco: Jossey-Bass.

Steinberg, M., & Dodge, K. A. (1983). Attributional bias in aggressive adolescent boys and girls. *Journal of Social and Clinical Psychology, 1*.

Toch, H. (1969). *Violent men.* Chicago: Aldine.

Conclusions: lessons from the past and a look to the future

Carolyn Zahn-Waxler

The initial, broad-based formulation of the issues to be addressed here – namely, the social and biological origins and interconnections of altruism and aggression in humans and animals – precluded the possibility of emerging with tidy, integrative statements or conclusions. Our major aims in the workshop on biological and social origins of altruism and aggression were, rather, (1) to begin to articulate what is not known, (2) to stimulate research interest in questions requiring an interdisciplinary approach, and (3) to create an opportunity for dialogue and collaboration between investigators with different areas of expertise in the biological and behavioral sciences. While we moved in this direction, we were humbled by the considerable research task ahead. A crucial problem is that both existing theories and projections for future research on altruism and aggression are determined by a thin, normative data base, regardless of the species studied.

In developmental psychology, there are few data based on strong, naturalistic, and experimental research methods regarding age-related changes in altruism and aggression. Prevailing theories, too, have contributed to a constrained view of prosocial and antisocial development in children. The child is commonly studied as an organism that is (1) detached from the environment in which it is reared and (2) disembodied from the future adult state, which would convey, perhaps more vividly, the possible complexities and extreme variations in altruism and aggression. Behaviorism and learning theory approaches have not encouraged exploration and analysis of emotions and motives underlying altruism and aggression. Social-cognitive theories have focused more on internal states, but predominant emphasis has been on (1) the role of intellect and reasoning, (2) uniformities across children at a given stage, and (3) analysis of change in age/stage that can be predicted from expanding cognitive capacities. Nor are other approaches, such as sociobiological theory, well equipped to explain individual differences and complexities in altruism and aggression.

If we assume that the complexity and variations in adult behavior evolve

303

from differences that begin in childhood (e.g., see Radke-Yarrow & Zahn-Waxler, 1984), there is a need to study patterns of variation that unfold developmentally. Research strategies will need to be adapted to index and accurately describe these patterns as well as the way in which they interact with socialization experiences. More naturalistic studies are called for, particularly those that will permit intensive study of children's relationships with significant persons in their lives (e.g., family and friends). Most of the existing research with children has been done within the school setting; this fact of research strategy cannot help but influence theories concerning the nature of altruism and aggression. It is commonly assumed that family patterns have little to do with the child's moral development (see Kagan, 1984). But some studies strongly suggest that these factors play a role in children's prosocial and antisocial behaviors (see reviews by Radke-Yarrow, Zahn-Waxler, & Chapman, 1983, Parke and Slaby, 1983); further research is required to delineate specific patterns of influence and directions of effect. When behavior is studied in the laboratory, it is important to continue to try to create microcosms that adequately represent extensions of children's existing social worlds.

These are not new messages (e.g., Radke-Yarrow, Zahn-Waxler, & Chapman, 1983). But if they are not followed in practice as well as in principle, the possibilities for conducting significant, relevant research are greatly diminished. There is a compelling need for continued research on the development of altruism and aggression. This is equally true whether the developmental perspective is framed in terms of changes over time within species or in terms of differences across species, across generations, or across cultures. More extensive examination of conditions of serious suffering and conflict would help determine adaptive and maladaptive functions of altruism and aggression.

We stand on the edge of a new era in which biological, sociobiological, and genetic approaches to the study of social behaviors are rapidly gaining prominence. It is too soon to say whether a serious fusion of past and current approaches can be achieved (see Cairns, Chapter 2). It is hoped that we will not simply bear witness to another nonproductive swing of the pendulum and a fruitless struggle between genetic and environmental explanations of altruism, aggression, and moral conduct specifically, and of adaptive and maladaptive patterns of psychosocial functioning more generally. The ability to care for others as opposed to the need to be cared for, the inability to control hostile impulses, and the capacity to channel aggression effectively are not only moral concerns – they have serious implications for quality of life and emotional well-being.

Empathy, aggression, and related personality characteristics of individuals are increasingly becoming part of the diagnostic criteria for a number of psychiatric disorders in children and adults. For example, failure to establish meaningful social bonds, to feel empathy, to feel appropriate guilt, to be able to refrain from hurting others, and so forth emerge repeatedly as descriptors in different diagnostic categories. Altruism is more frequently being used as a predictor variable in epidemiological and longitudinal studies of antecedents of emotional illness (e.g., see McCord, 1984). Recent work with autistic children is just beginning to provide systematic and rigorous assessments of empathy in these children. Concepts of altruism and aggression hence become increasingly important to theories of mental illness as well. Collaborations of psychiatrists and psychologists on risk groups and normal groups would thus be useful at several levels: in helping distinguish normative and non-normative patterns of altruism and aggression, in addressing questions of biology–behavior interactions, and in studying the etiology of different emotional disorders.

Many recent technological and methodological advances have been made in biological research. Instruments for measuring the functioning of the autonomic nervous system have become increasingly sophisticated. With regard to central nervous system functioning, methodological breakthroughs in measuring brain function and activity have also occurred, such as computer-assisted "pictures" (tomograms) of the brain and glucose uptake tests of activity in different regions of the brain. It is possible that in future decades some of these measures of brain function may be safely applied to children. The recently developed neuroanatomically based systems of Ekman and of Izard for coding discrete affects (and blends of emotion) by scoring facial muscle movements may provide yet another window into brain function. Advances have also been made in the construction of approaches to measure environmental influences on social–emotional development (e.g., see Radke-Yarrow, Kuczynski, Zahn-Waxler, Cytryn, McKnew, Cummings, & Iannotti, 1982). The biological and behavioral approaches need to be wedded in research designs as well as in conversations about what needs to be done.

Interconnections of altruism and aggression

Three chapters in this volume provide new empirical data on interrelations of altruism and aggression in children. As in past research, the patterns of association continue to be complex, not yielding readily to simple or uniform interpretations. Altruism and aggression may be either positively related, negatively related, or unrelated, depending on (1) the definitions used; (2) the particular types of altruism and aggression measured; (3) the

cognitions, emotions, and personality characteristics that mediate the behaviors; as well as (4) a host of other situational, biological, and environmental influences. Contrasting theoretical perspectives and the different
research methodologies that result may also contribute to the different
patterns of associations. For example, if one uses an animal model and
thereby emphasizes that which we have in common with other animals
(e.g., dominance hierarchies, primitive emotive systems), the patterns may
appear different from those of a model that includes mediating factors that
pertain more exclusively to humans, such as self-esteem and symbolic-
cognitive abilities.

Future research on connections between altruism and aggression might
benefit from a less literal, circumscribed focus on the meaning of "connections." It would also benefit from exploration of the antecedents and
correlates of opposites of altruism other than aggression – most notably,
many of the more subtle, self-serving, and manipulative behaviors of individuals that may compete with the maintenance of empathic connections
between people. The ontogeny of lack of concern may be another fruitful
area of investigation. But research on this topic will be difficult in view of
the problems associated with the ability to distinguish between enlightened
self-interest and selfishness.

The most common statistical approach used to examine interconnections
has been to examine correlations among altruism, aggression, and related
characteristics. This approach rests on a questionable assumption, namely,
that the same set of processes of influence and patterns of interdependency
will similarly characterize all children. If correlations are not strong, it is
usually assumed that measurement error is the reason, rather than the
likelihood that various subtypes of children contribute differentially to the
overall relationship. Complex patterns may be masked by an analytic approach that focuses on assumptions of linearity; quantitative increases in
aggression may reflect qualitative changes as well. Thus, a certain amount
of aggression may be adaptive and positively related to altruism; still higher
levels may reflect a level of hostility that is logically incompatible with
compassion (Yarrow & Waxler, 1975). The same is true with regard to
personality characteristics, expressions of emotion, and other variables that
may mediate both prosocial and antisocial behaviors. A given degree of
emotion (e.g., mild concern) may be effective in facilitating altruism, while
too much sadness may be disorganizing and may contribute to confusion
and withdrawal. As another example, with regard to self-esteem, feeling
good about oneself may be linked with consideration of others, but too
much self-esteem (e.g., that which borders on grandiosity) may be incompatible with caring.

Socialization practices

Questions about processes underlying connections between altruism and aggression have typically focused on determinants that are "embedded" within the individual. It would also be useful to begin to examine the forces outside the individual (e.g., family, culture) that will influence the complex flow and interplay of compassion and aggression within the individual. For example, in cultures, subcultures, or families that emphasize suppression or containment of emotions, what will be the impact on the interplay of altruism and aggression? Moreover, different cultures adopt different value systems with regard to the balance of competition, cooperation, and individualistic efforts, (e.g., see Madsen, 1971; Whiting & Whiting, 1973). What specific influences will the family and culture have in the differential balancing of these behaviors within the individual child? Or, within the family, what will be the influence of different discipline systems, different emotional climates, or different emotional states and moods of parents on the patterns of interconnection? How do child-rearing practices influence the interplay of kind versus hurtful behaviors or help us to understand or predict which will predominate in a given situation? For example, what is the conjoint influence on altruism and aggression of techniques traditionally examined in research, such as love withdrawal, reasoning, and power assertion?

The predominant research strategy has been to examine the influence of child-rearing practices on prosocial or antisocial behaviors but not on how they might affect the connection between the two response systems at a process level. Also, in research that assesses the relative effectiveness of different parental techniques, the tendency has been to place the strategies in opposition. For example, it is commonly concluded in summary accounts of discipline influences (e.g., see Zeigler, Lamb, & Child, 1982) that parental reasoning facilitates moral development and that power assertion hinders it, even though (1) appropriate combinations of both may be particularly effective (Zahn-Waxler, Radke-Yarrow, & King, 1979) and (2) there may be many different kinds of reasoning and power-assertive techniques, either of which could be beneficial or deleterious. It is important to begin to move beyond conceptions of child rearing that focus on specific actions directed toward children in specific kinds of situations or that assume a particular parental strategy to be uniform in influence.

Other environmental variables that may influence patterns of altruism and aggression include (1) the emotional relationship that the parent has with the child, (2) the emotional relationship that the parent has with others (spouse, friends), (3) the way the parent structures the outside world for the child and defines for the child who are members of the ingroup and the outgroup, and (4) the value systems and attitudes that are transmitted. Typically, the different components of environmental influence are not investigated concurrently. The paucity of well-developed research procedures for obtaining first-hand knowledge of family functioning carries considerable risk of oversimplification of socialization processes. There is a corresponding danger that we will stop studying these processes before the significant issues have been addressed.

There is a growing tendency to generalize that a good (empathic) relationship with the mother, a secure attachment to the caregiver, rational guidance from the caregiver, a good relationship with a peer, and a good feeling about oneself will predict heightened prosocial behavior in children and possibly diminution of aggression as well. Nevertheless, the lives and backgrounds of many individuals have been marked and sometimes marred by suffering, conflict, and strife, yet these persons emerge as compassionate and adaptively aggressive. Different developmental pathways and different socialization antecedents may yield similar outcomes; conversely, similar influences may have different effects on different children. Many more different patterns of sensitivity and insensitivity to the needs of others prevail in nature than have been incorporated into research paradigms and into existing theories of socialization antecedents of aggression, altruism, and moral development.

Oversimplification of the research issues has also resulted from the use of unidimensional research models that foster an either–or approach to questions of etiology. For example, some investigators emphasize the role of the peer environment in influencing children's prosocial and antisocial development, while other researchers emphasize the significance of the parental role. It would be valuable to study how parent and peer influences interact to determine the social interactions and relationships of the child. Some parents may play a more active role than others in constructing adaptive play environments and in creating opportunities for different kinds of friendship patterns for their children. While social-cognitive theorists discuss the elementary school years as the time when social relationships contain enough reciprocity to serve as a basis for facilitating prosocial behaviors, Youniss (Chapter 3) correctly points to the growing research evidence indicating that reciprocal interchanges are part of children's social repertoires even in the first years of life. Some parents may be better prepared than others to make use of this potential in children to facilitate the further development of early skills in this area. This process has not been investigated.

Furthermore, the early friendship patterns of young children will probably not be independent of their parents' (or caregivers') friendship patterns. Often children begin to play together because their mothers are friends; messages about quality of friendship and patterns of hurting, giving, and receiving will be complex and learned early. Even the personality and affective state of the parent (or caregiver) may influence the amount of time the child spends in interactions with other children, as well as the nature of those interactions (Zahn-Waxler, Cummings, Iannotti, & Radke-Yarrow, 1984). The interaction of parent and peer influence needs to be systematically investigated, as does the possibility that strong peer friendships and strong family ties each establish the potential for both exclusionary and altruistic behavior. Intimacy creates friction as well as close bonds.

Little firm knowledge is available to indicate the "normative" altruistic and aggressive behavioral patterns in children at different stages of development – or of environmental factors that may influence norms. Studies of at-risk populations may facilitate exploration of these issues. For example, studies at the National Institute of Mental Health (NIMH) have focused on variations in patterns of early development of altruism and aggression by comparing children of depressed and of normal mothers. Naturalistic and experimental methods were used to examine altruism and aggression toward parents, strangers, and peers in 2-year-old children (Zahn-Waxler, Cummings, McKnew, & Radke-Yarrow, 1984). Children of seriously depressed parents showed disturbances in the capacity to engage in friendly, sustained play with age mates and in the ability to share and cooperate with them. These children also showed inappropriate patterns of aggression, sometimes being overreactive, sometimes showing a lack of good judgment about when and where to display aggression (e.g., going after a strange adult), and sometimes showing displaced aggression (e.g., hitting their playmate when they were angry with their mother for having left them). While deviation from the norm, here, clearly reflected patterns of maladaptation, deviation may not always be indicative of psychopathology (see Zahn-Waxler, Cummings, Iannotti, & Radke-Yarrow, 1984, for a more extended discussion of these issues). For example, children of mildly depressed, but adequately functioning, mothers were similar to children of normal parents on most measures of social-emotional functioning. Children of mildly depressed mothers appeared to be particularly sensitive to the emotional states of others. This group showed less physical aggression toward playmates and more preoccupation with others in distress. Low levels of physical aggression could reflect a relative inability to engage in normal rough-and-tumble play and difficulty in defending oneself. In the animal literature, rough-and-tumble play is sometimes described as a mechanism for promoting assertiveness, competence, and social cohesion between animals. But in humans the willingness to refrain from hurting others might reflect the early development of a higher-level internalized norm or value regarding consideration for others. Similarly, children's heightened preoccupation with the distress of others alternatively could reflect too much empathy, or it could indicate a precocious sensitivity that may lead to adaptive empathy and understanding of others.

Developmental issues

The use of unidimensional theoretical models and the tendency to adopt a dichotomous approach to research issues creates a problem for the study of developmental processes as well as for socialization influences. In other words, we are most likely to assume that altruism and aggression either increase or decrease with age. Each hypothesis may reflect certain realities, but incisive exploration of the questions does not profit from an either–or juxtaposition of ideas about developmental processes. Different kinds of developmental trajectories for different children may depend on many different factors of socialization, circumstance, and temperament. A focus on age-related changes per se does not permit adequate investigation of the different developmental pathways. Furthermore, each child is subject to socialization pressures that may pull him or her in varied directions. Many societal norms dictate that as children grow older, they should show more consideration for others. At the same time, many socialization experiences act to dampen what we would view as natural early impulses to show concern for others. For example, a teacher may quickly take care of a child in distress in order to prevent the child from becoming overreactive and the distress from spreading through the classroom. To the extent that this is true, children would learn two things: (1) that people do not react emotionally to upset in others and (2) that if someone is hurt, someone else who is in charge will handle it.

Many socialization techniques are available to caregivers, some of which have been shown to be effective in naturalistic studies, both in facilitating altruism and in softening aggression (Zahn-Waxler, Radke-Yarrow & King, 1979). However, the most common reactions of parents in situations of another's distress were either to do nothing or to reassure the child that "everything is okay." This is consistent with the findings reported by Grusec and Dix in Chapter 8, indicating that many of the procedures demonstrated in the laboratory to produce internalization of moral standards tend in fact not to be used by parents.

It will be important to continue to study patterns of relationships between altruism and aggression from a developmental perspective. How do the connections between prosocial and antisocial behaviors change over time? To what extent do the social patterns investigated reflect stable individual differences (continuities) throughout development, even though they may take different forms at different ages and stages of development? To what extent do changing patterns reflect true discontinuities?

Most of the developmental research on prosocial behavior has consisted of cross-sectional interview studies of moral reasoning and social-cognitive changes in the understanding of issues regarding helping and hurting others. While these studies have been informative in their own right, they cannot (nor were they intended to) substitute for research on how children of different ages behave in situations calling for altruism or aggression. There continues to be a paucity of developmental research, longitudinal or cross-sectional, that is informative of quantitative and qualitative changes in altruism and aggression over time. (This is even more true of research on other species.) Nor are there adequate taxonomies or comprehensive descriptions of variations in behavioral repertoires of prosocial behavior and aggression at any given age or stage.

There are, however, deeply entrenched conclusions in the research literature about development, at least with respect to altruism, which is so commonly believed to increase with age. The data do not readily conform to these assumptions (e.g., see review by Radke-Yarrow et al., 1983). Not all forms of altruism uniformly increase over time. Marcus (Chapter 11) reports age changes in cooperation and sharing but not in help and physical comfort. Even the changes in cooperation and sharing are not large in magnitude and are restricted to particular settings, samples, and circumstances. The experimental literature, particularly studies with high-demand characteristics and/or requiring forms of altruism that tap children's cognitive capacities, favors older children. The NIMH research (Chapter 6) showed very few aspects of children's altruistic behaviors to increase with age (between the ages of 2 and 7).

Competing societal pressures for both increases and decreases in age in aggression also occur. Children are requested to control the aggressive impulses as they grow older, but the culture also offers many rewards (high status and successful models) for aggression if it can be reasonably appropriately channeled (and sometimes even if it cannot). Although forms and patterns of aggression change with age, there is increasing evidence that basic orientations begin early. Longitudinal studies indicate considerable stability in aggressive patterns over time, particularly in boys (e.g., Olweus, 1979; Loeber, 1982). There are also indications that the forms of aggression become more serious with age (see Chapter 2 by Cairns and 6 by the NIMH team), even though physical aggression commonly has been found to decrease over the preschool years. Cairns indicates that serious (violent) aggression begins in adolescence, after which it shows a decline with age in adulthood. A recent 20-year longitudinal study (Eron, 1982) indicates that adult criminality and antisocial behavior can be predicted from aggression in childhood. Of particular interest was the suggestion in the data that early prosocial behaviors (reflected in concern about interpersonal relationships, reluctance to harm others, and hence a possible susceptibility to guilt) play a role in inhibiting the expression of aggressive behaviors. All these factors will continue to make exploration of associations between altruism and aggression both difficult and complex.

The role of emotions: guilt and empathy

The emotions that underlie feelings of responsibility for the distresses of others are most likely to be guilt and empathy. The role of guilt in development and its links with altruism and aggression in children have been the subject of much speculation and theory but little research. Darwin (1872) was one of the first to characterize guilt as a higher-order socialized emotion and to distinguish it from other, more primitively based emotions. Freud (1958) and numerous others have discussed the role of civilization and acculturation in the expression of guilt.

Humans seem to be the only animals with strong propensities toward experiencing guilt. Dogs may be an exception to this generalization about species differences. Accounts of chimpanzees show their ability to make reparations for wrongdoing in sign language. Little is known about whether guilt is in their repertoire in the natural habitat, although appeasement gestures (which may be related to guilt) are common in some species. However, humans are unique in their capacities both for experiencing guilt and for shaming and blaming others, which would be expected to play a major role in the inculcation of guilt. In further research that examines the emotions that mediate altruism and aggression during the course of development, it will thus be useful to emphasize both those emotions that we have in common with other animals (e.g., empathy, anger) and those that are more specific to humans (e.g., guilt).

Research interest in how emotions are related to altruism and aggression continues at a high rate. Throughout this book, investigators repeatedly return to the concept of empathy (or concepts akin to it) as a facilitator of altruism and an inhibitor of aggression. Many major theories of the development of altruism make use of the assumption that empathy facilitates altruism (e.g., see Hoffman, 1982). Major intervention studies have been based on this hypothesis as well (e.g., the empathy-training studies of the Feshbachs, described in Chapter 7).

The degree to which empathy is viewed as a cognitive response, as an affective response, or as having elements of both is controversial. Most experimental studies of empathy are based on self-report data requiring the child to verbalize the emotion induced in the self by the emotion of another in hypothetical situations. There is considerable variation among children, however, in the extent to which they can accurately retrieve and label their own emotions and link them to the emotion states of others. This requires a degree of introspection, reflection, and linguistic competence that the young child may lack even though he or she is capable of empathic feelings.

The experimental literature commonly defines empathy as vicarious affect matching. The definition is not always restrictive in terms of which affects are (to be) vicariously matched; for example, it could be sadness in response to another's sadness, fear to fear, anger to anger, joy to joy, and so on. Such an approach often does not take into account the effects of variations in (1) the psychological meaning for the child of matching such different emotions, (2) how much emotion is being expressed and experienced, and (3) who is the recipient of the emotions.

Experimental studies have begun to demonstrate different outcomes for children's empathic feelings and behavior, depending on whether the sadness induced by another's affective state is directed toward the self or the victim (Barnett, King, & Howard, 1979). In real life and with young children, however, it is more difficult to determine the conditions that are likely to make the child feel sad and withdrawn versus those conditions that enable the child to show concern and extend himself to others in need. It would be of special interest here to examine the role of variations in inductive rearing practices. When does sensitization of the child to the plight of another lead to feelings of (empathic) concern for the other, and when does it produce sad feelings that engulf and overwhelm the child? The induction literature is equally complex with mixed findings (Radke-Yarrow et al., 1983) and failures to make distinctions between different kinds of reasoning. Rational guidance, lecturing, moralizing, and guilt induction could all be viewed as inductive techniques that inform the child of the affective state of the other. But the outcomes for children (e.g., empathy, guilt, despair, anger) could differ markedly, depending on the particular form of reasoning.

The nature and meaning of affect matching may be radically altered when one moves from the use of experimental paradigms to observational research procedures wherein the child's ongoing natural interactions with significant others are examined. For example, if one parent responds with anger to the other parent's anger and the child feels the respondent parent's anger, this could reasonably be defined as affect matching, but it might reflect many different processes (Cummings, Iannotti, & Zahn-Waxler, 1985). Whether this should be called empathy has yet to be decided; it may motivate aggressive behavior that is in defense of the victim, which can be viewed as a form of prosocial behavior (see Chapter 4). It is also common for young children who witness fights between others (e.g., adults) to become distressed and aggressive. Repetitions of exposure to the anger of others result in an intensification of aggression, particularly toward peers (Cummings, et al., 1985). Pure, laboratory assessments of empathy, then, do not always help in understanding behavior in the real world.

Lexicons and coding systems for scoring emotional reactions to distress in others often lump a variety of negative emotions, including concern, sadness, tension, and fear. These different emotions could result in different behavioral tendencies, and different intensities of each emotion could result in different behavioral orientations. Multiple emotions might also be induced that could, in turn, produce competing action or response tendencies; for example, fear and concern for a victim could simultaneously result in approach and avoidance tendencies (Zahn-Waxler, Friedman, & Cummings, 1983).

Other examples are illustrated as well. The evocation of sadness in response to another's distress (Fig. 1) might evoke an altruistic act, or it might produce withdrawal. Anger toward the perpetrator of distress (Fig. 2) could lead to sympathy for, and defense of, the victim, or it could become overgeneralized and directed toward the victim. Fear/tension also could result in competing response tendencies. Yet all these emotions and more have been construed as components of empathy, broadly defined.

Observations of facial expressions in the responses of 1–2-year-olds to distress in others indicate a very wide array of emotions, including interest, surprise, anger, fear, concern, sadness, smiles and laughter, and occasionally attempts to control or mask the emotions. Blends of these emotions also appear, with different emotions expressed simultaneously on different regions of the face or different emotions appearing in succession. A concerned look is also distinguishable and may provide a meaningful index of empathy. This can be seen in a facial configuration that combines mild sadness and interest (Fig. 3). Whether this is likely, more than other emotional reactions, to produce prosocial behavior or diminish antisocial behavior is still an empirical question. Also, it is still unknown whether children who externalize, rather than internalize, their emotions, and thus show their concern in facial expressions, are also more empathic in their

Figure 1. Sadness in a 2-year-old in response to mother's simulation of sadness.

Figure 2. Anger (threat stare) in a 2-year-old, directed toward "perpetrator" of mother's distress.

behavior (e.g., see Buck, 1979). Newer systems for coding emotions and use of multiple indices may help answer some of these questions. Although this discussion has focused on relationships between empathy and prosocial behavior, parallel questions regarding emotions that trigger aggression can be entertained as well.

Carefully controlled parametric studies of both human and infrahuman discrete reactions (facial, postural, gestural) to a range of negative emotions in others could do much to clarify some of the problems surrounding the concept of empathy. There is also a need to develop assessment procedures for making more global judgments about basic affective orientations to distress in others. There is some evidence (Chapter 6) of continuity over time in different emotional styles of prosocial and antisocial behavior when more psychodynamically (clinically) derived assessment procedures are used. Such assessments might help characterize different personality styles that

Figure 3. Facial configuration of concern and interest in response to another's distress.

may, in turn, be predictive of different prosocial and antisocial response orientations.

Retrospect and prospect

Earlier we referred to the large research tasks that lie ahead if we are to make significant strides in research on altruism and aggression. We have attempted to identify a few of the problem areas. Many more areas were left uncovered than we were able to consider, particularly with respect to biological issues and cross-species research. We continue to be concerned about the extent to which theories are developed in the absence of adequate data and come to represent entrenched beliefs about altruism and aggression.

It is important to ask critical questions about theory and data (old and new) on altruism and aggression. Do our theories provide us with insight and understanding that would not be possible if we did not exist as a science? How can the theories best be tested? In this process of translation from theory to research methods, what can be done to minimize the extent to which problems are reduced to trivial or minuscule issues that do little to advance knowledge? Such judgments ought not to be rendered quickly. But it would not hurt for investigators to engage in some introspection and assess successes and failures along the way. Often we seem more willing to criticize each other's theories, ideas, and data more than our own. The problem is similar to one described by Turiel (1983) in his analysis of the long-standing conflict between cognitive and socialization approaches regarding what is central to social development and behavior. With the advent of sociobiology and the increased recognition of the biological forces that shape social development, there is increased likelihood that biological issues also will enter into the conflict equation. These academic jousting matches, however, do not serve our science well. They prevent needed mergers between the different domains and theories.

In addition to evaluating our theories and data more carefully, it would help to explore the research culture in which aggression and altruism are studied. The study of such topics in psychology has sometimes been construed as a "soft" science. One outcome has been that we are often unwilling to use even "softer" areas as sources of hypotheses about the processes underlying altruism and aggression. Some of the most compelling insights about both compassion and brutality and how they influence relationships can be derived from philosophy, religion, literature, and drama. We would do well to try to incorporate into our thinking some of the collective wisdom that has emerged from these approaches in addition to considering how careful historical analyses of cultural records might shed light on changes in patterns of altruism and aggression over extended periods of time.

Our relative youth as a science has also made collaborative research difficult. There is a compelling need for persons with different areas of strength, skill, and expertise (e.g., biological, behavioral, theoretical, empirical, methodological) to work together. Our training as researchers emphasizes an individualistic approach. This begins in early training, when the student is required to do something unique and alone. The assumption is that the individual's scientific worth cannot be judged unless in isolation from others, with the result that collaboration becomes devalued until scientific status is established. This can be wasteful of many years of potential collaborative productivity. We might profit by the example of more established sciences, such as physics, in which collaboration in large projects is common, both during the years of student training and beyond.

In attempting to understand both the origins of altruism and aggression and the interplay of heredity and environment in their development, we might do well to heed the messages and follow the approaches suggested by Darwin more than a century ago. It is significant that of his two major works, one focused on evolution of the species and one on the evolution of emotions. It is clear that for Darwin the two were closely connected. He argued that to understand the nature and development of emotions, one had to view the phenomena in both humans and animals, in children and adults, in different cultures, especially primitive cultures, and in the mentally deranged. The same can be said for altruism and aggression, which often at their core are behaviors mediated by strong emotions.

Darwin also favored an approach requiring systematic detailed observations of behavior in the natural habitat. Implicit in his approach was the need for a taxonomy of the forms, functions, and elicitation contexts of emotions. Finally, time was required to reflect on the observations and consolidate them within a broader conceptual framework. As Cairns describes it in Chapter 2, "one begins with the analysis of a phenomenon, obtaining information about how it develops, what regulates it, and what are its functional consequences in adaptation, before offering explanations about its origins and determinants." Empirical research in this inductive mode is concerned with discovery, in contrast to empirical work in the hypothetical-deductive approach, which is concerned with demonstration. It is precisely this type of research, based on an inductive approach, that often has been missing in research on altruism and aggression.

Many of the constructs from sociobiology hold particular appeal because (1) they suggest to us how deeply in self and evolutionary history the motive forces for altruism and aggression are embedded and (2) they tell us to look to nature to view and understand these patterns of social organization. There are problems in this approach as well, however. Many of the ideas are the result of highly abstractly developed arguments that are based on very limited observations or on analyses of very primitive organisms. Generalizations of sociobiological principles to explain the social lives of more complex organisms may often be unwarranted (Bleier, 1984). Cairns (Chapter 2) expands on some of these issues with respect to aggression when he considers (1) the question of possible homologues of aggressive behavior in different species, (2) the different ways in which aggression may be manifested in different species, and (3) the extent to which aggression is instinctive rather than a product of learning in different species.

With respect to altruism, some of the problems of overgeneralization, when one moves from simple to complex organisms, are seen in kin-selection theory, which was developed to resolve the "paradox" of altruism. Altruism is typically defined by sociobiologists as "self-destructive behavior" performed for the benefit of others (Wilson, 1975). If altruism diminishes personal fitness, this would not be consistent with the concept of survival of the fittest. Altruism would be selected out, and selfishness would be selected in. Yet altruism in the real world exists to a significant degree. This puzzle was resolved by some sociobiologists, who proposed that individuals behave so as to maximize their inclusive fitness, rather than only their individual fitness, by increasing the production of successful offspring both by themselves and by their relatives (Hamilton, 1964). This process became known as kin selection. The percentage of genes shared is an important determinant of the amount of altruism displayed.

This theory has problems, however. It implies that we will be more altruistic to kin than to nonkin and for biological, not social, reasons. In real life, however, our biological and social worlds are usually totally confounded. Also, in humans, individual acts of violence and murder as well as altruism are very commonly directed toward family members. Furthermore, altruism can occur to outgroup members if the opportunities are made available. The theory does not readily explain the behavior of individuals who are quite capable of nurturing adopted children, particularly children from other cultures and races.

An attempt to extend kin-selection theory to explain kindness toward strangers is found in the genetic similarity theory proposed by Rushton, Russell, and Wells (1984). A gene is said to ensure its own survival by acting so as to bring about the reproduction of any organism in which copies of itself are to be found. Rather than behaving altruistically only toward kin, organisms are said to be able to detect other genetically similar organisms and to exhibit favoritism and protective behavior toward these "strangers" as well as toward their own relatives. Such a theory is difficult to test (e.g., by holding environmental influences constant), and the empirical evidence Rushton and co-workers bring to bear on this issue is scanty. This point of view also implies a theory that "assortative mating" (i.e., we select those most like ourselves to marry) is most common. It does not explain circumstances when "opposites attract" or where there is a search for complementarity in a mate. Such theories should be advanced with special caution, as they can be misused by others who for ideological reasons would grasp at any scientific evidence that would help explain and possibly justify maltreatment of outgroup members and others who are not in positions of control.

Careful systematic observations of family relationships are needed, especially those between caregiver and offspring in a variety of species, particularly the mammals. We are only beginning to learn about the rich family and social life and the extended arrangements for care of offspring that characterize many species. Because empathy is a component of caregiving, exploration of who cares for whom and how may help explain biological and social components of (the ontogeny of) concern for others.

Over the years, there have been many misconceptions about the sociability and capacities for caring of many animals. The wolf, for example, used to be viewed as a vicious and asocial animal. In fact, the wolf is a highly nurturant social being that is likely to adopt the offspring of wolves that have been killed. (In species that do not take care of nonrelatives, this lack of care has been evidence for kin selection.) Other mammals also show evidence of extended caregiving arrangements. Giraffes are observed to have "day-care" arrangements wherein designated adult animals are left in charge. If a young elephant is observed to be in distress (e.g., stuck in the mud), it may be offered help by any one of the adults, not just the mother. In some species of primates, the newborn is passed around to all the females, who may later share in the caregiving. Thus, while some animals (e.g., the wildebeest) are doomed if separated from their mothers, because no one else will adopt them, there is great variation across species as to whether other members of the group will care for orphans. In some species, the capacity to care for others, both affectively and instrumentally, extends well beyond blood lines and sometimes crosses species as well. The examples are particularly dramatic when they involve animals showing concern for humans in distress.

If progress is to be made in understanding the biological and social origins of altruism and aggression, conceptualizations and research methods will require significant expansion. I shall summarize here what I view as some needed new directions in research.

1. The construction of taxonomies of different kinds of caregiving, prosocial, and aggressive behaviors and emotions as they occur in nature and as they occur in different species is critical. Too often the focus is on only one kind or a few kinds of altruism or aggression in research procedures, with overgeneralization from the original concepts and operations.

2. Developmental studies, cross-sectional and longitudinal in design, would aid in the construction of these taxonomies of social behavior. Furthermore, they would provide more accurate bases for conclusions about the circumstances under which altruism and aggression become more or less significant components of our social repertoires as we mature.

3. Exploration of the etiology of individual differences in altruism and aggression at different stages in development is needed. While it is difficult and not always possible or desirable to label and classify different individuals as more or less altruistic or aggressive, these differences do exist in nature and understanding of individuals at the extremes is crucial.

4. Cross-cultural studies, adoption studies, and twin studies may help to elucidate the interplay of biological and psychosocial/environmental forces that influence children's altruism and aggression.

5. The motives, purposes, and goals underlying altruism and aggression were taboo topics of research for many years. However, opportunities can be created to examine the less overt and ostensibly less rational factors governing our social lives.

6. Parametric studies of affective reactions to the distress emotions of others (e.g., sadness, anger, distress, fear) in different species of animals will help explain the origins of our social and affective ties to others. Emotions are of special interest because they represent possible biological substrates of altruism and aggression. The search for biological markers, for indices of (affective) traits, as well as states underlying social behavior, is an important task for future research. The questions that need to be addressed can only be answered effectively through the conduct of multidisciplinary, multimethod research and a willingness to entertain seriously alternative points of view.

References

Barnett, M. A., King, L. M., & Howard, J. A. (1979). Inducing affect about self or other: Effects on generosity in children. *Developmental Psychology, 15*: 164–167.

Bleier, R. (1984). *Science and gender: A critique of biology and its theories on women.* New York: Pergamon (Athene Series).

Buck, R. W. (1979). Individual differences in non-verbal sending accuracy and electrodermal responding: The externalizing–internalizing dimension. In R. Rosenthal (Ed.), *Skill in nonverbal communication: Individual differences* (pp. 140–169). Cambridge, MA: Oelgeschlager, Gunn and Hain.

Cummings, E. M., Iannotti, R. J., & Zahn-Waxler, C. (1985). The influence of conflict between adults on the emotions and aggression of young children. *Developmental Psychology*, 495–507.

Darwin, C. (1872). *The expression of emotions in man and animal.* London: John Murray.

Eron, L. D. (1982). The consistency of aggressive behavior across time and situation. Presented at symposium on consistency of aggression and its correlates over 20 years, APA, Anaheim, CA.

Freud, S. (1958). *Civilization and its Discontents.* Garden City, NY: Doubleday.

Hamilton, W.D. (1964). The genetical evolution of social behavior. *Journal of Theoretical Biology,* I/II, 1–52.

Hoffman, M. (1982). Development of prosocial motivation: Empathy and guilt. In N. Eisenberg (Ed), *The development of prosocial behavior* (pp. 281–313). New York: Academic Press.

Kagan, J. (1984). *The nature of the child.* New York: Basic Books.

Loeber, R. (1982). The stability of anti-social and delinquent child behavior: A review. *Child Development, 53:* 1431–1446.

Madsen, M. C. (1971). Developmental and cross-cultural differences in the cooperative and competitive behavior of some children. *Journal of Cross-Cultural Psychology, 2:* 365–371.

McCord, J. (1984). Parental behavior in the cycle of aggression. S. Medrick, Symposium on Aggression and Family. The Family and Psychopathology. Meeting of the Society for Life History Research on Psychopathology, Baltimore, MD.

Olweus, D. (1979). Stability and aggressive reaction patterns in males: A review. *Psychology Bulletin, 86:* 852–875.

Parke, R. D., & Slaby, R. G. (1983). The development of aggression. In P. H. Mussen (Ed.), *Carmichael's manual of child psychology* (4th ed.). Socialization, personality, & social development, E. M. Hetherington (Ed.) (pp. 547–642). New York: Wiley.

Radke-Yarrow, M., Kuczynski, L., Zahn-Waxler, C., Cytryn, C., McKnew, D. H., Cummings, E. M., & Iannotti, R. (1982). Affective development in normal families and families with affective disorders. NIMH Research Protocol, Clinical Project Number 79-M-123.

Radke-Yarrow, M., & Zahn-Waxler, C. (1984). Roots, motives, and patterning in children's prosocial behavior. In E. Staub, D. Bar-tal, J. Karylowski, & J. Reykowski (Eds.), *The development and maintenance of prosocial behavior: International perspectives on positive morality* (pp. 155–176). New York: Plenum Press.

Radke-Yarrow, M., Zahn-Waxler, C., & Chapman, M. (1983). Children's prosocial dispositions and behavior. In P. H. Mussen (Ed.), *Carmichael's manual of child psychology* (pp. 470–545). (vol. IV, 4th ed.) New York: John Wiley & Sons.

Rushton, J. P., Russell, R. J. H., & Wells, P. A. (1984). Genetic similarity theory: Beyond kin selection. *Behavioral Genetics, 14* (3) 179–193.

Turiel, E. (1983). Interaction and development in social cognition. In E. Tory Higgins, D. N. Ruble, & W. W. Hartup (Eds.), *Social cognition and social development: A sociocultural perspective* (pp. 333–355). Cambridge: Cambridge University Press.

Whiting, J. W. M., & Whiting, B. B. (1973). Altruistic and egoistic behavior in six cultures. In L. Nader and T. W. Maretzki (Eds.), *Cultural illness and health: Essays in human adaptation* (Anthropological Studies, No. 9). Washington, DC: American Anthropological Association.

Wilson, E. O. (1975). *Sociobiology: The new synthesis.* Cambridge: Harvard University Press.

Yarrow, M. R., & Waxler, C. Z. (1976). Dimensions and correlates of prosocial behavior in young children. *Child Development, 47:* 118–125.

Zahn-Waxler, C., Cummings, E. M., Iannotti, R., & Radke-Yarrow, M. (1984). Young offspring of depressed parents: A Population at risk for affective problems. In D. Cicchetti and K. Schneider (Eds.), *Childhood Depression.* (No. 26, pp. 81–105). San Francisco: Jossey-Bass.

Zahn-Waxler, C., Cummings, E. M., McKnew, D. H., & Radke-Yarrow, M. (1984). Altruism, aggression and social interactions in young children of manic-depressive parents. *Child Development, 55:* 112–122.

Zahn-Waxler, C., Friedman, S., & Cummings, E. M., (1983). Children's emotions and behaviors in response to infants' cries. *Child Development, 54*: 1522–1528.

Zahn-Waxler, C., Radke-Yarrow, M., & King, R. A. (1979). Child rearing and children's prosocial initiations toward victims of distress. *Child Development, 50*: 319–330.

Zeigler, E. F., Lamb, M. E., & Child, I. L. (1982). *Socialization and personality development*. New York: Oxford University Press.

Index of names

Index of subjects

affective vocalization, 23, 48–9

age, assumptions about influence of, 310–12

aggression: altruism and, 7–9, 190–2, 305–7; defined, 7, 136

altruism: aggression and, 7–9, 190–2, 305–7; defined, 7, 21–2, 136

ambiguous provocation, responses to, 291–2

anger, 148; inhibition of, 146; see also rage

animal behavior, 191; altruism in, 19; child psychology and, 60; children's social behavior and, 110

animals: altruism in, 2; intraspecific interactions among, 39; misconceptions about, 321; neuropharmacology of social need in, 29–30; rough-and-tumble play of, 309–10; VMH lesions and social sensitivity of, 39; see also names of specific kinds of animals

antidepressants, play and tricyclic, 34

assertion: aggression and, 207–12; positive social behavior and, 213

attachment to others as motivation, 148–9

attack, aggression as result of, 137

attribution theory, internalization and, 218–24

authority, compliance with external, 220

behavior: aversive, 242–52; brain control of social, 22; consistency of, over time, 166–7; cooperative, 261–2, 265–7, 273; determinants of, 63–4; developmental aspects of, 303–4; disruptive classroom, 195; emotional circuits and sources of altruistic, 44; evaluation of human, 108–9; evolution of, 62; gene pool and altruistic, 91; genes and development of aggressive, 70–5; goals for, 143–4; helping, 267–9; influences on, 138–9; learning from, encouraged or discouraged, 152–3; meaning of altruistic, 214; mechanisms underlying helping and antagonistic, 42–3; motiva-

tion and, 144; personal selection of aims of, 139; reciprocity in aggressive, 156; rough play and aggressive, 109, 110; sequences between children's, 256–7; serotonin and, 34; sharing, 269–71; species similarities and differences in, 60–2; as structure, 82; survival value of altruistic, 21; see also maternal behavior; prosocial behavior; sexual behavior

behavioral biology, 83–4; child psychology and, 69; differences in conception and emphasis in study of, 69–70

benzodiazepine anxiolytics, 34

beta-endorphin, 23

biological approaches to altruism and aggression, 9–11

brain: distress vocalizations and, 23; emotive circuits of, 19–21; empathy development and evolution of, 4–5; hypothalamus of, 19; kin recognition and, 30; mediation of altruism by, 20; opiate receptors of, 29, 30; opioids of, 20, 22–5, 27–31, 37, 39, 43; studies of, 5

brain circuits, play and, 37–42

brain lesions, 45–6; distress vocalizations and, 23; ventromedial hypothalamic, 37–42

catecholamine activity, effects of reduction of brain, 45

catecholamine receptor-blocking agents, 34

chicks: effects of naloxone on, 29; imprinting of, 29–30

child abuse, 238; aversive behavior and, 242–52; behavioral characteristics of child and, 240–3; discipline confrontations and, 239; intervention procedures and, 251–2; parents' characteristics related to, 243–7

child-abusive families, 239–40

child development, study of, 59

child psychology: animal behavior and, 60;

333